THE FAMILY CIRCLE GOOD COOK'S BOOK

EDITORIAL STAFF

Managing Editors: Andrea Chesman and Lori Longbotham
Contributors: Georgia Chan Downard, Ceri E. Hadda, Mary B. Johnson, Jean F. Tibbets
Illustrator: Lauren Jarrett

FAMILY CIRCLE BOOK PUBLISHING & LICENSING

Editorial Director: Carol A. Guasti
Managing Editor: Christopher Cavanaugh
Editorial Intern: Lesly Atlas
Director: Margaret Chan-Yip
Marketing Manager: Jacqueline Varoli
Marketing Project Coordinator: Karen Dragotto

FAMILY CIRCLE MAGAZINE

Editor in Chief: Jacqueline Leo
Creative Director: Douglas Turshen
Executive Editor: Barbara Winkler
Food Editor: Jean Hewitt
Associate Food Editor: Diane Mogelever
Home Economist: Regina Ragone
Food Consultants: Jo Ann Brett, Beatrice Cihak, Paul E. Piccuito, David Ricketts, Robin Vitetta
Administrative Assistant: Sheena Gonzalez

THE FAMILY CIRCLE

Good Cook's Book

BY THE EDITORS OF FAMILY CIRCLE MAGAZINE

Produced by The Stonesong Press, Inc.
and Alison Brown Cerier Book Development, Inc.

SIMON & SCHUSTER

NEW YORK LONDON TORONTO SYDNEY TOKYO SINGAPORE

SIMON & SCHUSTER
Simon & Schuster Building
Rockefeller Center
1230 Avenue of the Americas
New York, NY 10020

Copyright © 1993
The Stonesong Press, Inc. and Alison Brown Cerier Book Development, Inc.
All rights reserved including the right of reproduction in whole or in part in
any form.

SIMON & SCHUSTER and colophon are registered trademarks of
Simon & Schuster, Inc.

Produced by The Stonesong Press, Inc. and Alison Brown Cerier Book
Development, Inc.

Designed by Martin Lubin

Manufactured in the United States of America

10 9 8 7 6 5 4 3 2 1

Library of Congress Cataloging-in-Publication Data
The Family Circle Good Cook's Book/by the Editors of Family Circle
Magazine
      p.   cm.
Includes index.
ISBN 0-671-76933-2 : $25.00
1. Cookery.   2. Food.   I. Family Circle (Mount Morris, Ill.)
II. Title: Good cook's book.
TX651.F33   1993
641.5—dc20   93-19597
                                                            CIP

CONTENTS

LIST OF CHARTS AND TABLES

INTRODUCTION

Have you ever searched frantically through cookbooks to find an emergency substitute for an ingredient? Or asked yourself if you were using your set of carving knives correctly? Or felt baffled by ever-changing nutritional advice, while trying to give your family healthy, balanced meals?

I know I've wished there were one *definitive* resource I could use to get the answers. And now there is: *The Family Circle Good Cook's Book*. You'll find everything you need to know about cooking in this one volume.

We give you techniques for preparing ingredients, taking you step-by-step through how to fold, zest, crumb, blanch, and chop by hand, as well as with the myriad of tools available. And we do it with easy-to-follow instructions and illustrations.

The chapter on kitchen appliances and tools will help maximize the use of your food processor, grinder, and blender to get through chores fast. Even your pizza baking stone can pull extra weight!

And because everyone is watching what they eat these days, you'll find our Healthy Eating chapter a godsend. Its clear, no-nonsense approach makes sense of terms like "good cholesterol," saturated fat, and "food pyramid." You'll find tasty suggestions for increasing the fiber in your diet, ideas for healthful snacks, and easy ways to make over your brown-bag lunch to pack a nutritional punch.

You'll also have great fun following our illustrations and techniques for garnishing and serving meals, displaying food, and decorating your table.

While this book is great for the beginner who is learning the ins and outs of cooking, it's also an invaluable tool for the experienced cook who wants information at her or his fingertips, fast. We're sure it will be as indispensable to you as your wooden spoon. And we want you to work with it in your own way. Use it to stimulate ideas, or as a problem-solver. (My personal favorite section is the one on saving failed recipes.) This book can be like a wise grandmother, always there to help with sound advice.

I invite you to sit down now and browse through this wonderful book. Discover all its advantages, keep it handy, and use it!

Jackie Leo

Common and Uncommon Ingredients

IN RECENT YEARS your local grocery store has probably become a global supermarket. No longer do you have to seek out specialty food stores for mangoes from the Caribbean, or cheese from France, or blue corn tortilla chips from New Mexico. Here's a look at those common and not-so-common ingredients we are cooking with these days—how to select them, store them, and use them to their best advantage.

*F*ruits

The fruits in this section are arranged by family: all of the berries are listed together, all the citrus fruits are together, all the melons are together, and so on. We grouped them together because within each family, the fruits are usually stored and prepared in the same way. For example, all berries should be stored unwashed and all citrus fruits will yield more juice at room temperature. If you are looking for just one specific fruit, here is a listing of the page number on which you will find that fruit.

The first food you see in most supermarkets is fruit because grocers know that displays of brightly colored, sweetly fragrant fruits are almost irresistible. But beware! No task in the supermarket is more challenging than picking out good fresh fruit.

Most fruits have a brief shelf life. Some, like pears and bananas, are picked green, and you must ripen them at home. Others, such as berries and grapes, are picked fully ripe and are prone to bruising and mold. The trick is to buy each fruit at its peak, or before its peak, and to avoid anything overripe or mushy.

To ripen fruit, leave it at room temperature in a basket that allows air to circulate. To speed ripening, poke a few holes in a paper bag, add the fruit, then close the bag and leave overnight. To further speed the ripening, enclose a ripe banana or apple with the unripe fruit.

Ripe fruits should be stored in the refrigerator in loosely packed plastic bags or in the crisper. Berries and cherries should not be washed before storing.

When cooking with fruit, be sure to use nonreactive cookware, such as stainless steel. Aluminum cookware may give the fruit an off-flavor.

APPLES AND PEARS

Harvested from late summer through the fall, apples and pears are good keepers that are available fresh throughout the year. Both are delicious for eating out of hand, for cooking in sweet and savory dishes, and for combining with cheese to make a sophisticated ending to a meal.

Once peeled, the flesh of apples and pears browns quickly. To retard the browning, toss with a little lemon juice, or cover the peeled fruit in water to which a few tablespoons of lemon juice has been added.

Apples and pears.
1 Crab apples 2 Apple
3 Pears 4 Apple 5 Quince
6 Asian pear

Apple Varieties

Some apples are better for eating out of hand than for cooking, because they lose their shape when they are cooked, or they produce a watery applesauce. Other apples are considered all-purpose because they are delicious raw, and they hold their shape well when baked in a pie, and produce a good, thick applesauce.

APPLE	DESCRIPTION
Cortland	Smooth, shiny red skin. Mild sweet-tart flavor. Excellent raw because it resists browning, in pies, or in cooked dishes.
Golden Delicious	Yellow apple. Sweeter than Red Delicious with juicy, crisp flesh. Good all-purpose apple with flesh that resists browning.
Granny Smith	Green apple. Moderately tart flavor. Prized for snacks, salads, and for use in cooking.
McIntosh	Bright red apple, often tinged with green. Very juicy, slightly tart flesh. Best eaten raw.
Mutsu	Yellow-green apple. Very crisp, sweet all-purpose apple. Also known as Crispin.
Red Delicious	Deep red apple with square shape. Very sweet, crisp, and juicy; good for eating raw and adding to salads.
Rome	Deep red apple with some yellow or green speckling. Slightly tart; the best choice for baking and cooking.
Winesap	Deep red apple. Moderately tart with slight hints of wine; excellent raw, cooked, or baked.

Pear Varieties

PEAR	DESCRIPTION
Anjou	Green with a red blush; round, heart-shaped; medium to large; short neck. Flesh is yellowish white, fine-textured, juicy, and sweet. Good for eating raw and cooking.
Bartlett	Popular summer pear. Turns yellow when ripe; bell-shaped; medium to large. Flesh is fine-grained and sweet. Good for eating raw or cooking; a favorite for canning.
Bosc	Russet-brown skin; long, tapering neck; medium to large. Crunchy, sweet, white flesh. Ideal for eating and baking.
Comice	Yellow-green, often with a red blush; round; medium to large. Flesh is very fine, extremely juicy. and not gritty. Famous as a holiday gift fruit. Excellent raw, not recommended for cooking.
Seckel	Late summer pear. Yellow-brown skin; egg-shaped; very small. The sweet flesh is ideal for eating out of hand, canning, and pickling.
Red Bartlett	Similar to Bartlett, differing only in its bright crimson skin.

Apples. Although good-quality fresh apples are available year-round, an apple just off the tree is indescribably sweet, juicy, and crisp. Apples are harvested ripe and should be stored in the refrigerator.

There are literally hundreds of varieties of these fruits grown around the world, though only a few types are available in the supermarket. For a description of these, see the table on page 4.

Pears. Pears are harvested green and should be left to ripen at room temperature until the fruit feels soft. If they are stored in their wrappers, they will ripen sooner. Some green pears, such as the Bartlett, will turn yellow when ripe, but others do not change color upon ripening. Once ripe, a pear deteriorates rather quickly. Store ripe pears in the refrigerator for three to five days.

Pears to be used fresh, eaten out of hand, or tossed into salads should be fully ripe. Pears used for cooking or baking should be firm and slightly underripe. For a look at pear varieties, see the table on page 4.

Asian pears, or apple-pears, are not true pears, although they taste more like a pear than an apple. The shape is usually round, with brownish yellow skin. The flesh is crisp and juicy like an apple. It is available in specialty markets from October to February. Select rock-hard fruits and eat out of hand.

Quinces. Another fruit that looks like a cross between an apple and a pear, a quince has yellow skin and hard, dry, yellow-white flesh that is quite tart. It is best enjoyed cooked and its high pectin content makes it an excellent choice for jams and jellies. Available in markets from October to December, large, firm yellow fruits that show no sign of green are the ones you want to select. Keep refrigerated in a plastic bag for up to two months.

BERRIES

"Doubtless God could have made a better fruit than the strawberry, but doubtless, God never did," so said Izaak Walton in the seventeenth century. And he's right, unless you consider the raspberry, the blackberry, the blueberry.... These delicate fruits of high summer, so delightful to eat plain or smothered in cream, are best enjoyed when local and in season. Out-of-season berries, now commonplace in the supermarket, are great for use as garnishes, but they generally lack the full flavor and sweetness of summer berries.

Berries are picked ripe and have a brief shelf life. Select berries that are bright, clean, dry, plump, and brightly colored. Avoid berries with packaging that has been stained by berry juice or shows any sign of mold.

Figure that a pint of berries will serve two to four people. Before storing in the refrigerator, sort through the berries and discard any that

▶ Apple corer, 140
▶ Apple corer/slicer, 140

Berries. 1 Cranberries
2 Blueberries 3 Gooseber-
ries 4 Blackberries 5 Boysenberries 6 Raspberries
7 Strawberries 8 Wild
strawberries

are bruised or moldy. Bruised flesh rots quickly, and the rot and mold tends to spread fast to other berries. Fragile berries, such as raspberries, should be laid out in a single layer on a tray to prevent crushing. Do not wash berries before storing.

Berries are easily preserved by freezing on a tray. Once frozen, the berries should be poured into airtight containers or bags and stored for up to one year at 0°F. They will retain their flavor and color, but the texture will soften. Frozen berries are best used in sauces, pies, and other desserts where texture is not important. They are too soft to be eaten out of hand.

Blackberries, boysenberries, dewberries, loganberries, and raspberries. These fragile berries are all related, though the flavor ranges from tart (the loganberry) to intensely sweet (the raspberry). Store these berries for no more than two days in the refrigerator. Wash in a bowl of cold water just before using; do not soak the berries. Use your hands to lift the berries gently out of the water. Drain on paper towels.

Blueberries. Also known as huckleberries, bilberries, whinberries, and whortleberries. Select plump, firm berries that are uniform in size. A dull appearance or soft texture indicates old berries. Blueberries sometimes are covered with a waxy, white bloom that is a natural protective coating. Blueberries can be stored in the refrigerator for only one to two days, so use quickly. They are particularly well suited to freezing and will keep for up to one year at 0°F.

A favorite method of freezing blueberries is to freeze them in a single layer on a tray. Once the berries are frozen, they can be poured into a resealable plastic bag. Then, when you need blueberries, you just pour out as many as you need at a time.

Gooseberries. These small, tart, firm berries are usually green with light stripes. Available in the summer months, they are generally served cooked and sweetened. Store in the refrigerator for up to one week. To clean fresh gooseberries, remove the blossom part and stem. Then wash in cold water and drain on paper towels.

Cranberries. Small, tart, firm cranberries are usually served sweetened and cooked, often in relishes. They mature in the fall and are sold fresh from October through December. Unopened packages of cranberries can be stored in the freezer at 0°F. for up to twelve months for use year-round. Look for firm, unblemished berries with a bright luster. Avoid soft and dull-looking berries.

Strawberries. Strawberries vary in size, shape, and color, with cultivated strawberries being far larger than the tiny, elongated, sweet wild strawberry. When buying strawberries, look for deep red color and a fresh green cap. Avoid greenish berries or ones with white shoulders—strawberries will not ripen off the vine. Refrigerate the berries immediately after purchase; they will keep for several days. Before serving, wash the berries with the caps on to avoid water absorption. To hull, use the tip of a paring knife to give the caps a light twist. Don't slice off the tops—you'll lose some of the fruit and transform the berry from an appealing heart shape to a triangle.

CITRUS FRUITS

Prized for their availability throughout the winter when other fruits are out of season, citrus fruits are also valuable for their tangy juice and aromatic peels.

Select fruits that are heavy for their size; this indicates juiciness. The fruit should be free of bruises or soft spots. A little green on the skin indicates cool growing temperatures, not unripe fruit.

Although you can keep citrus fruits for about a week at room temperature, they will last for about a month in the refrigerator. Many recipes call for the zest of an orange, lemon, lime, or grapefruit. This is the colored part of the peel, without the bitter white membranes. A zester peels off thin, curly strips, but a vegetable peeler can be used to shave off the zest.

A medium-size orange yields about 2 tablespoons of grated zest; a lemon yields 2 to 3 teaspoons of grated zest; a lime yields about 2 teaspoons of grated zest.

Citrons. Actually a variety of lemon, citron is used for its thick peel, which is candied and used in fruit cakes; its flesh is extremely sour. Candied citron should be stored in the freezer at 0°F., where it will retain its intense flavor for up to one year.

Grapefruit. There are many varieties of grapefruit, but all can be

Citrus fruits. 1 Lemon
2 Grapefruit 3 Lime
4 Tangerine 5 Orange
6 Ugli fruit 7 Clementine
8 Kumquats

divided into two types. White grapefruit has pale yellow flesh with a bright yellow rind. Pink grapefruit has pink flesh with a pinkish blush on its yellow rind. Fresh grapefruit will keep at room temperature for up to two weeks. You also can store grapefruit in the fruit bin of the refrigerator for about three weeks.

Kumquats. These taste and look like tiny oval oranges and are usually eaten with their skin, which is quite sweet, while the flesh is somewhat tart. They are often sold preserved in a heavy, sweet syrup, but you may find them fresh from November to March. Store fresh kumquats for up to a month in a plastic bag in the refrigerator. Fresh kumquats are eaten out of hand, sliced into fruit salads, or used as a garnish.

Lemons. Select fruits with glossy, fine-grained skin. Avoid fruits with soft spots at the stem, or with thick, hard skin, or with a spongy texture.

Store lemons in the refrigerator for two to three weeks. A cut lemon should be placed in an airtight container and will keep for up to two weeks.

Limes. Most limes found in the supermarket are Persian limes, though the tiny key limes, found mainly in Florida, are particularly aromatic. Regardless of the variety, look for limes with shiny green skin and avoid those with purple or brown scabs or soft spots.

Limes are the most perishable of citrus fruits. Store limes loose in the refrigerator for two weeks; after that they begin to lose flavor, though they still will yield juice.

Oranges. Most oranges are classified as *juice oranges* or *eating oranges*. *Valencia oranges* are a favorite for juice; they yield a sweet, golden juice with few seeds. Easy-to-peel *navel oranges* are good, seedless, eating oranges. *Blood oranges,* also good for eating, have a

Juice from Citrus Fruits

To extract the most juice from a lemon or lime, roll the fruit on the counter top before cutting. A lemon will yield 2 to 4 tablespoons of juice; a lime will yield 2 tablespoons of juice; and an orange will yield ⅓ to ½ cup of juice.

red or red and white streaked pulp. *Seville oranges* are bitter, used for making marmalade.

Fresh oranges are available every month of the year, although the peak supply is from December to March.

Choose firm, heavy fruits, free of soft spots or mold. Skin color is not an indication of ripeness because some ripe oranges have a tinge of green; brown mottling on the skin will not affect the fruit. Oranges will last at room temperature for up to a week, but for best results, store them loose in the refrigerator.

Tangelos. A cross between a grapefruit and a tangerine, a tangelo looks like a large tangerine and is similarly easy to peel. The fruit is juicy and has a tangy orange flavor. *Mineolas* are a variety with a distinctive knob at the stem end and deep coloring. *Ugli fruits* have bumpy, mottled, yellow-green skins with sweet, juicy flesh.

Choose heavy, firm fruits and store as you would oranges.

Tangerines and mandarins. Actually, tangerines are a type of mandarin, as are *clementines,* an especially tiny tangerine. These are all sweet and easily peeled fruits that make a great snack. The canned fruit that is called mandarin orange is usually the Japanese satsuma.

Choose heavy, firm fruits and store as you would oranges.

GRAPES AND CURRANTS

Both of these fruits are enjoyed fresh and dried, although the dried currant is actually a Black Corinth grape and not a currant at all!

Currants. Tiny, brilliantly red berries with a tangy flavor that is most prized in jellies. They are available in midsummer. Look for plump, firm, dry berries and store unwashed in the refrigerator in an uncovered bowl for one to two days.

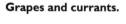

Grapes and currants.

Plumping Raisins

Some recipes call for plumping the raisins so they don't draw moisture from the batter. To plump raisins, soak in hot water for 10 minutes.

Dried currants are smaller than raisins but are similarly used.

Grapes. There are hundreds of varieties of grapes, most of which are used in wine-making. Of table grapes, the green Thompson seedless is the most popular. These are available from June to November. A popular reddish purple variety is the seedless Emperor grape, found throughout the winter and spring. The dark blue-black Concord grapes that appear briefly in September and October are a favorite for turning into jelly, though they can also be eaten out of hand.

Select plump, brightly colored grapes that are still firmly attached to their stems.

Store unwashed for up to a week in a perforated plastic bag in the refrigerator. Wash well before using.

Raisins. Most raisins start out as green Thompson seedless grapes, but two different processes of drying make for the popular dark and golden raisins. Store in a cool, dry place in an airtight container. If raisins become dry or form sugar crystals, rinse them with hot tap water or soak them briefly in water or cooking liquid before using in a recipe.

MELONS

Melons develop all their sweetness while still on the vine, but after harvest they become softer, juicier, and often more flavorful. What you want to buy are melons that had a chance to fully mature on the vine, but are not overripe. Select melons that are heavy for their size and well shaped. Avoid fruit that is cracked, wet, dented, or bruised. Often you can buy sliced or quartered melons, a good buy when a whole melon is just too large for your needs. Make sure the flesh of the melon looks firm and is the proper color for the variety.

Melons. 1 and **2** Cantaloupes **3** Crenshaw **4** Watermelon (small variety) **5** Casaba **6** Honeydew

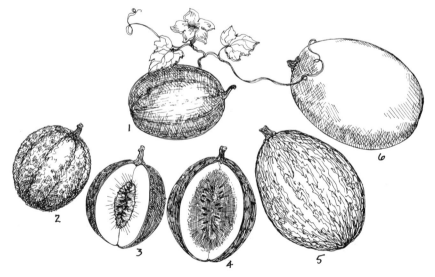

▸ **Adding dried fruits to batters, 265**
▸ **Plumping raisins in microwave, 257**

Keeping an uncut melon for a day at room temperature will bring it to full flavor. Then refrigerate and use within three or four days. Wrap cut melons securely with plastic wrap and store in the refrigerator for two to three days.

With the notable exception of watermelon, melons have a center filled with fibers and tiny, inedible seeds that should be scraped away before serving.

Cantaloupes. Also known as muskmelon, this popular melon has juicy orange flesh. Look for melons with a well-developed skin of netting over a yellowish, not greenish, rind. The stem end should be round, smooth, and slightly sunken. The melon should smell sweet, but not fermented.

Casabas. Some say the smooth, creamy white flesh of this melon is reminiscent of a mango. The golden rind is wrinkled, and the melon comes to a distinct point at one end. Casabas are in season in September and October. There is no strong scent to help you judge maturity, so look for melons that are slightly soft at the pointed end.

Crenshaws. A favorite among melon lovers, the salmon-colored flesh of the crenshaw is sweet, rich, and slightly spicy. It is available July through September. This is a melon you can sniff for signs of ripeness; it should have a spicy, sweet aroma.

Honeydews. At their peak from June to October, it's possible to find honeydews year-round. Select melons that have a slightly textured (as opposed to completely smooth), creamy (not white) rind. The stem end should give slightly to the touch. Some varieties have orange or pink flesh, though most are a pale green.

Persians. Persian melons look like large cantaloupes and can be selected by the same criteria, except the rind under the netting will stay green even when the melon is ripe.

Watermelon. Watermelons come in many different sizes and shapes, and seedless varieties are becoming more and more popular. Judge a watermelon by its appearance. The color, which may be solid or striped, should be deep and even, light to dark green, with the underside a creamy yellow (not white).

RHUBARB

Enjoyed as a tangy sour companion to strawberries in pies and in cakes, sauces, and chutneys, rhubarb is used as a fruit, though it is classed botanically as a vegetable. Only its stalks are eaten; the leaves are toxic.

Rhubarb stems range in color from deep red to light green with pink overtones, depending on the variety. No matter what variety you find, cook rhubarb with plenty of sweetener.

Available from January through August, rhubarb should be crisp and

Rhubarb.

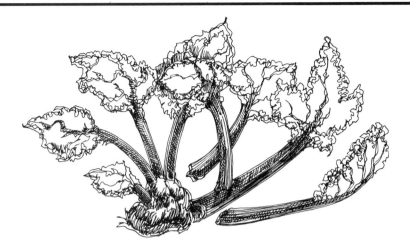

firm; avoid stems that are wilted or stringy. Store rhubarb in a perforated plastic bag in the refrigerator for three to five days. One pound of fresh rhubarb cooks down to two cups.

STONE FRUITS

Apricots, cherries, nectarines, peaches, plums—these are the fruits of summer. If you are lucky, you will find fruits that were left to mature long enough on the tree, for after harvest these fruits become no sweeter, though they will become somewhat juicier and softer.

Apricots. Finding a quality fresh apricot is difficult because an apricot harvested fully mature can rot in transport, while an immature apricot can rot before ripening. Still, they are worth seeking out for their rich, sweet flavor—something like a peach, with hints of wine and lemon. Look for deep color and a very slight softening of the fruit. Hold at room temperature until the fruit is soft but not mushy, then keep in the refrigerator for a few days. The flesh of cut apricots will discolor when exposed to air; brush or toss with a little lemon juice to prevent browning.

Since fresh apricots are so perishable, dried apricots are more reliable and offer intense apricot flavor.

To plump dried apricots, soak in hot water for about ten minutes, then drain before using in a recipe.

Cherries. Whether they be *sweet cherries* for eating out of hand or *sour cherries* for baking into pies, cherries should be used as soon as possible. Look for plump, firm, deeply colored cherries with stems attached, and avoid any that are soft or bruised. Cherries can be stored unwashed in perforated plastic bags in the refrigerator for two to four days.

Dried cherries are becoming more available and are good for use in baked goods and for snacks.

Stone fruits. I Peach
2 Sweet cherries **3** Apricots
4 Nectarines **5** Plums
6 Sour cherries

Maraschino cherries are sweet cherries that have been preserved and dyed a bright red color. They are used primarily for garnishing sweet alcoholic drinks and desserts. An opened bottle will last for about six months in the refrigerator.

Nectarines. With a flavor reminiscent of both apricots and peaches, nectarines have smooth golden flesh and smooth yellow-red skin. When buying nectarines, ignore the color, which may have a greenish cast. Instead look for fruits that give a little along the seam and have a sweet smell.

Ripen nectarines at room temperature for a day or so and store in the refrigerator in a perforated plastic bag for four to five days.

As with apricots, apples, and pears, the flesh of cut nectarines will brown when exposed to air. Brush or toss with a little lemon juice.

Peaches. Sweet, juicy, fragrant peaches are one of the highlights of summer. But take care to select peaches that have begun to soften and produce a sweet scent. Often peaches are picked when they are too green (avoid peaches with a greenish cast), or they may be held after harvest in temperatures that are too cold. The resulting cold injury produces fruits that look good on the outside but are mealy and dry inside. Look for peaches that are creamy or yellow, sometimes with blushes of red. Avoid hard peaches or ones with shriveled skin.

Hold the peaches at room temperature for a day or two so they become fully ripe. Then store in plastic bags in the refrigerator for up to two days.

Plums. Plums are available in wide assortment all summer long. *Casselmans* have tangy-sweet flavor and red color. *Friars* have deep black skin and a sweet-tart flavor. *Italian prune plums* have purple skins and golden green flesh. *Kelsey* plums are green and ripen to yellow-red. *Larodas* are colored red over yellow. *Nubianas* are purple-

♦ **Peeling peaches, 186**

black plums with red flesh. *Roysums* have sweet flavor and reddish blue skin. The popular *Santa Rosas* have red-purple skin and golden flesh.

Regardless of the plum variety, look for fruits with firm, but not rock-hard, flesh and deep color. A white bloom on the skin is a natural protective coating that doesn't affect the quality of the fruit.

Very hard fruits can be left to soften at room temperature for about a day. Refrigerate mature plums in perforated plastic bags in the refrigerator for three to five days.

Prunes are dried plums and can be handled just as you would raisins (see page 10).

TROPICAL AND MEDITERRANEAN FRUITS

Bananas. Bananas are picked unripe and, as they ripen, turn yellow or red, depending on the variety, and soften slightly. As a banana becomes more ripe, brown spots occur. Some people prefer a firm, slightly underripe banana, while others prefer them very ripe. Bananas will ripen at room temperature. To speed ripening, place the banana in a closed paper bag overnight.

Once ripe, a banana may be refrigerated. The skin will turn black, but the flesh inside will stay white for several days.

Mashed bananas can be frozen in airtight containers with a little lemon juice to prevent browning. Fresh or frozen and thawed mashed bananas make an excellent addition to French toast and pancake batter.

Carambolas. Also known as star fruit, this deeply grooved citrus fruit forms perfect stars when sliced. It is almost impossible to judge whether an individual fruit will be sweet or tart unless it has been marked by the greengrocer. A rule of thumb is that tart varieties have

Tropical and Mediterranean fruits.
1 Fig 2 Mango 3 Cherimoya 4 Pomegranate
5 Persimmon 6 Kiwifruit
7 Banana 8 Pineapple
9 Papaya

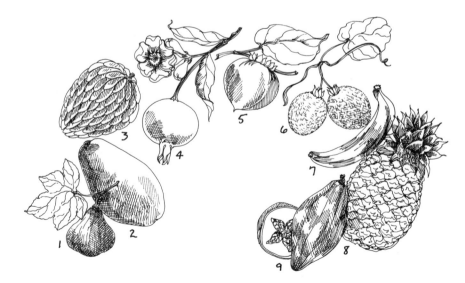

▸ **Plantains, 114**

very narrow ribs, while sweet varieties have thicker, fleshier ones. If the waxy skin is tinged with green, ripen at room temperature for a day or so before refrigerating. Brown on the spine indicates ripeness. There is no need to peel before using.

Cherimoyas. On the outside, this heart-shaped fruit is green with a patterned skin. Inside, its velvety pulp is custardy, tasting of papaya, pineapple, and banana. Buy pale green, even-colored fruit. Ripen at room temperature until the fruit is slightly soft, then refrigerate for one or two days.

The best way to eat a cherimoya is chilled. Slice it in half and eat with a spoon, discarding the black seeds as you go.

Dates. Dates are sold soft, semisoft, semidry, and dry. Whichever kind you buy, look for plump fruits with glossy skins. Seal in a perforated plastic bag and store in the refrigerator or freezer. Soft dates will last no more than a few weeks, but dry dates will keep indefinitely in the freezer.

Recipes usually call for chopped dates. The easiest way to chop them is to use a pair of kitchen shears and to dip the scissors in hot water between snips.

Figs. Fresh figs are harvested ripe from the tree, then rushed to the stores, where they must be consumed within seven to ten days of harvest. Look for plump fruits with unbroken skin and slightly yielding flesh. A fig should smell fresh, not sour. Refrigerate and use as soon as possible.

Black Mission figs are sold fresh and dried. These have a dark purple skin with pink flesh. Mostly sold fresh, *Brown Turkey* figs have brown skins and purple flesh. *Calimyrna* figs are usually dried, while *Kadota* figs with their pink flesh are usually canned.

Guavas. It is a challenge to find a guava that isn't overly ripe. A ripe guava—yellow, red, purple, or black in color depending on the variety—will be slightly soft and very fragrant. Eat it fresh or make it into a jelly. Store in the refrigerator for up to two weeks.

Kiwifruit. Light brown, fuzzy, egg-shaped kiwifruit has a distinctively fragrant sweet-tart flavor, with hints of strawberry and pineapple. The flesh is a bright green, dotted with small, edible black seeds. The brown skin should be peeled off with a knife and discarded. Kiwis add a bright splash of color to fruit salads and make lovely garnishes; they are also delicious to eat out of hand.

For the best eating, ripe kiwis should be as soft as a ripe pear. If the fruit is firm, ripen it at room temperature, then refrigerate for up to a week.

Mangoes. Juicy, refreshing fruit with a spicy sweet flavor that hints of peaches, mangoes are oval and slightly flat or rounded in shape and have yellow-orange to red skins when ripe. Mangoes are in season from January to September. Choose smooth, plump fruits that are

❧ **Kitchen shears,** 139

fairly firm; the color can range from green to deep orange. Most important, sniff the stem end: no aroma, no flavor. Leave at room temperature for a day or two to soften. Once ripe, mangoes should be refrigerated.

To peel, cut just the skin with the tip of a knife, starting from the stem and circling the fruit several times. Peel off the skin in sections. The flesh inside will cling to the large, flat seed. Cut the flesh to free it from the seed or scoop out the flesh with a spoon. Work over a bowl to catch the drips.

Papayas. Pear-shaped papayas, sometimes called papaws, have a greenish yellow exterior and golden orange flesh that is blandly sweet. Buy fruits that are mostly yellow and leave at room temperature for three to five days until soft and fragrant. Then store in the refrigerator for up to two weeks.

To serve, peel and scoop out the seeds before slicing or dicing the flesh. Sometimes papayas are used as serving shells for fruit or chicken salads.

Passion fruit. The drab, deep purple, wrinkled skin (the more wrinkled, the more ripe) belies a juicy mustard-yellow pulp and edible seeds inside. The fruit has a strong tart flavor. You can cut the fruit in half and eat it with a spoon or strain out the seeds and use the pureed flesh in mixed drinks, sorbets, and dessert sauces.

Persimmons. A ripe persimmon has vibrant red-orange skin and juicy sweet flesh. But an unripe persimmon is incredibly astringent and unappealing. The softer the flesh, the sweeter the flavor. Buy plump with the green cap intact and store at room temperature until *very* soft. Peel ripe persimmons and cube or slice for salads or baking or eating out of hand.

Pineapples. Fresh pineapples are available year-round, with peak supplies between April and June. A pineapple does not ripen after it is harvested.

Select a pineapple that is firm with a slight give and fresh-looking green crown leaves. A very slight separation of the eyes and a pleasant pineapple fragrance are the signs of ripe fruit. Store pineapple at room temperature and use within three days. Refrigerate until chilled just before serving.

Pomegranates. Pomegranates have a hard, dark red or purple striated skin. Inside the white-fleshed fruit is filled with glistening, crunchy, ruby-red seeds and a deep red juice. The seeds make striking garnishes for fruit, ice cream, and even poultry dishes. The seeds and juice can be crushed in a blender, then strained and the liquid used in a dessert sauce or drink.

Yields of Common Fresh Fruits

ONE POUND FRESH FRUIT	APPROXIMATE YIELD
Apples	3 medium, 3 cups sliced or diced
Apricots	10 medium, 3 cups cooked
Bananas	3–4 medium, 2 cups sliced, 1½ cups mashed
Cherries	2 cups pitted
Cranberries	4 cups
Grapes	2½ cups
Peaches	4 to 6 medium, 2 cups sliced
Pears	3 to 5 medium, 2 cups sliced
Pineapples	1½ cups cubed

Fresh Produce Availability

Buy fruits and vegetables when they're in season for freshest flavor, lowest cost. Farmers' markets and roadside stands are a great source of just-picked produce at great prices. The following produce reaches peak availability in the markets during the months indicated:

PRODUCE	PEAK AVAILABILITY
Apricots	June to August
Artichokes	Spring and Fall
Asparagus	March to July
Blueberries	June to August
Cantaloupes	April to October
Cherries	May to August
Corn, Sweet	July to September
Cranberries	September to December
Honeydews	February to October
Mangoes	March to August
Nectarines	January and February, June to September
Okra	April to November
Peaches	May to September
Peas, Sweet, Shelling	Spring and Fall
Persimmons	October to February
Plums and Fresh Prunes	June to October
Pomegranates	September to December
Pumpkins	September to December
Strawberries, Local	June to August
Tangelos	October to February
Tangerines	November to March
Tomatoes	July to September
Watermelon	April to September

The following fruits and vegetables, thanks to refrigeration and efficient transportation, are usually available year-round:

Apples	Lemons
Avocados	Lettuce
Bananas	Limes
Bean Sprouts	Mushrooms
Beans, Green	Onions
Beets	Onions, Green
Broccoli	Oranges
Brussels Sprouts	Papayas
Cabbage	Parsley and Herbs
Carrots	Parsnips
Cauliflower	Pears
Celery	Peppers, Sweet
Chinese Cabbage	Pineapples
Coconuts	Plantains
Cucumbers	Potatoes
Eggplant	Radishes
Escarole	Spinach
Garlic	Squash, Summer and Winter
Grapefruit	Sweet Potatoes
Grapes	Turnips and Rutabagas
Greens	

Vegetables

The vegetables in this section are arranged into groups that share similarities in terms of which part of the plant we eat. The beans and seeds are together, as are the leafy greens; the plants that offer edible fruits, such as tomatoes and eggplants, are in another group. Usually all of the vegetables in a group are similar not only in which part of the plant is edible, but in how we select these vegetables at the market, and how we store and prepare those vegetables at home. If you are looking for just one specific vegetable, here is a quick guide to finding it.

Appealing, fresh, crunchy vegetables are available year-round. Today's supermarkets stock a dazzling array of vegetables from all over the world, making it possible to enjoy vegetables as the backbone of a healthy diet.

When choosing vegetables, select those with bright, deep color and firm texture. Avoid vegetables with bruises, discolored spots, or cuts, which are invitations to decay. Smaller vegetables are more likely to be tender, with smaller seeds, than oversized vegetables. Fresh and frozen vegetables are usually higher in nutrients than canned vegetables, and usually have a fresh taste and firm texture as well.

Fresh vegetables, with the notable exception of potatoes, tomatoes, and onions, should be stored in the crisper drawer of your refrigerator. The sooner you eat a vegetable after harvesting, the richer it will be in nutrients, but most vegetables will keep for about one week in the refrigerator. Wash vegetables just before using.

Vegetables will retain more vitamins if microwaved or steamed in a small amount of water rather than boiled in water to cover. Most people prefer their vegetables cooked until tender crisp—firm, but not crunchy, with bright color.

For tips on preparing and cooking specific vegetables, see the table on pages 215–218.

BEANS, SEEDS, PODS, AND LEGUMES

Dried beans and legumes. Protein-rich, low-fat, low-cholesterol beans and legumes should be a part of everyone's diet. Besides being rich in nutrients and fiber, they are inexpensive and easy to prepare, though they sometimes require long, slow cooking.

One pound of dried beans will yield about 2½ cups uncooked beans or 5 to 6 cups cooked beans.

Canned precooked beans are high in quality and can be used in most dishes calling for cooked dried beans. Rinse and drain the beans before using.

Store dried beans at room temperature for up to one year or in the freezer indefinitely. For best flavor, buy in small quantities and use quickly.

For specific kinds of beans and cooking times, see the table on page 21.

Shell beans. Shell beans are beans removed from their pods and eaten fresh. Although theoretically any bean on its way to becoming a dried bean could be eaten fresh as a shell bean, not many varieties are commonly eaten this way. *Limas* and *broad beans*, or *fava beans*, are the most popular.

Beans, seeds, pods, and legumes. 1 Chickpeas 2 Snap beans 3 Corn 4 Lentils 5 Okra 6 Peas 7 Snow peas

▸ **Freezing vegetables, 295–296**
▸ **Microwave cooking of vegetables, 261–262**
▸ **Vegetable steamer, 157**

Beans and Legumes

Most beans should be presoaked before cooking. Lentils and split peas do not require presoaking.

BEAN/LEGUME	DESCRIPTION	COOKING TIME
Adzuki Beans	Small red, unusually sweet bean, used in Oriental cookery for both sweet and savory dishes.	3/4 to 1 hour
Black Beans	Also known as turtle beans. Small black beans. A staple in Central and South American cookery. Makes an excellent soup and combines well with cumin for flavoring.	1 1/2 hours
Black-eyed Peas	Small cream-colored beans with a black oval and cream dot in the center. Used as the basis for the Southern dish Hoppin' John.	1 hour
Broad Beans	Also known as fava beans. Large brown flat beans ranging in color from white to brown. Available fresh or dried.	1 hour
Cannellini Beans	White kidney bean. Popular in Italian cooking. Available canned.	1 1/2 hours
Cranberry Beans	Small, tan-colored, dotted with maroon.	1 3/4 hours
Garbanzo Beans (chick-peas)	Round, yellow-gold. Commonly used in Indian, Middle Eastern, and Mediterranean cooking. Available canned.	3 hours
Great Northern Beans	Medium-size white bean used in soups and for baked beans.	2 hours
Kidney Beans	Kidney-shaped; red; slightly sweet. Available canned. Commonly used to make chili.	1 1/2 hours
Lentils	Small, flat legumes in green, brown, yellow, and orange (red). Quick-cooking. A staple in Indian cooking.	15 to 20 minutes
Navy Beans	Small white beans. Holds shape well when cooked. Traditionally used for navy bean soup and Boston baked beans.	1 1/2 hours
Pinto Beans	Pink dotted with specks of red. Similar in taste to red kidney beans. Popular in the Mexican refried beans.	2 1/2 hours
Soybeans	Cream-colored; strong flavor. Slow-cooking. Processed into soy milk, tofu, soy flour, textured vegetable protein.	3 or more hours
Split Peas	Available in green or yellow. Makes an excellent soup flavored with a ham bone.	1 hour

Look for plump, moist pods with no sign of browning. Store in perforated plastic bags in the refrigerator for up to two days.

Snap beans. Beans eaten when the pods are tender, before the seeds have developed, are snap beans. *Green beans* and *haricot verts* have slender green pods. *Italian green beans* have broad, flat pods. *Yellow wax beans* have yellow pods. A *purple snap bean* will turn green when cooked. *Chinese yard-long beans* can measure one to two feet long, but they taste pretty much like regular snap beans.

Select slender, unshriveled pods with no signs of browning and no bulging, which would indicate mature beans within. Store in perforated plastic bags in the refrigerator for up to three days.

Corn. As soon as an ear of corn is picked, the sugars in the kernals start to convert to starch—which is why you should eat fresh corn as soon as possible. The recent development of supersweet varieties of corn give you a day or two leeway; nevertheless, the rule is to select corn that has been very recently picked or has been under constant refrigeration since picking.

Look for green, flexible husks; silks that are golden—not brown—and moist; and stem ends that are damp, pale green, and still flexible. If the ears can be inspected, look for tight, plump, regularly spaced kernels all the way to the tip of the ear.

It is possible to keep corn for up to two days in the refrigerator.

Okra. Gumbo wouldn't be the same without this green or purple, fuzzy-skinned, edible pod. When okra is sliced open it reveals lots of tiny white seeds and a slightly sticky liquid that becomes ropy and thick when cooked.

Select crisp pods without any signs of browning. Store in the refrigerator for up to three days.

Peas. Peas picked fresh from the garden are superior to any pea found in the supermarket. Like corn, peas should be rushed from field to pot because as soon as they are picked, the sugars in the peas begin converting to starch.

Shell peas, or *English peas*, are sweet green peas with an inedible pod. *Snow peas* are eaten only for the pod, before the peas inside have begun to develop. *Sugar-snap peas* have juicy edible pods and fully developed peas within.

When buying peas, look for plump, bright pods with no signs of shriveling or cracks. They will keep in the refrigerator for up to three days; shell just before cooking.

CABBAGE FAMILY

Members of the cabbage family—broccoli, brussels sprouts, cabbage, cauliflower (also known as brassicas or cruciferous vegetables)—pack a nutrition wallop, being high in vitamins A and C and in fiber. They are

⏶ **Grilling corn, 246**

also considered by some as important food for their anticancer properties. These vegetables store well in the refrigerator and lend themselves to steaming, stir-frying, and combining in casseroles.

These vegetables have strong flavors and odors that develop with overcooking, so cook until just tender.

Broccoli. Look for firm stalks with tight green heads. Heads that are light green or show yellow are no longer at their peak. Store in a plastic bag in the refrigerator for up to four days.

To prepare for cooking, remove the outer leaves and cut off the tough end of the stem. Peel away the outer layer of the stalk if tough or woody. Slice lengthwise into spears for steaming, or slice stems and cut into small flowerets for steaming or stir-frying.

Broccoflower. This cross between a cauliflower and a broccoli looks like a green cauliflower. Treat as you would cauliflower.

Brussels sprouts. Looking like miniature heads of cabbage, brussels sprouts are a delight when briefly cooked and a strong-flavored unpleasant mush when cooked too long. Look for bright green, firm heads and use quickly—within two days of purchase.

To cook, remove any loose outer leaves. For uniform cooking, slice in half or cut a small × in the bottom of each vegetable.

Cabbage. Cabbages come in several colors and varieties, but all are low in calories and high in vitamin C. *Green cabbage* has light green or white leaves; *red cabbage* is purple colored; and *savoy cabbage* has light green leaves that are crinkled and flexible, making it the cabbage of choice for stuffing.

Chinese cabbages, which are closer in flavor to celery than to cabbage, come in two varieties. *Napa* is slightly sweet tasting, with long white ribs and frilly, light green tips. *Bok choy* has long white stalks and large, dark green leaves.

Cabbage family. 1 Brussels sprouts 2 Cabbage 3 Broccoli 4 Cauliflower 5 Kohlrabi 6 Broccoflower

Select cabbages that are firm and heavy for their size. Avoid heads with splits or brown spots or wilted leaves. Cabbages will store for up to two weeks in the refrigerator.

Before cooking, remove the dark-colored outer leaves of green or red cabbage, if still attached. Remove the tough white core of green, red, and savoy cabbages. With Chinese cabbages, remove the stalk end as you would celery. Then slice or shred. Head cabbages can be cut in wedges and steamed.

Red cabbage will turn blue when cooked with an acid (lemon juice or vinegar).

Cauliflower. Usually white, there are novelty varieties in green (sometimes called broccoflower) and purple. All have firm, tight flowerets and a slightly sharp flavor. Cauliflower can be served as a cooked vegetable or it can be served raw or briefly blanched in a salad or with a dip.

Look for firm white heads without brown spots. Store in the refrigerator, tightly wrapped, for up to one week.

To prepare for cooking, remove leaves and woody stem. Leave whole or break into flowerets.

Kohlrabi. This odd-looking vegetable is a green or purplish globe topped with dark leaves on long stems. The flesh inside is white and tastes like that of a turnip.

During the months of June and July, look for firm, small bulbs with crisp leaves (if still attached). Store in the refrigerator for up to a week.

Treat the leaves as you would spinach. The bulb should be peeled, then chopped, grated, or julienned. Grated kohlrabi can be used in a slaw. Chopped or julienned kohlrabi can also be served as a cooked vegetable.

FRUIT VEGETABLES

Avocados. When ripe, the pear-shaped avocado has rich, buttery flesh that is eaten raw in salads and sandwiches or mashed to make guacamole.

There are many varieties of avocado, but most supermarkets label the avocados as California (usually Hass variety) or Florida. The Hass variety has a dark, bumpy skin and is richer in taste than the smooth, green-skinned Florida (or Fuerte) variety. It is also higher in calories and fat.

It is rare to find a ripe avocado in the supermarket. So look for firm, unblemished fruits and store for a few days at room temperature. To speed ripening, place the avocados in a paper bag or in a fruit basket near other fruit. Avocados are ripe when the flesh yields to gentle pressure.

To prepare avocados, slice in half, cutting the flesh around the large

Fruit vegetables.
1 Jalapeños **2** Dried pepper
3 Tomatillo **4** Sweet bell
pepper **5** Tomatoes **6** Hot
peppers **7** Eggplant **8** Avocado

Roasting Peppers

If you have a gas stove, place the pepper directly over the burner and roast, turning often, for about 10 minutes, until blackened and blistered. Or, broil it about 4 to 6 inches from the heat, turning often, for about 15 minutes. Place the charred pepper in a paper bag, close, and set aside for 15 minutes to loosen the skin. Peel off skin, discard seeds and membrane, then rinse.

▶ **Chinese or Japanese eggplant, 115**

pit. Twist the halves in opposite directions to separate. Then carefully lift the seed out with the tip of a knife.

Avocado flesh will turn brown when exposed to air. Treat the cut surfaces with lemon juice and keep tightly wrapped. It is a myth that placing an avocado pit in the bowl with guacamole will keep the dip from darkening. Tightly wrap with plastic wrap instead.

Eggplant. A wonderful vegetable to work with because it absorbs the flavors of herbs, spices, oils, and sauces so readily. It must be cooked before serving. European and Asian eggplants are purple skinned; a white variety has sweeter flesh but requires peeling. Baby eggplants can be purple or white and the flesh is sweet and tender.

Look for firm eggplants with glossy skin and no bruises. The flesh should yield a little to gentle pressure. It can be refrigerated for up to two days; eggplant tends to get bitter if not used soon after harvest.

Peeling purple eggplants is optional, though the skin can be tough and flavorless. Some recipes require slicing, salting, and allowing the eggplant to stand for about thirty minutes before cooking, to draw out the bitterness. If the eggplant is fresh and not overripe, it should not be bitter. Salting may be a good idea if the eggplant is to be fried, as salting prevents the eggplant from absorbing as much oil as it would otherwise.

Eggplant is best combined with other ingredients as in ratatouille or moussaka. It is also delicious grilled.

Peppers. Versatile peppers come in both sweet and hot varieties. They are picked green (young but still edible) or fully ripened, in which case they may be red, yellow, orange, or purplish black. Bell peppers are often enjoyed green, as are jalapeños and many other familiar hot peppers. Peppers can be enjoyed fresh, cooked, or dried.

A Guide to Chili Peppers

Some people just *love* hot peppers, and aficionados can go beyond the heat and distinguish the flavors among peppers. While one hot pepper *can* be substituted for another, they do have distinctive tastes and differing degrees of heat.

PEPPER	DESCRIPTION	SUBSTITUTIONS
Anaheim	Medium green fresh chili with a long, narrow shape; very commonly found in supermarkets. Slightly sweet and very mild.	New Mexico
Ancho	Dried poblano chili, dark brown in color. Has a slightly nutty flavor; may be fairly mild to medium hot.	Pasilla
Bird	Very tiny, very hot fresh chili, commonly found in Thai cooking.	Pequin
Chipotle	Smoked and dried jalapeño; quite hot. Available canned or dried.	None
Habañero	Known as Scotch bonnet in the Caribbean. Possibly the hottest of the hot peppers. Prized for its fruity, pungent flavor.	None
Hungarian Wax	Yellow, shiny pepper with subtle lemony flavor. Also called banana pepper. Mild to medium hot.	Jalapeño
Jalapeño	Popular and readily available. This short, fat green pepper is medium-hot and not terribly distinctive in flavor.	Serrano
New Mexico	Mild-tasting, long green chili, found green or red.	Poblano
Pasilla	Long, thin chili, usually found dry. Name means "little raisin" in Spanish—has a slight aroma of raisin. Has more flavor than the ancho. Very hot.	Ancho
Pequin	Orange-red dried pepper; varies in size from very small to about 2 inches long. Very, very hot.	Ground cayenne
Poblano	Long, irregularly shaped pepper with mild to medium-hot flavor.	New Mexico
Serrano	Fresh, tiny, thin green or red chili with very hot flavor; often used in fresh salsas.	Jalapeño

Select fresh peppers that are brightly colored, without bruises, soft spots, or cracks. Store fresh peppers in the refrigerator for about five days. Green (young) peppers keep longer than fully ripe peppers. Dried peppers should be stored in a cool, dark, dry place for up to one year.

Hot peppers should be handled with gloves (or slip your hands into plastic bags) to avoid burns to the eyes or skin from the hot oils they contain. To reduce the heat impact of a hot pepper, remove the seeds and membranes before chopping.

Pimientos are roasted sweet red peppers with the skins removed. They are available in jars, sometimes packed in oil.

◗ **Stuffed peppers, 402**

Tomatillos. Popular in Mexican cooking, these little husked tomatoes taste sour, with hints of lemon and apples. They are available fresh year-round. Select firm fruits with tightly fitting dry husks. Store in the refrigerator for up to ten days. Remove the husks and wash well before preparing in a recipe.

Tomatoes. Vine-ripened tomatoes are so superior in flavor to green-harvested tomatoes that many people prefer to use canned tomatoes when vine-ripened ones aren't available. *Plum tomatoes*, or *Italian tomatoes*, are often preferred in cooking because they are so meaty. *Beefsteaks* are sweet and juicy, perfect for salads and sandwiches.

In addition to fresh tomatoes, there are a number of canned and dried tomato products. *Tomato puree* is made from crushed, strained tomatoes. *Tomato paste* is a cooked down, thickened puree. *Dried tomatoes* are dried plum tomatoes, sometimes sold packed in oil. The flavor of these dried tomatoes is intense so they are used sparingly.

When buying fresh tomatoes, select tomatoes that are smooth, with no soft spots. They should feel firm, but not rock hard. Store tomatoes at room temperature.

GREENS FOR COOKING

While there is some overlap between greens for cooking and salad greens, greens for cooking encompasses those leafy vegetables that taste best cooked. These include chard, collards, kale, mustard greens, and turnip greens, as well as beet greens. Rich in vitamin A and calcium, greens make a valuable addition to the diet.

Look for crisp, deep green leaves and firm stems. Keep refrigerated in perforated plastic bags and use as soon as possible. Just before cooking, rinse and drain. If the greens are large, remove the leaves from the stems, which may be too tough or stringy.

Greens reduce considerably in volume when cooked. Allow about one pound of uncooked greens for two cooked servings.

Traditionally greens are slow cooked in broth flavored with salt pork or ham. A touch of lemon juice or vinegar enhances the flavor. Greens also can be briefly steamed and then stir-fried.

Broccoli raab. A green with tiny flowerets that resemble broccoli heads, this vegetable is also called broccoli di rape, rape, and rapini. You'll find it sold in bunches; look for small, firm stems and crisp, fresh leaves. Store in perforated plastic bags in the refrigerator for up to four days.

Its sharp, slightly bitter flavor makes this a green that is best cooked; steam or stir-fry until tender. It is delicious stir-fried in butter with a little garlic.

Chard. A member of the beet family with mild flavor, chard is also known as Swiss chard. Green chard has white stems and green leaves;

Greens for cooking.
1 Broccoli raab 2 Chard
3 Kale 4 Mustard greens
5 Collards

ruby chard has red stems with red veins running through the green leafy tops. Small leaves can be used fresh in salad. Chard can replace spinach in cooked dishes.

Collards. A member of the cabbage family, collards have large, silvery green, smooth leaves and tough stems. Before cooking, chop off the stems and remove the center veins.

Kale. One of the most nutrient-rich greens, crinkly leaved kale is a member of the cabbage family. It is at its best from the fall through early spring. Look for deep green, crisp leaves.

Mustard greens. Another green from the cabbage family, young mustard greens are peppery and pleasant, but older leaves can be bitter and tough. Look for small, brightly colored, frilly leaves.

Turnip greens. Another member of the cabbage family, turnip greens are best young and have slightly bitter flavor. Look for dull, rich green leaves with no brown edges or yellow spots.

GREENS FOR SALAD

Iceberg lettuce is the most popular salad green in America, but there are plenty of other greens to complement the mild flavor of lettuce and add excitement to the salad bowl.

Look for rich color and unwilted leaves. Greens that appear yellow are past their prime.

Store lettuce and other salad greens, uncut and unwashed, in open or perforated plastic bags in the coldest part of your refrigerator. Most greens will last about a week stored this way, although butterhead and other tender greens will keep only three to four days.

Greens should be well rinsed, leaf by leaf if necessary. You can dunk and swish the leaves in water, but don't leave them soaking. Leaves can be dried with towels or in a salad spinner. Leaves should be completely dry before being placed in a salad bowl. To refresh slightly wilted greens, wash, then pat dry. Wrap in paper toweling and place in plastic bags and return to the refrigerator for about an hour.

Arugula (rocket, roquette, rogula). With a distinctive peppery taste, arugula is used in combination with other milder greens. It is mainly available in the summer and it can be eaten raw or briefly sautéed. Discard the central stem if tough. Arugula will keep for two or three days.

Belgian endive (witloof chicory). Belgian endive has a mildly bitter taste that is quite pleasing with pepper greens like watercress or arugula. Belgian endive can be eaten raw or briefly blanched. This green is a creamy white with yellow tips. Look for small, tight heads, the whiter and firmer the better.

Belgian endive is very perishable and will become more bitter with age and exposure to light, so use it within a day or two of purchase. To store, wrap in a damp cloth and place inside a perforated plastic bag.

Use in salads, fill with dips on an appetizer tray, or braise lightly as a vegetable side dish.

Curly endive (chicory). These crisp, lacy, dark green leaves have a slightly bitter flavor. Use in salads or braise lightly.

Dandelion greens. Available mostly in the spring, the cultivated variety has a pleasantly bitter flavor that is milder in taste than the wild. Look for small, tender leaves. Treat as you would arugula.

Escarole (broadleaf endive). Escarole has irregularly shaped, slightly curling green leaves. Treat as you would curly endive.

Greens for salad.
1 Belgian endive 2 Watercress 3 Arugula 4 Spinach 5 Sorrel 6 Dandelion greens 7 Radicchio

Lettuce. Supermarkets stock a wide variety of lettuces. The familiar *iceberg* has crisp, bland, light green leaves; *butterheads (Bibb and Boston)* have soft, buttery leaves and form loose heads; *leaf lettuce* may be red or green with frilly edges and delicate flavor; and *romaine* has a bold taste and long, dark green leaves. Combining lettuce with sharp-flavored greens makes an interesting salad.

Mesclun. Sometimes it is possible to buy mixes of greens for salads. Mesclun is a mix that typically contains edible flowers, such as nasturtium, as well as baby lettuce, peppery arugula, and other herbs.

Radicchio. A red chicory that is prized for its lovely purple and white marbled leaves, radicchio is quite bitter and should be mixed with other greens.

Sorrel (sour grass). Sorrel's distinctive lemony snap makes it a good choice for an addition to salad bowls. It is also used as a potherb to flavor soups.

Spinach. Delicious raw or cooked, fresh spinach is available year-round. Look for broad, dark green, crisp leaves. Generally, it is better to buy loose spinach than to risk the prepackaged spinach, which may contain decaying or slimy leaves. Spinach tends to be quite sandy, so wash in several changes of water.

To store, open packaged spinach and remove any wilted leaves. Place spinach in a plastic bag and refrigerate for two to three days.

Watercress. Available year-round, watercress has a peppery flavor. It will keep for two or three days in a plastic bag in the refrigerator or with the stems submerged in a jar of water and the top leaves covered with plastic.

ONION FAMILY

Garlic. The most pungent of the onion family, garlic is strongest in flavor when used raw and mellows as it is cooked. It is available year-round and most varieties can be used interchangeably, with the exception of elephant garlic, which is a giant garlic with mild flavor. To substitute for regular garlic, double the amount used.

Buy firm, plump bulbs and store in a cool, dry, dark place. Remove cloves as needed.

Leeks. Less strongly flavored than onions, leeks can be used interchangeably with them in cooked dishes. Look for bright green, moist leaves. The bulb end should be fresh-looking and not shriveled. Smaller leeks are likely to be more tender than large ones. Store in the refrigerator in a plastic bag for up to five days.

Leeks can hold quite a lot of dirt inside. To clean, leave the root end intact but slice the leek in half lengthwise and then quarter lengthwise. Rinse under running water, fanning out the layers to expose all the inner leaves to the water. Then chop or slice to use in a cooked dish.

Onion family. 1 Garlic
2 Green onions 3 Red
onion 4 Yellow onions
5 Leeks 6 Shallots

Onions. Used extensively for flavoring, onions can be enjoyed green (scallions) or as mature bulbs. Among the bulb onions, for boiling there are the pickling onions and tiny white *pearl onions*; for boiling; for eating fresh in salads and sandwiches there are *Italian, Spanish, Vidalia, Walla Walla,* and *Maui onions*—all of them sweet onions with red, yellow, or white skins; and for cooking there is the familiar *yellow onion.*

Look for firm, dry bulbs with a papery outer skin. Avoid any that have begun to sprout. Select green onions with fresh, unwilted tops and clean white roots.

Yellow onions are good keepers; they will keep in a dry, well-ventilated place for several months. Green onions are the most perishable; they should be wrapped and placed in the refrigerator for about five days. Sweet onions will keep in the refrigerator for up to several weeks, depending on the variety.

Shallots. Shallots are the most delicately flavored of the onion family. They can be eaten raw but are most often used in cooked dishes. Shallots form cloves, as does garlic. The cloves are generally sold loose or as a partial head. The cloves should be peeled before you chop or mince them.

ROOT VEGETABLES AND TUBERS

Root vegetables may not be much to look at, but their deep, rich flavors, year-round availability, and low cost make them very valuable in the kitchen.

With the exception of sweet potatoes and Irish potatoes, store root vegetables loose in the refrigerator; don't put them in the vegetable crisper, which may be too humid for them. Look for leafy tops, which

♦ **Green onion garnishes,**
404

Root vegetables and tubers. 1 Jerusalem artichoke 2 Sweet potato 3 Yam 4 Turnip 5 Potatoes 6 Celery root 7 Beets 8 Carrots

indicate freshness, but trim them about one inch from the root as soon as you get the vegetables home.

Beets. Look for small vegetables—no more than one to two inches in diameter. Trim off the greens, wash, and store separately in a plastic bag lined with a paper towel. The greens will keep for three days; the roots for about one week.

Beets are easily peeled after they have been cooked and will retain better color if cooked first. However, you can peel with a paring knife, cut the beets into matchsticks and pan-fry to make a colorful, crunchy addition to a mixed dish of sautéed carrots and parsnips.

Carrots. This familiar sweet orange root is packed with vitamin A. It will keep in plastic bags in the refrigerator for at least two weeks.

Look for bright, crisp roots with no cracks. If the tops are attached, they should be fresh-looking. If the crown of a carrot has a green tinge, cut it off before serving, as the taste is bitter.

Carrots should be peeled or scrubbed before using. A slightly wilted carrot can be refreshed by soaking it in ice water for thirty minutes.

Celery root (celeriac). This softball-sized, irregularly shaped bulb is related to celery. It tastes and smells like celery, with overtones of walnut.

Select firm roots that appear heavy for their size. Refrigerate in plastic bags for up to one month. It is available from November through April.

Peel just before using and toss the flesh with a little lemon juice to prevent discoloring. Celery root can be sliced or shredded raw into salads, added to soups, or baked in creamy gratins.

Jerusalem artichokes (sunchokes). This mildly flavored, knobby tuber can be eaten raw or cooked. Eaten raw, the texture is crisp and the taste is sweet—just peel and slice. They can also be roasted whole, or sliced and deep-fried or pan-fried, or baked in a casserole.

Look for large, firm tubers. The more regular the shape, the easier to peel. Store in the refrigerator for up to two weeks.

Jicama. Pronounced HEE-cuh-muh, this tropical tuber has ivory flesh that resembles a water chestnut in texture. It is pleasingly crunchy and sweet both raw and cooked, but its best feature is that it does not soften or discolor when cut, so it is ideal to use as a garnish. It also does well as a crudité.

The size of a jicama can vary from ½ to 6 pounds. Look for unblemished tubers with a silken sheen. Store whole jicamas loose in the refrigerator for up to two weeks. Once cut, it should be covered tightly with plastic wrap, refrigerated, and used within one week.

Peel first, using a paring knife and removing the skin and fibrous underlayer.

Parsnips. The underappreciated parsnip looks like a carrot and can be treated like a carrot in cooked dishes. It has a very sweet flavor. Select small to medium parsnips and store for up to ten days in the refrigerator.

Potatoes. *Irish potatoes* are sometimes called white potatoes, but in fact they may be red, white, yellow, or even purple. Some varieties are sold as all-purpose potatoes, good for mashing, salads, and baking; others are best for specific purposes.

The thin-skinned *long white potato* is a good all-purpose potato; *round white potatoes* have a firm and waxy texture that is well-suited to boiling. *Russets*, or *Idahos*, are thick-skinned and best for baking. *Round red potatoes*, which are sometimes mislabeled as new potatoes, are good for boiling. Prized for their buttery flesh, *yellow potatoes*, or *new potatoes*, are good for boiling and frying. New potatoes are potatoes that have never been stored and may be red or white; they should be thin skinned and small.

Buy potatoes that are firm and smooth, with no signs of sprouting, wilting, or discolored spots (green spots should be cut away). Store in a cool, dry, dark place; in the summer, purchase in small quantities.

Radishes. There are several varieties of radishes to choose from, and all are served raw, except the Japanese *daikon,* which may be sliced raw into salads or cooked as you would turnips. Daikons are long white radishes with a mildly spicy radish flavor. *Red radishes* have bright red skins and pure white flesh; the flavor can be quite mild to rather spicy. *Icicle radishes* are milder white-skinned radishes and *French breakfast radishes* are an elongated version of the red radish. *Black radishes* have black skin and white flesh and are quite pungent.

Look for crisp radishes with no cracks or black spots. Store in a plastic bag for about one week. Radishes are eaten skin and all; just rinse off any dirt and remove the roots.

Rutabagas. Cousin to the turnip, rutabagas are large and round with tan, green, or purple skins and yellow flesh. Size makes no difference in taste; medium-size ones are somewhat easier to handle. They will keep for up to a month in the refrigerator. Cook as you would turnips, keeping in mind that rutabagas are sweeter and more strongly flavored.

Salsify (oyster plant). Salsify is a long, slender root that is found mainly in the early spring. A black-skinned cousin, known as scorzonera, is somewhat more difficult to find as it is imported from Belgium. In recipes the two varieties are pretty much interchangeable and have a very mild oyster flavor. Store in the refrigerator for up to two weeks.

Uncooked salsify discolors badly when peeled. The easiest way to handle this root is to peel it and slice or chop it into acidulated water (one tablespoon vinegar to one quart water). Alternatively, you can cook it whole and then peel it.

Salsify will leave a sticky residue on pots and utensils. Unlike other root vegetables, it should not be pureed; the process turns the salsify into a gummy mess.

Sweet potatoes. Much of what is sold as yams in this country are actually sweet potatoes. (Yams grow in the tropics and have brown skin and yellow or white flesh.) By any name, these tubers are delicious, with sweet, buttery flesh. Look for firm, medium-size potatoes; the darker the skin, the sweeter the flesh tends to be. Store in a cool, dark, dry place for up to a week.

Don't limit yourself to baked and candied sweet potatoes; treat as you would Irish potatoes, and serve sweet potatoes pan-fried, roasted, and in salads and gratins.

Turnips. Turnips come in a range of shapes and sizes, but the best turnips are harvested young, when they are sweet and tender enough to eat raw. Large, mature turnips have a stronger flavor and should be used in recipes that require longer cooking times.

Select blemish-free turnips that are heavy for their size. Refrigerate for up to one week. Peel before using.

SHOOTS AND STEMS

Artichokes. Artichokes are available year-round, but peak harvest time is in the spring, and it's then that you'll find the best price. Spring artichokes will be green; during the colder months, the chokes will have a purple tinge, which indicates frostbite—but there is no loss of flavor or texture.

Select artichokes that are heavy for their size, with tight, thick leaves. Artichokes that have been stored for too long will have leaves that are beginning to open, as well as black spots. Allow one medium-size artichoke per person.

Store in a plastic bag in the refrigerator for up to one week.

▸ Yams, 114

Shoots and stems. 1 Fiddlehead ferns 2 Artichoke 3 Asparagus 4 Fennel 5 Celery

Asparagus. Although fresh asparagus is available year-round, the peak season is April through May. Then the long, slender, edible stalks are available locally, and the delicate flavor is at its best. Both green and white varieties are grown, though the green is more common.

Look for spears that are crisp and well rounded, not ridged. The tips should be tight and free from damage. The spears may be thick or thin, but select ones of uniform thickness for uniform cooking. Allow about ⅓ pound per serving.

Asparagus will keep for up to four days in perforated plastic bags in the refrigerator. Wrap the bases in moist paper towels before placing in the plastic bags.

Celery. It may be a myth that celery has "negative calories" (meaning that digesting celery burns more calories than you consume), but there is no question that with five calories per stalk, celery is good for diets.

Look for bright green leaves on top of crisp, deep green to white stalks or ribs. Celery hearts are the most tender stalks, taken from the interior of the plant.

Wrap celery in moist paper towels, then place in a plastic bag in the refrigerator for up to two weeks. Slightly wilted celery can be refreshed in ice water for two to three hours.

Fennel. Florence fennel, or finocchio, is grown for its seeds (fennel seeds), its feathery tops, and its anise-tasting bulb. The bulb has the texture of crisp celery and is delicious raw or cooked.

Available from September through April, fresh fennel should have firm, crisp bulbs without cracks or soft spots. Remove the leaves and store in a perforated plastic bag in the refrigerator for a day or two.

If you are serving fennel as a vegetable, allow one bulb for every two people. Cut off and discard the upper stalks (reserving the feathery leaves to use as a potherb). Remove any wilted outer layers of stalks and cut off a thin slice from the bottom. Cut each bulb into quarters. The fennel is then ready for steaming (6 to 10 minutes).

Fiddlehead ferns. A wild (uncultivated) green that finds its way into specialty markets from April through June, fiddlehead ferns are the young, tightly curled green shoots of the ostrich fern.

Select firm, brightly colored ferns with tightly furled heads. Store in perforated plastic bags in the refrigerator for up to two days.

To remove the papery skins, wash in several changes of water. Drop into boiling water and cook until tender crisp, about 6 minutes. Drain off and discard the brackish cooking water. Rinse the fiddleheads, remove any remaining skins, and pat dry. The fiddleheads can then be briefly sautéed with butter and lemon or cooked in a cream soup.

VINE VEGETABLES

Chayote (mirliton or vegetable pear). A chayote is a pear-shaped squash with crisp flesh. Its skin is smooth or furrowed, light or dark green. Its mild flavor can be described as a cross between cucumber and summer squash. Look for chayote in the markets in early fall; it will keep in the refrigerator for up to two weeks.

Peel, then cook as you would summer squash. The single large, soft seed is edible.

Cucumbers. Cucumbers are available year-round, though the best Kirby, or pickling, cucumbers are to be found only in the summer. Reg-

Vine vegetables.
1 Summer squash 2 Zucchini 3 Acorn squash
4 Spaghetti squash 5 Pumpkin 6 Butternut squash
7 Chayote 8 Cucumber

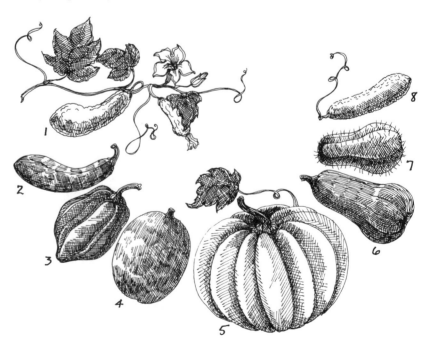

ular cucumbers are usually waxed to retard spoilage and must be peeled before eating. *Kirby cucumbers* are never waxed and can be eaten skin and all. *European*, or *seedless English*, *cucumbers* are usually wrapped in plastic wrap in lieu of waxing and are more expensive than regular cucumbers. Look for well-colored, firm cucumbers and store in the refrigerator for up to two weeks.

If the cucumber is mature and filled with seeds, you may want to seed it. Slice the cucumber in half lengthwise. Run a spoon down the length of the cucumber to scrape away the seeds and watery pulp that surrounds the seeds. The remaining cucumber will be crescent shaped when sliced.

Pumpkin. *Pie pumpkins*, or *sugar pumpkins*, are available from September through December in most grocery stores; their sweet flesh can be used in all manner of desserts from pies to ice cream to cheesecake.

To prepare a pie pumpkin, slice the top off the pumpkin. Scrape out the seeds and fibrous strings. Cut into large pieces and arrange in a single layer in a baking pan. Bake at 375°F. for 1 to 1½ hours, until tender. Allow to cool enough to handle. Scrape the pulp off the rind. Puree in a blender or food processor until smooth. If very watery, drain in a cheesecloth-lined strainer. Then use as you would canned cooked pumpkin. One 6-pound pumpkin will yield 2 cups of puree, enough for one pie.

Summer squash. Squashes that are harvested young and have tender, edible skin and seeds are called summer squash, though they are available fresh year-round. *Zucchini* has dark green skin and off-white flesh. Its flavor is quite bland—the moist flesh is used for everything from casseroles to chocolate cakes. *Yellow squash* comes in straight and crookneck varieties; its flavor is similar to zucchini. *Pattypan squash* has a unique scalloped shape and looks quite attractive stuffed.

The smaller the squash, the better. Look for squashes with shiny, unblemished skin, with an inch of stem still attached. One pound will serve four people. Store in a perforated plastic bag in the refrigerator for four to five days.

Winter squash. Sweet-fleshed, hearty, hard-shelled winter squash are available fresh in the fall and winter, but can be bought mashed and frozen throughout the year. There are many varieties available and each has a distinctive flavor (see the table on page 38). Select squashes that have no soft spots and are heavy for their size. When buying precut sections of large-sized squash, be sure the flesh is brightly colored and not bruised.

If you have a dry, cool (50°F.) basement, you can store winter squash for up to six months. Store cut squash in the refrigerator for up to one week.

Although each squash has a distinct flavor, and some are drier or

Winter Squash Varieties

SQUASH	DESCRIPTION
Acorn	Green, acorn-shaped; golden to bright orange meat. Flesh is sweet and slightly dry; often basted with a butter/maple syrup or brown sugar mixture as it bakes.
Butternut	Long, smooth, tan shell. Bright orange, sweet, nutty flesh.
Delicata	Elongated yellow shell, streaked with green and orange. Buttery flavored flesh described as a cross between corn, butternut squash, and sweet potatoes.
Hubbard	Irregularly shaped shell of pale gray with a tapering end; ranges in size from large to very large. Rich, smooth orange meat.
Turban	Round, orange skin; flattened bottom and knobby top. Bright orange flesh; very sweet and very rich.
Spaghetti	Pale gold shell. Yellow flesh resembles spaghetti strands when cooked. Not a true winter squash; prepared as a winter squash, but does not keep as well.

stringier when cooked, you can usually use them interchangeably in recipes, though you may want to adjust the seasoning depending on how sweet a variety you are using.

MUSHROOMS

Supermarkets and specialty stores now stock a wide array of fresh and dried mushrooms, some of them wild, most of them—even exotic ones, such as shiitake, oyster mushrooms, and enoki—cultivated.

Fresh mushrooms should be firm and plump with no bruises or wet spots. Place in a paper bag or on a tray in a single layer covered with dampened cheesecloth wrap for up to two days. Dried mushrooms will keep for about six months in a cool, dry spot.

Mushrooms are often quite dirty. They can be wiped clean with a damp cloth. Don't soak them in water, however; they will absorb water and become mushy.

Trim off the bottom part of the mushroom stem (discard the stem of shiitakes), then slice or chop.

Soak dried mushrooms in warm water until soft, about fifteen minutes. About three ounces of dried mushrooms is equivalent to one pound of fresh mushrooms.

Button mushrooms. The common white mushrooms found in supermarkets can be large or small. The flavor is mild.

Cèpe (Porcini). A member of the *Boletus edulis* species of wild mushrooms, cèpes are occasionally found fresh and more readily found dried. This mushroom is considered superior tasting to connoisseurs.

Chanterelles. The cap of the yellow-orange chanterelle is not distinctly separate from the stem as it is with other mushrooms. The flavor is sweet, vaguely reminiscent of apricots. Parboil before using.

♦ **Mushroom garnishes,**
405–406

Mushrooms. 1 Shiitake
2 Oyster mushrooms
3 Cèpe 4 Button mushrooms 5 Morel
6 Chanterelles 7 Enoki

Enoki. These mild-tasting mushrooms have long, slender stems with a tiny cap. They are often served raw.

Morels. Available in early spring and into summer, morels range in color from cream to dark brown. Sizes vary, but they all have hollow, conical caps and an aromatic flavor, reminiscent of hazelnuts or nutmeg.

Oyster mushrooms. An Oriental variety that was once found only in the wild, oyster mushrooms are now being cultivated and are increasingly common. The large, flowerlike cap is bluish gray in color and the flavor is mild.

Shiitake. These brown Oriental mushrooms have a tough stem (which is usually discarded) and a large brown cap. Available fresh or dried.

Nuts and Seeds

Nuts and seeds are good sources of protein and fiber, although high in fats and oils. They can be bought shelled or unshelled; raw, blanched, or roasted; whole, slivered, or chopped.

Buying nuts in the shell is generally the most economical; whole nuts last longer and are less likely to be stale. Most nuts yield easily to a nutcracker, a notable exception being the macadamia nut, which is most often bought shelled. To tell if a whole nut is fresh, shake it. You should not hear it rattle, unless it is a peanut. A rattle indicates the nut is dry and stale.

Nuts and seeds. I Pine
nuts (pignolia) **2** Sunflower
seeds **3** Sesame seeds
4 Coconut **5** Almonds
6 Hazelnuts **7** Walnuts
8 Peanuts

Because of their high oil content, nuts are prone to going rancid, which can be detected as an off flavor or odor. To avoid that, buy nuts in small quantities and store in airtight containers for several months in the refrigerator and up to a year in the freezer, depending on the nut.

Blenders and food processors can be used for chopping, using the pulse setting. Be very careful not to grind the nuts to a paste. When chopping nuts by hand, use the chopping technique described on page 185.

Almonds and hazelnuts can be used interchangeably in most recipes, as can walnuts and pecans. Walnuts can replace pine nuts in pesto for an interesting change in flavor.

Almonds. Almonds are used whole, slivered, sliced, chopped, and ground into a paste. Store in the refrigerator for up to nine months or in the freezer at 0°F. for one year.

Almonds sometimes require blanching to remove their papery brown skins. To do so, cover the nuts with boiling water and let soak for 3 to 5 minutes. Then drain, and rub the skins off with your fingers.

Brazil nuts. The large ivory-colored nuts have a rich, oily flavor and are most often eaten as a snack. Buy in small quantities as these are especially prone to going rancid. Store shelled and unshelled nuts in airtight containers in the refrigerator or freezer at 0°F. for up to nine months.

Cashews. You can buy cashews raw or roasted, but you'll never find cashews in the shell as the shell contains a caustic oil. Buttery flavored cashews are great for snacks. In cooked or baked dishes, they tend to become soggy. Store in an airtight container in the refrigerator for six months or in the freezer for up to one year.

Chestnuts. A favorite for roasting and serving at holiday time, chestnuts have a sweet flavor and a moist, crumbly texture. Buy whole, unshelled, and keep in the refrigerator in a plastic bag for about two weeks.

For use in cooking and for longer term storage, blanch the nuts by scoring an × on the flat side of each chestnut. Then boil in water to cover for about fifteen minutes. Drain and peel the chestnuts. The blanched nuts can be used immediately or stored in an airtight container in the freezer for up to twelve months.

Coconuts. Though we think of these as nuts, they are actually a fruit. Coconuts are used extensively in the cooking of the Caribbean and Southeast Asia.

Coconut water, the liquid inside the coconut, is used in mixed drinks in the Caribbean. *Coconut milk* is made by pressing hot water through grated coconut. *Coconut cream* is an enriched version of coconut milk; commercial coconut cream is often sweetened to be used in mixed drinks and should *not* be used as a substitute for coconut milk. The creamy, sweet white meat of the coconut is sold in cans or packages, shredded or flaked, sweetened or unsweetened. Canned coconut is closer to fresh in taste and texture and after opening will keep in a tightly sealed bag in the refrigerator for five to seven days. Dried coconut will keep for three to four weeks.

To buy a whole coconut, select a nut in which you can hear liquid sloshing. Uncracked, the nut will keep at room temperature for up to one month. To extract the coconut meat, pierce the eyes of the coconut with an ice pick or skewer and drain out the coconut water. Then bake the nut in a 400°F. oven for about fifteen minutes. This causes the meat to shrink from the shell. Smash the shell with a hammer and remove the flesh, flipping it out with a strong knife. Peel off the brown membrane with a paring knife. Then cut the meat into small pieces. The meat can be grated in a food processor fitted with a steel blade. Freeze any extra coconut for up to six months at 0°F.

To make coconut milk, combine 2 cups of cubed fresh coconut meat with 1¼ cups very hot water in a blender or food processor. Process for one to two minutes. Then cool for at least five minutes. Strain the mixture through a fine sieve lined with a double thickness of cheesecloth. Squeeze out all the liquid. This method yields about 1½ cups of fresh coconut milk.

Hazelnuts (filberts). The sweet, rich flavor of hazelnuts can be found in gourmet coffees, liqueur, and all manner of desserts. Hazelnuts are sold unshelled or shelled. Store in an airtight container in a cool, dry place for three months or for up to nine months in the refrigerator.

Usually the nuts are sold unblanched, but you will occasionally find them ready to use in specialty food stores. To remove the papery brown skins, toast in a 350°F. oven for five to seven minutes, then wrap the nuts in a clean kitchen towel and rub off the skins.

Macadamia nuts. Grown in Hawaii and California, these nuts are white, crisp, and sweet, with a high oil content. Because the shiny

Nut Yields

ONE POUND NUTS IN SHELLS	YIELD OF NUTMEAT
Almonds	1¼ cups
Hazelnuts	1½ cups
Peanuts	2 cups
Pecans	2¼ cups
Walnuts	1¾ cups

Peanut Butter: America's Favorite Spread

Peanut butter can be a simple paste of ground peanuts, or it can be sweetened, salted, and hydrogenated so that the oils don't separate out of the paste.

Ethnic recipes—Indonesian or Chinese, for example—that call for peanut butter are best made with unsweetened, unsalted, "natural" peanut butter.

All-natural peanut butters should be refrigerated after opening and will keep for about six months. Stir well before using. Other peanut butters will keep without refrigeration for three months, with refrigeration for six months. Unopened jars will keep for two years in a cool, dry spot.

Tahini: The Sesame Paste Spread from the Middle East

A spread made of ground sesame seeds, tahini is an essential ingredient in many dishes from the Middle East, including hummus. Refrigerate after opening and keep for about six months. Let it come to room temperature before using; then stir well to mix the separated oil back into the thick paste. Unopened jars will keep for about two years in a cool, dry spot.

brown shells are difficult to crack, macadamias are seldom sold in the shell. Most are sold in cans: shelled, roasted, and salted.

Peanuts. Although really a legume, peanuts are eaten and cooked like nuts. They are purchased shelled or unshelled; raw, roasted in oil, or dry-roasted; or made into peanut butter. Roasting brings out the buttery, nutty flavor of peanuts.

Raw peanuts in the shell can be stored for up to two months in an airtight container at room temperature, three to six months in the refrigerator, or for an indefinite period in the freezer. Roasted peanuts are more perishable but will keep for up to one month at room temperature, six months in the refrigerator, and for one year in the freezer.

Pecans. A true American ingredient, pecans are particularly identified with Southern cooking. Store unshelled pecans in a cool, dry place and use within six months. Shelled pecans are best kept under refrigeration in an airtight container; use within nine months or freeze at 0°F. for up to two years.

Pine nuts (pignolia, piñons). A flavorful ingredient in pesto, pine nuts are the ivory-colored, sweet-tasting kernels of a variety of pine tree. They are sold shelled or unshelled and always are raw or unroasted. They become rancid quite easily and should be bought in small quantities and kept refrigerated.

Pistachios. The pistachio nut has green flesh and a shell that is grayish white, thin, smooth, brittle—and often dyed red. They are used in pâtés and ice cream and for snacking. Pistachios are often found in Indian and Middle Eastern desserts. Whether shelled or unshelled, they can keep in the refrigerator for about three months or for up to one year in the freezer at 0°F.

Sesame seeds. Available with or without their hulls, the seeds can be used plain but have more flavor after being toasted. The tiny, flat seeds come in brown, red, and black varieties, as well as the familiar ivory. Store the seeds in the refrigerator or freezer for up to one year.

Sunflower seeds. Sunflower seeds are sold both hulled and unhulled, raw and roasted. The hulled seeds are commonly added to granola mixes and whole grain breads and add a nice crunch to salads. Store the seeds in the refrigerator or freezer for up to one year.

Walnuts. The mildly flavored *English walnut,* also known as the California or Persian walnut, is the most common variety of walnut. *Black walnuts* are native to America and intensely flavored, but difficult to remove from the shell and not widely available.

Walnuts are available shelled or unshelled. Shelled walnuts should be stored in an airtight container and refrigerated or frozen at 0°F. for up to one year. In the shell, they will keep at room temperature for about three months.

lavorings

ALCOHOL: WINES, LIQUEURS, AND HARD LIQUORS

In many recipes, wine, liqueur, or hard liquor is used for flavoring. It has been widely assumed that the alcohol is burning off in the cooking. Recent studies suggest that the amount of alcohol retained in cooked foods depends on the type of heat, the source of alcohol, and the

Liqueurs and Their Flavors

LIQUEUR	FLAVOR	USES
Amaretto, Crème d'Amandes	Almonds	Desserts
Calvados	Apples	Poultry, pork, and veal; desserts
Cassis	Black currants	Desserts
Cointreau, Curaçao, Grand Marnier	Oranges	Poultry; desserts
Crème de Cacao	Chocolate flavored with vanilla	Desserts
Crème de Menthe	Peppermint	Desserts
Fraise	Strawberries	Desserts
Framboise, Chambord	Raspberries	Desserts
Kahlua, Tia Maria	Coffee	Desserts
Kirsch	Cherries	Poultry; fondue; desserts
Kümmel	Caraway	Pork sausage; cabbage, sauerkraut
Mirabelle, Prunelle, Slivovitz	Plums	Desserts
Pernod	Anise	Fish
Poire William	Pears	Desserts

♦ Oriental wines, 115

Flavorings. 1 Mustard
2 Carob **3** Cocoa **4** Vanilla
5 Ginger **6** Horseradish

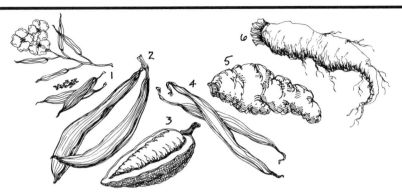

length of cooking, but some alcohol—anywhere from 5 to 85 percent—is retained in the dish no matter how it is cooked.

For the specific flavors that various liqueurs contribute, see the table on page 44.

CAROB

Anyone who expects chocolate and gets carob will be sorely disappointed, but used as a flavoring on its own—not as a chocolate substitute—carob is quite pleasing. It has a sweet, molasses flavor, slightly reminiscent of chocolate. It is sold as a powder or as sweetened chips. Store in a cool, dry place.

Carob is often touted as a healthier food than chocolate. While it does lack the caffeine of chocolate, it is not much lower in fat and calories (1 ounce of carob chips contains 140 calories and 7 grams of fat; 1 ounce of semisweet chocolate chips contains 143 calories and 10.2 grams of fat).

CHOCOLATE

Always a favorite flavor, chocolate comes in many forms (see table on page 45). Premium brands are often, but not always, superior in flavor to standard supermarket brands. But do beware of imitation chocolate products, which replace some or all of the cocoa butter with less expensive vegetable oils.

Chocolate should be stored in an airtight container in a cool, dry place. When the temperature exceeds 78°F., you may want to refrigerate it, but keep the chocolate very tightly wrapped so it doesn't absorb odors from other foods. Also, when bringing the refrigerated chocolate to room temperature, keep it wrapped. Otherwise condensation from the wrapper may drip on the chocolate, which would cause the chocolate to "seize" (described on page 268) when melted.

Chocolate that has been stored where it is too warm or too humid will develop a grayish "bloom." This doesn't affect the flavor or melting properties of chocolate.

For tips on working with chocolate, see page 268.

▶ **Melting chocolate in microwave, 257**

CHOCOLATE	DESCRIPTION	SUBSTITUTE
Unsweetened Chocolate	Also known as baking chocolate. The basic chocolate from which all other chocolate products are made. Roasted cocoa beans are pressed in special machines until the cocoa butter liquefies. The resulting chocolate liquor is then poured into molds to harden into 1-ounce cakes of pure chocolate.	For 1 ounce unsweetened chocolate: 3 tablespoons cocoa plus 1 tablespoon shortening or cooking oil.
Cocoa	Made by processing the chocolate liquor to remove most of the cocoa butter. Then it is cooled, pulverized, and sifted to produce unsweetened cocoa. Breakfast cocoa has slightly more cocoa butter than plain cocoa. Dutch cocoa has been treated with an alkali that darkens the cocoa and imparts a distinctive taste.	
Semisweet Chocolate	Used in baking; a blend of unsweetened chocolate, cocoa butter, and sugar. Sold as chips and bars. Can be used in place of bittersweet chocolate in a recipe.	For 1 ounce semisweet chocolate: 1 ounce unsweetened chocolate plus 1 tablespoon sugar.
Bittersweet Chocolate	Eaten out of hand; sometimes used in baking. A blend of unsweetened chocolate, cocoa butter, and sugar. Can be used in place of semisweet chocolate in a recipe, though it contains less sugar.	
Sweet Cooking Chocolate	Also known as German chocolate. Light, mild blend of unsweetened chocolate, sugar, and cocoa butter.	For 4 ounces sweet chocolate: 1/4 cup cocoa powder, plus 1/3 cup sugar, plus 3 tablespoons shortening.
Milk Chocolate	Sweet chocolate with milk added.	Semisweet or sweet cooking chocolate, ounce for ounce.
White Chocolate	Made of sugar, cocoa butter, dry milk solids, and flavorings.	Semisweet chocolate or milk chocolate, ounce for ounce.

CONDIMENTS AND SAUCES

Additional sauces can be found under Foods of the Orient, page 115–116. Unopened jars of these ingredients can be stored in a cool, dry place for up to a year; opened jars should be stored in the refrigerator and used within two to three months, unless otherwise noted.

Barbecue sauce. Dual-purpose barbecue sauce can be used as a glaze for grilled meats or it can be served as an accompaniment to meats as a tangier version of ketchup. Barbecue sauce usually is made with tomatoes, onions, mustard, brown sugar, and seasonings.

Chili sauce. Like barbecue sauce, chili sauce can be used as a recipe ingredient or a condiment. Chili sauce is usually made with tomatoes, sweet and hot peppers, vinegar, onions, spices, and sugar. It is usually spicier and thinner than ketchup.

Chutney. A traditional accompaniment to curries, chutney makes a delicious accompaniment to all manner of roasted meats. It is made from fruit, vinegar, sugar, and spices. The texture may be smooth or chunky, and the flavor may be sweet and mild or quite spicy.

Duck sauce. This sweet-and-sour condiment is sometimes called plum sauce. It can be made of either plums, apricots, or peaches, with sugar, vinegar, and spices added.

Ketchup. The all-American favorite for garnishing burgers and accompanying french fries, ketchup is made from tomatoes, vinegar, sugar, salt, and spices. Ketchup is often used as an ingredient in other sauces.

Mustard. Made from the ground yellow, black, or white seeds of the mustard plant, mustard adds a distinctive spicy flavor to foods. Over the years, many different blends of mustard pastes have been developed. Some are smooth, others are coarse-grained. All should be stored in the refrigerator and used as quickly as possible. After six months, the flavors of the best mustards fade.

American mustard is a smooth blend made with mustard, vinegar, and turmeric, from which it derives its bright yellow color. It is mild and slightly sweet, perfect on hot dogs and soft pretzels and necessary in deviled eggs.

Chinese mustard, or *English mustard*, is sold as a bright yellow powder (mustard powder) or as a blend made with the powder and water or vinegar. It is quite hot, though it loses its bite as it is exposed to air.

Dijon mustard is made from mustard seeds, salt, spices, and white wine or verjuice (an acid juice made from unripe green grapes). Dijon mustard is creamy gray-yellow in color and has a clean, sharp flavor, perfect for vinaigrettes and mayonnaises. Another French mustard is *Bordeaux mustard,* made with unfermented Bordeaux wine. It is darker, more acidic, and more aromatic than Dijon mustard, and it complements meat nicely.

Pepper sauce. Sauces made from aged peppers and vinegars are popular in the cooking of Louisiana and the Caribbean. *Tabasco* is an extremely hot version; *Louisiana-style hot sauces* are generally less hot. *Jamaican-style hot sauces* are usually both sweet and hot. Expect these sauces to last about a year at room temperature, whether they are opened or not. You can refrigerate them, but it won't extend their shelf life. If a sauce becomes discolored, throw it out. When a recipe calls for "liquid red pepper seasoning," use Tabasco sauce.

Soy sauce. Made from fermented soybeans, there are many versions of this salty brown liquid, but the best have no additives or artificial color. If you shake a bottle of high-quality soy sauce vigorously, a thick foamy head will form at the top.

⬧ **Mustard substitute, 301**
⬧ **Oriental condiments, 115–116**

Chinese light soy, not to be confused with various "lite" or *low-sodium American-made soy* sauces, is a light-colored soy with a delicate flavor. *Dark soy*, or *shoyu*, is darker in color, due to the addition of caramel. *Sweet soy*, also called *ketjap manis*, is a dark sauce made sweet with molasses. *Tamari* is a pure Japanese dark soy.

Soy sauce has a long shelf life and can be kept for up to a year at room temperature, opened.

Teriyaki sauce. A marinade for chicken or beef, teriyaki sauce usually contains soy sauce, wine or sake, sugar, ginger, and other seasonings. The sugar makes a nice brown glaze on meats that have been marinated in the sauce. Store opened bottles for up to a year at room temperature.

Worcestershire sauce. An unlikely combination of tamarind, molasses, sugar, anchovies, garlic, salt, and other ingredients gives Worcestershire sauce its unique flavor. It is generally used to season meats and gravies. The exact ingredients of Worcestershire sauce is kept a secret; "steak sauces" are generally imitations of the genuine sauce.

EXTRACTS AND ESSENTIAL OILS

The essential oils of certain flowers, fruits, nuts, and herbs are extracted and mixed with an alcohol base to form such familiar flavoring extracts as *vanilla extract*, which is the extract of the cured vanilla pod, the seedpod of an orchid. Other common extracts are almond, rum, maple, orange, lemon, banana, and mint. *Grenadine* is the extract of the pulp of the pomegranate.

Extracts can be stored in tightly capped dark bottles for about six months at room temperature. They don't spoil, but they change in flavor over time.

The same essential oils that make up extracts, but without the alcohol base, can also be found in drugstores and confectioners' supply stores to use in flavoring candy.

Rosewater and orange blossom water. In the Middle East and India, waters distilled from flowers are as common for flavoring as vanilla is here. Rosewater is used to flavor drinks and desserts. Gourmet shops will stock French rosewater, but less expensive floral waters can be found in Indian and Middle Eastern food shops. The waters will keep indefinitely, with a small loss of fragrance over time.

RHIZOMES AND ROOTS

Fresh ginger. A staple in Chinese cooking, fresh ginger is hotter and more flavorful than the ground, dried spice. The tan roots have bulging knobs growing at irregular angles. Look for plump rhizomes with unbroken skin.

Slice off what you need and store what's left, tightly wrapped, in the refrigerator. Fresh ginger will keep for two to three weeks. Or store in the freezer at 0°F. for about four weeks, again slicing off pieces as needed. You can also store the root, covered with dry sherry, in a jar. Keep in the refrigerator and slice off pieces as needed. Use the spiced liquid for salad dressings, topping off the jar each time you draw off some liquid.

To use fresh ginger, peel away the tan skin, then mince with a chopping knife, or add whole, unpeeled slices to marinades.

Horseradish. Horseradish is both a root and a prepared sauce; either way it is distinguished by its fiery flavor. The large woody root is found in the produce section from fall through spring. Store in a plastic bag for up to two weeks.

To make prepared horseradish, peel the root with a paring knife. Cut into 2-inch pieces and process in a food processor until fine textured, adding a little water or vinegar if the root is particularly dry. The horseradish will release burning fumes as it is processed. Remove the top of the food processor away from your face and avoid breathing directly over the bowl. Store prepared horseradish in a tightly sealed jar. It will lose potency as it is exposed to air.

Commercially prepared horseradish can be found in the dairy case of the supermarket. Store in the refrigerator for three to four months; over that time it will lose potency.

SALT

Salt—sodium chloride—is one of the oldest flavorings known. It does more than add a salty flavor to foods; it intensifies and balances flavors.

In some individuals, high intakes of sodium are associated with high blood pressure, and some medical experts recommend that everyone restrict sodium in their diets. For people who worry about sodium intake, herbs, spices, vinegar, and lemon juice can partially compensate for the lack of salt in a dish.

Salt will keep indefinitely when stored in a covered container.

Salt is available in a few different forms. *Table salt,* the most common household salt, contains additives to keep it from clumping. Some table salt is *iodized,* meaning that it has been treated with potassium iodide to prevent the formation of goiters, enlargements of the thyroid caused by an iodine deficiency. *Kosher salt,* also known as coarse salt, contains no additives and is the salt of choice for using on pretzels. *Pickling salt* is usually ground finer than table salt and contains no additives to cloud pickling brine. *Sea salt* is the salt crystals left when seawater evaporates. It contains minerals in addition to sodium chloride and is available in health food stores.

VINEGARS

When alcohol ferments, it produces vinegar, a very sour liquid flavoring. Vinegar is most commonly derived from grapes (*wine vinegar*) or apples (*cider vinegar*) or grains (*white,* or *distilled, vinegar*).

Keep vinegar tightly capped and store at room temperature. After a year, you may notice color changes or sediment forming, but the vinegar can still be used.

Flavored vinegars can be made with any vinegar as its base, although usually a wine vinegar is chosen. Fresh herbs or fruits, such as raspberries, are allowed to steep in the vinegar for about a week. Then the vinegar is rebottled and fresh herbs are added for show. Some favorite flavors are basil, garlic, thyme, and tarragon.

Balsamic vinegar. This brown-black vinegar has a mellow, slightly syrupy taste. It is made from a sweet white wine and aged for five to one hundred years in wooden barrels. It is more expensive than most vinegars, but it is prized for its mellow flavor. Inexpensive versions are made from briefly aged vinegars to which a caramelized syrup has been added. It is used in cooking and for salad dressings.

Cider vinegar. With the strong, distinctive taste of cider and a sharpness that is midway between wine vinegar and malt vinegar, cider vinegar is used mainly for pickles and fruit chutneys.

Distilled white vinegar. Made from grains, this colorless vinegar is used mainly for pickling. It is the most acidic tasting of the vinegars.

Malt vinegar. A favorite with fish and chips, malt vinegar has a slight nutty flavor. It is brewed from malted barley and usually is colored with caramel. Color, therefore, is no indication of strength.

Rice vinegar. Used in Oriental cooking, rice vinegar is sweet, with a subtle flavor, and is very lightly colored.

Wine vinegar. Wine vinegars are made from red wine, white wine, champagne, or sherry. The flavor varies, with sherry vinegar being quite sweet. In general, the price of the vinegar reflects the quality.

*H*erbs and Spices

In the kitchen we generally call seasonings herbs when they are the leaves of aromatic, nonwoody plants and shrubs—parsley, basil, oregano, for example. Spices, on the other hand, are derived from the roots, bark, seeds, fruit, or berries of perennial plants, such as allspice, cinnamon, and nutmeg.

Herbs can be bought fresh or dried. Some dried herbs, such as rosemary, are available ground. Spices are usually available whole or ground.

Herbs and spices.
1 Allspice 2 Bay leaves
3 Basil 4 Caraway 5 Marjoram 6 Rosemary 7 Parsley
8 Sage 9 Thyme 10 Cinna-
mon 11 Nutmeg 12 Cloves

Nothing matches the flavor of fresh herbs, but they are quite perishable. Look for healthy, green, aromatic leaves with no signs of yellow-
ing or wilting. Buy only what you need, and place the stems in about 2
inches of water, with a plastic bag loosely draped over the leaves. Store
in the refrigerator and change the water every few days; the herbs will
keep for up to one week. For longer storage, strip the leaves off the
stems, chop, then freeze. Fresh herbs will keep for two to four months
at 0°F.

When substituting fresh herbs for dried, multiply the amount by
three: Use three teaspoons of chopped fresh herbs for every one teaspoon of dried herb. To substitute dried herbs for fresh, divide by
three. If a recipe calls for three teaspoons (one tablespoon) of fresh
herbs, substitute one teaspoon dried.

When cooking with fresh herbs, you will get the most flavor if you
add some of the fresh herb during the last few minutes of cooking.

Dried herbs and whole spices have a shelf life of about one year at
room temperature; ground seasonings keep their flavor for about six
months. Their flavor is best if they are kept away from the heat of the
stove and out of direct light. Spices that are rich in oil—ground hot red
peppers (cayenne), paprika, chili powder, poppy seeds—do best in the
refrigerator.

One of the problems with herbs and spices is that most are packaged in containers that contain more than a year's supply. One way to
ensure your seasonings are fresh is to date the jars as you buy them
and throw them out after one year. You may find this too wasteful. An
alternative is to purchase herbs and spices in very small quantities from
health food stores or specialty shops. These bulk spices tend to be less

(continued on page 57)

Suggested Uses for Herbs and Spices

HERBS AND SPICES	FLAVOR AND FORM	USES	COMMENTS	COMPLEMENTS
Allspice	Flavor resembles a blend of cinnamon, cloves, and nutmeg. Sold ground or whole.	Savory and sweet dishes and pickles.	Used extensively in Jamaican cooking. Flavor intensifies with standing.	Works well with other sweet spices: cinnamon, nutmeg, cloves.
Anise	Tastes of licorice. Sold as seeds.	Mainly in baked goods and to flavor seafood, sweets, and creams.	Used in the cooking of the Mediterranean area. Pernod and ouzo are both alcoholic drinks flavored with anise.	Fennel.
Basil	A sweet, aromatic herb that tastes vaguely of cloves. Available fresh or dried; there are several different varieties of basil, including an opal red variety.	Soups, sauces, salad dressings, and seafood. The main ingredient in pesto.	Used extensively in the cooking of Italy and Southeast Asia. Holy basil and lemon basils are common Oriental basils; substitute mint or regular basil.	Oregano, thyme, garlic, tomatoes.
Bay leaf	Strong, pungent, almost bitter flavor. Available as whole, dried, or fresh leaves.	Poaching liquid of fish, tomato-based sauces, marinades, stews.	Flavor intensifies with standing. Usually removed when cooking is completed. Used in a bouquet garni.	Oregano.
Caraway	Pleasant, buttery flavor with sweet undertones. Sold as whole seed.	Baked goods, especially rye breads. Also in sauerkraut and with vegetables, potatoes, and pork.	Used in rye bread, aquavit (a Scandinavian liqueur, with anise, fennel, and coriander), and cheese.	Fennel and coriander.
Cardamom	Aromatic, sweet spice. Sold as whole seeds or ground.	Baked goods, hot spiced wines, and in curry blends.	Ten whole cardamom seeds (pods removed) equals 1/2 teaspoon ground cardamom.	Ginger and other sweet spices.
Celery Seed	Slightly bitter, tastes of celery. Sold as whole seed or ground and combined with salt.	Pickles, potato salad, coleslaw, relishes, salad dressings. Celery salt is also used in soups and sauces.	Celery salt is especially good in mayonnaise-type sauces and with hard-boiled eggs.	
Chervil	Delicate, anise seed flavor. Sold fresh.	Salads, chicken soup, eggs, and herb butters.	One of the traditional fines herbes. Does not dry well.	Tarragon, parsley, chives.

(table continues)

Suggested Uses for Herbs and Spices (*continued*)

HERBS AND SPICES	FLAVOR AND FORM	USES	COMMENTS	COMPLEMENTS
Chili Powder	A blend of spices, usually ground chili peppers, cumin, garlic, oregano, and sometimes allspice and cloves.	Mexican-style dishes; beans, meats, eggs, cheese, corn and cornmeal, rice.	Chili powder dominates a dish rather than enhances the flavors of the ingredients it is intended to season.	Cumin, garlic.
Chives	Delicate oniony flavor. Available fresh or freeze-dried.	Especially good with eggs, baked potatoes, and tomatoes. Makes a nice garnish for cream soups, potato salads, broiled fish. Pairs well with cottage cheese and yogurt.	Fresh chives are superior in flavor to dried. Freezing is a good way to preserve. One of the classic fines herbes.	Chervil, parsley.
Cilantro	Pungent, almost musty flavor. Available fresh or dried.	Salsas and other Latin American dishes; Oriental and Indian cooking. As an addition to curry, it is made into a paste with fresh ginger. Assertive flavor goes well with lamb and pork.	Although available dried, the flavor is very inferior to fresh. Also called fresh coriander and Chinese parsley.	Chilies.
Cinnamon	Pungent, sweet spice. Comes as stick or ground powder.	Baked goods, hot spiced drinks, creamy desserts, such as rice pudding, and fruits. Used in savory dishes from the Middle East and Spain.		Other sweet spices, apples, chocolate, vanilla.
Cloves	Sweet, warm flavor. Available whole and ground.	Spiced meats, curries, cooked apples and pears, hot spiced drinks.	Look for large, dark, plump cloves. Unpleasant to bite into, so securely fix into an apple or onion when simmering in a liquid or use ground spice. Flavor intensifies on standing.	Cinnamon, nutmeg, allspice.
Coriander	Sweet spice with slight citrusy flavor. Available as round, brittle, easily crushed seeds and powder.	In curries and to flavor vegetables *à la grecque,* lentils, and apples.	Flavor is enhanced when seeds are lightly toasted in ungreased frying pan.	Sweet spices, curry spices.

Suggested Uses for Herbs and Spices (*continued*)

HERBS AND SPICES	FAVOR AND FORM	USES	COMMENTS	COMPLEMENTS
Cumin	Pungent, earthy, slightly sweet, slightly oily flavor. Available as whole seeds and powder.	Essential in both curry powders and chili powders. Used to season beans (especially black beans and chick-peas), meats, fish, rice, and couscous.	Looks like caraway, but is more powerfully flavored. Use ground cumin and cumin seed interchangeably in recipes.	Any curry or chili powder spice.
Curry Powder	A blend of spices, often turmeric, fenugreek, cumin, coriander, ginger, and cayenne. Comes in mild and hot blends.	Curries with all manner of meats and vegetables. Also flavors rice, soups, and yogurt-based or mayonnaise-based dips.	Use sparingly, unless you want the flavor to overpower all other ingredients. Cook slowly to bring out best flavor and to avoid a raw curry powder taste.	
Dill	Light, lemony and buttery flavor. Available as fresh or dried greens, whole seed head, or seeds.	Pickles, fish, lamb, eggs, vegetables, cottage and cream cheese.	Used extensively in Scandinavian cooking.	
Fennel	Slight licorice flavor. Available as fresh greens or seeds.	Greens are used to season eggs, fish, lamb, pork; seeds are added to sauces and to season Italian sausage.	Can be used interchangeably with dill. Used extensively in Italian cooking.	
Filé Powder	Grassy flavor. Available as a powder.	Flavor and thicken gumbo and other Creole soups and stews.	Add just before serving; becomes stringy when cooked. A powder made of dried sassafras leaves. Creole cooks learned the secrets of filé powder from the Choctaw Indians.	

(table continues)

Suggested Uses for Herbs and Spices (*continued*)

HERBS AND SPICES	FLAVOR AND FORM	USES	COMMENTS	COMPLEMENTS
Garam Masala	Sweet spice mix.	Curries.	Sprinkle on at the end of the cooking time. There are regional variations in the spice mix. A typical one might contain coriander seeds, cinnamon, cumin, cloves, cardamom, mace, and peppercorns. Greatly enhances foods flavored with supermarket curry powder.	Curry powder.
Ginger	Hot, spicy, sweet. Available as fresh or candied root, ground powder, and in syrup.	Baked goods, desserts, meat dishes, pickles, cold and hot beverages, fruit compotes. Used extensively in Oriental and Caribbean cooking.	Crystallized ginger is used as a confection or a condiment, not as a spice.	Other sweet spices, chilies, garlic.
Mace	Similar to nutmeg, but more delicate. Available ground.	Baked goods, desserts, marinades, pickles. In Italy it is used in cream and cheese sauces.		Nutmeg.
Marjoram	Sweet-scented herb, similar to oregano, but more delicate. Available fresh or dried.	Meats, chicken, cheese, eggs, tomato sauces, vegetables.		Basil, thyme, savory.
Mint	Aromatic, sweet flavor with cool aftertaste. Available fresh or dried.	Candies, desserts, drinks; is combined with boiled new potatoes and peas and seasons fresh pea soup, tabbouleh (grain salad), and other Middle East dishes. Makes a cooling sauce combined with cucumbers and yogurt.	There are many varieties of mints, including spearmint, peppermint, apple mint.	Oranges, chocolate, basil.
Nutmeg	Sweet, warm, slightly bitter. Available as whole seed or powder.	Sweet dishes—particularly rice pudding, apple pies, and spiced fruits—and hot spiced drinks. Combined with cheese in Italian dishes. Goes well in savory dishes with spinach and potatoes.	Freshly grated nutmeg is superior in flavor to ground. A whole nutmeg will keep for several months, sometimes for years.	Cinnamon, ginger, mace.

Suggested Uses for Herbs and Spices (*continued*)

HERBS AND SPICES	FLAVOR AND FORM	USES	COMMENTS	COMPLEMENTS
Oregano	Aromatic, with pleasantly bitter overtone. Available fresh and dried or ground.	Tomato-based dishes, vegetables, meats, seafood, cheeses.	Essential to Italian cooking.	Basil, thyme.
Paprika	Sweet flavor, reminiscent of the sweet peppers from which it is made. Available ground. Also available in hot varieties.	Garnish for light-colored foods—potato salads, broiled fish or chicken, etc. Used extensively in Hungarian cooking and is the principal seasoning in Hungarian goulash and veal paprika. Also used in fish and vegetable soups in Spain and Portugal.	Hungarian paprika is often of higher quality than supermarket brand paprika.	
Parsley	Pleasant, mild, grassy flavor. Available fresh and dried.	As a garnish, to flavor soup stocks, added to salads.	Fresh parsley is superior in flavor to dried; readily available year-round. Flat-leaved Italian parsley has more flavor than curly-leaved. For a different flavor, it can be used as a substitute for chervil or cilantro. One of the fines herbes and traditionally included in a bouquet garni.	Garlic, lemon.
Pickling Spice	Pungent, somewhat sweet blend.	Pickles, sauerbraten, pot roast.	A blend of whole and crumbled herbs and spices. Tie the spice in a cheesecloth bag for easy removal.	
Poppy Seeds	Pleasant, nutty flavor.	Baked goods, especially Eastern European.	Dark, shiny color indicates freshness. Dull-looking seeds are probably old.	
Poultry Seasoning	A blend of herbs, primarily ground thyme and sage.	Poultry.		Thyme, sage, rosemary.
Pumpkin Pie Spice	Sweet, aromatic blend of ground cinnamon, nutmeg, cloves, and ginger.	Pumpkin pie and other baked goods, custards, and fruits.		

(table continues)

Suggested Uses for Herbs and Spices (*continued*)

HERBS AND SPICES	FLAVOR AND FORM	USES	COMMENTS	COMPLEMENTS
Rosemary	Aromatic, reminiscent of pine needles. Available fresh, dried, ground.	Lamb, game, duck, rabbit; good in tomato sauces and soups.	Use sparingly; a little goes a long way. Can overpower delicate fish, cheese, egg dishes.	Thyme, tarragon, savory.
Saffron	Pleasantly bitter flavor. Available as whole "threads" or ground.	An essential ingredient in arroz con pollo, paella, bouillabaisse, and risotto alla milanese. Used in yeast breads, rice, chicken dishes, soups, sauces, and with seafood.	Crush before using. Dyes food a pleasant yellow. Use sparingly; 1/4 teaspoon for each pound of meat or fish and each cup of rice.	
Sage	Aromatic and slightly bitter. Available fresh, dried, or ground.	Sausage, chicken, fish, pork, veal, stuffing, potatoes, sauces, and vegetables.	Use sparingly.	Thyme, rosemary, savory.
Tarragon	Astringent, bittersweet, aniselike flavor. Available fresh or dried.	Egg dishes, chicken, fish, ham. Good in salads and dressings. Used to season Béarnaise sauce.	Best enjoyed fresh or as a flavored vinegar; dried tarragon develops a haylike taste. Use sparingly.	
Thyme	Aromatic outdoorsy-scented herb, reminiscent of lemon and mint. Available fresh, dried, ground.	Meat, poultry, fish. Essential to clam chowder. Good with tomatoes and cheese. Used in a bouquet garni.	Seasons many Cajun and Creole dishes.	Basil, marjoram, oregano, rosemary.
Turmeric	Musky, slightly bitter taste. Available ground.	Curries, pickles, cream sauces, and with chicken and fish.	Gives curries and prepared mustard their characteristic bright yellow color. Used extensively in Indian cooking.	Curry powder.

Herb Combinations

A *bouquet garni* is a small herb bouquet, most often made of sprigs of fresh parsley and thyme plus a bay leaf, tied in cheesecloth. Other seasonings such as celery or garlic may be included. Dried herbs can be used in place of the fresh. The bouquet garni is dropped into stocks, stews, sauces, and soups as a seasoner and is removed before serving—usually as soon as it has flavored the dish.

Fines herbes is a mixture of minced fresh or dried parsley, chervil, tarragon, and, sometimes, chives used to season salads, omelets, and other dishes.

expensive than supermarket brands, and they may even be fresher and more flavorful.

For suggested uses of various herbs and spices, see the table on page 51–56.

G rains and Flours

FLOURS

Of all the ingredients we buy in the supermarket, flour may be the least standardized. A bag of all-purpose flour milled in the South, where more biscuits and cakes are made than breads, is likely to have a high proportion of soft wheat in it. Flour sold in the Northeast, where more bread baking is done, is likely to have a higher proportion of hard wheat. (Hard and soft refer to different types of wheat.)

How well a flour has been stored and whether it has absorbed moisture from the air will also affect the outcome of a recipe. White flour and those flours without the germ (including degermed cornmeal) can be stored at room temperature in airtight containers for six months to a year. Whole grain flours will keep for no more than a month at room temperature. In the refrigerator or freezer, whole wheat and cornmeal will keep for up to a year. Other flours should be used within three months.

Before using refrigerated flours in a recipe, bring to room temperature.

Many times a package will note that the flour is *bromated*. This means that potassium bromate has been added to help the flour produce lighter baked goods.

While supermarkets stock wheat flours, cornmeal, and the occasional other flour, health food stores are the best sources for most whole grain flours.

Buckwheat flour. Buckwheat flour comes as a light flour (ground without the hull) and dark (ground with the hull); the dark kind is stronger in flavor. It is used to make pancakes, crêpes, and Russian blini. Because it contains no gluten, it must be combined with another flour for baking.

Cornmeal. *Degermed cornmeal* has the germ removed and *stone-ground cornmeal* comes from the whole grain. The texture can be coarse or powdery fine. The color may be white, bright yellow, or blue-gray. *Blue cornmeal* has a toastier flavor than yellow cornmeal, although all three can be used interchangeably in recipes. *Masa harina* is a finely ground corn flour mixed with limewater and used to make tortillas.

Grains. 1 Buckwheat
2 Rice 3 Rye 4 Wheat
5 Millet 6 Oats

For Italian polenta you will get best results with a coarse-grained Italian cornmeal. If you are unable to find Italian cornmeal at a specialty store, make polenta with a blend of fine-ground and coarse-ground cornmeal.

Oat flour and oat bran. High in fiber and protein, oat flour is made from finely grinding oats. Oat flour can be bought in health food stores, or you can make a small quantity yourself by processing rolled oats in a blender. Because it has no gluten, oat flour must be combined with other flours in baking. Oat bran is the ground outer layer of the oat. It is considered an excellent source of fiber.

Rice flour. Ground from either white or brown rice, rice flour is mainly used as a thickener. You can make it in small quantities in a blender by processing dry rice grains until you have a fine powder.

Rye flour. A strongly flavored flour, rye comes in dark and light varieties. It makes a very heavy loaf of bread, unless combined with significant amounts of white flour.

Soy flour. Made from ground soybeans, soy flour is rich in protein, iron, and calcium. It is used to enrich baked goods made with wheat flour. Because it contains no gluten, it must be combined with other flours for baking.

Triticale. A hybrid of wheat and rye, triticale is used in bread making.

Wheat flour. When it comes to wheat flour, there are many choices. Suitable for most baking and thickening purposes, *all-purpose flour* is a combination of soft and hard wheats. It is available both bleached (chemically whitened) or unbleached, which is higher in nutrients.

Cake flour is milled from soft wheat. Because it is lower in gluten, it

⟩ **Substitute for cake flour,**
301

is a good choice for cakes, cookies, and pastries, and a poor choice for bread and pasta. If a recipe calls for cake flour, you will get the best results by using it. However, if you must substitute all-purpose flour, measure the flour as called for, then remove 2 tablespoons of flour for each cup.

Bread flour is high in gluten; it is made entirely of hard wheat. Substitute all-purpose flour, cup for cup.

Found mainly in the South, *self-rising flour* is all-purpose flour with salt and leavening added. One cup of self-rising flour contains 1½ teaspoons of baking powder and ½ teaspoon of salt. You can substitute all-purpose flour and adjust your recipes accordingly. *Instant flour* is finely processed so it can be used as a thickener. Do not bake with it.

Semolina is a high-gluten flour made from durum wheat. It is used in Italian cooking to make gnocchi and in Indian cooking to make pancakes called dosas. In many recipes, farina or cream of wheat can be substituted for semolina.

Whole wheat flour is milled with the entire wheat grain. It is richer in taste and flavor than white flour. Look for stone-ground whole wheat, which has better flavor and more vitamins. Sometimes whole wheat flour is called *graham flour.* Graham crackers are made with whole wheat flour.

Wheat bran is the thin, papery outer covering of the wheat grain. It is added to breads and sprinkled on breakfast cereals for extra roughage.

Wheat germ, the heart of the wheat kernel, is mainly sprinkled on breakfast cereal or mixed into yogurt for extra nutrition. Keep raw wheat germ in the refrigerator to prevent rancidity.

GRAINS

A diet based on grains and lots of vegetables, with meat just for flavoring, is a healthy diet. To keep this diet interesting, it helps to eat a wide variety of grains, beyond the familiar rice.

Whole grains are best fresh, and they keep in airtight containers for only about a month. In the refrigerator they stay fresh longer, four to five months. Pearl barley and hominy, however, will keep for up to a year in a cool spot. A whole grain will have an off odor when too old, indicating the oils in the grain have gone rancid.

Supermarkets carry many whole grains. Health food stores that do a big business tend to be the best source of whole grains because the selection is usually broadest and the stock turns over quickly.

For cooking instructions for grains, see page 219.

Barley. *Pearl barley,* also called soup barley, is the polished grain with the bran removed. It cooks in 45 to 60 minutes. *Quick-cooking*

Popcorn

Whole popped kernels of corn make a healthy high-fiber snack, as long as no butter is added for flavoring.

Popcorn should be stored at room temperature for one to two years. If you find yourself with old popcorn with a high percentage of kernels that won't pop, you can add water to recondition it. For each 3 cups of kernels, add 1 tablespoon of water to the jar. Shake well and leave the popcorn on the shelf for two to three days, shaking the jar occasionally. The kernels should absorb all the water and then be ready for popping.

♦ **Couscoussier,** 165

barley cooks in 10 to 12 minutes; follow the package directions. *Pot barley* or *Scotch barley* is the whole grain, with only the outer hull removed. It takes several hours of cooking to tenderize this grain.

Buckwheat groats. Also known as kasha, buckwheat groats have a distinctive nutty flavor. They retain the best texture if they are combined with an egg before cooking.

Bulgur. The quick-cooking grain of cracked wheat has a sweet, nutty flavor. It makes an excellent base for a salad, as in tabbouleh, but can also be combined with herbs and vegetables and simmered in stock to make a delicious pilaf.

Couscous. These small, golden grains of semolina pasta look like tiny beads. The quick-cooking form cooks so quickly it makes an instant side dish. You can also combine it with peas and diced cooked chicken or meat for an instant meal.

Hominy. Dried and hulled corn, hominy has a slight corn flavor. It is sold dried and canned. Dried hominy must be soaked like beans before it is cooked.

Most often, hominy is ground and eaten as grits. *Grits* are prepared as a cooked cereal. Grits can be made from white or yellow corn. They come in regular, quick-cooking, and instant forms. Follow the package directions. Grits can be served as a breakfast food and as a side dish with meat.

Posole, a pork stew with hominy, is a Southwestern specialty.

Millet. Familiar as bird seed, the tiny round grains of millet resemble mustard seeds. It has a slightly nutty flavor and chewy texture and can be used as a substitute for rice.

Oats. Whole oats, called oat groats, are rarely eaten. The groats are usually steamed and rolled, then used in baked goods and to make oatmeal. *Quick-cooking oats* are similar to *rolled oats* and can often be interchanged with rolled oats in a recipe. *Instant oatmeal* has been pre-cooked and is often flavored with sugar and salt. It cannot be used in a recipe that calls for rolled or quick-cooking oats. *Steel-cut oats* are also known as Irish oatmeal; they take considerably longer to cook than rolled oats.

Quinoa. An ancient Peruvian grain that has just recently been imported to the United States, quinoa (pronounced KEEN-wah) has a sweet, nutty flavor. It is very high in protein compared to other grains.

Rice. Literally the most popular grain in the world, there are more than 40,000 varieties of rice. Today's choices include white and brown rice, long-, medium-, and short-grain rice, unprocessed, converted, and seasoned rice. *Basmati rice* is an aromatic long-grain rice, as is *Tex-mati,* which is sold both as white and brown rices. *Arborio* is the short-grained rice used to make Italian risotto. A *short-grained Japanese rice* is the best choice for sushi. *Brown rice,* which may be long-, medium-, or short-grained, has a nutlike flavor and can be used interchangeably with white rice, if the recipe is adjusted for brown rice's longer cooking time. *Converted rice* has been partly cooked; follow the package directions for cooking.

White rice, if it isn't preseasoned, will keep indefinitely in airtight containers at room temperature. Brown rice will keep for about one month at room temperature or six months in the refrigerator.

Wild rice. The seed of a rare aquatic grass, wild rice has a distinctive nutty flavor and chewy texture. It is particularly good when mixed in a cooked dish with white or brown rice. Wild rice will keep indefinitely at room temperature in an airtight container.

*P*asta and Noodles

Pasta's recent rise in popularity is no quick-fading trend. Low in fat and calories, with no cholesterol if made without eggs, pasta can be considered a health food. A meal of pasta leaves you feeling well fed and satisfied.

Fresh pasta commands a premium price at supermarkets and specialty food stores. Often these fresh pastas are flavored with tomatoes, pepper, saffron, or spinach, and make a colorful dish. But fresh pasta is not necessarily superior to dry pasta, so let your taste guide you. Dry noodles and fresh pastas often contain eggs, while most dry pastas do not.

Fresh pasta should be refrigerated and used within five days. It cooks quite quickly. For longer storage, freeze fresh pasta. Add it directly to boiling water to cook; do not thaw first.

Dry pasta has the advantage of coming in a wide variety of shapes. It can be stored indefinitely in a closed package.

Suggested serving sizes on packages of pasta tend to be quite meager. Figure 1 pound of fresh pasta will yield three to four main course

Pasta and noodles.
1 Tortellini 2 Ravioli
3 Penne 4 Fettuccine
5 Spaghetti 6 Capellini
7 Conchiglie 8 Orecchiette
9 Ditali 10 Rotini/fusilli
11 Ziti 12 Farfalle
13 Rigatoni

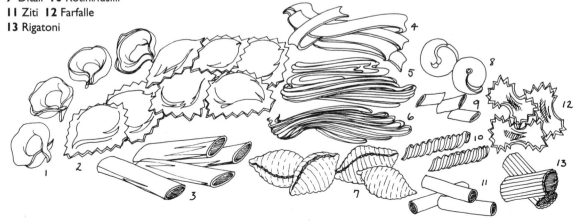

servings; 1 pound of dried pasta will yield four to six main course servings.

For tips on cooking pasta, see page 220.

PASTA SHAPES

Pasta shapes can be used interchangeably, although there is general agreement that small pasta shapes are good in soups; long, thin shapes should be served with thin sauces; curled shapes are nice for holding chunky meat sauces; and short, ridged shapes hold cream sauces well. (For a description of Oriental Noodles, see the chart on page 116.)

The same shape may be called by different names in different regions of Italy. Here's a description of several pasta shapes. Cooking times vary; follow the directions on the package.

Spaghetti types. Good with oil-based sauces and tomato sauces.
Capellini—very thin "angel hair"
Vermicelli—very fine spaghetti
Spaghetti—comes in thin (spaghettini), medium (spaghetti), or thick diameters (spaghettoni)

Flat egg noodles. Flat shapes rolled by hand or machine.
Linguine—very narrow pasta ribbons
Fettuccine (also called tagliatelle)—narrow pasta ribbons
Tagliarini—thin tagliatelle
Lasagna—straight- and ripple-edged; much wider than fettuccine

Soup pastas. Tiny shapes.
Alphabets
Anelli—"little rings"
Anellini—smaller rings
Ditalini—thimbles
Orzo, or rosamarina—like tiny grains of rice
Farfallini—bow ties

Macaroni types. Hollow tubes.
Rigatoni—ribbed tubes, 1½ to 3 inches long; traditionally served baked in a sauce
Ziti—"bridegrooms"; tubular macaroni
Penne (mostaccioli)—cut like quills (or little "mustaches")
Elbow macaroni—curved tubes

Stuffed pastas.
Agnolotti—"fat little lambs," square or circular ravioli
Anolini—round or ring-shaped ravioli, served in a sauce or broth
Cannelloni—large 4-inch to 6-inch tube

♦ Pasta making and cooking
equipment, 151

Manicotti—large tubes
Tortellini—pasta triangles stuffed, folded over, and shaped into rings
Tortelloni—stuffed pasta bundles
Ravioli—pasta pillows with filling
Cappelletti—little hats

Specialty shapes. Whimsically shaped pasta; may be large or small.
Cavatelli—short curled noodle formed like a shell with scalloped edges
Conchiglie, Conchigliette—shells in various sizes, from tiny sizes for
soup to shells large enough to stuff
Farfalle—butterflies
Fusilli—twisted strands of spaghetti
Orecchiette—"little ears," pasta curls
Rotini—short twists

L eavening Agents

Leavening agents make batters and doughs rise and become light and
porous. The most common leavening agents are air and steam. Air is
incorporated into the batter during stirring and beating, and helps to
lighten the batter. When heat is applied some of the liquid in a batter is
converted into steam. Cream puff shells are leavened by steam.

Baking powder. A common ingredient in quick breads and cakes,
baking powder is made of baking soda plus acid. When combined with
moisture or heat, the baking soda reacts with the acid and produces
bubbles of carbon dioxide gas, which cause the batter to rise and
become light.

Most baking powders available in the U.S. are double-acting; that is,
they produce gas once when mixed with liquid, and again in the heat
of the oven. Unless a recipe specifies otherwise, assume that double-
acting baking powder is required.

If you find yourself out of baking powder, make this substitution:
For 1 tablespoon of baking powder, mix together 1½ teaspoons of
cream of tartar with 1 teaspoon of baking soda.

Sodium-free baking powders are available in health food stores, but
these are usually single-acting powders, which create carbon dioxide
gas only once, when it comes in contact with liquid. Use double the
amount the recipe calls for.

Baking powder begins to lose potency after six months or when
exposed to humidity or steam. To test its potency, add one teaspoon of
powder to ⅓ cup hot water. If it bubbles furiously, it is still active. If
not, it's time to buy a new can.

Baking soda. Bicarbonate of soda and sodium bicarbonate are the chemical names for baking soda. The chemical releases carbon dioxide gas when it comes in contact with moisture and acid. When baking with baking soda, the batter must supply the acid, usually in the form of buttermilk, soured milk, chocolate, molasses, lemon juice, or cream of tartar.

Cream of tartar. A naturally occuring acid that combines with baking soda to create carbon dioxide gas to lighten batters. Cream of tartar is also beaten with egg whites to increase their volume and stability. Store in a cool, dry place for up to one year.

Yeast. These tiny organisms gobble up sugar in dough and release carbon dioxide gas bubbles, which enable the dough to rise. *Active dry yeast* is dried granules of yeast that become active when mixed with liquid. *Quick-rising active dry yeast* is a new strain of yeast that makes dough rise more quickly. It can be substituted for regular active dry yeast, tablespoon for tablespoon, but rising times will be reduced (see page 284 for substituting quick-rising yeast for regular yeast). *Compressed yeast* or *fresh yeast* comes in moist cakes. This form of yeast is viable for about two weeks in the refrigerator, though it can be stored in the freezer for up to six months.

If you have doubts about the rising power of your yeast, test it by combining a small amount with an equal amount of sugar. Dissolve in warm water. The mix should become foamy within five minutes. If not, the yeast should be replaced.

*T*hickeners

Agar-agar. Derived from seaweed, agar-agar is sold as a powder or in long strips or blocks. It dissolves in boiling water and can absorb up to twenty times its own weight. It is used in Oriental cooking instead of gelatin and has the advantage of being able to set up foods without refrigeration. Gelatin may be substituted for agar-agar.

Arrowroot. Arrowroot is a tasteless, fine, dry white powder ground from the root of a plant found abundantly in the Caribbean. While arrowroot may be unfamiliar to many cooks, it is the thickener of choice for fruit sauces and pie fillings. It makes a sparkling, clear sauce.

Arrowroot's thickening powers are activated at a lower temperature than either cornstarch or flour, which makes it useful in cream sauces that should not boil. It is a good thickener to use with fruit because, unlike cornstarch, it is not broken down by acid.

Add arrowroot during the last ten minutes of cooking as it becomes less effective the longer it is cooked. Like cornstarch, arrowroot has

♦ **Making yeast bread, 282–287**

double the thickening power of flour. To substitute arrowroot for flour, use half as much.

Cornstarch. A fine white powder, cornstarch dissolves readily in cold liquids; it is used to thicken sauces, puddings and fruit-pie fillings. Cornstarch must be brought to boiling temperature to release its starch. Sauces thickened with cornstarch have a clear, translucent quality.

Store in an airtight container at room temperature for up to two years. Cornstarch has double the thickening power of flour.

Gelatin. Gelatin comes as a fine powder that will dissolve in hot water and then form a transparent jelly when chilled. Flavored gelatins will keep on the shelf for up to a year, while unflavored gelatin will keep for about three years in an airtight container.

Gelatin can be fussy to work with. It won't set if it is combined with certain fresh fruits—pineapple, kiwifruit, figs, guava, papaya, and ginger root. Unflavored gelatin dissolves best if softened in cold or cool water before it is added to the hot liquid.

Pectin. Pectin occurs naturally in fruits, particularly apples. When cooked, it will allow fruit juices to gel. The riper the fruit, the less pectin it contains. So if you are making jelly without the addition of commercial pectin, select slightly underripe fruits. Also, fruits that are tart even when ripe—apples, Seville oranges, quinces, and red currants—have more pectin than sweet fruits, such as strawberries and grapes, so they are better choices for making jams and jellies without commercial pectin.

Commercial pectin is available as a liquid or powder. It is devised to be used with a very specific amount of sugar and lemon juice, so follow the manufacturer's directions exactly. "Light" pectins allow you to make jams and jellies with less sugar.

Store pectin at room temperature and use by the sale date indicated on the package.

Tapioca. Extracted from the roots of the tropical cassava plant, tapioca is used to make puddings and to thicken fruit fillings for pies. It is the thickener of choice to use when the pie is to be frozen because it will retain its ability to thicken even when reheated (unlike flour and cornstarch).

Quick-cooking tapioca is most frequently used. *Pearl tapioca* must be soaked before making into pudding. *Tapioca flour* can sometimes be found in Oriental food stores for use only as a thickener. Store all forms of tapioca in airtight containers at room temperature for up to two years.

Sweeteners

The desire for sweet foods is instinctual—we are born with it. But that doesn't mean we can't cut back on sweeteners without losing flavor. If you are looking to lighten up the desserts you make, try substituting undiluted frozen fruit juice concentrates, such as apple and white grape, for some of the sugar in your favorite recipes. Or use dried fruits for sweeteners. Here is a look at the more conventional sweeteners we use in cooking and baking.

Dry sugars will keep indefinitely at room temperature in airtight containers.

Baked goods made with honey, maple syrup, or molasses are moister than those made with sugar and will last longer.

Brown sugar. Brown sugar is a mix of granulated white sugar and molasses—*dark brown sugar* has more molasses in the mix than *light brown sugar*. They can be used interchangeably in recipes, though the flavor and color may be affected.

Store brown sugar in an airtight container. If it becomes hard, heat in a 250°F. oven until it is soft enough to spoon. Return to an airtight jar with an apple slice or a slice of bread and leave the slice in overnight.

Confectioners' sugar. Also known as powdered sugar, confectioners' sugar is granulated sugar that has been crushed and screened. The degree of fineness is indicated by the number of X's—4X is fine, 6X is very fine, and 10X is ultrafine. Cornstarch is mixed with 10X sugar to prevent it from caking.

Corn syrup. *Light corn syrup* is bland and a little less sweet than sugar, *dark corn syrup* has more flavor. Both are prone to mold and fermentation, so check the expiration date on the label. Store in a cool, dry place. Dark corn syrup can be used as a substitute for molasses in baking.

Sweetener sources.
1 Sugar cane 2 Corn for syrup 3 Sugar maple 4 Clover for honey

Granulated sugar. *White granulated sugar* is the sweetener most commonly used. *Superfine sugar* is a finer grind of sugar that dissolves more readily. It is often used to sweeten icings and whipping cream.

Honey. Honey is made by honeybees from flower nectar and is flavored and colored by the flowers used to produce it. Clover, sage, orange, and alfalfa blossom are the most common kinds of honey. It is sold as a liquid or still in the honeycomb.

Honey can be substituted for sugar in most recipes by reducing the amount of liquid called for in the recipe by ½ cup for each cup of honey used. Its sweetening capacity is comparable to that of sugar.

Store honey at room temperature in a tightly covered container. Cold temperatures increase crystallization. To liquefy crystallized honey, place the jar in a pan of warm, not hot, water until the honey returns to its liquid state.

Maple sugar. Old recipes often called for maple sugar, though it is rare to see that now. Maple sugar is maple syrup that has been boiled to the hard sugar stage. It is often sold in specialty stores molded into leaf or animal shapes.

Maple syrup. As anyone who lives in maple syrup country can attest, nothing beats the taste of fresh maple syrup. Made by boiling down the sap of the sugar maple tree into a syrup consistency, maple syrup is much more intensely flavored than commercial pancake syrup, which is corn or cane syrup blended with a small amount of maple syrup or maple flavoring.

Maple syrup is graded by color and flavor. U.S. Grade A Light Amber or Fancy is the lightest in color and flavor. U.S. Grade A Medium Amber and U.S. Grade A Dark Amber are darker in color and have a more pronounced maple flavor. U.S. Grade B is very dark and intensely flavored, best used for baking. The producer has little control over the grade of syrup produced; it is the result of many factors, including the weather. Although light amber commands the best prices, many people prefer the richer flavor of medium or dark amber.

Pure maple syrup can be expensive, but because its flavor is so intense, less is needed to flavor pancakes and waffles. The most economical way to purchase syrup is by the gallon. Pour the syrup out of the gallon tin into glass quart canning jars, leaving plenty of headspace. Leave one quart of syrup in the refrigerator and store the rest in the freezer. The syrup itself will not freeze, but the cold temperatures will help it to retain flavor.

Substitute maple syrup for sugar as you would honey.

Molasses. This thick dark to light brown syrup is made either by boiling down sugar cane juice or separating the liquid from raw sugar in the process of making granulated sugar. Molasses is rich in iron and distinctive in flavor. *Blackstrap molasses* is heavier in flavor than either light or dark molasses.

Unsulphured molasses is a finer grade of syrup, lighter in color and with a more noticeable cane-sugar flavor. Store in a cool, dry place. It cannot be used as a substitute for other sweeteners.

Sorghum. A dark, sweet syrup used primarily in the South for cooking and baking and as a table syrup. Store at room temperature for up to one year.

Sugar substitutes. Those who are on restricted diets find that low-calorie chemical sugar substitutes can replace sugar in some, but not all applications. Because sugar substitutes are vastly sweeter than sugar, they cannot be used in baking goods without radically affecting the texture of the final product. Also, *aspartame* (sold under the brand name NutraSweet) breaks down in the presence of heat and must be added to recipes after all cooking is completed. *Saccharin* leaves a bitter aftertaste, which can sometimes be masked by using fruit juice.

Turbinado sugar. This is raw sugar that has been steamed cleaned, leaving the sugar crystals blond-colored and delicately flavored with molasses. You can find turbinado sugar in health food stores. It can be used in place of brown sugar.

*F*ats and Oils

Of all the ingredients we cook with, fats and oils are cause for the most concern—because of the role they play in adding calories and cholesterol to our diet. They also perform dozens of needed cooking chores, from holding together mayonnaises to tenderizing pie crusts to adding flavor to salads.

If the fat or oil is solid at room temperature, like butter, it is considered a saturated fat. Saturated fats have been shown to increase the amount of cholesterol carried in the blood. Unsaturated fats, liquid at room temperature, like corn oil, help to lower blood cholesterol. Monounsaturated oils, such as olive oil and canola oil, are better at lowering blood cholesterol than polyunsaturated oils, such as safflower, soybean, and corn oils. So monounsaturated oils are the ideal choice for cooking and baking—at least from a nutritional standpoint.

Some fats and oils are interchangeable in cooking, others lend distinctive flavors to dishes. An oil with a high smoke point is particularly good for deep-frying, because the oil allows you to cook at a high temperature without burning or imparting a scorched, smoky flavor to the food.

Oils should be stored in tightly sealed bottles in a cool, dark place to prevent changes in flavor. Fats derived from animals should be kept refrigerated. The refrigerator is fine for most oils, although some will become cloudy when cold.

♦ Diet and fats, 358, 370–375
♦ Nutrient values of fats and oils, 390

Sources of vegetable oils.
1 Walnut **2** Olive
3 Avocado **4** Corn
5 Coconut **6** Sunflower
7 Sesame

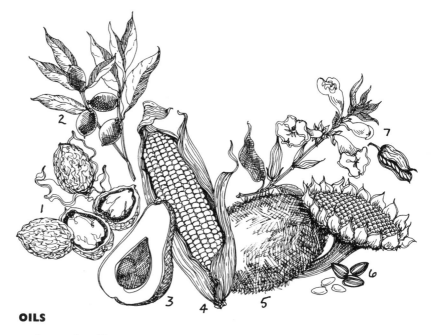

OILS

Avocado oil. A monounsaturated fat with a high smoke point and delicate, buttery flavor, avocado oil is used for cooking and for salad dressings. Store in a cool, dark place for up to six months.

Canola oil. Derived from rapeseed, canola oil is a neutral-tasting monounsaturated oil, which makes it perfect for baked goods. Store in a cool, dark place for six to twelve months.

Coconut oil. High in saturated fat, coconut oil is most frequently used in commercial baking. It is also found in recipes from the Caribbean; substitute peanut oil for a more healthful dish. Coconut oil is not sold in the United States for home baking.

Corn oil. A good all-purpose, neutral-tasting oil.

Grapeseed oil. Only recently has this mild-tasting oil been found in the U.S., although it is a staple in French and Italian cooking. Store in a cool, dark place for up to six months.

Olive oil. High in monounsaturated fats, olive oil is a good choice to use in cooking but it is too distinctively flavored for baking. Olive oil comes in several grades, and oils from Spain taste different from Italian oils, which are different from Californian oils.

The most expensive, cold-pressed *extra-virgin olive oil,* is deeply colored and fragrant with the aroma of green olives; it is low in acidity and a good choice to use in salad dressings. *Virgin olive oil* is made from the second pressing of the olives, it is a little lighter and less fruity than extra-virgin, and a little higher in acidity. *Pure olive oil* is made from successive pressings of the leftover olive pulp and is still higher in acidity. It is an excellent oil to use in cooking as it has a very mild fla-

▶ **Chili oil, 115**

vor and a high smoking point. Some producers have developed "light" versions of olive oil. These oils are light in flavor but they are suitable to cook with.

Keep olive oil in a dark, well-sealed jar or tin for up to two years. When the room temperature exceeds 80°F., it is a good idea to refrigerate the oil. It will become cloudy and thick when cold. Bring to room temperature before using.

Palm oil. An oil high in saturated fat. Although it is used by some commercial bakeries, it is not sold for home use.

Peanut oil. The preferred oil for Chinese stir-fries, peanut oil has a high smoke point. Cold-pressed peanut oils, available at specialty food stores, have a distinctive peanut flavor, while most supermarket brands taste quite neutral. Store in a cool, dark place for six to twelve months.

Safflower oil. A light, tasteless oil that is the most unsaturated of the unsaturated oils, good for baking and cooking. Store in a cool, dark place for six to twelve months.

Sesame oil. The dark-colored Oriental sesame oil is used to add a distinctive flavor to Chinese dishes. Domestic sesame oils still have a nutty flavor, but are somewhat lighter and good to use in salad dressings. Because of its low smoking point, sesame oil is often combined with another oil for cooking. Buy in small quantities and store in a cool, dark place for two to four months.

Soybean oil. A light oil, good for cooking, but avoid it for deep-frying, because of its tendency to foam. Store in a cool, dark place for six to twelve months.

Sunflower oil. A very light, tasteless oil, good for cooking and baking. Store in a cool, dark place for six to twelve months.

Walnut oil. A rich, nutty oil used in salad dressings. Store in a cool, dark place for about two months.

FATS

Animal fats. Once used by frugal housewives who wasted nothing, animal fats are less likely to be used today because of their high concentration of saturated fats. Chicken fat, called *schmaltz,* and beef fat, called *suet,* and *lard,* from pork, are prepared for cooking by a process known as *rendering.*

To render animal fat, cut the fat into cubes and melt it slowly over low heat. Strain the liquid fat through cheesecloth. The fat will harden at room temperature and can be stored in the refrigerator for up to six months.

Suet and lard are usually found in the meat case of the supermarket. Suet is often fed to birds, while lard is used to make tender, flaky piecrusts.

Butter. See Dairy Foods, below.

Margarine. Most margarines are made from vegetable oil and are similar in texture and cooking properties to butter, though with a higher smoke point. It is considered inferior in taste to butter and equivalent to butter in calories and fat, but it is much lower in cholesterol.

Margarine is available in regular and diet versions, and it comes as a stick and in a tub or squeeze bottle. Diet or light versions contain more water and less fat and cannot be substituted for butter in baking. Whipped versions have air added to make them more spreadable, which also makes them unsuitable for replacing butter in recipes.

Although stick margarine can be substituted for butter in cooking and baking, it is best avoided where a rich buttery flavor is desired, as in croissants and shortbread.

Margarine keeps best tightly wrapped in the refrigerator or freezer. It will last for up to six months in the refrigerator, twelve months in the freezer.

Solid Vegetable Shortening. Made from vegetable oils, solid vegetable shortening can be used for deep-frying or baking. It is available plain or butter-flavored. Solid vegetable shortening keeps for up to a year on a cool shelf. For a longer shelf life, keep refrigerated.

 airy Foods

In these days of cholesterol watching, dairy products have lost some of their appeal. Still, they contain most of the nutrients we require—proteins, vitamins, and minerals, especially calcium.

Low-fat yogurt, skim milk, and skim milk soft cheese can address our worries about fats. And an occasional splurge with cheese and butter and cream is probably good for our souls.

BUTTER

Butter is made by churning liquid cream into a solid. It is used as a table spread and for cooking. It comes in stick form and whipped. *Whipped butter* is not suitable for use in cooking or baking. When a recipe requires butter, it means *stick butter,* unless otherwise specified.

Butter may be salted or unsalted. Salted butter keeps slightly better than unsalted butter. The two can be used interchangeably as long as

Dairy foods.

the salt is adjusted for in the recipe. Unsalted butter is sometimes identified as sweet butter.

Butter absorbs odors readily, so while it will keep for months in the refrigerator, it must be protected by a tight wrapper. Once the original package is opened, butter should be stored tightly in plastic wrap. Butter will keep from one to three months in the refrigerator and for up to five months in the freezer.

Butter, especially salted butter, burns at a fairly low temperature, which makes it tricky to cook with. If you want to fry in butter, you can add a little oil to prevent it from burning or you can use clarified butter.

To clarify butter, melt it over low heat without stirring. Then pour off the clear liquid on the surface—that is the clarified butter—leaving behind the milk solids.

Clarified butter, sometimes called *drawn butter,* is used for cooking and for dipping seafood and artichokes. In Indian cooking, clarified butter is called *ghee*.

CHEESE

Milk curdled by the action of heat, rennet (a natural enzyme), or bacteria, or some combination of the three, separates into curds and whey. The curd, and sometimes the whey, is then made into cheese.

Cheese is often described by texture. A *hard cheese*, such as Parmesan, is usually grated before it is used. *Firm to semisoft cheese*, such as Swiss, Cheddar, or Gouda, can be sliced or grated. These cheeses are often eaten out of hand and may have a crumbly texture, such as Roquefort. *Soft cheeses* may be smooth, like Brie, or curdy, like cottage cheese. (For a description of various cheeses and their uses, see the table on pages 74–76.)

Compared to all the cheese made around the world, the selection at

Processed Cheeses

Cheese that undergoes further processing, such as pasteurization, or that has additional ingredients added for flavoring, improving the texture, or extending the shelf life, is known as processed cheese.

Cold-pack cheese and *cold-pack cheese food* **are blends of cheese, mixed to attain a smooth consistency and often flavored. Keep refrigerated for two to three weeks.**

Pasteurized processed cheese **is a blend of shredded fresh and aged cheese that is reformed into loaves (which can then be sliced) or rounds. American cheese is a pasteurized processed cheese. If unopened, it will keep until the date stamped on the package. After opening, it will keep for three to four weeks in the refrigerator.**

Pasteurized processed cheese food **is similar to pasteurized processed cheese, but it has added nonfat dry milk, which softens the texture and makes it easy to spread. It also melts faster. Keep unopened at room temperature for up to six months; after opening, refrigerate for three to four weeks.**

Pasteurized processed cheese spread **is even easier to spread because it has more moisture content. It is lower in milk fat, too. Pasteurized process cheese spread is packaged in jars, tubes, and pressurized cans. Some are flavored with olives, onions, or pimientos. Keep unopened at room temperature for up to six months; after opening, refrigerate for three to four weeks.**

most supermarkets is fairly limited. If you are interested in serving unusual cheeses—perhaps as a dessert course—you will find the best selection at specialty cheese shops.

The softer the cheese, the more perishable it is. Soft cheeses will keep in the refrigerator for one to two weeks; keep well wrapped. Hard cheeses will keep for weeks in the refrigerator, if wrapped tightly. Mold on hard cheeses can be cut away and the remaining cheese can be safely eaten.

Different cheeses respond differently to heat and some melt more readily than others. When cooking with cheese, keep the heat low; when making a cheese sauce, add the cheese at the last minute. Overcooked cheese will become tough and chewy.

Cheese is an extremely versatile food. As an appetizer, it can be served with crackers or bread. Rounds of Brie are sometimes baked *en croûte* (in a crust) or simply baked until runny and served on a bed of greens (goat cheese is good this way, too). Cheese can be cubed into salads or crumbled into salad dressing. It is used plain in sandwiches or melted in toasted sandwiches. Cheese is made into sauces and soups, and baked in casseroles. Finally, complemented by fruit and wine, a tray of assorted cheeses makes a satisfying and sophisticated ending to almost any meal.

▶ **Cheese plane, 138**
▶ **Cheese knife, 128**
▶ **Presenting cheese, 400–401**

(continued on page 77)

Guide to Cheeses

CHEESE	DESCRIPTION	USES	COMMENTS
Soft Cheeses			
Brie	Edible white crust, creamy yellow interior. Mild to pungent flavor.	For appetizer and dessert trays, and in cooking.	Look for wheels that yield to the touch and run a little; center should not be collapsed.
Camembert	Gray-white edible crust, with creamy interior. Flavor is slightly acidic and earthy.	Appetizer and dessert trays.	Interior should be soft, almost runny. Flavor ranges from mild to pungent, depending on age of cheese. Serve at room temperature.
Cottage, Ricotta	Creamy white, curdlike, low calorie. Delicately mild in flavor. Soft enough to be spooned.	Perfect in appetizers, cooked dishes, desserts, cake fillings and frostings. Cottage cheese is often eaten plain.	
Cream, Neufchâtel	Creamy white spread, mild and slightly acidic in flavor. May be whipped for easier spreading; sometimes flavored. Neufchâtel is lighter and lower in fat and calories than cream cheese.	As a spread for bread and bagels, in cheesecake and other desserts, cake fillings, and frostings.	
Liederkranz, Limburger	Soft, bacteria-ripened cheese with strong to overpowering flavor.	Eaten out of hand.	An acquired taste.
Mascarpone	Creamy white cheese, eaten with a spoon.	For desserts, and with fruit or sugar and cinnamon.	
Semisoft Cheeses			
American	Processed cheese of uniform texture made from domestic Cheddar. Mild flavor; pale yellow, orange, or white. Smooth texture.	Sandwiches and casseroles.	Available as individual slices or loaves.
Bel Paese	Mild, sweet flavor; creamy interior; waxy.	Team with fruit for dessert. Also good as appetizer.	
Blue (Bleu)	Strong flavor; marbled with blue-green mold; crumbly. Some of the more popular types include Roquefort, Stilton, and Gorgonzola.	Appetizers, salads, dressings, desserts.	Look for moist cheese with veins that stand out against background.
Brick	Mild flavor when young, strong when old; light yellow to orange; small holes in cheese.	Appetizers, sandwiches, salads, desserts.	Similar to Muenster.

Guide to Cheeses (*continued*)

CHEESE	DESCRIPTION	USES	COMMENTS
Semisoft Cheeses (*continued*)			
Feta	Salty, sharp flavor; soft, crumbly texture.	In salads and in cooking.	Made from sheep's, goat's, or cow's milk. Available in jars or packaged in brine or vacuum-sealed packages. Not eaten out of hand.
Gorgonzola	Creamy, delicately flavored blue cheese.	Appetizers, salads, dressings, desserts.	Italy's most famous blue cheese.
Mozzarella	Soft, white, with a round shape. Fresh mozzarella is quite soft. Mild in flavor, a bit chewy.	On pizza and in other baked Italian dishes. Fresh mozzarella is delicious as an appetizer, in salads.	Also available shredded. Made from either whole milk or skim; cow's milk or buffalo milk (in Italy). Fresh mozzarella will keep for only one or two days.
Muenster	Mild to mellow flavor; creamy yellow interior with orange rind; smooth; waxy.	Appetizers, sandwiches, in cooking.	European Muenster is sharper in flavor and darker in color than American Muenster.
Roquefort	Rich, strong, creamy blue cheese; smooth, firm, and buttery.	Appetizers, salads, dressings, desserts.	Considered the premier blue cheese.
Semihard Cheeses			
Cheddar	Mild to very sharp flavor, depending on age, which is marked on package; cream to orange color; smooth.	Very versatile; used for sandwiches, cooked dishes, salads, snacks, desserts.	Available shredded, sliced, and in bricks.
Colby	Mild to mellow flavor, light yellow to orange, slightly granular texture.	Sandwiches, cooked dishes, snacks.	American Cheddar type.
Edam	Mild, nutty, buttery flavor; small holes; mealy texture; thin rind with red wax coating.	Appetizer and desserts trays; snacks.	Similar to Gouda, but slightly harder due to its lower fat content.
Fontina	Delicate nutty, slightly smoky flavor; ivory colored; semisoft to firm texture, depending on age; natural rind, small holes.	Cooking, snacking.	Cheese of choice for fondue; good melting qualities.
Gjetost	Sweet, caramel flavor; golden brown; buttery.	Dessert; snacks.	Pronounced YED-ost.

(table continues)

Guide to Cheeses (*continued*)

CHEESE	DESCRIPTION	USES	COMMENTS

Semihard Cheeses (*continued*)

CHEESE	DESCRIPTION	USES	COMMENTS
Gouda	Mild, buttery cheese; small holes, soft texture; thin rind with yellow wax coating.	Appetizer and dessert trays; snacks.	
Gruyère	Nutty, faintly tasting of caramel; smooth, firm, pale, Swiss-type cheese.	Good all-purpose cheese, excellent for sauces, toppings, salads, soufflés, omelets; also good for snacking.	Good melting qualities; doesn't get stringy when melted.
Monterey Jack	Mild to mellow flavor; creamy white; semisoft to firm in texture, small holes.	Used in cooking (particularly Tex-Mex dishes), for sandwiches and snacking.	
Port du Salut	Mellow to robust flavor; creamy yellow interior; smooth and buttery.	Appetizers or desserts.	
Swiss (Emmenthaler)	Sweet, nutty flavor; pale yellow; large holes throughout; smooth, firm texture.	All-purpose cheese, good for appetizers, sandwiches, cooking, snacking.	The best Swiss comes from Switzerland; American Swiss is often slightly bitter. Milder in flavor than Gruyère. Stringy when melted.

Hard Cheeses

CHEESE	DESCRIPTION	USES	COMMENTS
Asiago	Sharp flavor; hard, smooth texture.	Grated into cooked dishes.	
Parmesan	Sharp, salty flavor; golden color; hard, grainy texture.	Grated into typically Italian dishes, especially soups, pastas and sauces.	The best are labeled Parmigiano-Reggiano.
Provolone	Mellow to sharp, smoky flavor, often salty; semifirm to hard, smooth texture, depending on age; light brown outside, light yellow inside; sometimes lined with rope marks.	Younger, softer cheese used for sandwiches, snacking; older cheese for cooking.	
Romano	Sharp, piquant flavor; light yellow color; hard, dry texture.	Grated into typically Italian dishes, especially soups, pastas, and sauces.	Though different in flavor, can be used interchangeably with Parmesan. The best Romanos are Pecorino Romanos.
Sapsago	Grassy, herby flavor; pale green in color; hard dry texture.	Grated into cooked dishes.	Low in fat; addition of clover gives it its characteristic color and taste.

CREAM

Cream comes in various forms, depending on the amount of milk fat it contains. All cream is more perishable than milk; it should be kept well chilled and used within one to four days, or frozen for up to two months. Commercial whipped cream in aerosol cans, however, will keep for up to one month.

For long-term storage, cream can be frozen for up to a month and then used for cooking. However, it will no longer be good for whipping or adding to coffee.

Half-and-half. Made by combining equal amounts of whole milk and light cream, half-and-half is used as a table cream for coffee, cereal, and desserts. It contains between 10.5 and 18 percent milk fat. Expect half-and-half to last for three to four days in the refrigerator, or four months in the freezer. Ultrapasteurized half-and-half will keep longer than regular half-and-half.

Light cream. Used as a table cream and for cooking, light cream contains between 18 and 30 percent milk fat.

Light whipping cream. Contains between 30 and 36 percent milk fat and can be whipped.

Heavy whipping cream. Containing not less than 36 percent milk fat, this is the best to use for whipping cream. It is also called heavy cream. One cup of whipping cream will yield two cups of whipped cream. For directions for whipping cream, see pages 265–266.

CULTURED DAIRY PRODUCTS

Buttermilk. Tangy buttermilk is made when special bacteria is added to skim milk. The resulting thick liquid is low in calories (one cup has ninety calories) and fat; it is used as a beverage, in salad dressings, and in baking, where it adds tenderness and flavor to the finished product.

Buttermilk is generally sold in quarts in the dairy case, although it is available as a powder. Liquid buttermilk should be kept refrigerated and will last up to two weeks without spoiling; however, the flavor is best if used within one week.

When substituting buttermilk for regular milk or cream in baking, counteract its higher acid content with 1 teaspoon of baking soda for every 1½ cups of buttermilk.

If you don't have buttermilk on hand, you can make soured milk (see page 301). You can also substitute unflavored yogurt for buttermilk in recipes.

Dry buttermilk powder can be used in any recipe calling for buttermilk. For each cup of liquid buttermilk, use ¼ cup buttermilk powder and add an additional cup of water to the batter.

Crème fraîche. Popular in French cooking and recently available in the United States, crème fraîche is akin to sour cream, but it is creamier and milder in flavor. It is used in cooking and to spoon over fresh fruits and desserts. If you find it in the supermarket, plan to use it within one month.

To make your own crème fraîche, combine 1 cup of heavy cream with two tablespoons buttermilk in a large jar. Cover and set in a warm place for twelve to eighteen hours, until thick. Then refrigerate; it will keep for about one week.

Sour cream. Cultured sweet cream becomes sour cream with its own tangy flavor and stiff consistency. It will keep for up to four weeks in the refrigerator.

Sour cream gives baked goods a rich taste and tender crumb. It also makes a delicious cream sauce when added to a gravy at the end of cooking (do not let it boil). To prevent the cream from separating (which it will do if it gets too hot), mix two tablespoons of flour into each cup of cream.

Yogurt. Tangy, creamy yogurt is becoming indispensable in the kitchen as a low-fat substitute for sour cream in baked goods, salad dressings, and desserts. It is available plain or flavored. Some yogurt has gelatin added to give it a more puddinglike consistency.

Yogurt is considered a healthful food when it is made with low-fat milk because it is a good source of calcium. The live cultures in some yogurts are also valuable for maintaining digestive health.

ICE CREAM AND FROZEN DESSERTS

There are an incredible number of choices when it comes to ice cream these days—premium brands, supermarket brands, low-fat frozen desserts made with or without dairy, ices, sherbets, sorbets.

When buying a frozen dessert with the idea of consuming fewer calories than you would if you bought premium ice cream, read the labels carefully! Often what the desserts lack in calories from fats they make up with calories from sugar. Some soy-based frozen desserts contain even more fat than premium ice cream.

Whatever you buy, look for packages that are frozen solid and clean. A sticky surface indicates that the ice cream has thawed and refrozen.

Keep ice cream in the coldest part of your freezer. At 0°F. it will keep for one to two months. If you store it in the freezer compartment of your refrigerator, use it within a week.

When you return a partially used container of ice cream to the freezer, slip it into a plastic bag and seal it first. Any ice cream that has completely thawed should be discarded.

Ice cream. The most expensive, the most fattening, and often the most delicious ice cream is labeled *premium*. Usually there is less air whipped into the ice cream as it is freezing. By contrast, *supermarket* *brands* contain less cream and yolk and more air, making them significantly lower in fat and calories.

French custard ice cream. This ice cream contains a higher percentage of egg yolks, making the ice cream richer and smoother. Most homemade ice creams are based on this formula.

Ice milk. Ice milk contains less fat than ice cream, but it is often higher in sugar.

Sherbet. Usually this is a mixture of milk, sweetener, fruit or juice, and gelatin or egg whites for smoothness.

Sorbets and ices. Sorbets, ices, and frozen fruit bars are made from fruit or juice, sugar, and water. They contain no eggs or milk, though they may be quite high in sugar.

Frozen yogurt. Similar in fat to ice milk, frozen yogurt may or may not be a diet dessert, depending on what is mixed in or added on top. Because it is pasteurized, it no longer contains active yogurt cultures.

MILK

Milk is the basis for all dairy products. It is available in many forms. Keep milk well chilled, and don't leave it out on the table for extended periods of time. If consistently stored at 40°F., milk will keep from one to five days beyond the "sell by" date marked on the bottle. Whole milk generally keeps longer than skim or low-fat milk.

Acidophilus milk. For people who have trouble digesting milk, acidophilus milk can make a big difference. The milk—skim or low-fat—is treated with bacteria that help break down milk once it is in the digestive track.

Evaporated milk. Milk from which 60 percent of the water has been removed is called evaporated milk. It has been processed to be stable in a can. Although not good for drinking, it is used in baking. When a recipe calls for evaporated milk, it is usually referring to whole evaporated milk. Evaporated low-fat and skim milks are also sold.

To substitute evaporated milk for 1 cup of whole milk, combine ½ cup evaporated milk with ½ cup water.

Lactose-reduced low-fat milk. Also for those who have trouble digesting milk, this milk has its lactose reduced to only 30 percent.

Low-fat milk. This can contain anywhere from .5 percent to 2 percent milk fat. It can be used interchangeably with whole milk in most recipes.

Nonfat dry milk. Available as a powder, this is skim milk with the water removed. It reconstitutes in water. The flavor is not the same as fresh skim milk, but it can readily be used in cooking. Sometimes the powder is added to baked goods and breads to boost the product's protein content.

◗ **Milk substitutes, 301**

Skim milk. Skim milk, or nonfat milk, contains less than .5 percent milk fat.

Sweetened condensed milk. Used in baking and as a coffee lightener, sweetened condensed milk is sweetened whole milk from which more than half the water is removed. Although they both come in cans and have a similar viscous consistency, sweetened condensed milk and evaporated milk cannot be used interchangeably.

Whole milk. Whole milk contains at least 3.5 percent milk fat. Unless otherwise specified, recipes that require milk mean whole milk. However, in most instances you can substitute low-fat milk with no impact on flavor or texture.

*E*ggs

Where we once used eggs freely, now we must be concerned with the cholesterol contained in egg yolks and the risk of salmonella that both the whites and yolks present. Nonetheless, eggs remain a staple in most kitchens because of the valuable roles they play in leavening baked goods and binding together ingredients in pancakes, fritters, and the like. For preparation tips, see pages 267–268.

BUYING EGGS

Shell color does not indicate the quality, taste, texture, or nutritional value of eggs. Commercial chickens lay white or brown eggs, depending on the breed. If you buy directly from the farm, you may be treated to any color egg, including blue or green, again depending on the breed.

Eggs are graded by freshness and by size. Grade AA eggs are fresher than Grade A; Grade B eggs, usually sold to institutions, are older and sometimes misshapen. Eggs are also graded by size—extra large, large, medium, small. Unless otherwise stated, most recipes require the use of large eggs.

Look for eggs that are clean and free from cracks.

FRESHNESS COUNTS

Fresh eggs are superior in flavor to old eggs. If you can't buy eggs straight off the farm, check the packing date code on the bottom of your egg carton. The three-digit code represents the date (from 001 to 365, the days of the year). Eggs can be safely stored in the refrigerator for four to five weeks after purchase, though after two weeks they are no longer the best choice for whipping or for any dish where the

Egg Safety

Farmers and egg producers, particularly in the eastern United States, are having great difficulty eradicating salmonella bacteria from their chickens. Those who handle raw eggs and those who eat uncooked or barely cooked eggs (in Caesar salads, eggnog, hollandaise sauce, homemade mayonnaise, soft-boiled eggs) run the risk of contracting salmonella, or food poisoning.

To minimize the risk of salmonella, keep eggs refrigerated, discard leaking or cracked eggs, keep utensils that come in contact with eggs scrupulously clean, and always cook eggs to at least 160°F. Be sure to wash your hands after handling eggs.

Forget about those recipes, like eggnog, that call for raw eggs and avoid soft-boiled eggs and sunnyside-up eggs. Make meringues with a hot sugar syrup (see Techniques, page 281). Eggnog can be made with a cooked custard base.

When cracking eggs, don't allow the egg to come in contact with the outer shell. Use an egg separator rather than pass the yolk from eggshell to eggshell.

The danger of salmonella is greatest for the elderly, infants, pregnant women, and people with illnesses or compromised immune systems. Healthy adults should use discretion and common sense when it comes to eating raw eggs.

appearance or texture of the egg matters—as in scrambled or fried eggs.

The only way to accurately gauge the freshness of an egg is to crack it open. A fresh egg has a cloudy white and a high-standing yolk. An older egg will have a less cloudy white and a flatter yolk. An egg that has gone bad will have a definite odor.

STORING EGGS

Store eggs, unwashed, in their original carton, large end up (to keep the yolks centered). Don't use the egg rack provided in many refrigerators—the unprotected eggs are kept too warm and are exposed to odors, which they will absorb through their shells.

Leftover egg whites can be stored for up to four days in a covered glass container in the refrigerator or in the freezer for up to one year. Either keep each white in a separate container, or store in convenient size batches (for example, three to use in a meringue).

Leftover yolks should be covered with water and stored in a covered glass jar for two to three days. Drain off the water before using the yolks in custards and sauces.

Hard-cooked eggs in their shell will keep for up to a week in their shells.

EGG SUBSTITUTES

If you are concerned about the cholesterol you eat, consider substituting egg whites for whole eggs in baked goods, such as cookies, where the egg is used for structure, but leavening is provided by baking soda or baking powder. To make the substitution for a whole egg, mix a teaspoon of vegetable oil with 4 teaspoons of water and 1 egg white. Or, if you want to avoid fat altogether, substitute 2 egg whites for 1 whole egg.

There are also several commercial egg substitutes on the market, most using egg whites as a base. They vary in flavor and you must experiment to find a brand you like. Commercial egg substitutes can be stored in the freezer at 0°F. for up to one year. After thawing, keep in the refrigerator and use within seven days.

DUCK AND GOOSE EGGS

Duck eggs and goose eggs are richer tasting than chicken eggs, but the whites are not suitable for whipping. Use in omelets, custards, and mousses.

*F*ish

Fish holds a place of honor in a healthful diet, because it is high in protein and low in fat. The fish with the most flavor—salmon, tuna, mackerel, swordfish—are also high in Omega-3 fatty acids, which play a role in reducing blood cholesterol.

Until recently, most fish was caught in the wild. Today we are eating more and more farm-raised fish. Most of the trout, catfish, salmon, striped bass, and sturgeon you find in the markets are farm-raised.

SELECTING FISH

Select fish that are as fresh as can be. Fillets and steaks should be plump and moist. The grain of the meat should look firm and tight, not ragged or fuzzy. Whole fish should have clear, bright eyes, pink or red gills, and shiny, elastic skin. If you are buying frozen fish, make sure the packaging is intact, and there is no evidence of ice or leaking blood. It should be free from odor.

Fresh fish should be cooked the same day you buy it, though it can be held in the coldest part of the refrigerator, tightly wrapped, for up to two days. If possible, keep the fish on a pan of crushed ice. Frozen fish should be left in its packaging and stored at 0°F.; lean fish will keep for

⧫ **Nutrient values of fish,**
390–391

Fish. 1 Flounder 2 Trout 3 Whitefish 4 Bass 5 Bluefish 6 Tuna 7 Swordfish

four to six months, oily fish will keep for about two months. Thaw overnight in the refrigerator in the original wrapping.

If you are buying a whole fish: One that is *round* or *whole,* is just as it came off the boat—in need of a cleaning to take care of the gills, guts, and scales. If the fish is *drawn,* it has had its organs, gills, and scales removed. A *dressed* fish has been gutted and scaled and the head and fins removed. Small fish prepared this way are called *pan-dressed.*

A *fillet* is the side of a fish that has been cut lengthwise from the backbone. A fillet may be anywhere from ¼ to 1 inch thick. A *steak* may be ⅝ to 1 inch thick and is a crosscut slice of fish from one of the larger types of fish, such as tuna. The bone is usually left in.

Allow four to five ounces of fish steaks or fillet per serving; allow eight ounces of drawn or dressed fish.

CAVIAR AND ROE

Most caviar, which is lightly salted sturgeon eggs (roe), comes from beluga, sevruga, and osetra sturgeon. These fish are found in the Mediterranean and Caspian seas. The best caviar, like beluga, is composed of whole (not broken), crisp, firm eggs; they should pop when eaten.

Beluga is considered the finest caviar. It is black in color and is fairly large grained. *Sevruga* is small-grained and greenish black. *Osetra* is larger-grained and may be golden brown, slate gray, or bottle green in color.

Although the roe of other fish can be made into a caviarlike product, the USDA says that only imported sturgeon roe can be called caviar. If

(continued on page 86)

Oily Fish versus Lean Fish

Fish is often divided into two categories: lean and oily. Lean fish have firm white flesh and a very mild flavor. Many times a recipe will require a specific fish that just isn't available—or perhaps a different fish looked fresher and more appealing at the store. You can usually substitute one lean fish for another and one oily fish for another.

When cooking fish, moist cooking methods—steaming and poaching—are most successful with lean fish, as are cooking in a sauce, broiling with a butter baste, or microwaving. The flesh of oily fish contains enough fat to keep it from drying out even on a grill. Oily fish have flesh that is rich in taste and color.

The big challenge in preparing any fish is cooking it just to the point of doneness, without overcooking. Properly cooked fish *just begins* to flake easily. The juices are milky white. By contrast, an undercooked fish will resist flaking, is still translucent, and the juices are watery. Overcooked fish looks dry, has no juices, and the flesh falls apart when prodded with a fork.

Guide to Fish

FISH	DESCRIPTION
Anchovy	Small, slim, silvery fish. Usually salted and canned in oil, to be used as seasoning. Anchovy paste is made from anchovies, oil, and herbs; a little goes a long way.
Bass, Largemouth and Smallmouth	Freshwater, bony fish.
Bluefish	Oily fish with dark blue-red flesh. Good grilled, broiled, or smoked. The meat lightens as it cooks and has a distinctive flavor.
Catfish	Freshwater; usually farm-raised. Sweet white flesh. Lends itself to a variety of cooking methods; a favorite preparation is coated with cornmeal and pan-fried.
Cod	Firm, white, large-flaked lean meat. Lends itself to a variety of preparations. Immature fish is called scrod. Salt cod is also readily available.
Flounder	Fine-flaked, lean white fish; delicate in taste. Can be used interchangeably with sole (and is sometimes labeled as sole, though sole is more delicate and requires gentler cooking).
Grouper	Lean, firm, large-flaked flesh with mild, sweet flavor.
Haddock	Large-flaked, lean white fish; delicate in taste. Is always sold skin on. Can be used interchangeably with cod. Finnan haddie is smoked haddock fillets.
Halibut	Large-flaked, lean white fish; delicate in taste. Cooks very quickly.
Herring	Flavorful, soft, dark, fatty flesh that turns ivory when cooked. Fresh herring is very perishable. Popular canned in a vinegar brine. Kippered herring are salt-dried and then cold smoked.
Mackerel	Distinctively flavored, fatty red flesh that cooks to ivory; small-flaked. Highly perishable; cook on same day as purchased.
Mahimahi	Tender, white, sweet, lean flesh. Can be dry. Plan to marinate or cook in a sauce.
Monkfish	Called the "poor man's lobster." Mild, sweet white flesh reminiscent of lobster. Low in fat and firm in texture.

LEAN FISH		OILY FISH	
Cod	Orange roughy	Bluefish	Smelt
Flounder	Pollock	Herring	Striped mullet
Grouper	Sea bass	Lake trout	Sturgeon
Haddock	Shark	Mackerel	Swordfish
Hake	Tilapia	Pompano	Trout
Halibut	Turbot	Salmon	Tuna
Ocean perch	Whiting	Shad	

Guide to Fish (*continued*)

FISH	DESCRIPTION
Orange Roughy	Tender, white, lean flesh; sweet delicate flavor. Usually available as fresh-frozen fillets.
Pollock	Grayish, firm, lean white flesh turns white when cooked and has a delicate, slightly sweet flavor. Resembles haddock and cod.
Pompano	Firm, white, moderately fatty fish; sweet, mild flavor.
Red Snapper	Large-flaked, lean white fish, mild flavor. Sold whole or as skin-on fillet. If skin is not on, it may not be red snapper.
Salmon	Pale pink, fatty meat, large flakes, mild flavor. Sockeye has darker meat than chinook (the most expensive salmon), coho, or pink. Most Atlantic salmon is farm-raised, with pink to red or orange flesh.
Sea Bass	Fatty to lean white meat with a mild flavor.
Skate	Firm, lean white flesh is reminiscent of scallops in flavor.
Smelt	Tender, mild-flavored, fatty meat. There are freshwater and seawater varieties. Cooked whole.
Sole	Lean white meat; mild flavor. Most sole sold in the United States (usually as lemon sole, gray sole, or rex sole) is actually flounder. For real sole, look for imported Dover sole.
Swordfish	Fatty, firm, short-grained, light meat; distinctive flavor. Cooks quickly.
Tilefish	Lean, firm meat; delicate flavor. Buy whole or in fillets or steaks. Suitable to all methods of cooking.
Trout, Brook	White to deep red/orange flesh, moderately fatty, mild flavor. Averages less than 1 pound. In the U.S. it is often considered the finest trout.
Trout, Sea	Off-white meat, light textured, milk flavor that varies in quality. Sometimes somewhat oily.
Tuna	Firm, moderately fatty. Albacore has white meat; bigeye and bluefin have dark red meat; yellowfin has reddish meat.
Whitefish	Delicate, white, fatty flesh, mildly sweet. Makes a good substitute for freshwater trout.

you can't afford the steep price of the real stuff, sample other roes. *Lumpfish roe* is died black to resemble beluga caviar or red and makes a credible garnish. *Salmon roe* is red and is an acceptable substitute. Smoked *cod roe* is used to make *taramasalata*, a Greek dip.

Caviar is highly perishable. The best comes in bottles or tins, stored at 32°F., and no higher or lower. Some caviar is pasteurized to extend its shelf life, though pasteurizing does affect the flavor.

Store unopened caviar between 29°F. and 32°F. for one to four weeks. Once opened, the caviar should be used within a day or two. Pasteurized caviar will keep on the shelf for two to four months; opened it will keep in the refrigerator for one to two weeks.

If you splurge on real caviar, serve it simply with a little lemon, perhaps some chopped hard-cooked egg, and toast.

SHAD ROE

Shad roe is a delicacy found only in the spring when the fish spawn. The roe is contained in two deep red egg sacs. The sacs are thoroughly washed, then cooked. They may be dredged in flour and fried, poached and added to scrambled eggs, or grilled.

*S*hellfish

Shellfish may be the only creatures that we can consistently eat fresh, because shellfish are widely available live. Actually, this is necessary as shellfish are highly perishable and should be eaten within twenty-four hours of purchase.

Shellfish are divided into two categories: crustaceans, which have pincers and antennae; and mollusks, which have hinged shells. Additionally, squid and octopus fall into the mollusk grouping.

With all shellfish, if you are buying live specimens, be sure they *are* alive. Crustaceans should be active; mollusks should have tightly shut shells or shells that shut when tapped. If you are buying fresh shellfish—cooked or uncooked—it should have no fishy odor. Frozen shellfish should be solidly frozen with no traces of ice and no dry spots that would indicate mishandling or thawing.

To keep in the refrigerator, place the shellfish in a shallow tray and cover with a clean, damp towel. Never store shellfish in water or ice, which would draw moisture out of the shellfish and spoil the texture.

Boiling, poaching, steaming, baking, grilling, broiling, and frying are appropriate to all shellfish (except that lobsters and crayfish aren't fried). If you are using a dry heat method—baking, grilling, or broil-

Shellfish. **1** Oyster
2 Mussels **3** Shrimp
4 Crayfish **5** Lobster
6 Scallop **7** Squid **8** Crab
9 Clams

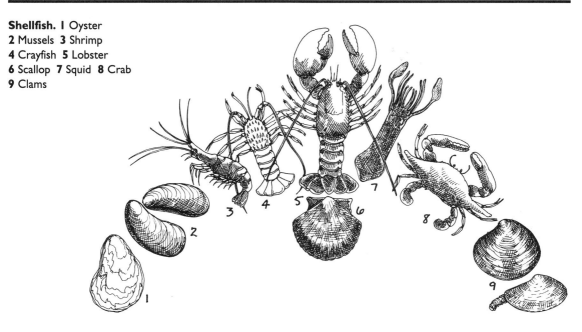

ing—be sure to baste frequently with a flavored oil or butter. All shell-fish cooks quickly; with overcooking it becomes tough and dry.

Canned shellfish will do in a pinch for soups, sauces, and casseroles. Generally the flavor and texture are inferior to fresh shellfish. Most are packed in a very salty brine. Rinse well before adding to a dish.

Bottled clam juice can be used in recipes calling for fish stock or for enriching a fish stock. It is very strongly flavored and salty.

CRUSTACEANS

Crabs. A variety of crabs are harvested in the U.S. *Blue crabs* are small, ranging from ¼ to 1 pound in weight. On the West Coast, one finds the *Dungeness crab,* which can weigh anywhere from 1½ to 3½ pounds. Alaskan *king crabs* are huge—6 to 20 pounds in weight. Their legs can be up to three feet long and are filled with long pieces of red-flecked white meat.

Stone crabs are a Florida delicacy. Because the crabs are in short supply, fishermen harvest only one claw and return the crab to the ocean to grow another, a process that takes about eighteen months. The fishermen cook the claws immediately, then chill or freeze the meat; otherwise the meat would adhere to the shell. Before serving, crack the shells with a mallet so the meat can be extracted. The meat is sweet and firm and can be served hot or cold.

Frozen *soft-shell crabs* are available year-round, but live ones are only available from May to September. Their delicate flavor makes them worth seeking out. Although all crabs go through a soft-shell stage,

◗ **Broiling soft-shell crabs, 227**
◗ **Preparing crabs for cooking, 190–191**
◗ **Sautéing soft-shell crabs, 210**
◗ **Steaming crabs, 212, 390**

when they have outgrown their old shell, it is mainly the blue crab that is sold as soft-shell.

BUYING CRABS You can buy crabs whole—live, fresh, or frozen—or you can buy just the claws, usually cooked and frozen. You can also buy fresh or frozen crabmeat. It comes as lump meat (highest in quality; nice, fat lumps), flaked meat (high quality, small flakes), or claw meat (stringy, dark, often tough). Imitation crabmeat does not come close to the sweet original in taste.

When buying live crabs, look for active specimens and plan to cook them within one day. Don't cook any that have died. Crabs do slow down under refrigeration, but you can tell they are alive by slight movements of their legs.

It's hard to gauge how many live crabs to buy. In an informal setting, where boiled crabs are dumped onto a paper-covered table and no one is concerned about the mess, people eat well beyond expected limits. Here's a general rule of thumb.

For one serving: ½ to 1 whole Dungeness crab
1 pound blue crabs
2 soft-shell crabs
½ pound crab legs
3 to 4 ounces crabmeat

SOFT-SHELL CRABS Soft-shell crabs are graded by size: jumbo (up to seven inches across), prime, and medium (which are quite small). Generally allow two per main course serving. Fresh soft-shells are generally superior in taste and texture than frozen soft-shells; they are also more expensive.

You must deal with live soft-shells as soon as you bring them home, by cleaning and cooking or cleaning and storing at 33°F. for a few days. (You can clean and freeze soft-shells, but you can also buy frozen soft-shells at a reduced price, so why pay a premium price for live crabs if you plan to freeze them?) For instructions on how to clean soft-shell crabs, see page 191.

Crayfish (crawfish, crawdad). These freshwater critters look like miniature lobsters. You'll find them sold whole, live, or boiled. For instructions on how to remove the meat from crayfish, see page 191.

Lobster. A first-time encounter with a whole cooked lobster can be intimidating, but it is not really difficult to remove the meat from the shell. At the table, a nutcracker and a small fork or pick are used to extract the flesh. In the kitchen, you can use a large knife.

Lobsters are available live and cooked. Frozen cooked tails are available also.

When buying live lobsters, pick out the most active lobsters in the

▶ **Boiling lobsters, 198**
▶ **Extracting meat from lobsters, 190**
▶ **Roasting lobsters, 240**

Shrimp Sizes and Recommended Uses

These sizes are based on industry standards. Stores may have their own definition of small, medium, and large, so check the count-per-pound for an accurate
idea of the size of the shrimp. In bulk grading, some individual shrimp may be
slightly larger or smaller than expected. These sizes refer to uncooked, headless
shrimp.

Large Sizes	Suggested Preparations
Extra colossal (under 10 per pound)	Cocktails, stuffed, baked, broiled, fried, grilled, sautéed
Colossal (under 15 per pound)	
Extra jumbo (16 to 20 per pound)	
Jumbo (21 to 25 per pound)	
Extra Large (26 to 30 per pound)	
Large (31 to 40 per pound)	

Medium Sizes	Suggested Preparations
Medium large (36 to 40 per pound)	Cocktails, casseroles, Creole, curried, fried, grilled, gumbo, broiled
Medium (41 to 50 per pound)	

Small Sizes	Suggested Preparations
Small (51 to 60 per pound)	Soups, salads, casseroles, Creole, sauces
Extra small (61 to 70 per pound)	
Tiny (more than 70 per pound)	

tank. A lobster should curl its tail and wave its claws and antennae as it
is lifted from the water.

Lobsters are priced according to size, which has nothing to do with
taste or quality. *Chicken lobsters* weigh about 1 pound each, *quarters*
weigh about 1¼ pounds, *large*, or *selects*, weigh from 1½ to less than
2½ pounds, and *jumbos* weigh over 2½ pounds. The jumbos are just
as sweet and tender as the chickens. Generally one chicken or quarter
lobster is served per person; though many adults are capable of—and
happy to—eat two or more.

Prawns. What you buy as a prawn is probably a jumbo shrimp,
unless you happen to live in Hawaii, where prawns are farmed. Prawns
are large, freshwater shellfish with longer legs and a more slender body
than shrimp. Treat as you would shrimp.

Shrimp. There are several different varieties of shrimp harvested in
the U.S., ranging in color from gray to pink, depending on whether
they were harvested from the Gulf of Mexico or the Atlantic. *Rock*

shrimp from Florida are sweeter and more like lobster than other varieties of shrimp. Differences among other varieties are hard to discern.

Fresh or previously frozen shrimp should feel firm and smell clean. Dark spots on the body are usually natural coloration and not spoilage. Shrimp is graded by size or by how many shrimp to the pound (see page 89). There is no difference in taste or quality; but the larger the shrimp, the less work to peel and devein, and the more expensive.

Figure on getting about three servings per pound of unpeeled shrimp and about five servings per pound of cooked peeled shrimp.

In the U.S., shrimp is usually sold with the head removed. If the head is on, you have a bargain, because the heads have a lot of flavor. You can leave the heads on for a dramatic presentation in paella, or to add extra flavor in a gumbo, or you can remove the head and use it to make stock. To remove the head, hold the body of the shrimp in one hand and with the other grasp the hard shell at the base of the head. Gently pull the head from the body with a slight rocking motion. The head should pull off easily. Rinse the body.

Shrimp can be peeled and deveined before or after cooking; but cooked in the shell, they will have more flavor. For peeling and deveining instructions, see page 189. Rock shrimp have a tough, rigid shell that requires cutting with scissors or kitchen shears.

As with all shellfish, shrimp is best eaten on the day it is purchased. However, it can be kept for up to two days in the refrigerator.

MOLLUSKS

Clams. There are many varieties of clams, some tougher than others and more suitable for chowder than for frying. But in general you can substitute one type of clam for another.

From the East Coast, *hard-shell clams* and *littlenecks* are the sweetest and most tender; *cherrystones* are larger; *chowder clams* are the toughest and are usually minced to use in soups and sauces. *Soft-shell clams* include *steamers, squirt clams,* and *belly clams.* These all have necks that stick out between the shells and are a good choice for steaming, though they can be fried or used in chowder. On the Pacific Coast, you will find hard-shelled *littlenecks* that are unrelated to the East Coast clams of the same name; *razor clams* are a soft-shell variety. *Geoducks* are the largest clam found in the States; these Pacific clams are usually used in soups and chowders.

BUYING CLAMS You can buy clams live or shucked. When buying live clams, look for moist, unbroken shells. The shells should close when gently tapped. Clams in the shell will keep for up to two days, though the sooner they are consumed, the better.

Shucked clams should be plump; their liquor should be clear. They are sold by the pint or gallon. There are about eighteen shucked clams to a pint. They will keep in the refrigerator, covered in brine, for about three days. For longer storage, three to four months, store in the freezer. If there is not enough brine to completely cover the clams, make up more by combining ½ teaspoon of salt with 1 cup water. Or use bottled clam juice.

For instructions on preparing clams, see page 191.

Mussels. Farm-raised mussels are meatier and more grit-free than wild mussels. They are available year-round and can be purchased fresh, canned, smoked, or frozen. When purchasing mussels in the shell, allow about one pound per person. Mussels in the shell will keep for up to two days, though the sooner they are consumed, the better.

Just before cooking, scrub the mussels under cold running water and remove the beard by pulling it off. If you wish to shuck the mussels before cooking, shuck as you would for clams, taking care because mussel shells are more easily broken than clam shells.

Leftover cooked mussel meat can be stored in the refrigerator for two to three days.

Oysters. The unique briny taste of oysters makes them a favorite among seafood lovers. Each variety of oyster has its own distinctive taste.

When buying live oysters, look for ones that are kept in a tank of salt water. The shells should be closed and intact. They should not be buried in ice because ingesting fresh water is fatal to them. Store oysters with their cupped shell down, so the liquid that provides the interior environment they require doesn't run out.

Clean oysters by scrubbing well with a brush, then place them in a single layer on a dish or tray. Cover with a damp towel and refrigerate for up to two days—though the oysters will be at their peak for only a day or so.

Oysters should be cooked immediately after shucking (for instructions on how to shuck, see pages 191–192).

When buying shucked oysters, look for oysters in liquid that is clear, not cloudy. Small oysters are preferable in stews because they fit better on the spoon. Shucked oysters covered in their own liquor will keep for up to two days, or they can be frozen for up to three months. Shucked oysters should be cooked just until they look plump and opaque and begin to curl at the edges.

Scallops. Scallops are usually sold fresh, already shucked, which makes them very convenient to prepare. They are also very quick cooking.

Sea scallops are large, averaging 10 to 30 per pound. They are available year-round and taste briny, sweet, and tender. *Bay scallops* are quite small (50 to 100 per pound) and expensive, with a distinctly sweet, rich, nutty taste. Bargain-priced bay scallops are probably *calico scallops*. These tiny (150 to 250 per pound) scallops are tougher and have less flavor than bay scallops.

Whatever variety you buy, select scallops that are firm and sweet-smelling. Refrigerate fresh scallops covered in their own liquid in a closed container for up to two days.

Scallops can be broiled, sautéed, poached, grilled, stir-fried, or deep-fried. They are also a good choice for seviche.

Squid and octopus. Squid and octopus are both ink fish and fairly similar in looks and taste. The ink is flavorful and used to season many Italian dishes, particularly risotto. If you are looking for recipes for these delicately flavored critters, you will have best luck in Italian, Greek, Spanish, Portuguese, and Oriental cookbooks. Squid is sometimes known by its Italian name, calamari. Both are sold fresh, frozen, or precooked.

When buying fresh squid or octopus, look for firm, bright meat. The thin speckled skin should not be torn or damaged. The eyes should be distinct and the tentacles firm and whole. Small octopus, under two pounds, are more tender than larger ones. Large octopus and squid over eight inches long should be pounded to tenderize after they are cleaned. Most octopus you buy will already be cleaned. To prepare squid for cooking, see page 192.

*P*oultry

Poultry—chicken, turkey, duck, goose, and other game birds—can be bought fresh or frozen, whole or in parts, free-range or mass-produced, plain or preseasoned. Our choices seem to expand each time we visit the supermarket.

SELECTING POULTRY

Fresh is almost always better—tastier, with moister flesh—than frozen, but a lot harder to come by. Often birds are sold as fresh but have been held at such cold temperatures that the flesh is actually icy. A lot of blood in the package (or liquid in the case of a turkey covered with opaque wrapping) is an indication that the bird has been frozen and then thawed, which is something to be avoided.

You will pay premium prices for "free-range" or "organic" or "natural" birds. These are birds that are allowed to forage for food in the barnyard. In the case of organic birds, any supplemental feed is produced without chemicals. Often these birds are tastier than mass-produced birds and are handled with greater care. It may be worth the extra money if you plan to roast the bird or serve it in a simple fashion.

♦ Nutrient values of poultry, 391–392

If your intention is to bury the bird in spice anyway—or marinate and roast it over wood chips—then the premium price may not be worth it.

It used to be the case that only chickens were sold in parts—breast meat with or without the bone, drumsticks, wings and so on. These days turkey is sold as boneless breast cutlets or thighs, whole breasts, leg quarters, not to mention ground, made into sausage, hot dogs, and a variety of cold cuts usually made from pork or beef.

Look for plump, moist birds with unbroken, unbruised skin. There should be little or no evidence of blood in the package. There should be no smell.

If you are buying a frozen bird, make sure the bird is completely frozen. Don't choose a package that seems to be filled with frozen liquid, which would indicate that the bird had been thawed at some point.

When buying poultry with the bone in, allow about 1 pound per person, though with a big turkey, you may be safe by allowing ½ to ¾ pound per person. With fatty ducks and geese, allow 1½ pounds per person.

STORING POULTRY

When you get your poultry home, place still-frozen poultry directly into the freezer. Fresh poultry should be kept in its original wrapper and frozen or used within one or two days. In the freezer, store chicken, turkey, duck, and goose at 0°F. for up to six months. Giblets may be stored in the freezer at 0°F. for two to three months. Ground turkey may be left frozen for up to three months.

COOKING POULTRY

Poultry is so adaptable, there isn't a cooking method that can't be used successfully. The mild tasting flesh lends itself to baking, roasting, broiling, grilling, stewing, braising, frying, stir-frying, pan-frying, and poaching.

Before cooking, remove any visible fat. If you wish to remove the skin, slip your hand between the skin and flesh and pull the skin. It will pull off fairly easily. Discard the skin. Removing the skin significantly reduces the amount of fat and cholesterol in the meat, but it does mean that the meat is vulnerable to drying as it cooks. You can also remove the skin after cooking, which will allow the flesh to stay moist without increasing its fat content.

Marinating skinless chicken is one way to keep the meat moist. By using vegetable oil in a marinade you replace some of the saturated fat with unsaturated fat, while keeping the meat moist and flavorful.

Whether you are cooking poultry whole or in part, and by whatever

▶ **Deboning poultry, 193**
▶ **Grilling poultry, 252–253**
▶ **Roasting poultry,**
  228–230, 231, 232, 233
▶ **Steaming poultry, 212**

method you choose, you will want to be sure to cook it thoroughly. Undercooked poultry is quite unpleasant, with chewy red flesh that runs with red juices.

Poultry is done when the juices run clear, the drumstick moves easily in its socket, and the meat near the bone no longer shows pink. A meat thermometer is handy for testing doneness on large birds. It should register between 180°F. and 185°F.

CHICKEN

The most versatile of all poultry, one could eat chicken in a different style every night for over a year. When buying chicken, allow ½ pound per person with the bone, or ¼ pound per person boneless. In addition to whole chickens, you can buy whole cut-up chickens, or just breasts, leg quarters, drumsticks, wings, or thighs.

Broiler-Fryers. These all-purpose birds weigh between 2½ and 4 pounds. They are suitable for any cooking method.

Capons. Capons are young roosters that have been castrated and fattened up—usually to the tune of 6 to 10 pounds. Noted for having a huge proportion of breast meat and being extremely tender, capons are usually roasted. But they can be prepared in any way you would fix broiler-fryers.

Roasting Chickens. A little larger than broiler-fryers, these are good for roasting and grilling whole.

Stewing Chickens. Rarely available, a stewing chicken is an older bird that will weigh between 4½ and 7 pounds. Less tender but often more flavorful than other chickens, they make a good soup stock or stew.

White Meat versus Dark Meat, Skin versus No Skin

There are those who won't touch the dark meat on a chicken, others who say only dark meat is fully flavored. White meat is lower in fat and cholesterol. White meat without skin is the lowest in fat and calories of all. For more nutritional breakdown of different birds, see the table on pages 391–392.

3.5 OUNCES CHICKEN	PERCENT FAT	CALORIES	CHOLESTEROL
White meat, no skin	1.7	114	58 mg
White meat, with skin	11.1	186	67 mg
Dark meat, no skin	4.3	125	80 mg
Dark meat with skin	18.3	237	81 mg

Rock Cornish Hens. A cross between a Cornish and a White Rock chicken, these miniature chickens are best broiled or roasted. Allow one per person.

GAME BIRDS

Game birds are distinguished from other poultry by having more flavor and leaner meat. Generally speaking, game birds do not have the gamy flavor that some game meats acquire, but it all depends on the diet of the bird. Wild birds will have more flavor than farm-raised, free-range game birds. Because the meat has a lot of character, these birds are fine simply grilled and presented on a bed of greens; on the other hand, they stand up well to stewing and braising in more complex, spicy sauces. Game birds have a particular affinity to sauces made with tart fruits and to stuffings that include nuts and mushrooms.

It is not necessary to bard game birds with fat (wrap them in bacon) to keep the flesh moist. Farm-raised game birds are not as lean as their wild cousins and, in any case, quick cooking or braising in plenty of liquid will keep the flesh moist.

Pheasants and ducks have tough muscular legs that require longer cooking than the breasts. You can make a rich stock with the legs of the birds, and serve just the breast and thigh meat.

In general, allow about 1 pound per person; but with the tiny birds, allow one or two birds per serving.

Duck. Pekin (Long Island) ducks are easily found in the supermarket. They have dark, rich, mild-flavored meat that lacks the gamy taste of other birds.

Partridge. Smaller than a pheasant (average weight 1 pound) and more gamy tasting, free-range partridges are available year-round.

Pheasant. This large bird (average weight 2 to 3 pounds) tastes like a strongly flavored chicken. The legs are usually quite tough and should be used to make stock or braised slowly to tenderize.

Quail. Tiny quail have mild, dark, very lean meat. Avoid overcooking. These usually weigh about 5 ounces each; allow two per serving.

Squab. Immature pigeons, squab have rich, dark meat. They tend to be very expensive. They usually average about 1 pound each; allow one per serving.

TURKEY

We are eating more turkey these days, and with good reason. Turkey is an excellent nutritional bet—even better than chicken. Three ounces of white meat from a turkey contains 135 calories, 3 grams of fat, and 59 milligrams of cholesterol. Three ounces of chicken breast meat without skin contains 147 calories, 4 grams of fat, and 72 milligrams of cholesterol.

Handling Poultry Safely

Because a very real danger exists of contracting salmonella from mishandled poultry, it is a good idea to be concerned with cleanliness and proper temperatures in the kitchen.

☐ Keep all poultry in its original wrapper and use or freeze within twenty-four hours.

☐ Thaw frozen poultry in the refrigerator, allowing five hours per pound. If you find you need to speed up the thawing process, place the packaged bird in the sink or in a large pan. Cover with cold water. Allow 30 minutes of thawing time per pound, and change the water two or three times an hour. Always keep the bird completely immersed in the water.

☐ Always wash your hands, countertops, and utensils with hot, soapy water between each step of food preparation.

☐ Always cook poultry thoroughly. Poultry is done when a thermometer registers 180°F. to 185°F. at the thickest part of the thigh. (Breast meat should measure 170°F. to avoid dry, overcooked meat.)

☐ When stuffing a large turkey, fill the cavity with no more than ¾ cup of stuffing per pound. Smaller birds can be filled with no more than ½ cup of stuffing per pound. Bake extra stuffing in greased baking pans. Be sure the stuffing has reached the safe temperature of 160°F. before removing the bird from the oven. Do not stuff your bird until just before roasting. Store cooked stuffing separately from the bird.

☐ Cooked poultry should be kept hot (140°F. to 160°F.), or stored in the refrigerator at 40°F. or lower.

☐ Leftovers should be thoroughly warmed. Gravy should be bubbling.

Whole turkeys. Whole turkeys can weigh as little as 6 pounds or as much as 24. Prebasted birds are often moister than unbasted birds, but the flavor may not be better. If you buy an unbasted bird, slip a little herbed butter under the skin of the breast for moist meat without the chemicals of the prebaste. Allow ½ to ¾ pound of turkey per person for large birds; ¾ to 1 pound per person for turkeys under 12 pounds. Then add some extra weight for leftovers.

If you have a choice of a hen or a tom, select a hen if you prefer white meat, a tom if you prefer dark meat.

If you have bought a frozen turkey, allow plenty of time for thawing. Keep the bird in its freezer wrapper and thaw in the refrigerator, allowing five hours of thawing time for every pound of bird. A 12-pound bird will take 60 hours or two and a half days.

Many birds come equipped with little pop-up devices that register when the turkey is cooked. Although these are fairly reliable, it is best to test for doneness as the cooking time elapses. Allow 20 minutes per pound for a stuffed bird; 18 minutes per pound for an unstuffed bird. For safety, check to make sure the stuffing has reached a temperature of 160°F. before removing the bird from the oven.

Turkey breast. You can buy half or whole breasts, with the bone or without, perfect for roasting. A 4-pound to 6-pound breast with the bone will roast in 1½ to 2¼ hours—great with stovetop stuffing.

Turkey breasts are available sliced as *cutlets,* excellent for grilling, broiling, or slicing for stir-fries.

Turkey breast tenderloins are the whole muscle on the inside of the turkey breast, while *turkey breast tenderloin steaks* are ½-inch-thick lengthwise pieces cut from the tenderloin. High-quality pieces of meat, these tenderloin pieces are good for grilling, broiling, or slicing for stir-fries.

Other turkey parts. *Thighs* are all dark pieces, with or without the bone, good for broiling, grilling, or slicing for stir-fries.

Hindquarters are dark meat pieces with the thigh and drumstick, weighing between 2 and 5 pounds. There's a lot of bone there, so allow at least 1 pound per person. Dark-meat drumsticks are also available; these are best roasted or braised, or used for soup stock. Or, for a lovely feast, marinate the drumsticks and grill, taking care to keep the meat from drying out.

Wings are all-white pieces with the bone; they weigh between ¾ pound and 1½ pounds. There's more bone than meat there; a wing is best used for soup stock.

Ground turkey is lean, inexpensive, and versatile. As a burger, it tastes best with bits of herbed butter worked into the patty, which undermines its healthy nutritional profile. Ground turkey is excellent, however, in meatballs, meat sauces, and casseroles, where its bland flavor can be boosted by other ingredients.

In addition to all the turkey parts, there are plenty of other turkey products, including sausage, hot dogs, and luncheon meats. Some are quite good. You'll have to sample them to find the products that please you.

Meat

Buying meat at the supermarket is a fairly easy process, because most stores voluntarily comply with industry standards for labeling.

First, the label identifies what type of meat it is, be it lamb or beef or pork. Then it specifies where the meat comes from on the animal—sirloin, for example, is the hip area. Next, the label identifies the specific retail cut—roast or chop, for example. If the meat is processed—boned or smoked, for example—this is on the label, too.

Beef, veal, and lamb—but not pork—are all graded. *Prime* is the highest grade. *Choice* is the next highest—most supermarkets stock mainly choice meats. *Select* is the next grade. If you are looking to trim fat from your diet, select meat may be a good choice, as it is leaner meat. Use moist cooking methods with select meat and avoid overcooking, which will dry out and toughen the meat.

When buying meat, look for moist, springy, and well-colored meat. You should not see dry or discolored spots. There should be no odor. Avoid packages that contain liquid. The drier the package, the fresher tasting the meat. The presence of liquid could indicate that the meat was previously frozen.

Buy ¼ to ⅓ pound of boneless meat per serving. If the meat has a bone, allow ½ to ¾ pound per serving. Very fatty or bony meats, such as ribs, may only stretch as far as 1 pound per person.

Meat should be stored in the coldest part of your refrigerator; how long depends on the cut. It can be frozen for long-term storage; again the time depends on the cut. To prevent the meat from drying out, be sure it is sealed in an airtight package.

Frozen meat should be defrosted in the refrigerator, not at room temperature. You can also use a microwave, following the oven manufacturer's directions.

The USDA recommends that all meat be cooked to at least 160°F. to kill any microorganisms that could spoil the meat or cause food poisoning. This means cooking all meat to medium at least. Those who prefer their meat rare should take extra care that their meat is handled properly before cooking to minimize the risk of food poisoning. Proper handling includes keeping the meat under constant refrigeration and handling with clean utensils.

Whether you cook meat to rare or well done, an accurate meat thermometer is invaluable.

Nutrient values for meat, 391–392

The most tender cuts of meat usually come from the back and loin, rump and round end of the animal—parts of the animal that are exercised the least. These cuts are suitable for cooking with dry heat—

grilling, broiling, pan-frying, and roasting. Less tender cuts should be cooked with moist heat—braising or cooking in liquid. You can tenderize tough meat with marinades that contain acid (vinegar, lemon juice, wine), which breaks down the tough connective fiber in the meat. For example, skirt steak, which is a tough cut, is marinated and then grilled to make fajitas.

For nutritional information on beef, lamb, pork, and veal, see the table on pages 391–392.

BEEF

Prime beef is the juiciest, most tender, and most flavorful beef. It is also the most expensive because it is aged. This is beef that you will want to buy and cook immediately—freezing it to enjoy later will undermine its quality. *Choice meat,* handled properly, will also be tender and delicious.

Cuts of beef. 1 Boneless arm pot roast 2 Chuck steak 3 Brisket 4 Shank 5 Standing rib roast 6 Filet of beef tenderloin 7 Flank steak 8 Loin 9 Porterhouse steak 10 T-bone steak 11 Club steak 12 Sirloin steak 13 Rolled round roast 14 Rump roast 15 Tip steaks (if left whole, Tip roast)

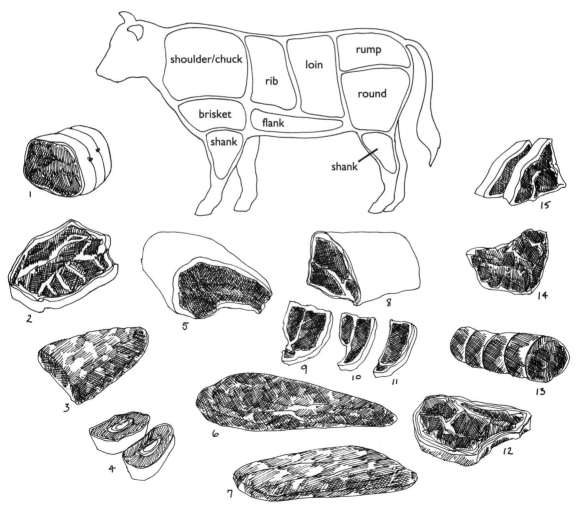

Cooking Beef

For a discussion of the various cooking methods, refer to Chapter 3.

CUTS OF BEEF	BEST WAY TO COOK
Shoulder/Chuck	
Boneless top blade roast or steak	Braise
Boneless shoulder pot roast or steak	Braise
Boneless arm pot roast or steak	Braise
Blade pot roast or steak	Braise
Short ribs	Braise; precook, then barbecue
Brisket and Foreshank	
Corned beef brisket	Braise, cook in liquid
Fresh beef brisket	Braise, cook in liquid
Shank crosscut	Braise, cook in liquid
Ribs	
Standing rib roast	Roast
Rib-eye roast (Delmonico)	Roast
Rib-eye steak (bone in or boneless)	Broil, grill, pan-fry
Back ribs	Braise, roast
Flank	
Flank steak (London broil)	Broil or pan-fry if high quality; braise
Flank steak roll	Broil or pan-fry if high quality; braise

Look for bright red color. Beef that looks brown is not spoiled, but it has been under lights for a while. It should be cooked soon after purchase. Look for fine-textured meat and soft bones. The exterior fat on the beef should be white, not yellowed. Yellowed fat is usually found on older or grass-fed animals whose meat is less tender. The fat should be crumbly-looking. Marbling of fat throughout the meat will dissolve during cooking and provide automatic internal basting for the juiciest meat.

Ground beef is frequently labeled as to the percent of lean meat contained in the mix. Ground beef has not less than 70 percent lean, meaning 30 percent of the meat by weight is made of fat. Lean ground beef or lean ground chuck is not less than 77 percent lean, meaning 23 percent of the weight is fat. If you are concerned about fats and calo-

Cooking Beef (continued)

CUTS OF BEEF	BEST WAY TO COOK
Loin	
Top loin steak	Broil, grill, pan-fry
Tenderloin roast (filet mignon)	Roast
Tenderloin steak (filet mignon)	Broil, grill, pan-fry
T-bone steak	Broil, grill, pan-fry
Porterhouse steak	Broil, grill, pan-fry
Club steak	Broil, grill, pan-fry
Chateaubriand	Broil or sauté
Bottom and top sirloin steaks	Broil, grill, pan-fry
Sirloin steak	Broil, grill, pan-fry
Top sirloin roast	Roast
Rump	
Rump roast	Roast, braise
Round	
Round tip steak	Braise; broil, grill, pan-fry if high quality
Round steak, top	Braise or broil, if high quality
Round steak, bottom	Braise, pan-fry
Bottom round roast	Braise, roast
Top round roast	Roast
Round tip roast	Roast, braise
Eye round roast	Braise, roast

ries, you may want to select a lean mix, keeping in mind that ground beef derives some of its flavor and pleasing moistness from the fat.

Ground beef is more perishable than other beef cuts. It is usually higher in fat than other cuts. Store ground beef for one to two days in the refrigerator or up to three months in the freezer. *Steaks, roasts,* and *chops* may also be frozen for up to six months at 0°F. Other beef cuts will keep for three to five days in the refrigerator and for six to twelve months in the freezer at 0°F.

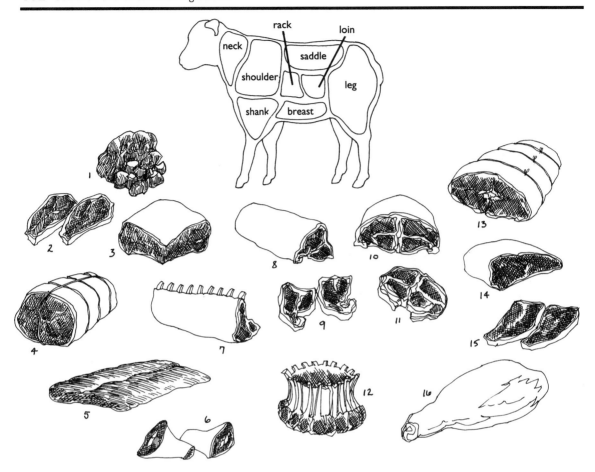

Cuts of lamb. **1** Neck **2** Shoulder blade chops **3** Shoulder **4** Boned rolled shoulder **5** Breast **6** Shanks **7** Rack **8** Loin **9** Loin chops **10** Double loin **11** Double chops **12** Crown **13** Saddle **14** Sirloin **15** Sirloin chops **16** Leg

Cooking Lamb

CUTS OF LAMB	BEST WAY TO COOK
Boneless shoulder roast	Roast, braise
Shoulder blade chop	Braise, broil, pan-fry
Rib chop	Broil, pan-fry, roast
Rib roast	Roast
Loin chop	Broil, pan-fry
Noisettes/medallions	Roast, pan-fry

LAMB

A favorite in the cooking of Greek, Middle Eastern, Italian, Indian, Spanish, and French cooking, lamb pairs well with strong seasonings—garlic, ginger, mustard, pepper, oregano, cumin, chilies, and citrus. Recent increases in domestic production has made lamb more available than ever.

Look for pinkish red meat with a thin layer of firm white fat surrounding it. Meat from older lamb is darker. Certified American lamb is guaranteed to be less than a year old; it will be tender and the meat mildly flavored. *Baby,* or *milk-fed, lamb* is marketed at six to eight weeks old. *Spring lamb,* which is available year-round, is marketed between five and six months of age. *Yearling lamb* comes from an animal between one and two years old. *Mutton* is from sheep older than two years. Both yearling lamb and mutton will be tougher and gamier in taste than lamb. Grain-fed domestic lamb will be milder in taste than imported lamb, which is grass-fed.

Although most lamb is tender, the most tender cuts come from the loin and rib. Supermarkets rarely carry a full selection of lamb cuts, but you can always ask the butcher to cut what you want. The leg can be boned and butterflied for barbecuing and broiling, or rolled for roasting. Kabobs can be cut from the boneless leg meat. See the table below for a listing of cuts and their recommended cooking methods.

Lamb roasts and chops are best served rare, with the meat still showing pink.

PORK

Pork producers are calling pork "the other white meat" these days with good reason. Today's pork is leaner and lower in cholesterol than ever before. It compares favorably with white meat chicken (see the table on pages 391–392).

Cooking Lamb (continued)

CUTS OF LAMB	BEST WAY TO COOK
Loin roast	Roast
Sirloin chop	Braise, broil, pan-fry
Boneless leg roast	Roast
Whole leg	Roast
Spareribs	Braise, broil, roast
Shank	Braise, cook in liquid

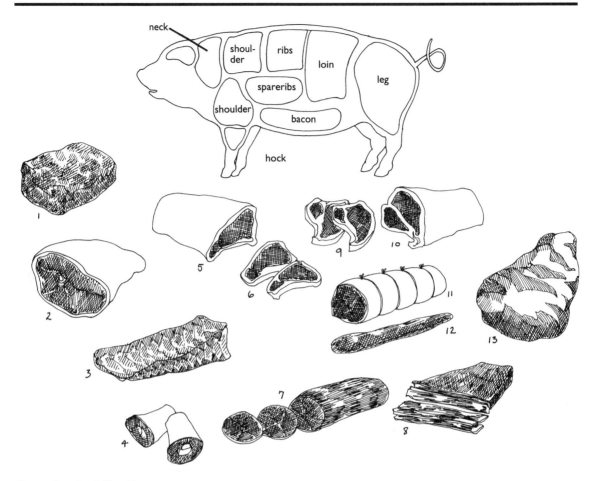

Cuts of pork. 1 Shoulder butt 2 Picnic shoulder 3 Spareribs 4 Hocks 5 Rib roast 6 Rib chops 7 Canadian bacon 8 Bacon 9 Loin chops 10 Loin roast 11 Boned rolled pork loin 12 Pork tenderloin 13 Whole ham

Look for pork that is pale pink with firm white fat. Nearly all cuts are tender; how you cook the meat will affect the tenderness and moistness of the meat more than the cut.

Cooks used to overcook pork to destroy the trichinella parasite that causes trichinosis. That parasite, we now know, is destroyed at 137°F. Still of concern is salmonella bacteria, which is destroyed at 160°F. The USDA recommends cooking pork to 160°F., while some cooks maintain that pork is overcooked at that temperature and should only be cooked to 140°F.

The pig is famous for having every part edible "except the squeak." For roasting, choose the loin, shoulder, or leg. Chops, which are cut from the loin, rib, or shoulder, are tender, but must be cooked over low heat or braised to prevent them from drying out.

Many parts of the pig are processed, smoked, or cured in some way.

Hams

HAM	DESCRIPTION
Bayonne	A mildly smoked ham from France. Similar to prosciutto, but cured in a wine mixture. Like prosciutto it is eaten raw, but not sliced quite as thin.
Black Forest	Very heavily brined, smoked ham from Germany. The robust flavor of the flesh goes well with sourdough bread.
Prosciutto	Fine-quality ham from Parma, Italy, where the hogs are raised on a diet of chestnuts or whey from the making of Parmesan cheese. Cured with a mixture of sugar, pepper, allspice, nutmeg, coriander, and mustard. Then hams are pressed, steamed, and rubbed with pepper. Serve raw, very thinly sliced. It pairs nicely with melon or fresh figs.
Smithfield	Virginia ham that comes from hogs raised on a diet of peanuts. The meat is given two curings of salt and saltpeter, then heavily smoked with hickory and rubbed with pepper. Hams are aged for up to eighteen months. The ham must be soaked in cold water for 12 to 24 hours to remove excess salt. The meat is rich, salty, and rather dry.
Virginia	Fully cooked boneless ham, sometimes studded with cloves. The ham comes from pigs that feed on peanuts and acorns and the meat is usually smoked over hickory and applewood.
Westphalian	Rich, dark-colored German ham from hogs raised on a diet of sugar beets. Cured with a mixture of salt, sugar, and saltpeter, then smoked over ash or beech with a bit of juniper and aged.

Bacon. Meat cut from the side or back of a hog is cured and sometimes smoked to make bacon. There is a lot of variety in the curing process—some bacon is sugar-cured, some maple-cured, and some hickory-smoked. Regardless of flavor, look for bacon that has a good proportion of lean striping. It should be firm, fine-grained, and well colored. Avoid any meat that looks moist or slimy.

Low-salt versions are often just as flavorful as regular bacon, with one-third less sodium.

In its original vacuum-sealed packaging, bacon can be kept for about one week past its sale date. Opened packages should be stored in the refrigerator and used within one week. Slabs of bacon bought in specialty food stores should be stored tightly wrapped and will keep in the refrigerator for several weeks. For longer storage, keep frozen at 0°F. for up to two months.

Allow about two to three slices of bacon per serving.

Cuts of Meat: Some Basic Terms

What is a chop anyway? Or a fillet? Here are a few of the names you'll see on labels at the meat counter.

Chop. A usually tender cut of pork, lamb, or veal that has been taken from the loin or rib area. It may be boneless or include a bone.

Cutlet. A small, thin, boneless piece of meat— usually cut from the leg of veal or chicken or turkey breast.

Escalope. A thin slice of meat or fish, slightly flat-tened. It cooks quickly and is most often sautéed in oil or butter.

Fillet. A thin, boneless piece of meat or fish.

Kabobs (also kebabs). Cubes of meat, fish, or poultry and/or vegetables threaded on long skewers and grilled over coals or under the broiler.

Roast. A large piece of meat. Tender cuts are cooked with dry heat (roasted), while less ten-der cuts may be braised (as in a pot roast).

When cooking bacon, start with a cold skillet or baking sheet to pre-vent curling and burning. Drain on paper towels to remove excess grease.

Canadian bacon. Canadian-style bacon is the cured and smoked pork loin. It is closer to ham in appearance and taste than it is to regu-lar bacon. It is also leaner than regular bacon.

Store in the refrigerator for three to four days or in the freezer for six to eight weeks. Canadian bacon comes both fully cooked and uncooked. If cooking is necessary, broil or pan-fry.

Ham. While *ham* refers to the hind leg of a hog, it can also mean any cut of the hog that is cured with salt, smoked, and sometimes aged.

Buying ham involves making a lot of choices. Hams are available whole, as halves, or in slices, bone in, partially deboned, or boneless. It may be smoked (which is usually most desirable and most expensive) or not. The highest quality and most expensive cut is the butt half, with the bone in. The shank half is good, but will contain tough tendons. Boston butt hams and shoulder hams will be fattier. Many hams are sold "ready to eat"; others must be cooked—to 160°F.—first.

When buying ham, look for fine texture and pink color. The meat should feel firm to the touch, not spongy.

Canned hams are boneless and fully cooked. Most are made from pieces of ham that are pressed and formed under pressure into their characteristic ham shape. There is a lot of difference among brands so you must experiment to find one you like. Store in the refrigerator unopened for six to twelve months; opened it will keep for up to seven days. Freeze leftover meat for up to one month at 0°F.

Country hams are dry cured, smoked, then aged. There may be a layer of mold on the surface, which should be scraped off before you cook the ham. A whole country ham will keep indefinitely in a cool, dry place, but eventually it becomes unpleasantly dry. Plan to store it for no more than six to twelve months for the best eating.

Uncooked, dry-cured ham should be treated like any other uncooked meat. Store in the refrigerator for three to five days.

Ready-to-eat-ham should be kept in its original packaging and stored for about seven days in the refrigerator or for about three months in the freezer. *Sliced ham* will keep for only about one month in the freezer at 0°F.

Baked, cooked, or boiled ham is available at the deli counter, sliced to order. Like all cold cuts, sliced ham should be refrigerated and kept for about three days. In vacuum-sealed packages, ham will keep for about a week beyond the last sale date.

Salt pork. Dry-cured salt pork is a fatty piece of meat used mainly for seasoning. Store for up to a month in the refrigerator. Do not freeze.

RABBIT

Farm-raised rabbit is available dressed, cut up, and ready to cook. The meat is very much like chicken, just a little denser and drier. You can substitute rabbit for chicken in recipes; for best results, select recipes that involve stewing or braising.

VARIETY MEATS

Organ meats and meats from nonfleshy parts of the animal are called variety meats. They come from beef, lamb, pork, veal, and poultry. They tend to be high in fat and cholesterol.

Variety meats are quite perishable; use within twenty-four hours of purchase or freeze for longer storage (two to four months).

Of all the variety meats, chicken (and goose) and calf livers are the most popular. They are tender and mildly flavored. Liver is an excellent source of iron.

Look for liver with a bright, shiny surface and plan to use it within twenty-four hours.

To prepare for cooking, wipe the liver with a damp cloth. Remove the thin outer skin and veining.

Never overcook liver or use too high a heat, both of which will result in tough meat.

Sweetbreads. The thymus gland from the neck or throat of calves or lamb is eaten as sweetbreads. Sweetbreads are the most delicately flavored of the variety meats and the most expensive. Look for moist whitish meat and use on the day of purchase.

To prepare for cooking, soak them for at least 1 hour in cold water to release any blood, changing the water two or three times. Then cover with acidulated water (water with lemon juice or vinegar), bring to a boil, reduce the heat, and simmer for 2 to 5 minutes. Firm them by plunging them into cold water, then drain. Trim away any cartilage, tubes, connective tissue, or tough membrane.

Tongue. Beef tongue is the most popular, but the tongue of calves, lamb, and pork is also eaten. Smaller-size tongues have the best texture. You can buy tongue fresh, pickled, or smoked.

To prepare for cooking, scrub well with a scrub brush. Soak for one hour in cold water. Tongue is usually simmered for several hours.

Before serving, split the skin and peel it off. Trim away any small bones and gristle at the root end.

Tripe. Tripe is the muscular lining of the four stomachs of ruminant animals—usually beef or veal. Honeycomb tripe is the most desirable. It is yellow-beige in color and quite chewy in texture.

Tripe is usually sold parboiled. Cut it into pieces, wash thoroughly, then cook.

❧ **Sautéing liver, 208**

VEAL

The most delicately flavored meat, veal is fine-grained, with no marbling and only a thin layer of external fat. Traditionally, veal comes from young milk-fed calves whose movements are restricted to keep the meat tender. The meat is almost white in color. Alternatively, some veal is raised "naturally," with the veal calves given a more balanced diet and allowed more movement, resulting in a darker meat. This "natural" veal is considered tastier by some; others claim it is less tasty, less tender, and not worth the premium price.

Because veal is so lean, it should be cooked at low to moderate temperatures—pan-fried, braised, or roasted, but not broiled.

The cuts of veal are similar to those of beef, but they are smaller in size. All cuts are tender. Veal scaloppine, sometimes called scallops, is the most expensive cut. These thin, boneless slices are pounded to make them even more tender. Breast of veal, shoulder, and shanks are less expensive cuts. The shank is used to make osso buco.

Cuts of veal. 1 Neck 2 Shoulder blade chop 3 Rolled shoulder 4 Breast 5 Shank 6 Rack 7 Rib chops 8 Loin 9 Loin chops 10 Sirloin 11 Leg 12 Cutlets 13 Scallops

Guide to Sausages

SAUSAGE	DESCRIPTION
Fresh Sausages	
Bockwurst	German-style sausage made from veal or veal and pork. Flavored with onions, parsley, and cloves.
Bratwurst	German-style sausage made from pork and veal. Looks like a fat hot dog. Flavored with allspice, caraway, and marjoram. Usually served broiled or fried.
Chorizo	The Mexican version of chorizo is a rusty-red sausage flavored with garlic, chili powder, and other spices. There are several regional variations. Spicy and coarse textured.
Country Sausage	Pork sausage made into patties or links. Flavored with sage, sometimes smoked.
Frankfurter	Hot dog. May be made with pork, beef, turkey or a combination.
Italian Hot Sausage	Pork sausage flavored with coriander.
Kielbasa	In Poland, refers to any number of garlicky fresh sausages. Sold either fresh or fully cooked.
Knockwurst	Garlicky, precooked beef or pork sausage. Sold in short, thick links. Often served with sauerkraut.
Vienna Sausages	Pork and beef, sometimes veal. Flavored with onions, mace, and coriander.
Cured Sausages	
Braunschweiger	German-style pork sausage. Mild, smoky flavor accented with onions, mustard seed, and marjoram.
Cervelat	Many varieties. Resembles salami, but is milder and sweeter. Always smoked.
Chorizo	Spanish version of this pork sausage is flavored with cayenne, pimiento, or other hot chili peppers. Resembles pepperoni in size and shape. Longaniza is the Portuguese version.
Mortadella	Made of finely ground pork patterned with green flecks of pistachio nuts and white cubes of fat. The best mortadellas come from Bologna and are flavored with white wine and coriander. The American version of this is bologna and may be made of pork or beef.
Pepperoni	Italian-style air-dried sausage made from beef and pork. Can be quite spicy. Often served on pizza.
Salami	There are many regional variations. Originally from Italy; now there are Danish, German, Hungarian, and Jewish salamis. Usually a mixture of lean pork and pork fat, sometimes beef. Flavored with wine or rum, peppercorns, fennel or garlic, paprika, and sometimes sugar. Sometimes smoked.

VENISON

The meat of any antlered game, venison is similar to beef, but leaner and gamier in flavor. Treat as you would beef, being sure to marinate and slow-cook tough cuts. Trim away any excess fat from the meat, as it is the fat that carries the gamy taste.

*B*everages

COFFEE

It's a passion and an addiction. Those who drink coffee cannot do without it and everyone has an opinion on what makes the best cup.

Coffee flavor is determined by the type of bean used, the climate and soil in which the bean was grown, and how the bean was roasted. Most coffees are actually a blend of two or more beans. Some coffees are further flavored with spices, liqueurs, chocolate, or extracts. Which coffee you will prefer is strictly a matter of taste.

For the best-tasting coffee, buy whole beans from a store that roasts its own or at least turns over its stock rapidly.

Store the beans in an airtight container in a cool, dark place or freeze; do not defrost before using. Whole beans will remain fresh in the refrigerator for about two weeks. Ground coffee from freshly roasted beans will stay fresh in the refrigerator for about a week. Unopened

Beverage sources.
1 Coffee beans **2** Grapes for wine **3** Hops for beer **4** Tea leaves

▸ **Nutrient values of beverages, 393**

Brewing Better Coffee

Regardless of the type of coffeepot you use (see page 161), a few guidelines for making coffee always apply.

☐ **Start with a clean pot; the residue of coffee oils from previous brews will affect flavor.**

☐ **Measure your ground coffee accurately. The exact amount of coffee to use will vary depending on whether you like strong or weak coffee. The rule of thumb is to allow two tablespoons of coffee (one coffee measure) for every six ounces of water for brewed coffee; double that amount for espresso.**

☐ **Use fresh, good-tasting cold water. If your tap water has an off flavor, use bottled spring water.**

☐ **If you are using a nonautomatic drip coffee maker, place the ground coffee in the filter. As soon as the water boils, pour a little over the coffee to moisten it and release the flavors. When all the water has drained through the filter, pour in the remaining water.**

vacuum-packed coffee and jars of instant and freeze-dried coffees can be stored, unopened, at room temperature for at least six months. Once opened, for best flavor, use up these coffees within a month.

Whether you grind your own or purchase your coffee ground, the grind you select depends on how the coffee will be brewed. The shorter the brewing time, the finer the grind. Thus, espresso is ground very fine and coffees for drip pots are ground finer than coffee for percolators.

Decaffeinated coffee has been processed to remove about 97 percent of the caffeine; some flavor is lost in the process as well. The caffeine may be extracted by volatile solvents, which leave no residue, or by the Swiss water process, where the beans are first steamed and then the caffeine layer is scraped away.

Instant and *freeze-dried coffee* are both concentrated extracts of brewed coffee; freeze-dried versions tend to be more flavorful.

Figure that 1 pound of coffee beans will yield approximately 40 cups of brewed coffee.

TEA

There are many who claim that there is nothing more comforting than a hot cup of tea—be it a cup of orange pekoe with plenty of sugar and milk or a soothing cup of mint tea.

♦ **Coffee grinders and mills, 143–144**

How to Make a Proper Pot of Tea

To make a pot of tea—herbal or regular—start with fresh cold water and bring to a boil. Preheat the teapot by filling with hot tap water and letting stand for a minute. Pour out the hot water and dry the pot. Add the tea, allowing 1 teaspoon of loose tea per cup plus one for the pot. Gently pour the boiling water over the tea leaves. Replace the lid on the pot and allow the tea to steep for 3 to 5 minutes. Stir the pot once, then pour the tea into cups through a strainer. Serve with sugar and milk or lemon slices.

Basically there are three types of tea. *Black teas* are made from fermented tea leaves; the flavor of these teas is strong, rich and mellow—like Darjeeling. *Oolong,* or *semifermented, teas* are not quite as strong and rich as black teas. *Green teas,* the kind found in Oriental restaurants, are the mildest teas. Many teas, such as Earl Grey and Lapsang Souchong, are made of blends of the different teas.

Herbal teas are made from various herbs or blends of herbs. Lacking caffeine, they are a valuable alternative to brews made from tea leaves.

You can purchase tea in convenient tea bags or as loose leaves. If you are buying loose teas, it is best to purchase only a small amount at a time as the tea will lose flavor and absorb odors over time. Store teas, each in a separate airtight container, in a cool place for up to one year. Figure that 1 pound of tea leaves will make 125 cups of brewed tea.

BEER

An alcoholic brew, beer is made from grains and hops. Most of the beer sold in the United States is the pale, light-bodied *lager* beer. The taste is light, smooth and clean, with plenty of malt and not too much hops. *Light beer* is usually a lager type made to have fewer calories and less alcohol. *Ale* was originally a malt liquor made without hops. Today ale can mean beer or it can mean a brew that is slightly bitter, with more body than a lager beer. Its color ranges from pale to dark. *Stout* is very dark, its head is creamy, and its taste sweet. *Porter* is halfway in appearance and flavor between ale and stout.

Most beer deteriorates in light, which is why it is sold in colored glass bottles or cans. Keep under refrigeration.

WINE

Wine enhances any meal, whether it is used as a flavoring or as a beverage.

As a flavoring, the rule of thumb is to cook only with wines you would also drink. If an opened bottle of wine has become too vinegary to drink, it will not be good to cook with. Likewise, so-called "cooking wines" available in supermarkets are simply low-quality wines with added salt (originally added to keep the cook from drinking) and are not as good as regular table wines.

Generally, the best red wines for cooking will be young and dry. They don't need to be expensive. Quality inexpensive white wines are harder to find. For a smooth taste, substitute dry vermouth for white wine in recipes.

Wine can be served as an aperitif before a meal to stimulate the appetite. Any wine will do, including sherry and vermouth. Dessert wines are usually sweet and full-bodied, such as port, tokay, muscat, sweet vermouth, cream sherry, and sauterne.

In between there are the table wines, which can be red, white, or rosé. Rules governing which wine to serve with which food are no longer held in such high regard, though it is always safe to serve red wine with red meats and white wine with poultry and fish. Try to match robust wines with hearty foods and light wines with delicately flavored dishes.

To calculate how much wine to buy, figure that you will get four to six servings per 750 ml bottle of a table or sparkling wine. Because dessert and aperitif wines are served in smaller glasses, you will get ten to twelve servings per 750 ml bottle.

Store wine in a cool, dark place. Wines sealed with corks should be stored on their sides to prevent the corks from drying.

Foods of the Caribbean

Many of these foods are available in ordinary supermarkets. Others can be found in neighborhood Spanish bodegas, West Indian food shops and specialty food stores. In addition to the foods listed here, Caribbean dishes often contain coconut (page 41), tamarind (page 116), and sweet potatoes (page 34). Tropical fruits—bananas, guavas, papayas, pineapples (pages 14–16)—are also important Caribbean foods.

Substitutes for some of the foods are offered. Be aware that while these substitutes will work in most recipes, they will not provide authentic taste.

FOOD	DESCRIPTION	SUBSTITUTES
Annatto Seeds (achiote, roucou)	Brick-red seeds. Heat in oil to provide a characteristic yellow color and elusive flavor found in Hispanic dishes. Available as a paste made with pepper, vinegar, salt, and garlic or as a paste made with lard called *manteca de achiote*.	Saffron
Breadfruit	Large green fruit, 10–12 inches in diameter; bumpy skin. Available fresh or canned. Use like a potato—roasted in the skin or peeled and fried.	None
Callaloo	Leafy, green vegetable. (Also a soup by the same name.) Available fresh or canned.	Spinach
Conch	Shellfish, similar to abalone. Tenderize by beating the meat with a paddle or heavy object until flattened. Available fresh or frozen.	None
Pigeon Peas (gungo)	Mottled, brown, round pea. Cooked with rice, stewed, and added to soups. Available canned and dried. Fresh pigeon peas are green.	Black-eyed peas
Plantains	Member of the banana family, but only eaten cooked. The green, unripe fruit is eaten, as well as the ripe black fruit. It is fried, sautéed, or baked.	Unripe bananas
Salt Fish (bacalhao, morue)	Widely available in the States. Buy salted boneless fillets packaged in 1-pound boxes. Before using, soak in cold water for several hours or overnight to remove the salt. To quickly desalt, place the fish in cold water to cover and boil until the fish tastes palatable. How long to boil will depend on how salty the fish is; different processors use different amounts of salt. Once desalted, drain the fish and flake with a fork.	None
Yams	Can be waxy, dry, or hard; bland or sweet; with yellow or white flesh. Prepared in the same way as sweet potatoes.	Sweet potatoes

Foods of the Orient

For a description of Oriental noodles, see page 116. For a description of soy sauce, see pages 46–47.

FOOD	DESCRIPTION	SUBSTITUTES
Asafetida	Powdered herb that releases the flavor of onions when cooked. It has a very strong odor and should be used sparingly. Used in Indian foods.	Onion powder
Bean Sprouts	The sprouts of mung beans. Look for crisp fresh sprouts with no sign of browning. Store in the refrigerator in a plastic bag.	None
Black Beans	Salted and fermented beans, used for flavoring. Come in 8-ounce plastic packages and will keep indefinitely.	Soybeans cooked until soft and seasoned generously with soy sauce.
Chili Oil	Oil, usually sesame oil, that has been steeped with hot red peppers. Used in cooking and adds very hot flavor to a dish. You can make your own by slowly cooking several dried chili peppers in sesame oil until the peppers turn black. Strain out the peppers. Make it in small quantities; a little bit goes a long way. Store in the refrigerator for up to two months.	Sesame oil
Chili Paste	A seasoning paste made of hot chilies, garlic, salt, and oil.	Mashed fresh chilies
Chinese or Japanese Eggplant	Longer and narrower than a European (purple) eggplant, with tender, edible skin.	European eggplant; use it peeled
Coconut Milk	A staple in Thai cooking. Look for unsweetened canned milk. To make coconut milk, see page 41.	Whole milk flavored with coconut extract
Fish Sauce	A staple in the cooking of Vietnam and Thailand, fish sauce is a very salty liquid that is used like soy sauce. Its fishy odor mellows as it cooks.	None
Hoisin Sauce	Thick reddish-brown sauce made from soybeans, garlic, chili peppers, and molasses. Used in poultry, pork, and seafood recipes. Also used in barbecue marinades.	None
Lemongrass	Citrusy, grassy flavor. Used extensively in the cooking of Thailand, Indonesia, and Vietnam. Comes with a white bulb attached to long green stems. Select the heaviest, greenest stalks. To store, strip off the outer leaves, wrap tightly, and store in the refrigerator for a few weeks or indefinitely in the freezer. To prepare, lightly pound the tough upper stems to release their essential oils. Then slice or chop; they can be used to flavor soups and sauces but should be removed before serving. The tender, pale inner leaves and bulb are edible if finely minced. Dried lemongrass can be substituted for fresh; soak in warm water to cover for about 30 minutes before using.	Grated zest of ½ lemon for 1 stalk lemongrass
Litchis	Delicately perfumed white fruit. Usually found canned. To prepare a fresh litchi, peel, then cut in half and remove seed.	None
Mirin	Japanese sweet rice wine, used in cooking.	Sweet sherry
Miso	A salty paste of fermented soybeans used in Japanese cooking to flavor soups and sauces. May also contain rice, wheat, barley.	None
Oyster Sauce	A staple in Chinese cooking, oyster sauce is a thick brown sauce that is both sweet and salty.	None
Rice Wine	Also called Chinese cooking wine. Can be clear or golden.	Pale, dry sherry
Sake	Dry rice wine from Japan, used in cooking and for drinking.	Pale dry sherry or vermouth

(table continues)

FOOD	DESCRIPTION	SUBSTITUTES
Sesame Oil	Made from pressed, roasted sesame seeds. Dark in color and distinctively flavored.	None
Star Anise	Star-shaped spice with a strong anise flavor.	Anise seed
Szechuan Peppercorns	Not related to black peppercorns or to chili peppers. Clean, spicy, woodsy flavor.	Black peppercorns and anise
Tamarind	Tart flavoring used extensively in the cooking of India, Thailand, and the Caribbean. Fresh tamarind pods are available from May through November, and packages of prepared pulp are available year-round. When buying pods, look for long pods with brown, furry skin. The pods will store well in the refrigerator for several weeks. To use, crack open the pods and squeeze out the sticky, thick pulp. Take the pulp from the pods or package and soak in hot water for 15 minutes, then drain. Discard the pulp and use the liquid.	None
Tofu (bean curd)	Made from soybeans in a process that resembles the making of cottage cheese. Choose firm and extra-firm tofu for stir-fries. Soft tofu can be blended or whipped for non-Oriental dishes. Buy fresh tofu in bulk in health food and Oriental food stores. It should be firm and fresh-smelling. Store in water in a covered container in the refrigerator, and change the water every day. Will keep for seven to ten days. Or purchase in aseptic container and store in a cool place. Use by the expiration date marked on package.	None
Wasabi	Japanese horseradish. Not related to Western horseradish root. Bought as a green powder and reconstituted with the addition of water. Essential for sushi and sashimi.	None

Oriental Noodles

NOODLE	DESCRIPTION	COOKING INSTRUCTIONS	SUBSTITUTES
Bean Thread Noodles (cellophane noodles)	Made from mung bean starch. Transparent, thin, crunchy.	Soak in warm water until soft—15 to 20 minutes—drain, then use in salads, spring rolls, or other dishes. Presoaking is not necessary when added to soups 15 minutes before soup is done.	None
Ramen Noodles	Japanese egg noodles. Sold both fresh and dried.	Boil in plenty of water until just tender, 3 to 5 minutes.	Any wheat-based thin pasta, such as vermicelli
Rice Sticks (rice vermicelli, rice noodles)	Dried rice-flour noodles in several different widths.	Soften in warm water for 15 to 30 minutes, drain, then use in soups and stir-fries.	None
Soba	Japanese noodles made with buckwheat and wheat flour. Best served cold with a spicy dressing.	Boil in plenty of water until just tender, 5 to 6 minutes.	None
Udon	Flat, thick Japanese wheat-flour noodle made with egg.	Boil in plenty of water until just tender, 5 to 6 minutes.	Linguine

STORAGE TIME

The following storage times are only approximate, since successful storage depends on factors such as the type of freezer and/or refrigerator, how often it's opened, heat and humidity, and quality of containers and packing materials. For best results, try to use food *before* it reaches its maximum storage time; after that its quality will quickly diminish.

Maximum Recommended Freezer Storage Time at 0°F.

FOOD	STORAGE TIME (MONTHS EXCEPT WHERE NOTED OTHERWISE)
Beef, Veal, Lamb—uncooked, fresh	
Roasts, steaks and chops	6
Ground meat	3
Liver, heart and kidneys	3 to 4
Beef, Veal, Lamb—cooked	
Roasts	4 to 6
Stews, meat in gravy or sauce, meat loaves, meatballs	2 to 4
Pork—uncooked, fresh	
Roasts and chops	3
Ground pork and fresh sausage meat	1 to 3
Liver	1 to 2
Pork—smoked and cured	
Bacon (slab and strip), ham, frankfurters	2
Sausages	1 to 2
Pork—cooked	
Roasts	2 to 4
Stews, meat in gravy or sauce, meat loaves, meatballs	2 to 4
Poultry—uncooked, fresh	
Chicken	6
Turkey, duck, goose, game	6
Giblets	2 to 3
Ground meat	3
Poultry—cooked	
Chicken	4 to 6
Turkey, duck, goose	2 to 4

(table continues)

Maximum Recommended Freezer Storage Time at 0°F. (*continued*)

FOOD	STORAGE TIME (MONTHS EXCEPT WHERE NOTED OTHERWISE)
Seafood—uncooked, fresh	
Lean, white fish (e.g., haddock, cod)	4 to 6
Fatty fish (e.g., salmon, mackerel)	2
Shucked clams and oysters, scallops, shrimp	3 to 4
Seafood—cooked	
Fish (all varieties)	1 to 2
Crab and lobster	2 to 3
Shrimp	1 to 2
Shellfish in sauce (tomato, cream, etc.)	1
Dairy Products	
Butter	5
Cream, whipped	2
Hard cheeses	6
Ice cream, sherbet, ices	1 to 2
Margarine	12
Eggs (yolks, whites)	12
Vegetables	up to 6
Herbs, fresh	6
Fruit	
Apricots and peaches	12
Cranberries	12
Raspberries, strawberries, blueberries	12
Baked Goods—breads, rolls	
Breads, yeast	6
Breads, quick	2
Rolls, muffins	2 to 4
Sandwiches (all fillings except those made with may-onnaise, cream cheese, jelly, or hard-cooked egg)	2 to 3 weeks

Maximum Recommended Freezer Storage Time at 0°F. *(continued)*

FOOD	STORAGE TIME (MONTHS EXCEPT WHERE NOTED OTHERWISE)
Cakes and cookies	
Baked cakes (e.g., angel food, cheesecake, ginger-bread) and cookies (unfrosted)	4 to 6
Baked cakes and cookies (frosted or filled)	2 to 4
Baked fruitcake	12
Cookie dough	4
Pies	
Unbaked pie shells	2
Unbaked fruit or mincemeat pies	2
Baked pies	1
Other Precooked Foods	
Combination dishes (e.g. stews, casseroles)	4 to 8
Potatoes	
French-fried	4 to 8
Scalloped	1
Soups	4 to 6

Maximum Recommended Refrigerator Storage Time

FOOD	STORAGE TIME (DAYS EXCEPT WHERE NOTED OTHERWISE)	NOTES
Fresh Meats (uncooked)		
Organ meats	1 to 2	
Ground, cubed and slivered meat	2	
Steaks, chops	3 to 5	
Roasts	5	
Cooked Meats (including leftovers)	3 to 4	
Cured and Smoked Meats		
Sliced ham, luncheon meats, sausages	2 to 3	Refrigerate in original wrapper or loosely wrap with plastic wrap
Frankfurters	4 to 5	
Ham roasts	1 week	
Bacon	1 week	
Fresh Poultry (uncooked)	2 to 3	Remove giblets and refrigerate separately
Cooked Poultry (including leftovers)	2	Remove stuffing and refrigerate separately
Fresh Seafood (uncooked)		
Live lobster and crab	6 to 8 hours	Bring home packed in seaweed in double thickness of plastic bag. Place in larger plastic bag; refrigerate. Never cover with water
Shellfish (clams, mussels, oysters, scallops)	1	Unshucked, in their liquor in an airtight container
Shrimp (shelled or unshelled)	1 to 2	Store in plastic bags
Fish	1 to 2	Clean and dress before refrigerating, loosely wrapped
Cooked Seafood (including leftovers)	1 to 2	
Smoked and Pickled Fish	1 to 2 weeks	

Maximum Recommended Refrigerator Storage Time (*continued*)

FOOD	STORAGE TIME (DAYS EXCEPT WHERE NOTED OTHERWISE)	NOTES
Dairy Products		
Butter	1 to 2 weeks	
Cheese, cottage, cream, processed and spreads	1 to 3 weeks	
Cheese, hard and semihard	3 to 9 months	For long storage, wrap cheese in cheesecloth moistened with vinegar; keep moist. Remove any mold that develops
Cheese scraps	2 to 3 weeks	Grate; store in airtight containers or sturdy plastic bags
Eggs		
Whole, raw	10	Keep small end down in egg carton
Whites, raw	1 week	Store in airtight metal container
Yolks, raw	2 to 3	Cover with cold water; store in airtight container
Whole, hard-cooked	10	Store in or out of shell. Wrap unshelled eggs in foil or plastic
Vegetables, fresh, raw		
Artichokes	3 to 5	
Asparagus	3 to 4	Wrap bottoms in moistened paper towel
Beans	3 to 5	
Beets	2 weeks	Remove all but 1 inch from tops. Rinse if sandy
Broccoli	3 to 5	
Brussels sprouts	3 to 5	
Cabbage	3 to 7	
Carrots	2 weeks	Remove all but 1 inch from tops. Rinse if sandy
Cauliflower	3 to 5	
Celeriac	3 to 7	
Celery	3 to 7	Rinse if sandy
Chayote	3 to 5	
Cucumbers	1 week	
Eggplant	3 to 5	
Fennel	3 to 5	
Leeks	3 to 7	
Lettuce	3 to 7	Wash and dry well. Do not break up until serving time

(table continues)

Maximum Recommended Refrigerator Storage Time (*continued*)

FOOD	STORAGE TIME (DAYS EXCEPT WHERE NOTED OTHERWISE)	NOTES
Mushrooms	1 week	Do not trim or wipe until serving time. Cover loosely or place in brown paper bag or cardboard carton
Okra	3 to 4	
Parsnips	2 weeks	Remove all but 1 inch from tops. Rinse if sandy
Peas	3 to 5	
Peppers	3 to 5	
Plantains (very ripe only)	1 to 2	
Potatoes, new	1 week	Refrigeration is optional, maintains best flavor
Salsify	3 to 7	Rinse
Scallions	3 to 7	
Spinach and other greens	3 to 8	Wash and dry well. Do not break up until serving/cooking time
Squash, summer	1 week	
Tomatoes (very ripe only)	2 to 3	Store unwrapped, uncovered
Vegetables—cooked (including leftovers)	2 to 4	

Fruits, fresh, raw

Note: Uncut avocados, bananas, melons, and pineapples should be stored at room temperature unless very ripe.

Berries	2 to 3	Pick over and discard bruised, moldy berries. Cover loosely with a cloth
Soft fruits	3 to 7	Discard bruised or moldy fruits. Cover loosely OR: Store in perforated plastic bags
Firm fruits	1 to 2 weeks	Same storage guidelines as for soft fruits
Cut-up raw or cooked fruits	3 to 5	Store in airtight containers

Miscellaneous Foods

Brown sugar	3 to 6 months	Store in airtight container in high-moisture drawer
Cereal, cooked	3 to 4	Cool quickly, cover tightly, and refrigerate
Coffee, ground	1 week	Store in original can
Condiments (e.g., mustard, ketchup)	2 to 3 months	Refrigerate, tightly closed, after opening
Custards and Mousses	1	Cool quickly, cover, and refrigerate immediately
Custard and cream cakes and pies	3 to 5	Same as for custards and mousses

Maximum Recommended Refrigerator Storage Time (*continued*)

FOOD	STORAGE TIME (DAYS EXCEPT WHERE NOTED OTHERWISE)	NOTES
Fruit juices (fresh, canned or thawed frozen)	5 to 7	
Gelatin, prepared	3 to 4	Cool quickly, cover, and refrigerate
Gravies, Sauces	2 to 3	Cool quickly, cover, and refrigerate
Lard	2 to 8 weeks	Store in original or other airtight container
Maple syrup	2 to 4 months	Refrigerate tightly closed after opening
Margarine	2 to 4 weeks	
Mayonnaise	2 to 3 months	Refrigerate tightly closed after opening
Nuts, shelled	3 to 4 months	Store in airtight container
Pasta, cooked	3 to 4	Cool quickly, cover tightly, and refrigerate
Pudding, leftover	3 to 4	Cool quickly, cover tightly, and refrigerate
Rice, cooked	3 to 4	Cool quickly, cover tightly, and refrigerate

Maximum Recommended Pantry Shelf Storage Time

FOOD	STORAGE TIME (MONTHS EXCEPT WHERE NOTED OTHERWISE)	NOTES
Bread	2 to 4 days	
Cakes (without custard or whipped cream filling or frosting)	1 to 2 days	Fruitcakes should be wrapped in cheesecloth soaked in liqueur, whiskey, or rum, then foil, and stored in a cool, dark place
Canned foods (other than fruits and vegetables)	1 to 2 years	
Cereal, dry	2 to 3	Transfer to airtight container for long-term flavor and crispness
Cocoa Powder	6	
Coconut	6	Refrigerate after opening
Coffee (unopened vacuum-packed can)	6	Store open cans and freshly roasted ground coffee in refrigerator or freezer and use within 1 month

(table continues)

Maximum Recommended Pantry Shelf Storage Time (*continued*)

FOOD	STORAGE TIME (MONTHS EXCEPT WHERE NOTED OTHERWISE)	NOTES
Coffee, instant powder or granules	6	Once opened, consume within 1 month
Cookies	1 week	Store soft, bar, and crisp cookies separately. Soft cookies should be stored in airtight containers. Bar cookies can be stored in their baking pans, tightly covered with aluminum foil or plastic wrap. Crisp cookies should be stored in loosely covered container in dry climates, in tightly covered container in humid areas
Cornmeal	2 to 3	Transfer to airtight container
Cornstarch	3 to 6	Transfer to airtight container
Crackers	1 to 2 months	
Cream of tartar, baking powder, soda	6	Store away from stove or heat
Dehydrated Foods (potato flakes, instant milk powder)	6	
Drink Mixes	6	
Fish, dehydrated	1 year or longer	After opening, wrap package in plastic bag or transfer to airtight jar or tin; store out of direct light
Flour	2 to 3	Transfer to airtight container
Food Coloring	1year or longer	
Freeze-dried Foods	Indefinitely	Once opened, should be tightly rewrapped as per package instructions
Fruit, dried	6 to 12 months	After opening, wrap package in plastic bag or transfer to airtight jar or tin; store out of direct light
Fruits and vegetables, canned	3 years	After opening, transfer to covered container and refrigerate
Herbs, dried	6 to 12 months	Store in cool, dark place
Honey, Preserves, Jams, Jellies, Pickles, and other condiments	1 year or longer	Refrigerate after opening
Maple Syrup, Maple-Flavored Syrup, Molasses	Indefinitely	If mold develops, discard
Mixes (cake, pudding, soup)	6	

Maximum Recommended Pantry Shelf Storage Time (*continued*)

FOOD	STORAGE TIME (MONTHS EXCEPT WHERE NOTED OTHERWISE)	NOTES
Nuts, unshelled	6	Once shelled, store in refrigerator or freezer
Oil, vegetable	6 to 12	Discard if rancid
Onions	1 to 4 weeks	Store in cool, dark, dry place
Pasta	3 to 6	Transfer to an airtight container
Peppercorns	1 year or longer	
Pies (without custard or cream)	3 to 4 days	Refrigerate
Popcorn, unpopped	1 year	Store in airtight containers
Popcorn, popped	2 weeks	
Potatoes	1	Store in cool, dark, dry place. New potatoes maintain flavor better if refrigerated
Potatoes, sweet, and yams	1 week	Store in cool, dark, dry place
Pumpkin, Rutabaga	1	Store in cool, dark, dry place
Rice	Indefinitely	Transfer to an airtight container
Salt	1 year or longer	Store near stove to maintain dryness and free flow
Shortening, solid	6 to 12	For long-term storage, refrigerate
Squash, Winter	1 to 3 weeks	Store in cool, dark, dry place
Sugar	6	To preserve moisture of brown sugar, tightly rewrap in plastic or airtight container after opening package and store in high-moisture drawer in refrigerator
Tea	1 year	
Turnips	1 week	Store in cool, dark, dry place
Vanilla and other extracts	6	Store away from heat
Vegetables, dried	1 year or longer	After opening, wrap package in plastic bag or transfer to airtight jar or tin; store out of direct light
Vinegar, prepared Salad Dressing, Peanut and other nut butters	6	After opening salad dressings and nut butters, refrigerate
Wild Rice	Indefinitely	Transfer to an airtight container
Yeast, dried	As per package expiration date	Keep in very cool place or refrigerate

CHAPTER 2

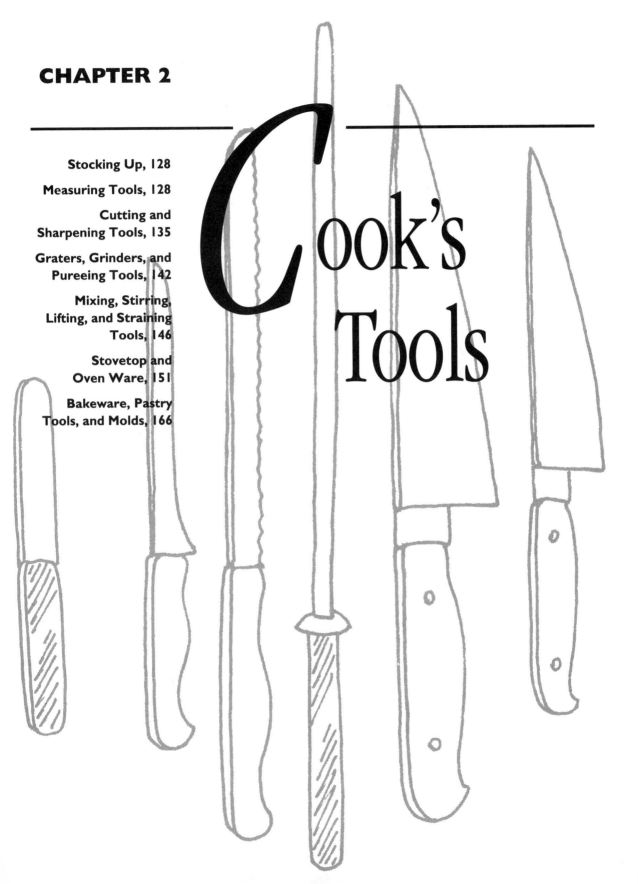

Cook's Tools

WITH THE DAZZLING ARRAY OF COOKWARE and kitchen gadgets available, it's fun to outfit a kitchen—but with so many choices, it can also be a bit daunting. Should you buy a knife exclusively designed to fillet fish and a gadget just for pitting cherries and olives? Do you really need a fish poacher or an asparagus steamer? What types of pots and pans are the best to buy? Here are some facts to help you create your dream kitchen.

Remember, whenever you buy cookware—whether you are adding to an existing collection or starting from scratch—buy the best you can possibly afford. Fine tools will last a long time and will perform consistently well. Most fine, heavy-gauge cookware can be found in the kitchenware sections of large department stores, kitchenware specialty shops, and restaurant supply stores. Other good sources are those mail order houses that deal exclusively in specialty cookware and bakeware.

Stocking Up

To help you make smart shopping choices, we've created some quick-read lists—a list of *essential* cookware you will need to turn out the most simple of meals, a list of *desirable* cookware that makes cooking and baking more efficient and pleasurable, and a list of *luxury* cookware to help you create a wide range of sophisticated recipes with ease.

Use this table as a checklist for your kitchen, then turn to the different sections of this chapter to read about the specific equipment we call for.

Measuring Tools

Many consider cooking to be an art, but it is also a science where accurate measures can make a difference. No kitchen is complete without a complement of measuring tools—a cup to measure cake flour, a thermometer to monitor a roast's internal temperature, a timer to clock a simmering stew.

Most of the measuring devices now made in the United States are marked in both American and metric calibrations, which makes it easy for you to follow recipes from cookbooks written anywhere in the world.

After you invest in measuring tools, take proper care of them. Store measuring spoons and cups so that other utensils can't knock against and dent them, which could result in inaccurate measures. Occasionally

(continued on page 132)

Kitchen Tools and Ware

ESSENTIAL COOKWARE	DESIRABLE COOKWARE	LUXURY COOKWARE

Measuring Tools

Measuring spoons	Set of glass graduated measuring cups (1 to 4 cups)	Deep-fat thermometer
Dry-measure cups		Candy thermometer
Liquid-measure cups	Additional set of measuring cups and spoons	
Oven thermometer	Weight scale	
Kitchen timer	Meat thermometer	
	Rapid-rise thermometer	
	Refrigerator/freezer thermometer	

Cutting and Sharpening Tools

8-inch high-carbon stainless steel chef's knife	5-inch utility knife	Cheese knife
	10-inch slicing knife	Cleaver
3- to 4-inch high-carbon stainless steel paring knife	5-inch steak knife	Clam knife
	Boning knife	Oyster knife
10-inch bread knife	Tomato knife	Decorating knife
Kitchen shears	Grapefruit knife	Radish decorator
Swivel blade paring knife or vegetable peeler	Cheese plane	Mandoline
	Poultry shears	Apple corer/slicer
Straightening steel	Channel knife	Butter curler
Sharpening stone	Zester	Butter slicer
Chopping board	Apple corer	Egg slicer
	Melon ball scoop	Cherry and olive pitter
	Pizza wheel	
	Poultry lacers	

Graters, Grinders, and Pureeing Tools

4-sided stainless steel box-style grater	Rotary shredder (Mouli grater)	Coffee mill
Potato masher	Marble or porcelain mortar and pestle	Meat grinder
Citrus juicer		Juice extractor
	Pepper mill	Meat tenderizer
	Food mill	
	Electric blender	
	Electric food processor	
	Garlic press	
	Meat pounder	
	Nutcracker	

Kitchen Tools and Ware (*continued*)

ESSENTIAL COOKWARE	DESIRABLE COOKWARE	LUXURY COOKWARE

Mixing, Stirring, Lifting, and Straining Tools

ESSENTIAL COOKWARE	DESIRABLE COOKWARE	LUXURY COOKWARE
Long kitchen spoon	Additional wooden, metal, and slotted metal spoons	Carving forks
Long slotted kitchen spoon		Tea strainer
Wooden spoon	Assorted sizes of whisks	
Medium wire whisk	Portable electric mixer	
Rotary beater	Standing electric mixer	
Two rubber spatulas (1- by 2-inch and 3- by 5-inch blades)	Pastry blender	
	Assorted sizes of rubber spatulas	
Long, thin metal spatula	Assorted sizes of metal spatulas	
Solid pancake turner		
Slotted pancake turner	Metal scrapers	
Kitchen tongs	Assorted sizes of ice cream scoops	
Long two-pronged fork	Assorted sizes of ladles	
Footed colander	Large strainer	
Medium-size strainer	Small strainer	
	Skimmer	
	Cheesecloth	

Stovetop and Oven Ware

ESSENTIAL COOKWARE	DESIRABLE COOKWARE	LUXURY COOKWARE
1- and 2-quart saucepans with lids	3-quart saucepan plus additional saucepans	Vegetable steamer
10-inch skillet	Double boiler	Asparagus steamer
6-inch skillet	12-quart stockpot	Griddle
Tea kettle	Folding stainless steel steamer insert	Paella pan
Coffee maker		Deep fryer
Shallow roasting pan and folding rack	All-purpose steamer	Chicken fryer
	Pressure cooker	Stovetop broiler
6-quart Dutch oven	Trivet (steamer rack)	Fondue pot
9-inch square baking dish	Small sauté pan	Chafing dish
	Large sauté pan	Deep roasting pan
	Omelet pan	Bean pot
	Crêpe pan	Ramekins
	Waffle iron	Terrine
	Wok	Pots de crème

Kitchen Tools and Ware (*continued*)

ESSENTIAL COOKWARE	DESIRABLE COOKWARE	LUXURY COOKWARE

Stovetop and Oven Ware (*continued*)

	Heat diffuser	
	Splatter shield	
	Egg poacher	
	Additional assorted sizes of baking dishes and casseroles	
	Gratin dish	
	Assorted sizes of custard cups	
	Assorted sizes of soufflé dishes	
	Microwave browning dish	
	Grill baskets	
	Skewers	
	Bulb baster	
	Basting brushes	

Bakeware, Pastry Tools, and Molds

ESSENTIAL COOKWARE	DESIRABLE COOKWARE	LUXURY COOKWARE
Mixing bowls (graduated set)	Rolling pin	Copper bowl
Sifter	Pastry cloth	Marble pastry board
Cookie sheet	Two square 9-inch baking pans	Pie weights
Two round 9-inch layer-cake pans	Jelly-roll pan	Brioche mold
9- by 13-inch baking pan	9- by 5- by 3-inch loaf pan	Popover pan
9-inch pie plate	Pizza pan	Cornstick pan
Muffin pan	Springform pan	Aspic and gelatin molds
Cooling rack	10-inch tube pan	Ice cream molds
Pastry brush	12-cup Bundt pan	
	9-inch tart pan with removable bottom	
	9-inch quiche dish	
	Cake cooling racks	
	Cookie press	
	Cookie cutters	

Kitchen Tools and Ware (*continued*)

ESSENTIAL COOKWARE	DESIRABLE COOKWARE	LUXURY COOKWARE

Bakeware, Pastry Tools, and Molds (*continued*)

	Pastry cutters	
	Pastry wheel	
	Pastry crimper	
	Additional pastry brushes	
	Dredger	
	Pastry bag	
	Pastry tips	
	Cake-decorating turntable	
	Parchment paper	

Miscellaneous Essentials

Manual or electric can opener		
Bottle opener		

What the Asterisks Mean

As you read through this chapter, notice that we have put one asterisk (*) next to the essential cookware, two asterisks (**) next to the desirable cookware and three asterisks (***) next to the luxury equipment.

▸ **Standard bar equipment, 423**

verify your scale's accuracy by placing a 5-pound bag of flour on it; then adjust or accommodate any inaccuracy. A medium-range thermometer is also easy to check: Place the probe of the thermometer into boiling water; it should read 212°F., the temperature of boiling water at sea level. If it doesn't, adjust your recipe accordingly.

CUPS, SPOONS, AND SCALES

Measuring spoons.* A good set of measuring spoons is essential to accurately add small amounts of herbs, spices, extracts, baking powder, and such. Choose durable stainless steel over aluminum or plastic spoon sets, which are prone to dent and warp, making them inaccurate. Measuring spoons usually range from ¼ teaspoon to 1 tablespoon, although some sets start with a ⅛ teaspoon and go up to 1½ tablespoons.

Dry-measure cups.* A nest of four cups accurately measures dry ingredients in ¼ cup to 1 cup increments; a nest of 5 cups includes a ⅓ cup measure. Fill to the rim for an accurate measure (see page 197). Stainless steel dry-measure cups are more durable than plastic or aluminum.

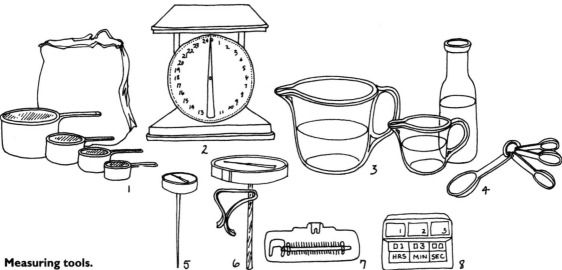

Measuring tools.
1 Dry-measure cups
2 Weight scale 3 Liquid-measure cups 4 Measuring spoons 5 Rapid-rise thermometer 6 Candy thermometer 7 Oven thermometer 8 Kitchen timer

Liquid-measure cup.* A see-through, well-marked cup is necessary to measure liquid ingredients precisely (see page 197). The finest liquid-measure cups—all of which are transparent—have spouts for dripless pouring, are made of ovenproof glass, and range in size from one to eight cups. Large-size glass measures are convenient for use in the microwave.

Weight scales.** Measuring by weight is far more accurate than measuring by volume. Both dieters and professional bakers rely on scales. You can choose from one of three types. A *balance scale* operates like a seesaw. Measured weights are set on one tray and ingredients on the other. When the weights of both trays match, a pointer lines up with a central marker. Balance scales are precise, frequently made of cast iron, and last a lifetime. Their drawback is that it takes considerable time to balance the beam.

The highly accurate *beam scale* is favored by professional bakers. Once ingredients are placed on its suspended tray, two weights are slid along a calibrated beam until the beam becomes level. The scale's gradations are well spaced and marked, the sliding weights are easy to move, and the removable tray makes it convenient to transfer the measured ingredients.

A *spring scale* measures the weight of an ingredient by how much it compresses its inner spring coil. The scale is convenient and sturdy enough for home use, though the spring tends to wear out with extended commercial use. Domestic scales should measure in increments from 1 ounce, to gauge small quantities, up to at least 12 pounds, to measure large amounts.

♦ **Measuring techniques,** **197**

THERMOMETERS

Oven thermometer.* A thermometer to monitor an oven's heat fluctuations and hot spots should be able to withstand temperatures over 600°F., and be well marked and easy to read. Mercury thermometers give more precise readings than liquid-in-glass or dial types. To check your oven's heat, stand the thermometer in various positions on both the top and bottom shelves, note the differences, then accommodate when baking or roasting.

Meat thermometers.** There are two types of thermometers that measure the internal temperature of roasting meat and poultry. Bimetallic thermometers register the correct temperature on a dial's scale. With liquid-in-glass thermometers, a liquid expands or contracts along a calibrated scale. Both types indicate when meat has reached a sufficient internal temperature to kill all harmful bacteria, and both usually read temperatures from 120°F. to 200°F. Liquid-in-glass thermometers are more accurate by 3°, but since they have thicker probes that make bigger holes and let out more juice, bimetallics are the better choice. The liquid-in-glass thermometers made for the microwave are similar to those made for conventional ovens, except that their calibrated scale is made of plastic rather than metal.

Rapid-rise (or instant-read) thermometer.** Once this thermometer's probe is inserted into a roast, its sensor signals the temperature of the surrounding meat to a microelectronic circuit for an instant readout. The thermometer is accurate to within .1°F. Most read temperatures between 68°F. and 220°F. A rapid-rise thermometer can be used to spot-check the temperature of microwave preparations and doughs, as well as meat.

Refrigerator/freezer thermometer.** With a scale that ranges from -40°F. to +80°F., this thermometer monitors the internal temperature of a refrigerator or freezer. Since frozen foods should be stored below 0°F. to keep them safe from bacteria, this gauge is particularly useful for maintaining high quality of foods.

Deep-fat thermometer.*** This thermometer has a 95°F. to 400°F. scale, a clip to hold it to the side of a pan, and a heat-resistant plastic handle to prevent burns. A thermometer is important when deep frying because it indicates when oil reaches its proper temperature. If food is added to oil that is not hot enough, the food absorbs the oil rather than being sealed by it. Since it has a moderately high scale, this thermometer can also be used to check boiling sugar syrup when making candy or jam.

Candy thermometer.*** A candy thermometer is critical to accurately monitor sugar syrup temperature for making candies or preserves. The temperature indicates the moisture content of the sugar syrup. Less concentrated syrups (those with more water) boil at lower temperatures and are used to make chewy fudge and fondant. Concentrated syrups (those with little water) boil at higher temperatures and are the bases for hard candies. Before using a candy thermometer—all of which have glass casings—take care to place it in hot water to warm it before adding to the hot syrup as the boiling syrup may crack the glass if it is not warmed beforehand.

TIMERS

Kitchen timers.* Often you can tell when food is done just by its aroma, but a timer with an alarm assures greater accuracy. There are two types of timers with alarms. Spring-action timers tick off seconds on a rotating dial. Even better are the precise battery-powered digital timers, which have easy-to-read liquid-crystal displays and shrill, attention-getting alarms. Some can monitor three functions at once, each channel able to clock blocks of time from 1 second to 10 hours.

Cutting and Sharpening Tools

Fine knives are among the most important cooking utensils you will own. You will rarely prepare a meal without using one to chop, mince, or slice. Razor sharpness makes these jobs easier and quicker. So don't skimp on your budget when it comes to these invaluable tools.

When buying any knife, it's most important to consider the blade's metal. For many centuries, good knives were made of carbon steel—an alloy of carbon and iron that is similar to cast iron. Carbon steel is still used because it holds an excellent edge, but it corrodes easily and stains on contact with acidic foods. Stainless steel, which became readily available early in the twentieth century, became a popular knife-making alternative. It resists corrosion and is very strong, but it has difficulty keeping an edge and is nearly impossible to sharpen. (Stainless steel remains the best metal for specialty cutting tools like lemon zesters, pizza cutters, and mandolines.) The successor to both metals, high-carbon stainless steel, is now considered the finest knife making steel. It holds an edge, resists pitting and abrasion, and is easy to sharpen.

Whichever knife metal you select, the blade should be forged (hammered into its basic shape) rather than stamped (die cut from a steel sheet). Because of the greater attention needed to forge blades, they become tougher and heavier.

A finely constructed, forged knife will have a *tang*—the unsharpened, rear end of a blade that extends the entire length of its handle with a shape to match. The full tang is obvious because manufacturers

Knife Nomenclature

A fine knife is forged in high-carbon stainless steel, has a full *tang* (the unsharpened rear end of the knife located inside the handle), and displays a *bolster*—a thick band of steel that runs directly along the heel and up to the spine. The handle should feel comfortable and have tight joins and flush rivets.

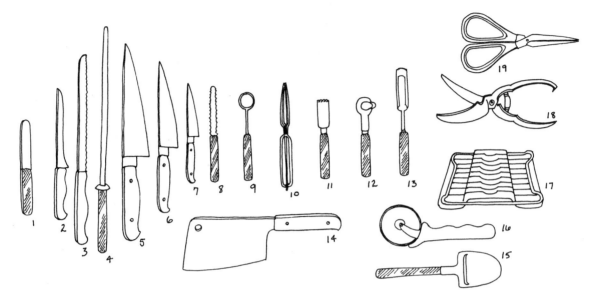

Cutting and sharpening tools. 1 Clam knife 2 Boning knife 3 Bread knife 4 Sharpening steel 5 8-inch chef's knife 6 6-inch chef's knife 7 4-inch paring knife 8 Grapefruit knife 9 Melon ball scoop 10 Vegetable peeler 11 Zester 12 Channel knife 13 Apple corer 14 Cleaver 15 Cheese plane 16 Pizza wheel 17 Egg slicer 18 Poultry shears 19 Kitchen shears

proudly sandwich it between a handle's two sides. A full tang—versus the equally descriptive three-quarter, half, or rat-tail tang—increases the stability of the knife and contributes to its overall balance.

You should also consider handle shape, composition, and finish. The sleek, simple profile that chefs prefer promises the most comfortable hold, and a durable, hard plastic covering supplies the most hygienic, nonslip grip. All handle joins—the tang to its covering, the cover to the bolster, and the rivets to hold them in place—should be flush. Not only do smooth joins enhance a smooth grip, they discourage dirt and grease from collecting.

Pick up a prospective knife before buying it—it should feel secure and balanced in your hand. If it does not feel balanced, the knife will be tiring to use.

At home, protect your investment with proper care and storage. Use a knife on a wood or polyethylene chopping board that is slightly resilient. Avoid chopping, mincing, or cutting on glass, ceramic, metal, or hard plastic since striking against such hard surfaces will dull the blade edge. Wash by hand instead of in a dishwasher, where blade edges might become nicked. If you need to clean stained carbon steel blades, gently rub their sides with a dampened cork dipped in scouring powder. Finally, store knives separately—in a knife block, on a mounted magnetic bar, or in sheaths in a drawer.

Keep your knives sharpened with the techniques described on page 184.

Start out with a chef's knife and a small paring knife for general purpose use, and a straightening steel and sharpening stone to keep them

♦ **Knife techniques, 184–194**

Knife Cutting Edge Shapes

Plain tapered edge. **This is the general-purpose edge found on most household knives and is made by successive coarse to fine grindings.**

Serrated edge. **This looks and acts like a saw. Found on bread and some cake and steak knives, this edge doesn't cut food as much as it rips it apart.**

Wave edge. **This resembles a series of arcs. It is found on tomato knives, some bread knives, roast beef slicers, and grapefruit knives—and excels at cutting juicy or delicately textured foods. Its sequence of half moons expands the actual cutting surface, while the points (which end along the cutting edge) protect the sharp edges of the arcs.**

in tip-top condition. After using these, you'll discover which of the more specific knives or cutters described in this chapter you may need or want.

BASIC BLADES

Chef's knife.* This blade's rigid, triangular shape with its large, gently curved edge is ideal for quickly chopping, slicing, dicing and mincing vegetables and herbs. It is considered the most important cutting tool because it performs so many tasks so well. Blade lengths range from 5 to 14 inches, the most popular of which is 8 inches.

Paring knife.* This blade's profile matches that of the chef's knife, but its 3- to 4-inch blade enables you to get closer to what is being cut. It is great for delicate and detailed cutting, trimming, peeling, paring, and decorating.

Utility knife.** The slightly curved cutting edge and sharp tip of this 5-inch blade make it good for slicing cooked meats and poultry, and for salads and moderate amounts of chopping. A *fish fillet knife*, which looks like a utility knife, is 2 inches longer, more thinly profiled, and flexible; it is used to bone fish before cooking.

Slicers.** Fairly narrow 10- to 14-inch blades are used to cut even slices from cooked or cured fish and meat. The thinnest, most flexible slicing blade is used for salmon. The carefully ground indentations that run perpendicular to its blade edge prevent the chance of friction, snagging, or pulling that create uneven slices. A ham slicer's slightly broader, less limber, tapered-edge blade cuts the drier and denser textures of cooked ham and turkey better. Since it has no need to pierce, only to slice across meat, it has a blunt tip that won't tear thin slices as you transfer them from board to platter. A roast beef slicer has the

▶ **Filleting fish, 187–189**
▶ **Paring, 181, 186**

widest, stiffest blade, with either a wave cut or the similar granton edge of the salmon slicer. This allows the blade to slip through softer, juicier meats yet maintain its course on a downstroke. A general-purpose slicer is actually a cross between a ham and roast beef slicer: It is 10 inches long, barely flexible, moderately narrow, and sharply tipped.

Bread knife.* This knife's 10-inch blade easily reaches across a large loaf for single-stroke slicing. Its serrated or wave-cut edge is designed to bite into a crisp, hard crust, and then rip through the bread's softer interior without squashing the loaf.

Steak knife.** This knife's small, narrow blade has a cutting edge that sweeps up to a high tip. This extends that part of the blade used most often when cutting down and drawing through a juicy steak or chop. Steak knife blades measure 4 to 5 inches.

Boning knife.** With a high, strong tip that accurately pierces flesh and a narrow, flexible blade that sticks close to carcass contours, this knife is perfect for separating flesh from bone. A 5-inch blade is considered the most practical length.

Tomato knife.** This narrow, rigid, wave-cut blade deftly slices fruits or vegetables with smooth skins and soft centers, such as plums and kiwifruit. Its edge virtually saws through a tough exterior, thereby preventing any undue pressure that would crush and juice a delicate fruit. Five-inch tomato knives are also used to slice salami.

Grapefruit knife.** This 4-inch, double-edged blade is curved to mirror the profile of the fruit half about to be hollowed, bluntly tipped to deter penetration into bitter peels, and either serrated or wave-cut to saw through stringy pith.

Cheese plane.** When drawn across a block of semifirm cheese, the slicing edge that juts below this tool's spade-shaped head cuts, lifts, and serves the thinnest possible sheets of cheese. It is especially good for slicing paper-thin sheets of strong cheeses that might otherwise be too pungent to enjoy.

Cheese knife.*** This blade's full, flat edge supplies a substantial slicing surface while its etched sides prevent semifirm cheese from sticking and pulling the blade off its cutting course. The knife's offset handle allows you to press forcefully downward to cut through a wheel or brick without the fear of jamming your knuckles against the cutting board.

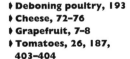
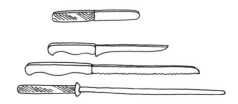

Cleaver.* The only way to split cartilage and bone is with a heavy, near-rectangular cleaver. Its weight (about 2 pounds) adds momentum to the downward swing motion while its axlike channel edge protects the tool from heavy impact. Blades measure from 6 to 9 inches, the smallest being the most practical for home use.

SHEARS

Kitchen shears.* The 4-inch-long, sharply tipped blades of these shears readily notch dough, cut twine, snip chives, and fin fish. The finest have forged, stainless steel blades, one of which is serrated. They measure 8 inches in overall length and are finished with plastic-coated handles to enhance gripping.

Poultry shears.** These 9½-inch-long shears (as measured by their overall length) are strong enough to cut through chicken and duck carcasses and slightly curved to follow poultry's rounded contours. One of its blades is serrated to prevent the flesh from slipping as the blades advance; the other is notched to secure a small bone as it is cross cut. When buying, be sure the shears have textured handles for a secure grip and display a pivot screw that allows for pressure adjustment and disassembly.

CLAM AND OYSTER KNIVES

Clam knife.*** This tiny, sharp-edged spatula is tailor-made to slip between a clam's shell. Once in, it is squeezed further through then twisted to spread the shells open, break the vacuum, and free the flesh.

Oyster knife.*** This short, rigid, sharply tipped blade is used to open oysters. Poke the tip into the oyster's hinge, twist to separate its two shells, then slide the blade under the meat to free it. The stubbier, arrow-shaped oyster knives are used mainly to open such wider, flatter oyster varieties as the Belon.

PEELERS, CORERS, AND GARNISHING BLADES

Vegetable peelers.* A good peeler has a slotted blade with two sharp edges to suit right- or left-handed motions, a sharp tip to dig out potato eyes, and a swivel-set to follow closely vegetable bumps and hollows. Some are fitted with carbon-steel blades and others are available with stainless steel. Style—either straight or harp-shaped—is a matter of preference.

Channel knife.** This tool's short, flat blade has a bulging V-shaped tooth that lies perpendicular to its tip in order to scrape away thick, decorative strips from lemon, orange, lime, and grapefruit peels. These strips can then be candied to garnish tarts or sorbets or can be served in cocktails. You can also draw this blade down a cucumber, carrot, lemon, or lime to neatly groove it before slicing.

Zester.** When drawn across an orange, lemon, or lime peel, this blade's tiny, sharp-edged holes produce thin, decorative citrus wisps to flavor sauces, marinades, and frostings or to top custards. Since the holes barely scrape the surface, they leave behind the bitter white pith that lies under all citrus peels.

Decorating knife.*** This 4-inch-long, corrugated, stainless steel blade is designed to crinkle-cut root vegetables and create ripple designs on cream cheese spreads and icings. Its inch-long, sharp, straight front edge can be used for preliminary peeling and trimming.

Radish decorator.*** This tongslike device made of cast aluminum handles with stainless steel blades is used to quickly notch radishes into decorative roses. Place a trimmed radish in the cupped end of one arm, squeeze the handles, and the tiny blades located on the other arm end score a deep hub-and-spoke pattern into the vegetable. A brief ice-water bath then causes the radish flesh to contract or "bloom."

Mandoline.*** Use this tool, which resembles a carpenter's rectangular plane, to rapidly slice such firm, crisp foods as potatoes, apples, onions, carrots, and beets into uniformly thin or thick, plain or waffled wafers, or julienne strips. The 16-inch-long frame, which may be made of wood, plastic, or, ideally, stainless steel, has two adjustable stainless steel cutting blades: one straight and one rippled.

Apple corer.** This narrow, troughed, 4-inch blade with its sharp, ringed tip cores apples neatly. Drive the tip into the center of the fruit to encircle its core, twist to completely sever the core from its surrounding flesh. Withdraw the knife and the core comes out as well.

Apple corer/slicer.*** This device, which resembles the hub and spokes of a small wheel, is used to core and section apples or pears in one stroke. Set the tool's open, dropped center around a fruit's stem end, then push down on the high-set handles; the core remains cradled while the surrounding fruit wedges are freed for eating or cooking. Cast aluminum and stainless steel apple corer/slicers are made to section 8, 12, or 14 wedges.

Melon ball scoop.** This tiny, sharp-edged, stainless steel scoop easily cuts fleshy fruits or vegetables into neat ball shapes. The best have a tiny hole in the center of the bowl to break the suction that develops while scooping. Scoops can also be used to hollow cherry tomatoes and mushrooms before filling. They are manufactured in both round and oval shapes.

Pizza wheel.** A stainless steel pizza wheel should be strong to prevent wobbling or bending under pressure, fitted with an offset handle to be comfortable to use, and finished with a finger guard to protect the working hand from slipping onto the blade. Make sure the wheel rotates smoothly and easily before you buy.

Butter curler.*** This inch-wide stainless steel blade may look like a miniature shepherd's crook, but it is used to create tight, individual, scalloped-shaped butter portions. The notching creates decorative ridging while the distinct hook gently directs newly shaved butter into tidy, uniform shapes.

Butter slicer.*** The 17 evenly spaced wires stretched across this tool's cast aluminum frame draw through a chilled 4-ounce butter stick to slice it evenly into 2-teaspoon pats. Some apportion 14 pats, but all measure 8 inches long.

Egg slicer.*** Set a peeled hard-cooked egg into the cradle of an egg slicer's contoured base, then draw down its hinged top. Its braced wires will neatly pinch, press, and slip through an egg's firm white and creamy yolk to make picture-perfect slices. Another version cuts eggs into wedges.

ACCESSORIES

Poultry lacers.** The easiest way to truss a bird for roasting is with a handful of these tiny, ring-capped stainless steel skewers. Insert them ladderlike through the skin on both sides of the cavity, then anchor with twine. You can also use them to secure stuffed pork chops or fish, by pinning the edges together or using the same lacing technique.

Cherry and olive pitter.*** Place a cherry or olive—stem side up— in the cupped ring at the end of one of this tongslike tool's 7-inch arms and compress the handles for the corresponding rod to pierce the fruit and punch out its pit. The finest pitters are spring-loaded to powerfully retract once compressed.

Straightening steel.* To maintain the sharp edge on your knives, you need this long, chrome-plated steel shaft. A 12-inch length supplies enough surface to draw a sizable blade. Its chrome finish creates a surface harder than the blade being filed against it. Select a moderately coarse rather than a finely grooved steel when buying. The ceramic rods that are available sharpen rather than straighten blades.

Sharpening stone.* There are two common varieties of sharpening stones: those made entirely of man-made silicone carbide and those with a surface embedded with diamond dust. Both are available in brick shapes with coarse to fine grits, although the latter is also manufactured in shaft form. When buying, select a double-grit stone with a medium-coarse side and a medium-fine side; both are preferred over electric knife sharpeners, which tend to wear away blades more rapidly.

Chopping board.* Polyethylene (plastic) boards are waterproof and warp-resistant, and for some years they have been touted as more sanitary than hardwood chopping boards. However, it has been discovered that wood is actually safer, as, unlike plastic, it quickly kills any food-poisoning bacteria left behind when the board is washed. Still, it is important to carefully clean all chopping boards after use.

Graters, Grinders, and Pureeing Tools

One glance at the kitchen tools that grate, grind, crack, puree, or juice, and it's easy to imagine that they are the latest from innovative engineers. They make short work of altering food texture, are user-friendly, and easy to clean.

Yet many of these presses, pounders, and sieves have been kitchen staples for centuries. The mortar and pestle that crush herbs, spices, and nuts predate recorded time. The rudimentary stones that ground Neanderthal grain are the forerunners of the buhrstones found in today's coffee mills, and the rasps that shred cheese are similar to those used in Dante's day.

Many of these tools are single-purpose and have no peer at performing their task—grinding pepper, tenderizing meat, or juicing lemons, limes, and oranges, to name a few. Others, like the food processor, are

Graters, grinders, and pureeing tools. 1 Pepper mill 2 Rotary shredder 3 Grater 4 Food mill 5 Citrus juicer 6 Mortar and pestle 7 Blender 8 Potato masher 9 Meat pounder 10 Meat grinder

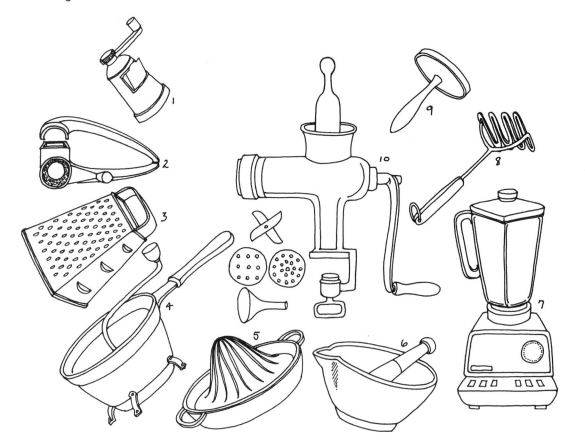

multipurpose and seem like an assistant in the kitchen—kneading dough, grinding meat, and grating cheese. With so many available tools, only you can decide which suit your needs and which are truly worth the sometimes sizable investment.

GRATERS

Graters.* Steel sheets with coarse to fine rasplike perforations are designed to grate nutmeg and lemon peel and to shred cheese, cabbage, carrots, and potatoes. Some are flat, finished with plastic-coated handles, and are easy to store. The most popular general-purpose version, however, is the *four-sided box grater* that has three different grating surfaces plus one slicing plane. A *rotary grater* is fitted with one arm to clamp down on food held in its other arm's hopper, pushing it against a hand-cranked perforated drum to shred. It requires less exertion to operate and grates 1/3 cup of food at a time.

Rotary shredder.* Often regarded as the poor person's food processor and commonly called the "Mouli grater" in deference to the French firm that first popularized it, this hand-cranked machine juliennes, shreds, and slices. Most rotary shredders come with five interchangeable stainless steel shredding disks for various degrees of coarseness and are fitted with folding feet that spread out to straddle bowls.

GRINDERS

Mortar and pestle.* These have been used for centuries to reduce dried herbs, spices, and chilies to powder and fresh herbs and nuts to paste. Marble and porcelain mortars and pestles are preferred because they don't absorb or impart flavor or react with any food being processed. Wood and brass ones are also available. All have unglazed or rough bowl interiors to maximize friction.

Pepper mill.* To enjoy peppercorns at their pungent peak, grind just before use. Peppermills come in many different styles and are manufactured in materials such as wood, cast aluminum, or pewter. The best have a screw to adjust the grind on the top rather than a handle.

Coffee mill.** You get the finest flavor and best aroma when you make coffee from freshly roasted beans that you grind yourself. An electric mill feeds the beans directly between two buhrstones, where they are ground uniformly, then flung into a removable container. Most coffee mills have a gauge that ranges from 1 to 8 to regulate the desired grind, from coarse to near powder, depending on which type of coffeemaker you will use. When buying, don't confuse a coffee mill with what manufacturers call a coffee grinder, a device that works on the principle of a blender: its two bottom-based blades chop or rechop

◗ **Grate,** 180
◗ **Coffee,** 110–111

anything they come in contact with, making evenly sized granules nearly impossible to achieve.

Meat grinder.*** A meat grinder saves time, energy, and trouble when you need to chop large quantities of fish, meat, or poultry. To use, drop the food into the grinder's hopper and turn the handle to set the large metal screw (called the "worm") in motion. The worm catches food between its treads and advances it toward and through cutting blades and onto a perforated coarse or fine disk. Sturdy manual meat grinders are manufactured in cast iron and are fitted with clamps to hold them firmly to kitchen counters.

PUREEING TOOLS

Food mill.** A hand-cranked food mill simultaneously purees and strains ingredients. Once food is placed in its hopper and the handle turns, a spring-loaded, semicircular blade pushes food through a perforated disk. Hooks on the base allow the rig to be set atop an empty bowl when working. The finest food mills are made of stainless steel and have three interchangeable disks for various degrees of coarseness.

Blender.** The best way to attain supersmooth soups and shakes and satiny sauces is with a blender. Many varieties are available, but the best seem to be the simplest. Look for a simple two-speed type with a strong motor, straight, angle-set blades, and a large, tight, see-through container. Remember that a blender is most effective when it is no more than half full.

Food processor.** For saving both time and labor in the professional and home kitchen, nothing beats a food processor. It slices, shreds, chops, cuts, grates, grinds, mixes, and kneads. Various models come with 1-cup to 16-cup work bowl capacities, the largest of which are fitted with the most powerful and sturdiest motors. Of these larger processors, choose one that sits atop its direct-drive motor rather than one located beside its belt-driven motor. Food processors are often packaged with an S-shaped blade, dough blade, and shredding and slicing disks. Optional attachments include a juice extractor, citrus press, thick-slicing disk, and french-fry and ripple-cut disks.

Potato masher.* A favorite for pureeing white potatoes, sweet potatoes, and parsnips, this tool's thick, rigid, zigzag wire head easily cuts and crushes cooked starchy root vegetables. Because it's small, the masher is convenient to use in the same pot that the drained vegetables were cooked in.

Garlic press.** A good garlic press has a basket large enough to contain four garlic cloves, perforations that can be cleaned easily, and two sturdy, medium-length handles to supply ample leverage and to distance your hands from clinging aroma. Garlic presses are manufactured in either cast aluminum or stainless steel.

JUICERS

Citrus juicer.* The pointed dome of a juicer is perfectly shaped to remove the juice from a halved lemon, lime, orange, or grapefruit. It can be made of porcelain, plastic, glass or, ideally, durable stainless steel. The dome should have distinct ridges to crush flesh and channel juices, a perforated base gulley to strain out pulp and seeds, and a convenient pouring spout on its receptacle.

Juice extractor.*** Many people swear by the vitamin power of juice made in this electrical device from such hard raw vegetables as carrots and beets and such delicate herbs as parsley and chives. Once food is fed into its chute and onto a rotating cutting disk, it shreds food fibers to expose the maximum amount of flesh. This pulp is then thrown to the sides of a spinning strainer basket where, thanks to centrifugal force, all juice is drawn out and into a surrounding jacket, from which it is then funneled out and into an awaiting cup or bowl.

MEAT TENDERIZERS

Meat pounder.** The broad, flat face of a meat pounder is used to flatten veal and chicken to a uniform thickness prior to sautéing or stuffing. Choose the chromed-steel models, which can be effectively cleaned. The pounder should be heavy to do a good job. Remember to first moisten the pounder with water before using to prevent meat from sticking and tearing.

Meat tenderizer.*** This mallet's striking surfaces are designed to pierce and sever the long, tough muscle fibers of both thin and thick cuts of meat. The tool is cast in aluminum in a single piece so its hammerhead remains intact even with vigorous pounding.

NUTCRACKERS

Nutcrackers.** The two most popular nutcrackers allow you to crack shells easily and neatly. A hinged nutcracker's two 7-inch arms provide plenty of leverage to crack shells, and its two inset ridged grips firmly grasp large or small nuts. A wooden nutcracker's bowl cradles a nut as its turned screw bears upon a nut until it cracks. Hinged nutcrackers are manufactured in enameled, nickel-plated, or stainless steel, while wooden ones are commonly available in cherry, oak, or walnut.

*M*ixing, Stirring, Lifting, and Straining Tools

Almost every kitchen has a crock full of spoons, whisks, spatulas, skimmers, ladles, and strainers at the ready to stir sauces, flip pancakes, skim stocks, serve soups, and drain pasta. You will find you use these tools often, so look for durable materials—either heavy-gauge stainless steel that can't rust, bend, or buckle, or high-quality plastic or dense wood to use with nonstick or otherwise treated surfaces. Look for skimmers and strainers that are rigidly framed to prolong their shape and life; spoons and ladles made of single-piece construction so there are no weak, easy-to-snap spots; and full-tanged forks that are far stronger than their half or pintail relatives.

Before buying a tool, evaluate its practical design. Ladles with deep bowls are better able to transfer liquids neatly from stockpot to tureen; flat skewers prevent threaded foods from slipping when they're turned; and whisks with wires welded inside silicone-capped handles are resilient and easy to clean.

Mixing, stirring, lifting, and straining tools.
1 Skimmer 2 Ladle 3 Solid pancake turner 4 Slotted pancake turner 5 Rubber spatulas 6 Long, thin, metal spatula 7 Two-pronged fork 8 Slotted spoon 9 Whisks 10 Wooden spoons 11 Strainer 12 Portable electric mixer 13 Footed colander 14 Standing electric mixer

Also consider a tool's size. Turners should be long enough to keep your hands from heat, yet small enough to get in close to flip food deftly. Colanders should be big enough to drain rapidly, yet small enough to fit in a sink.

Your own cooking habits are the final factors to weigh when buying kitchen utensils, particularly those that mix ingredients. A few whisks and a rotary beater may be enough for you, if all you want to do is aerate batters and remove lumps from sauces. Or you may be content to own a portable electric mixer to complete those and a few heavier chores, such as whipping potatoes and mixing frosting. If you are a serious baker, however, you won't be happy without a powerful standing electric mixer to make short work of all your kneading, beating, and whipping tasks.

SPOONS, WHISKS, AND BEATERS

Metal spoons.* A variety of long-handled, shallow-bowled, solid, slotted, and perforated metal spoons are used to stir, mix, baste, and transfer foods. The finest are made of inflexible stainless steel in single-piece construction; "no join" means there is no spot weld to break. Metal spoons should measure approximately 12 inches.

Whisks.* With their elongated or bulbous head shapes and flexible or firm wires, a variety of whisks are designed to efficiently perform specific tasks—to emulsify or blend ingredients or to incorporate air into liquids. The three most common types of whisks are the long, moderately stiff sauce whisk; the flat, lightly pliant roux whisk; and the rounded, flexible balloon whisk, which has no peer for whipping egg whites into massive peaks. Convenient lengths range from 10 to 14 inches. The best are manufactured in stainless steel with uniformly thick, silicone-capped handles.

Rotary beater.* The two 4-bladed whisks suspended in this tool's frame make it an effective tool to quickly beat egg whites and moderate amounts of fairly fluid batters. Choose one with a stainless steel frame and blades, smooth-turning gears, and a comfortable, yet sturdy handle.

Portable electric mixer.** This is superb for tackling moderate mixing chores—from beating batters to whipping potatoes. A fine portable electric mixer is lightweight and well balanced with a comfortable handle, easy access to controls, and a stable heel rest. The best have an electronic sensor that allows them to maintain a steady mixing speed.

Standing electric mixer.** A fine heavy-duty countertop mixer is designed to mix, aerate, or knead light to heavy batters and doughs with relative ease. The machines have large, stationary stainless steel

♦ **Mixing techniques, 181, 266–267**

bowls with beaters that rotate as they travel in a circle to effectively reach every part of a mixture. The motor should be powerful to prevent overheating and heavy to deter vibrating or walking during operation. The best standing electric mixers come equipped with a wire whisk for whipping cream, a flat beater for mixing batters, and a dough hook for kneading bread. Attachments can include a pasta maker, food grinder, sausage stuffer, and vegetable slicer/shredder, among others.

MISCELLANEOUS MIXING TOOLS

Rubber spatulas.* The flat, wide, flexible blade of a rubber spatula is tailor-made to remove the last lick of batter from a bowl or to fold beaten egg whites into a soufflé base. Synthetic rubber spatulas with handles range in overall length from 10 to 20 inches and carry 1- by 2-inch to 3- by 5-inch blades. The handle-free ones, called cornes, measure 3 by 5 inches. What size spatulas to buy is a matter of preference; a good set to start out with would have blades that measure 1 by 2 inches and 3 by 5 inches.

Pastry blender.** These multiple, U-shaped wires capped with a comfortable wooden grip are used to quickly cut fat into flour to create the best doughs for pastry. The wires should be medium thick and semiflexible to sustain the rapid bouncing work motion, deep to reach well into bowls, and securely bolted to their handle for a long life.

LIFTING TOOLS

Metal spatulas.* The long, broad, round-tipped stainless steel blades of metal spatulas are designed to spread icings, smooth batters, and lift freshly baked foods from their pans. Their blades should be long in order to frost cakes with a minimum number of strokes, superthin to slip beneath oven-fresh cookies and pastries, and semiflexible to ease out sheet cakes from jelly-roll pans. Like better knives, straight and off-set spatulas should have full tangs and comfortable grips.

Pancake turners.* A good turner has a flexible head to slide easily into a pan and under food. It should be broad enough to lift bacon, fried eggs, hamburgers, or pancakes, and slotted to simultaneously drain off cooking grease. Turners with stainless steel heads are durable, but shouldn't be used in nonstick or anodized aluminum pans; for these, use nylon or wood utensils that won't scratch coated pan surfaces.

Tongs.* Long stainless steel tongs are like dependable, heatproof fingers that grip, turn or transfer foods from sizzling pots to serving platters and plates. The easiest work like tweezers. Pivot-sets act like scissors, requiring a push and pull motion to close and open. Tongs with long, scalloped-edged (versus saw-toothed) jaws provide stronger grips and are available in 6½- to 16-inch lengths.

Kitchen forks.* A fine fork must be made of carbon or stainless steel, with long, thick, inflexible tines to lift heavy roasts from pans and turn searing meat in pots or on grills. A 12-inch length will distance your hands comfortably from hot foods, and the long, strong tines will supply ample lifting leverage. Two types of forks are made for the various kitchen tasks: The longer tined, barely bowed chef's fork is ideal for roast and grill work; the smaller-tined, lightly bowed pot fork is better suited for stovetop work. As with fine knives, fine forks have full tangs.

Carving forks.*** Two distinct table carving forks are styled to secure differently shaped roasted meats or grilled poultry, though both are made of carbon or stainless steel. Both have two tines to anchor meat and an overall length of roughly 10 to 12 inches to maximize leverage and keep your hands comfortably away from hot foods. A fork with curved tines is designed to press against the contours of a large roast or big bird and a straight-tined fork is better equipped to anchor flatter meat cuts, such as London broil and skirt steak. Both should have full tangs.

Metal scrapers.** Broad, inflexible blades with large, moderately dull working edges are meant to scrape and lift the last trace of food from working and cooking surfaces. Those with traditional handles push across griddles to pry off burned-on bits of food. Dough scrapers have sharpened blades to divide pastry and bread doughs quickly and cleanly and to scrape the flour and bits of hardened dough off your work surface. The sturdiest metal scrapers are made of stainless steel and have textured grips. Griddle scrapers have a trapezoid shape and are fitted with a 3- to 4-inch working edge. Dough scrapers are rectangular and measure 6 inches across the front.

SCOOPS AND LADLES

Ice cream scoops.** You can use the deep, round bowl of an ice cream scoop to shape and apportion such soft foods as mashed potatoes and rice, as well as ice cream. The tapered tip makes it easy to slice down and sweep across foods while the spring-set blade assures their clean release. Scoops with oval- and tower-shaped working heads are also manufactured, the best of which have smooth-to-operate, cog-regulated mechanisms. The insulated cast aluminum ice cream scoops have no moving parts, simply an ingenious addition that makes them work: a salt-based fluid housed in the aluminum handle that absorbs body heat. The metal remains warmer than the frozen dessert through which it's driving, making it easy to sweep through the firmest-packed ice creams or sherbets.

Ladles.** Long, deep-bowled ladles of various sizes are indispensable for serving soups and stews, pouring measured amounts of batter, or apportioning punch. Those with deep cups promise neater transfers. They should be made of single-piece construction, which makes them stronger and, with no joins to catch foods or liquids, more hygienic. Stainless steel ladles will prove to be most durable, though ladles are available in plastic or tinned steel.

STRAINERS

Colander.* A freestanding perforated bowl that quickly separates food from liquid, a colander should be moderately large in order to hold a pound of cooked pasta, a rinsed head of lettuce, or washed grape clusters. If possible, select a colander with feet. They are manufactured in tinned steel, enameled steel, porcelain, anodized and nonstick aluminum, and stainless steel.

Strainers.* A general-purpose bowl strainer should have a medium-coarse mesh surface to quickly drain cooking water from vegetables and a sturdy frame to maintain shape. Select freestanding bowl strainers or those fitted with hooks and handles that straddle pot rims because they don't require a second hand to balance them. Strainers are manufactured in tinned steel or the more durable stainless steel with 2½- to 14-inch diameters.

Skimmers.** These are used to remove solids from liquids and are available in four different head styles, depending upon their use. The perforated, barely bowled metal disk and gridded-wire skimmer are particularly good for fishing doughnuts or fish fillets from hot fat. A saucer-shaped fine mesh skimmer will quickly skim off the gray foam (albumen) that rises to the surface of stocks. The shallow bowl of a Chinese skimmer mirrors that of its wok to make sweep and scoop motions easy to execute when stir-frying.

Cheesecloth.** Originally a wrap for freshly made cheese, this cotton cloth is used more often to strain and shape foods. Tie it around chopped celery and aromatics for a bouquet garni; wrap it around a soon-to-be-poached salmon to ensure its shape; or line a colander with it to clear poured stock or rendered fat. Cheesecloth is strong and durable because it is woven, not knitted. Most people use cheesecloth once, then discard it rather than bother with washing it, but it can be reused.

Tea strainer.*** The mesh bowl of a tea strainer must be tightly woven in order to trap every spent leaf as steeped tea is poured from pot to cup. Some have a wire handle; others are inset into a frame that

♦ **Tea,** 111–112

Proven Pasta Performers

If you're serious about pasta, your kitchen should include some of the special tools available to make, cook, and serve it.

☐ *Pasta machines.* These knead, pull, and press dough sheets, then cut them into a variety of shapes. Both manual and electric versions are sold. The manual version, coupled with a food processor to mix the dough, is just fine for small quantities.

☐ *Ravioli cutters.* Utensils that stamp out neat, uniformly shaped packets, which will cook evenly, from assembled dough sheets.

☐ *Pasta pot.* This looks like a small stockpot and is fitted with a perforated basket that simultaneously removes and strains pasta once it's done.

☐ *Pasta fork.* This resembles a pronged stainless steel scoop and handily moves small amounts of pasta from boiling water to bowl or from buffet platter to plate.

straddles a cup as tea is poured. Tea infusers—both the two-part hinged spoon and ball varieties—act as perforated tea containers that are removed after brewing. Tea strainers are available in tinned or rust-resistant stainless steel.

Stovetop and Oven Ware

Just as fine artists depend on top-quality paints, brushes, and papers to create their masterpieces, you can rely on superior cookware to turn out culinary classics.

Anytime you buy cookware, first consider its material. The best cookware conducts heat uniformly and efficiently and responds rapidly to temperature changes. Once the material is selected, carefully examine a prospective vessel's construction. Pick it up; the pot should be relatively heavy to withstand frequent use, have a thick base, and be stable when empty. Lightweight pans dent, wear quickly, and conduct heat unevenly, creating "hot spots" that tend to burn food. Look at the handles, too; the finest are sturdy, heatproof, provide a comfortable grip, and are well attached to the body of their pot with either rivets or spot welding. If the pot comes complete with a cover, examine it closely. The fit should be snug and the cover finished with an obvious "skirt"—ideally a sloped riser or a rim that fits inside the pot. Finally, inspect the surface for nicks, gouges, and scratches. Metals should be

⁌ **Pasta, 61–63, 220**

Stovetop and oven ware.
1 Steamer insert 2 Casserole 3 Soufflé dish 4 Gratin dish 5 Saucepan and lid 6 Wok 7 Bean pot and cups 8 Double boiler 9 Roasting pan and folding rack 10 Crêpe pan 11 Sauté pan and lid 12 Tea kettle

smoothly polished or finished, ceramics evenly glazed, and nonstick surfaces uniformly coated.

Try to resist the seeming economy of buying a packaged set of cookware instead of a few well-designed, hard-wearing items. It's better to have cookware in materials to suit particular chores and in sizes that conform to your personal needs. Not only will you enjoy their effectiveness, you'll reap the rewards of their lifelong service.

BASIC POTS

Saucepans.* Deep, straight-sided pans that hold heat well and limit evaporation are ideal for preparing sauces, heating small amounts of vegetables, rice, or pasta, and melting butter. Two- to 6-quart saucepans are manufactured in all the standard metals and finishes; smaller-capacity plastic saucepans are made for microwave use, which is where heatproof glass also finds its best use. For general purpose,

(continued on page 156)

Cookware Composition and Care

No one material excels in all cooking tasks—whether it's to fry, bake, steam, stir-fry, or sauté. One may be a fine heat conductor but a poor heat retainer, making it impractical for long, slow simmers. Another may absorb heat slowly but retain it for a long time, making it great for stovetop searing. The following describes the characteristics of the most common materials that are used in pots and pans described in this chapter.

MATERIAL	ADVANTAGES	DISADVANTAGES	CARE
Aluminum	A very good heat conductor. Also durable and inexpensive.	Reacts with acidic and alkaline foods, discoloring and imparting a metallic taste if exposure is prolonged. Storing any foods—especially acidic foods—in aluminum should be avoided. (Anodized aluminum is coated with a hard, dense oxide film, the result of an electrolytic process that improves its corrosion resistance and makes it less reactive with certain foods. Calphalon is the brand name for a line of anodized aluminum pots, pans, and bakeware.)	Cool before washing to safeguard against buckling. Wash in hot, soapy water and dry immediately. Remove discoloration by boiling for 10 minutes in a solution containing 2 tablespoons of cream of tartar for each quart of water.
Brass	Good, uniform conductor. Durable, inexpensive, and resists corrosion.	Tends to discolor.	Wash in hot, sudsy water; then rinse and dry immediately.
Carbon Steel	Good heat conductor. Relatively quick to absorb and convey heat.	Vulnerable to rusting. Its iron content reacts with acidic foods. (Black steel bakeware, which is heat-treated carbon steel, is more resistant to corrosion.)	Season before first using: Wash, dry, and brush the inside of the pan with cooking oil. Heat for 15 minutes over a medium flame. Then wash, dry, and coat any food contact surfaces with a light layer of oil. Wash both carbon and black steel in hot, soapy water and soak instead of scouring to remove any burned-on bits of food; dry immediately.

(table continues)

Cookware Composition and Care *(continued)*

MATERIAL	ADVANTAGES	DISADVANTAGES	CARE
Cast Iron	Retains and conveys heat uniformly. Sturdy, heavy, and warp-resistant.	Slow to heat. The iron content reacts with acidic foods, adversely affecting their flavors, and also is prone to rusting and pitting.	Before its first use, season by washing with soapy water, rinse, and dry. Brush with a neutral-tasting cooking oil on all food contact surfaces. Add another 2 inches of oil to the pan and heat for 1 hour in a 300°F. oven. Remove from the oven, cool to room temperature, then discard the oil and wipe the pan dry. After each use, wash, dry, then wipe with a lightly oiled paper towel. Never use abrasives as they will ruin the seasoning.
Copper	A fine conductor of heat, and also durable and resistant to corrosion. Because it can react toxically with some foods, copper is almost always lined with tin, stainless steel, or silver.	Does not retain heat well. Expensive.	To protect the linings from scratches, use nylon or wood utensils. To prevent blistering, never place the pans on a flame when empty or overheat them. Wash in hot, soapy water and dry at once. Soak to remove any burned-on foods; never scour. Use a commercial copper polish to brighten the exterior as necessary.
Glass, Ceramics (earthenware, stoneware, and porcelain), and Ceramic Glass	Retains heat well. Nonreactive, usually microwaveable (they should have no metal content or trim), and occasionally suitable for stovetop use (check the manufacturer's directions).	Poor heat conductors. Glass and ceramics can crack with radical temperature changes and, for safety's sake, should always be used on top of a diffuser. (There is a potential danger of lead poisoning from cooking, storing, or serving in some decorative glazed ceramic ware from abroad, so use questionable ceramic dishes for decoration, not cooking.)	Wash in hot, soapy water and soak to remove any burned-on food. To avoid scratching glazes, refrain from scouring.

Cookware Composition and Care (*continued*)

MATERIAL	ADVANTAGES	DISADVANTAGES	CARE
Phenolic Resins	Sold under the tradename Bakelite. Allows microwaves to pass through so that food cooks. The plastics are easy to clean, relatively inexpensive, and can withstand low conventional-oven heat.	Brittle. Does not conduct heat well.	Wash in hot, sudsy water and scour to remove burned-on foods.
Porcelain on Metal	Cast iron and steel are frequently coated with a highly durable glass to prevent corrosion, resist stains, and prevent reaction with acidic foods. The characteristics of all pots and pans that are coated with frit (the fused or calcinated material used in glassmaking) then fired remain similar to their bare metal: good heat absorption and adequate heat conduction.	The porcelain-enamel coating is fragile, can chip, and may crack if exposed to radical temperature changes.	Wash in warm, sudsy water with a cloth; soak in soapy water to remove burned-on foods or stubborn stains and avoid scouring. Use only wood or nylon utensils when working with coated metal pans.
Stainless Steel	Durable, corrosion-resistant, and nonreactive	Notoriously poor heat conductor; as a result is almost always combined with aluminum, copper, and/or carbon steel to improve conduction. This is achieved by fusing a copper or aluminum disk to the bottom of a vessel or by sandwiching—"cladding"—these metals together in various combinations.	Wash in hot, sudsy water and scrub with a nylon pad.
Tinned Steel	As reliable as it is economical. The baker's choice for most specialty pans and plaques.	The coated metal tends to discolor and cannot be heated above its 449°F. melting point.	Wash in hot, sudsy water and dry immediately. Soak to remove stubborn food particles, but resist the temptation to scour, as it will scratch the surface.

Microwave-Safe Cookware

These days it's not hard to find cookware that is safe for the microwave—basically, most ceramics, glass, china, and pottery are safe. To test whether a certain dish is microwave safe, place it in the microwave oven next to (not touching) a glass measuring cup that contains ½ cup of water. Microwave on high for one minute. If the dish becomes very warm or hot, it should not be used in the microwave.

Paper towels and paper plates labeled microwave safe can be used in the microwave if the food is moist and the total cooking time is less than 10 minutes on high power.

clad metal pans are more durable than those with finishes, which tend to wear off. A good, basic selection of saucepans includes 1-, 2-, and 3-quart sizes.

Double boiler.** A double boiler makes preparing smooth, egg-based sauces or custards almost foolproof. Essentially two stacked saucepans, it can convey only gentle heat from the boiling water held in its lower saucepan, so the warming egg ingredients in the top pan don't curdle as readily as they emulsify. Double boilers have 3-cup to 2-quart capacities. Both pan and insert hold the same measure. Avoid aluminum double boilers, which will discolor eggs, and light-gauge enameled steel double boilers, because they chip easily.

Stockpot.** A tall, narrow, straight-sided pot is perfect for preparing the liquid base for soups and sauces. Its substantial height enables it to hold the large amounts of bones, meat, and vegetables that are needed to prepare stock, while its tight diameter restricts evaporation during the standard 4- to 6-hour simmers. A 12-quart stockpot with sturdy handles is recommended, the best of which are manufactured in clad stainless steel, stainless steel with an aluminum disk base, or anodized aluminum.

STEAMERS

Steamer inserts.** Any tightly covered, sizable saucepan or pot can be converted into a steamer if you have a perforated steamer insert. A folding metal one has 1-inch legs to suspend food above simmering water. Its stainless steel overlapping leaves (like those of a flower's petals) create sides that expand to 9 inches and contract to 5 inches, thereby allowing it to fit into variously sized pots and pans. Lidded bamboo steamers, which allow steam to vent through their slatted bases, are designed for use in a wok and are often stacked atop one another. Slower-to-cook foods are straddled above the wok's simmering water, then left to steam; when a meal's quicker-to-cook foods

Nonreactive Cookware

When a recipe calls for *nonreactive cookware*, you should use pots and pans that will not be affected by the acid in citrus juice, vinegar, fruits, wine, or tomatoes. Cookware made of glass, enamel, enameled cast iron, stainless steel, and most nonstick finishes are safe to use. Anodized aluminum is also nonreactive. Pots made of unlined aluminum, copper, or cast iron may react with the acidic foods to produce an off flavor or discolor the food.

require heating, their steamers are set above those already in action—carefully timed so that everything is ready at once. Bamboo steamers have diameters of 4 to 11 inches.

All-purpose steamer.** This 4-piece stackable steamer is dependable for general-purpose use. It comes with a base pot, two perforated steamer inserts, and a cover. It is large enough to contain the water needed to complete its task and balance the two inserts. It should have a snug-fitting cover to prevent steam from escaping. Steamers are manufactured in aluminum or stainless steel with 3- to 8-quart capacities.

Vegetable steamer.*** This two-part, tin-lined copper pot is as handsome as it is adept at steaming and serving vegetables. Its tall, tight, 1½-quart base limits evaporation to allow for lengthy steaming. Its perforated insert is bow-sided to expand capacity and enhance balance.

Asparagus steamer.*** This tall, tight stainless steel container with its basket insert is used to steam asparagus stalks upright. Since asparagus stalks are thicker and therefore require more cooking than their slender, more delicate tips, this cylindrical pot is designed to boil the bases as the tips steam. Thanks to the handled basket, it simultaneously removes and drains them once they are cooked to perfection. Cylindrical asparagus steamers come in 3½- and 6-quart sizes.

Pressure cooker.** This pot operates by using superhot steam to cook food quickly. Once its cover is hermetically sealed to create a pressurized environment, the contained cooking liquid can boil at 250°F. rather than 212°F., water's boiling point in an open vessel at sea level. Consequently, cooking times are reduced, fuel is saved, and food flavors are retained. A fine pressure cooker is made of a nonreactive metal that disperses heat evenly. It should be fitted with two safety valves—one to release excess steam and the other to prevent any premature opening if internal pressure is still present. Popular pressure cooker capacities range from roughly 5 to 9 quarts and are especially useful for preparing braises, stews, and beans that usually require lengthy cooking.

Trivet/steamer rack.** This three-footed, 5-inch-wide ring transforms any saucepan or shallow roaster into a workable bain marie (hot water bath) fit to cook steamed puddings, custards, or terrines. Its small band of aluminum promises complete hot water access to an onset pot, while its grooved surface creates traction for sure placement.

PANS FOR FRYING

Skillet (frying pan).* A shallow, flare-sided pan made of a heavy-gauge, heat-conducting metal is unmatched to rapidly cook foods in

▶ **Steaming, 183, 211, 212**

Nonstick Surfaces

Polyfluoroethylene—whose trade names include Tefal, Teflon, and Silverstone—and silicone are the thermoplastic coatings that are referred to as "nonstick" surfaces on pots and pans. Neither affects the heat conductivity of its underlying metal, yet both resist adhesion and are nonreactive. The pans they coat allow reduced-fat cooking and are easy to clean. However, they must be treated with care. The coatings eventually wear off through use and should be used with plastic, rubber, or wood utensils that are less likely to scratch their surfaces.

After use, keep them clean with hot, sudsy water and soak in warm water to remove any burned-on bits of food instead of scouring.

small amounts of fat. The pan's thick base should spread heat evenly; its low sides make it easy to turn and lift foods, while the slope of the sides helps to disperse steam and enhance a clean fry. Skillets are manufactured in all the standard metals with diameters that range from 6 to 14 inches.

Sauté pan.** Chefs constantly slide this wide, shallow, straight-sided pan across a burner to quickly cook foods in small amounts of hot fat. The pan's wide, flat bottom supplies ample room on which to shake and toss foods as they cook, while its generally 3-inch-deep sides deter foods from accidentally flying out during such spirited maneuvers. Good sauté pans with 6½- to 14-inch diameters are manufactured in tin-lined copper, clad stainless steel, and stainless steel with an aluminum disk bottom.

Omelet pan.** The traditional omelet pan is wide and low with gently curved, outwardly sloping sides. Its roughly 10-inch diameter accommodates standard 3-egg omelets. The 2-inch-deep sides invite the rapid-fire stirring needed initially to fluff the setting eggs, while curved sides make it easy to roll the folded omelet out and onto an awaiting warmed plate. Fine, heavy-gauge aluminum or carbon steel omelet pans must be seasoned before first use.

Crêpe pan.** A low carbon steel pan with widely flared sides is used to produce the feather-light French pancakes called crêpes. The pan's sides are shallow and angled so a spatula can be slipped easily under the crêpe to turn it. Dessert crêpe pans measure 6½ inches in diameter while entrée crêpe pans measure 7¼ to 9½ inches. All are manufactured in carbon steel and must be seasoned before their first use.

Griddle.*** A thick cast-iron griddle is ideal for cooking pancakes, bacon, eggs, and minute steaks. The cast iron absorbs and conveys the high heat needed for short-order cooking without the chance of its

♦ Sautéing, 182, 207–211

warping or buckling. Its having no true sides, meanwhile, makes it easy to maneuver food with a spatula. Square and round cast-iron griddles measure 9 inches to 12 inches and fit neatly atop a single burner; oblong griddles can measure 20 inches by 9 inches or 20 inches by 11 inches and straddle two burners. All must be seasoned before their first use.

Paella pan.* A broad, shallow pan with outwardly sloping sides supplies plenty of space for preparing paella, the national dish of Spain. Its large diameter prompts the immediate heat contact to quickly cook the chicken, pork, sausage, and shrimp before the saffron-scented rice, tomatoes, clams, and mussels are added. The pan is fitted with two handles for easy transfer from rangetop to table. (Paella is always served directly from its pan.) Diameters range from 14 inches (the most popular) to 20 inches.

Waffle iron. A good manual waffle iron is made of lightweight aluminum to rapidly conduct the high heat needed for stovetop baking and easy maneuvers. Its grid surface should be encircled with a runnel to catch excess batter, while its handles are best capped with stay-cool wood or hard plastic. There are two distinct types of manual waffle irons: deep grid surfaces to create Belgian waffles and a shallow iron to make standard waffles. Electric waffle irons range from those that make shallow waffles to those that have changeable grids for making the shallow or Belgian variety, as well as plates for grilling sandwiches. Most have nonstick surfaces, and all should be moderately weighty with skid-free feet.

Wok. You will find the wide, deep, round-bottomed wok the ultimate Oriental cooking vessel. Its smooth, deep bowl shape evenly diffuses heat and extends the actual cooking surface on which to stir-fry, steam, braise, boil, smoke, and simmer foods. Round-bottomed woks have diameters that range from 12 to 30 inches and must be balanced atop separately sold metal wok rings. A good choice is a 14-inch diameter wok in carbon steel. Woks are also available in aluminum, anodized aluminum, and cast iron. Electric woks are also available.

Deep fryer.* A good deep fryer must be wide enough to accommodate quantities of food without crowding, deep enough to hold hot oil to both immerse food and account for oil's bubbling rise, and fitted with a basket for easy retrieval. Deep fryers are manufactured in aluminum or carbon steel with 2- to 8-quart capacities for home use. The 4-quart size is most convenient—and should be used in conjunction with a deep-fat thermometer. Electric deep fryers are also available.

Chicken fryer.* A wide, 3-inch-deep cast-iron pan is well designed to fry chicken. It is deep enough to hold a generous layer of oil and to thwart excessive splattering, while its cast-iron surface retains and disperses heat uniformly. All chicken fryers are fitted with a side spout to pour off oil when the cooking is complete. Manufacturers suggest these pans be used for casserole cooking, provided acidic foods (which would react with this metal) aren't included. Cast-iron chicken fryers require seasoning before first use.

SPECIALTY POTS AND PANS

Egg poacher.** An international array of utensils is made to help you turn out picture-perfect poached eggs. The small ceramic container from England with its screw-on cap is filled with a dab of butter and an egg, then placed in simmering water, which actually coddles the egg. The oval, perforated stainless steel bowl from France is footed so it can stand and support a poaching egg in barely bubbling water. The indented pan insert from America contains three shallow, round, non-stick bowls and sits above a covered pan's simmering water to steam cook eggs. All create eggs with their whites well contained; a feat some consider nearly impossible if one of these tools isn't used.

Stovetop broiler.*** Also called a grill pan, this ridge-bottomed, shallow cast-iron pan is set on a burner over high heat and used to broil steaks, lamb chops, hamburgers, and fish. It heats evenly, is warp-resistant, and—with an 11½-inch diameter—fits neatly atop one burner. Its ridged bottom lifts food above fat for clean, rangetop broiling.

Fondue pot.*** Designed for tableside cooking, traditional cheese fondue pots, which are made of glazed earthenware, sit atop a frame with a candle-warmer beneath. The pot can only withstand and transmit gentle heat, so the cheese won't overheat and separate to make the fondue stringy. The pot's 9-inch diameter provides sufficient room in which to dip and swirl bread-laden fondue forks. Cheese fondue pots usually have 2-quart capacities. They can also hold melted chocolate for dipping fruit and broth for gently cooking Oriental-style meat and vegetable tidbits.

Chafing dish.*** A good chafing dish has a food tray and an underlying water pan set in a sturdy frame above an adjustable fuel compartment. Simmering water is added to the water pan before use and it keeps hot hors d'oeuvres or entrées at their perfect serving temperature during buffets and banquets. Be sure to place your chafing dish on a thick cork pad to protect the tabletop's finish from this pan's heat. Chafing dish capacities range from 3 pints to 7 quarts and are available in a wide variety of materials, from silverplate to tin-lined copper to stainless steel-lined copper.

Tea kettle.* A stout container with a high-set, stationary handle and a well-angled spout is the ideal vessel in which to boil water rapidly. It maximizes heat contact, is easy to fill, and is safe to pour. Aluminum, clad stainless steel, and tin-lined copper are all excellent quick-to-heat

(continued on page 162)

A Look at Coffee Makers*

No kitchen is complete without a coffee maker, but which kind is best? The answer depends on what you want in a coffee maker—and that includes convenience and taste. Here's a look at the most popular types.

Filter-drip coffeepot. Once its plastic cone is fitted with a disposable paper or permanent gold insert, filled with a measured amount of coffee grounds, then set atop its carafe and near-boiling water added, this popular coffeepot produces a quick, aromatic brew. International favorites that require no paper filters include the 4-part French porcelain version with its cylindrical strainer and the 3-part Italian Neapolitan pot that must be upended for water to pass from its boiling container into its serving carafe. As is the case in every filter-drip coffeepot, water has full contact with grounds to properly extract flavor, the filter prevents the passage of coffee grounds, and the brewed coffee remains true to taste in the nonreactive glass, porcelain, or stainless steel carafe. Manual and electric filter-drip coffeepots are available with 6- to 12-cup capacities.

Percolator coffeepot. Both stovetop and electric models work in much the same way as their filter-drip cousin. Near-boiling water is passed through filter-held grounds to produce a rich, aromatic beverage. The water boils, vents up through the pot's central stem, and across the grounds suspended in its filter. With stovetop percolators, you have to watch the coffeepot and remove it from the heat to halt the brewing. Percolator coffeepots come with 2- to 50-cup capacities, and the larger their capacity, the more likely they are to be electric.

Plunge-filter coffeepot. This framed glass carafe is designed to both brew and serve coffee. Near-boiling water is poured onto the grounds and the water and coffee grinds mix in the pot. After due time has passed for flavor extraction, the pot's screen filter is inserted into the container and depressed to trap the spent grounds at the base of the pot for the coffee to be served. Plunge-filter coffeepots are manufactured with 3- to 12-cup capacities; the most durable have chromed-steel (not plastic) frames.

Espresso maker. This three-part, pinch-waisted coffee maker is used to brew strong Italian coffee. Water is heated to a boil in its base; as steam, it funnels up a central shaft, through filter-held coffee grounds, and up into the top half of the pot, where it collects and from where it is poured. Manual espresso machines are manufactured in cast aluminum with 1- to 14-demitasse-cup capacities. Electric espresso makers are also available.

◗ Coffee, 110–111

metals. All tea kettles should be sweetened every now and then by boiling water in them with a few tablespoons of baking soda.

STOVETOP ACCESSORIES

Heat diffuser.** When set atop a burner, this chromed-steel pad protects ceramic dishes or glass carafes from direct heat as their contents keep warm. The diffuser's two disks, sandwiched air space, and gridded surface all contribute to temper and disperse rangetop heat. The pad is preferred over a wire trivet that raises a carafe or baking dish above an electric element or a ridged enameled plate that fits on a gas burner because it is more stable. Heat diffusers with 8-inch diameters fit neatly over a burner.

Splatter shield.*** Placed on a skillet or chicken fryer, a lightweight, perforated metal disk is terrific for curtailing excessive splattering. Its 11½-inch diameter tops any number of variously sized skillets while its mesh (or perforated) surface allows food steam to pass, but blocks most airborne oil. Good stovetop splatter screens are usually finished with stay-cool, plastic-capped handles. Plastic shields made for the microwave look like domed pot covers with narrow, concentric slots that deter grease from splattering.

OVEN ROASTING PANS

Shallow roasting pan.* A good roasting pan has 2-inch sides to expose meat or poultry to as much oven heat as possible. It should be fairly large to accommodate all sizes of meat or poultry and moderately heavy to prevent warping. Before buying an aluminum, stainless steel, enameled steel, or tin-lined copper roasting pan, measure your oven; a roasting pan should sit at least 2 inches away from each of your oven's four walls.

Deep roasting pan.*** A 19- by 13- by 6-inch covered pan is preferred by many to roast a large bird or cut of meat. The food is easily contained: the depth deters splattering in the oven, and the standard, dimpled dome lid bastes as it covers meat by directing condensed steam droplets back onto the roast. Yet, rather than truly roast, these pans create a moist environment in which foods steam cook rather than dry roast. As with the shallow roasting pan, select one that is moderately heavy so it won't buckle, and look for one fitted with sturdy handles for safe transfers. It should allow at least a 2-inch clearance space in the oven to circulate heat properly.

Roasting rack.* A chromed steel wire roasting rack is crucial to expose as much flesh as possible to oven heat and to distance food from rendered fat and juices. The most versatile racks fold to various

▸ **Roasting, 227–240**

V-shaped positions and support loins, saddles, or birds. They are easy to store and more practical than having one flat rack designed to hold standing rib and crown roasts and one V-shaped rack that suits poultry and larger cuts of meat. A vertical roaster is also made that supports upended chickens, ducks, and geese while they cook. Although manufacturers imply that the vertical roaster reduces cooking time due to the heat it channels internally, this roasting rack's genuine merit lies in its ability to drain off the excessive, rendering fat from roasting ducks and geese.

Dutch oven.* The precursor to today's Dutch oven straddled the stoked hearth of yore where it slowly simmered meats and broth. Hefty cast iron was the favorite metal then—as it is now—because it absorbs, retains, and conveys heat better than any lighter weight metal. The finest of these modern, low, wide casseroles are enamel-coated so acidic foods can't react with the bare metal. They also have snug-fitting lids to block escaping steam. Round casseroles come in 4- to 10-quart capacities; the oval ones are to prepare whole poultry or long cuts of meat, and have 3- to 6½-quart capacities.

FOR THE MICROWAVE

Microwave browning dish.** This microwave-safe baking dish has a metal surface on the bottom. When brushed with butter or oil and pre-heated in the microwave, the dish will allow sandwiches and other similar small pieces of food to brown.

BAKING DISHES

Baking dishes.* Porcelain, earthenware, and ovenproof glass versions of shallow roasting pans come in handy when preparing layered and sauced entrées. Their compositions allow the slow, steady heat conduction that best cooks foods like lasagna and moussaka, while their 2-inch sides make serving easy. Oval, square, and round porcelain and earthenware baking dishes are superb for use in microwave ovens.

Begin your collection with a 9-inch square baking dish and add on, depending on the quantity of food you cook.

Gratin dish.** To enjoy the crisp golden brown crusts that crown sauced crabmeat, potatoes, and chicken, you'll need a low, wide, slope-sided dish. It is shallow and broad to expose a maximum amount of surface for crusting, and fitted with outwardly sloping sides to disperse as much food steam as possible for proper browning. The opposite-set handles that handsomely finish a gratin dish makes it easy to remove from beneath a broiler's flame. Oval gratin dishes are available with lengths that measure 10½ to 17½ inches; round ones are 4¾ to

9½ inches in diameter. Gratin dishes are manufactured in porcelain and earthenware.

Bean pot.*** This bulbous, glazed earthenware, covered pot is used to slowly cook the New England favorite, baked beans. It is nearly as deep as it is wide to promote uniform baking, and tight-necked and capped to minimize liquid evaporation. Bean pots are available with 2- to 6-quart capacities.

Custard cups.** These tall, slope-sided porcelain containers are used to bake and present single servings of custard and rice pudding. They are made of ceramic to uniformly conduct gentle heat and curved in profile to make it easy to reach every spoonful of a creamy dessert. Porcelain, glazed earthenware, and ovenproof glass custard cups with 5- to 8-ounce capacities can also be used to bake popovers and melt chocolate.

Ramekins.*** These small porcelain containers look like miniature soufflé dishes and are used to prepare and serve the individual, cheese-based custards called ramekins. They are twice as wide as they are deep to convey a water bath's even heat and crafted in porcelain so as not to alter delicate egg flavor or color. Three-ounce to 16-ounce ramekins are also used for serving individual pâtés and baked eggs.

Soufflé dish.** This round, deep, straight-sided porcelain container is tailor-made to produce a high-rising soufflé. It is round to heat evenly and tall with straight sides to support and upwardly direct an expanding egg-based mixture. Soufflé dish exteriors are traditionally fluted to duplicate the pleated paper case that was often used to prepare soufflés. Ovenproof glass and stoneware soufflé dishes are also manufactured with 1- to 4-quart capacities. A 2-quart soufflé dish is a good all-purpose size.

Terrine.*** This long, lidded, enameled cast-iron mold is unsurpassed for baking the ground meat mixtures called terrines. The heavy metal conveys heat gently and uniformly; the tight shape promises neat slices; and the vented lid traps steam to prevent a hard, top crust from forming as it bakes. Oval, octagonal, and round terrines are also available in earthenware and porcelain. So, too, are charming bisque ones whose lids come crowned with realistic game heads to indicate the type of terrine within. Terrines commonly come in 1- to 2-quart capacities.

Pots de crème.*** Small, covered porcelain pots are used to prepare and present individual servings of rich custard creams. Once a whisked egg mixture is poured into each cup, they are baked in a water bath; each cup is immediately removed and, if served hot, covered with a cap to prevent a top skin from forming. If served cold, the pudding is cooled, traditionally topped with a candied violet, then capped and served. Pots de crème are only manufactured in porcelain,

Exotic Cookware

There are numerous single-purpose pots and pans that are highly effective and often so unique in shape and style that they are frequently used to serve the dish they help to cook. You probably do not *need* these items, but if you have the space for them, they can be fun and helpful to own.

☐ *Fish poachers.* Oblong, low, lidded pots that are fitted with a rack to cradle, cook, and remove a whole fish.

☐ *Couscoussier.* It looks like two stacked bulbous pots but is in fact a bottom pot and steamer insert that are used to stew and steam couscous, a North African semolina-based dish.

☐ *Chestnut pan.* Looks like a frying pan with a perforated bottom and is used to roast chestnuts above a fire.

☐ *Blini pan.* Resembles a tiny, 4¾-inch-wide skillet and is used to prepare the rich, yeast-leavened Russian pancakes called blini.

☐ *Sugar boiler.* Looks like a straight-sided and spouted saucepan. It is only manufactured in heavy-gauge copper to respond rapidly to heat, a crucial factor when boiling sugar syrups.

which conveys the necessary gentle, uniform heat that won't curdle custard. Capacities range from 2 ½ to 8 ounces.

FOR THE BARBECUE

Grill basket.** A hinged, wire frame is a terrific tool to hold small, awkwardly shaped, or otherwise delicate foods as they grill. The best have wide-set, heavy-gauge wires to expose as much surface as possible to flames and are fitted with a latch to secure closings. Look for baskets that are hinge set rather than linked with open rings because they hold food more firmly. In addition to general-purpose ones, uniquely shaped grill baskets are made to hold hamburgers, hot dogs, kabobs, or fish. Some have nonstick surfaces, but they are more frequently manufactured in chromed steel. Remember to lightly brush steel grill baskets with oil before using.

Skewers.** Long, flat stainless steel skewers with looped heads are perfect for threading cubed food for grilling. The food won't slip when the skewers are turned, and the end cap makes it easy to handle as well as prevent food from falling off. Bamboo, chromed, and stainless steel skewers are manufactured in lengths from 4 to 14 inches. Serve appetizers on 4-inch skewers, while 10- to 12-inch lengths are standard for entrée kabobs. If you are using bamboo, remember to soak the skewers in water for 30 minutes before use to prevent burning.

♦ **Barbecuing, 178, 241–254**

BASTING UTENSILS

Bulb baster.** To keep roasting meat and poultry moist and flavorful, use this long syringe to apply melted fat and juices. Its ½-cup capacity suctions and dispenses rapidly while the 10-inch length creates an easy reach across large roasts and a comfortable work distance. Many come complete with injector needles and brushes for cleaning the inside of the shaft. They are manufactured in see-through plastic or glass, or in stainless steel, the most durable.

Basting brush.** A wide natural-bristle brush with a long, angled handle can't be beat for basting grilling meat with melted fat or marinade. Natural bristles pick up and dispense liquids far more efficiently than synthetic, while a crooked handle eases the reach behind meats or poultry yet keeps hands far from white-hot embers. Brushes with 12-inch handles are recommended; the best are braced with a seamless nylon ferrule.

*B*akeware, Pastry Tools, and Molds

Glistening tarts, feather-light cakes, lacy cookies, and crusty breads all begin with fine-quality ingredients that are measured accurately and mixed properly, then baked in a few specialized pans.

For starters, you should have a reliable mixer, a few bowls, and spatulas. For pies and tarts, you will need a rolling pin and pastry brush. To decorate cakes, you may want a pastry bag and a few decorator tips. From that point on, it's up to you to decide how you want your pastry to look, then to purchase the appropriate round, square, or rectangular pans. But before buying any pan or mold, consider size and general shape in relation to the doughs and batters you intend to bake. A yeast dough, for example, won't rise high in a shallow pan or on a flat sheet. Batter poured into too broad a pan burns easily, and into too small a pan, overflows.

Also consider a baking pan's finish, as it helps to develop or deter the dark crust that's welcome on breads but unwanted on cakes. Dark steel, for instance, rapidly absorbs and conveys oven heat to produce dark crusts, whereas shiny, tinned steel and aluminum deflect some oven heat to produce golden crusts.

Like baking pans, other food molds are made of various materials to suit particular tasks. Ice cream and gelatin molds, for example, are made of aluminum, tinned steel, or stainless steel to quickly transmit a refrigerator's chill. Butter and candy molds, on the other hand, are most often made of plastic to enable you to release the food with a sharp twist.

▶ **Basting, 178**

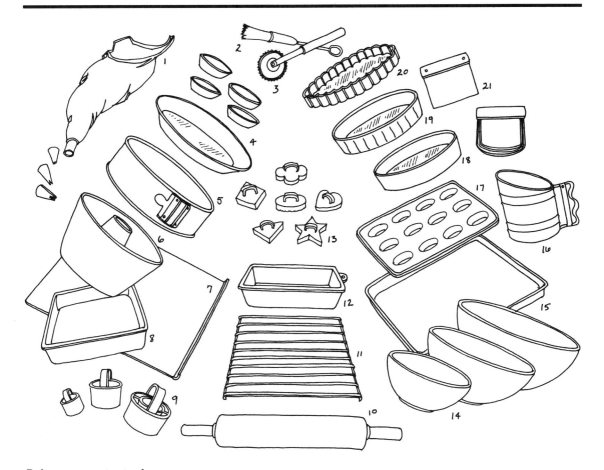

Bakeware, pastry tools, and molds. 1 Pastry bag and tips **2** Pastry brush **3** Pastry wheel **4** Pie plate **5** Springform pan **6** Tube pan **7** Cookie sheet **8** Square baking pan **9** Pastry cutters **10** Rolling pin **11** Wire cooling rack **12** Loaf pan **13** Cookie cutters **14** Mixing bowls **15** Jelly-roll pan **16** Sifter **17** Muffin pan **18** Layer cake pan **19** Quiche dish **20** Tart pan with removable bottom **21** Pastry scraper

The range of quality for metal bakeware and molds is broad. Lightweight ones are readily available, but they are sure to dent and quick to buckle with use. The heavier-gauge, reinforced pans and molds found in kitchenware shops and some department stores last many years. They may be costlier, but they more than pay their way through their long life and the better-looking, finer-quality products they create.

MIXING BOWLS

Mixing bowls.* A graduated set of bowls is needed in any kitchen to mix ingredients, assemble salads, whip cream, cool gelatin, and heat food in a microwave oven. Narrow, deep bowls are particularly good for mixing and beating as their tall sides readily contain ingredients; they are also good for protecting rising yeast doughs from drafts. Broad bowls are better suited for quickly cooling hot liquids because they allow better air circulation.

Emergency Baking Dish and Pan Substitutes

You can usually substitute a pan of equal volume if you don't have the exact baking pan suggested by a recipe. However, some rules do apply: If your pan is made of glass instead of the metal suggested or is shallower than the one recommended, reduce the baking time by 25 percent; and if the pan is deeper than the one recommended, increase the stated baking time by 25 percent.

IF A RECIPE SUGGESTS:	YOU MAY SUBSTITUTE:
4-Cup Baking Dish	9-inch pie pan
	8- by 1½-inch round layer-cake pan
	7⅜- by 3⅝- by 2⅝-inch loaf pan
6-Cup Baking Dish	10-inch pie pan
	8- by 2-inch round layer-cake pan
	9- by 1½-inch round layer-cake pan
	8 ½- by 4½- by 2-inch loaf pan
8-Cup Baking Dish	9- by 2-inch round layer-cake pan
	8- by 8- by 2-inch square cake pan
	9- by 9- by 1½-inch square cake pan
	9- by 5- by 3-inch loaf pan
Three 8-Inch Layer-Cake Pans	Two 9-inch square cake pans
Two 9-Inch Layer-Cake Pans	Two 8-inch square cake pans
	13- by 9- by 2-inch baking dish

You might start with a set of light to medium-weight, 1- to 4-quart bowls that rest flat on a work surface. Stainless steel bowls are great for multipurpose work, but ovenproof glass and plastic ones are a near necessity for some microwave preparations.

Copper bowl.*** A broad, round-bottomed, unlined copper bowl is unquestionably the best vessel in which to beat egg whites to their maximum volume. The breadth and round shape of the bowl invite rapid aeration and smooth whisk strokes, while the unlined metal reacts electrolytically with egg whites to produce the stablest foam possible. Copper bowl sizes—as measured by their top diameters—range from 9 to 12 inches. The heaviest usually have a rolled wrap-around rim and will maintain their shape far better than lighter-weight bowls.

PASTRY TOOLS

Sifter.* A single-mesh stainless steel sifter is used to remove lumps and uniformly aerate flour for baking. Recipes will say whether the flour should be sifted before measuring.

Some sifters have double and triple screens and can be battery pow-ered or spring set, both of which leave one hand free for any necessary stirring or mixing. But the simpler the sifter, the less there is to break. Sifters come with 1- to 8-cup capacities; a 3-cup size should suffice for most baking tasks.

Rolling pin.** A long, smooth, handle-free wooden cylinder is pre-ferred by professionals for general-purpose rolling chores. No handles allow the close hand-to-pastry contact that promotes even rolls and uniformly thin doughs; a 20-inch barrel covers maximum surface and is easy to wipe clean. If you opt for a two-handled wooden rolling pin, select one with bearing-set handles rather than stationary or dowel-set ones. Specialty rolling pins include those with grid-faced wooden bar-rels to mark pasta sheets for ravioli, ribbed plastic barrels to incorpo-rate butter into puff-pastry dough, hobnailed wooden barrels to notch Swedish hardtack dough, and carved wooden ones with multi motif barrels to emboss springerle cookie dough. When buying any rolling pin, inspect its barrel to make sure it's free from nicks and gouges.

Pastry cloth.** When set on a flat surface, a medium-sized, plastic-coated cotton cloth is a good alternative to a marble slab for rolling out pastry dough. It requires a minimum amount of flour so it won't offset a dough's proper flour-to-fat ratio, plus the cloth facilitates moving the dough from countertop to pie pan.

Pastry board.*** A medium to large polished marble slab is the ulti-mate surface on which to roll dough. It is naturally cool, so dough doesn't stick or require further flouring, and supersmooth to ease rolling. A marble board can also be used for cooling candy syrups.

BASIC BAKING SHEETS AND PANS

Cookie sheet.* A flat, rimless, heavy-gauge aluminum sheet has no peer for baking cookies. It should be thick to prevent buckling, which might occur at high baking temperatures, heavy aluminum to conduct heat evenly, and sideless to allow full, hot-air access to batters. Cush-ioned, or insulated, cookie sheets—which are actually two thin alu-minum sheets sandwiching an air pocket—temper heat and conse-quently are particularly good for the longer baking (but little browning) required for meringues. If you have a problem with overbrowning cookies, you may want to invest in a cushioned cookie sheet.

Layer-cake pans.* Bakers favor heavy, seamless aluminum baking pans because they are easy to maintain and quick to heat. Their straight, shallow sides promote a batter's even rise while their rolled edges and medium weight promise long-lasting, clean shapes. Two-inch deep, round layer-cake pans range from 3 to 24 inches in diame-ter; square ones measure 8 x 8 x 2 inches and 9 x 9 x 2 inches.

Single-Purpose Baking Pans

Special breads and cakes often require particular molds to help their specific dough or batter achieve its characteristic shape. These pans may be made of tinned or black steel or plain or nonstick coated aluminum. Black steel promotes the development of a good crust. The pans include:

☐ *Pullman bread loaf pan.* **A long, covered loaf pan that bakes perfect, brick-shaped, close-textured breads for sandwiches and canapés.**

☐ *Baba au rhum mold.* **Looks like a giant thimble and is used to bake small, yeast-raised, rum-soaked cakes.**

☐ *Savarin mold.* **A low, wide, sleek ring mold used to bake a sweet, similarly named yeast cake that is then soaked in liquor and filled with glazed fruit or whipped cream.**

☐ *Panettone pan.* **Looks like a tall, tight, tinned-steel pail and is used to bake the famous Milanese Christmas cake or a buttery brioche mousseline.**

☐ *Madeleine plaque.* **These individual, shallow, shell-shaped molds help to turn out the buttery tea cakes called madeleines.**

Square and rectangular baking pans.* Professionals rely on high-quality, straight-sided, heavy aluminum rectangular baking pans that heat quickly and uniformly and are harder to dent than lightweight pans. They are readily available in kitchenware stores, but if you have access only to lightweight pans, remember to line their bottoms and sides with buttered parchment or baking paper to prevent batters from overbrowning.

Jelly-roll pan.** Sheet cakes and jelly rolls are best produced in a broad, shallow, rectangular pan. It exposes the maximum amount of batter to oven heat, so it bakes quickly and remains moist. Select a moderately heavy aluminum pan with a rolled rim that will maintain its shape. Remember to line the pan with parchment paper before adding batter to be sure the cake will release cleanly.

Loaf pan.** A simple, hollow-brick mold is essential to bake neatly shaped, round-topped breads and cakes. Depending on the type of loaf you prepare, there's a pan to suit your needs. Tinned steel is recommended for pound cakes, fruitcakes, and meat loafs; since the shiny metal deflects some oven heat, crusts don't brown before the center is done. Black steel molds better suit yeast breads; the steel absorbs and conveys heat to develop a crackling crust.

Pie plate.* When given a choice, professional bakers select two different types of pie pans, depending upon the kind of pie they are baking: Aluminum pans are picked for filled pies and black steel is chosen

♦ **Rolling a cake roll, 273**
♦ **Breads, 274, 282–287**

for unfilled ("blind") pies. Since shiny aluminum deflects some oven heat, a crust won't overly brown before its center is cooked; while black steel rapidly absorbs and transmits oven heat to quickly bake and brown a blind pastry crust. Glass pie plates are also fine to use, but reduce the oven temperature by 25 degrees when you bake in them. Standard pie pan diameters measure 8 inches, 9 inches, and 10 inches.

Pie weights.*** Scatter a number of these aluminum pellets on a piece of aluminum foil on the bottom of an unfilled pastry shell to prevent any blisters from forming on the crust as it bakes. Their weight deters air bubbles from forming and breaking through while their quick-to-heat aluminum composition helps bake the crust from the top. Remove the weights by lifting the aluminum foil sheet when the crust is half baked.

Ceramic pie weights are also manufactured and similarly packaged in 1- and 2.2-pound packages. (If you don't have pie weights, you can make do with uncooked rice or beans.)

Muffin pans.* Muffin pans generally come in three sizes—miniature (1⅞ inches by ¾ inch), regular (2¾ inches by 1½ inches), and large (3¾ inches by 2 inches). When buying, select a muffin tray manufactured in a fairly heavy gauge of metal—ideally tinned steel, nonstick coated, or plain aluminum; it will conduct heat well and last for years.

Pizza pans.** Two distinct types of pizza pans are available, depending upon the type of pie you want to enjoy: A flat, round one turns out the classic, thin-crusted, Neapolitan-style pizza and a 1½-inch deep, flare-sided one creates the deep-dish, Chicago-style pizza. The

For Perfect Pizza

If you're serious about preparing pizza, the following cookware will surely come in handy:

☐ *Round black steel baking sheets or deep dish pizza pans.* These rapidly conduct high oven heat for crispy crusts.

☐ *Perforated flat pizza pans.* These allow oven heat to reach the bottom of a dough to prevent it from being soggy.

☐ *Baking stone.* This is an unglazed, porous ceramic slab that transfers steady high heat and can absorb a dough's water to encourage a crisp crust.

☐ *Pizza peel.* This flat, wooden utensil shaped like a shovel slips under a pizza (or loaf of bread) to neatly transfer it to or remove it from an oven.

☐ *Pizza wheel.* Small metal wheels with handles for cutting straight slices. Wheels with 2½-inch diameters are fine for flat pizzas; those with 4-inch-wide wheels suit both flat and deep-dish pies.

◗ **Pies, 275–279**

Butcher's Twine

A skein of pure cotton twine can help to truss a chicken, stuff fish, bind a standing rib roast, even secure the collar on a souf-flé dish. Two types of unwaxed twine are made for kitchen use: the stout cotton is preferred over the less manageable thin linen, which won't stretch. Butcher's twine is frequently available in 50-yard skeins.

best quality pans are made of black steel, which absorbs and conveys heat rapidly and thereby develops crisp brown crusts. Flat, lightweight aluminum perforated pizza pans also produce superb results when used in conjunction with flat black steel pizza pans or baking stones.

Springform pan.** Dense fruit- and honey-cakes, as well as cheesecakes whose crumb crusts can't be unmolded easily, should be prepared in a springform pan. The sides snap open and are removed after baking to leave the base holding the cake completely intact. Tinned steel springform pans carry 6- to 12-inch diameters; silicone-coated ones are available with 10- and 12-inch diameters.

Tube pan.** Deep, round tube pans are most often used for baking and cooling angel cakes. The pan's towering central vent conveys heat to the batter's core to evenly bake it and later supports the upended cake as it cools. Some tube pans have removable bottoms for easy, postbake releases; the majority of these are manufactured in light-weight aluminum. Most recipes require a 9-cup-capacity tube pan measuring 10 inches by 4¼ inches.

Bundt pan.** This tall, broad, fluted cast aluminum ring is used to bake the popular, dense-crumb Bundt cake. The flutes add character and extend the amount of surface to dredge with sugar or a poured frosting, while the central hole promotes uniform baking and later eases slicing. Plain and nonstick Bundt pans with 12-cup capacities are manufactured, as are Bundtlette trays fitted with six 1-cup molds.

Tart pans.** A shallow black steel tart pan with a removable bottom is perfect for blind-baking golden brown pastry crusts. Use tinned steel pans when baking filled tarts because the shiny metal deflects some oven heat so the filling cooks completely before the crust becomes too dark. Round tart pans are available with diameters that measure from 4½ to 12½ inches.

Quiche dish.** This low, fluted porcelain dish is used to create the classic savory custard tart called a quiche. Its 1½-inch-deep sides expose most of its filling to oven heat so it sets rapidly, while its oven-proof porcelain assures uniform heat absorption and transmission. Handsome porcelain quiche dishes, which are ideal for conventional or microwave oven-to-table serving, are available with 5¼- to 12-inch diameters.

Brioche mold.*** The broadly flared, deeply crimped sides of this mold are designed to extend the actual crust of the buttery, egg-rich yeast bread called brioche. The molds are manufactured in tinned steel, porcelain, ovenproof glass, and black steel, which retains and conducts the constant heat that guarantees deliciously browned crusts.

Popover pan.*** Once this tray's tall, tapered black steel cups are preheated and slicked with oil, they are ready to produce the most feather-light, highest-rising popovers. Each cup's deep sides immediately set a proportionately large amount of batter, so internal steam has

◗ Tarts, 280

nowhere to go but up—taking with it the still-setting batter. A popover tray's six molds contain 5 ounces each.

Cornstick pan.*** Once an oven is heated to 500°F. and a seasoned, heavy cast-iron cornstick pan is set in to it to preheat, no other pan is better equipped to bake and brown this quick bread. The weighty cast iron won't buckle at that high temperature, while the charming notches and grooves that resemble a kerneled ear of corn actually expand the amount of surface to sear and set a loose batter. Cornstick pans are available with 5, 7, or 9 molds.

Cooling racks.** Footed round and rectangular wire racks dependably support freshly baked cakes and pastries as they cool. Their thin, tightly set wire surfaces prevent uneven settling while their small feet ensure that air circulates beneath a pastry as well as above it. Cake racks can also double as icing grates to hold foods as they are glazed with molten aspic or melted chocolate.

CUTTERS AND DECORATING TOOLS

Cookie press.** Fit the barrel of a cookie press with one of its accompanying cutting disks, fill the press with dough, attach its cover, and create picture-perfect cookies by pressing or cranking the top shaft or lever to neatly pipe out dough. Presses are usually sold with a variety of cutting disks and occasionally tips and tubes for piping out mashed potato platter garnishes or filling jelly doughnuts and eclairs.

Cookie cutters.** Plastic and metal cookie cutters come in all shapes and sizes to stamp out various shapes from rolled cookie dough.

Pastry cutters.** An assortment of round and oval, plain and fluted, rigid metal stamps are used to cut dough for pastry cases, biscuits, and doughnuts. The sides of pastry cutters should measure about 1½ inches high to contend with thin or thick sheets of dough, be moderately sharp to make clean cuts, and be finished with a rolled rim and soldered joins to maintain shape.

Pastry wheel.** A good pastry wheel has a sharp round blade so it won't tear or pull a carefully prepared dough sheet. It should also have a handle with a finger guard to prevent slips onto the tool's perpendicular wheel. The blade should be rigid to prevent buckling and securely attached to its axle. Small pastry wheels with zigzag (versus straight) edges are called pastry jaggers and are often used to cut the decorative strips for latticework pie and tart crusts.

Pastry crimper.** These tiny stainless steel tweezers with their two jagged working jaws are used to make the decorative borders on pies and tarts. Their toothed edges grip, score, and sever dough easily and the 4-inch length limits the warm hand contact that helps a dough's gluten to develop and toughen pastry.

◗ **Cookies, 274–275**

Pastry brushes.* Small, natural-bristle pastry brushes are kitchen workhorses for applying egg washes to doughs, fruit-based glazes to cakes and tarts, and melted butter to cake pans. The natural bristles absorb and dispense greater amounts of liquid than synthetic ones, so basting goes quickly. The finest pastry brushes are bonded firmly to their handles with tight nylon ferrules to prevent shedding. Flat brush heads measure from ½ to 4 inches in width and a 1½-inch head is the most versatile.

Dredger.** The delicate dusting of flour on dough, sugar on strudel, or cinnamon on cappuccino is best achieved with a dredger. The tiny holes in its perforated cap permit the barest amount to pass while its tight surface encourages accurate aim and a neat work area. Tin-lined copper, aluminum, and stainless steel dredgers are manufactured with 1-cup capacities; those with recognizably larger holes are meant to hold and dispense grated cheese.

Pastry bag.** A cone-shaped nylon bag is favored for piping decorative icing onto cakes, filling eclairs with pastry cream, and finishing platters with piped potatoes. The bag's nylon prevents the frequently high-fat fillings from seeping through while the double layering at its tip strengthens the bag at its most vulnerable point. Pastry bags are manufactured in 7- to 24-inch lengths; the most versatile is 16 inches.

Pastry tips.** Virtually dozens of tips are made to insert into a pastry bag to create scrolls, seashells, leaves, and petals with icing. Avoid tips made from tinned steel and nickel-plated brass. Instead choose stainless steel or polycarbonate ones; they'll remain rust-free and burrless for many years to come. A basic set of six pastry tips includes a fine writing tip, two star tips, and one each of leaf, petal, and ribbon tips. Many use a two-part plastic coupler (a threaded conical tube and fitted nut) to change these tubes for different effects in the middle of piping. The coupler fits securely into a filled pastry bag where its cone-shaped tube extends beyond the bag, creating an external threaded anchor for the twist-on coupling nut that cradles the selected decorating tip.

Cake decorating turntable.** Cake decorating experts and aspirants alike always set a boarded cake atop a stable, rotating turntable in order to reach its entire surface. The finest turntables have a sturdy pedestal to provide unquestionable support and a pivot-set aluminum disk that spins smoothly and easily. Turntables with cast iron or cast aluminum bases are available in addition to durable polystyrene ones that may drag with some weight but are still good for the occasional icer.

▸ **Cake decorating, 269**

MOLDS

Aspic and gelatin molds.* The quickest way to chill, set, and release a gelatin-based sweet or savory dish is in a copper, tin, or stainless steel mold. Those with simple lines reproduce neatly and release easily. These should sit level in order to set their contents properly. Stars, turbans, melons, horseshoes, and fish are popular shapes with 2½- to 8-cup capacities.

Ice cream molds.* Hollow metal bricks, logs, cones, and half spheres—some plain, some fluted, all lidded—are used to produce spectacular ice cream presentations. Wipe the inside of the desired form with a neutral-tasting oil, such as mineral oil, then freeze it before filling so softened ice cream will adhere to the mold's sides. Ice cream molds, which go by such specific names as portative mold (square), bombe mold (sphere), biscuit glacé mold (brick), and yule log ice cream mold (trough), are manufactured in tinned and stainless steel.

Parchment paper. A roll of clean, convenient, greaseproof paper is great for baking, steaming, microwaving, and cake decorating. It guarantees a cake's clean release if the layer-cake pan is lined with it; it traps moisture to steam cook a fish fillet if wrapped around it; and it pipes out the neatest bead of icing when rolled into a cone and filled. Parchment paper is most often available in 20-foot by 16-inch rolls.

◗ **Preparing baking pans, 264**
◗ **Steaming in parchment paper, 211**

CHAPTER 3

Cooking Techniques

COOKING IS THE MOST DELIGHTFUL COMBINATION of art and science: a little bit of technique, a lot of tasting and adjusting. Here are a few tricks you can easily master—such as how to chop vegetables for a stir-fry and how to cut butter into a pastry dough so it turns out flaky—so that your foods will look and taste as wonderful as a professional's.

Recipe Terms

Have you ever been stumped by a recipe instruction? Here are some quick definitions to help you figure out any recipe.

Al dente   An Italian phrase meaning "to the tooth," used to describe vegetables and pasta at the perfect stage of doneness—tender, but with enough firmness to be felt between the teeth.

Aspic   A jelly made principally from the cooking liquids of beef or poultry. The liquids will gel by themselves, but are often strengthened with additional gelatin and used for coating and garnishing cold foods.

Bake   To cook cakes, pies, cookies, breads, other pastries and doughs, as well as casseroles, fish, ham, etc., in the oven by dry heat.

Barbecue   To roast meat, poultry, or fish over hot coals or similar open heat, basting with a seasoned sauce. Also, the food so cooked and the social gathering at which it is served.

Baste   To ladle pan fat, marinade, or other liquid over food as it roasts in order to add flavor and prevent dryness.

Batter   A flour, liquid, and/or egg mixture of fairly thin consistency.

Beat   To stir vigorously with a spoon, eggbeater, or electric mixer.

Blanch   To plunge foods quickly into boiling water, then into cold water as a preliminary cooking step. Tomatoes and peaches are blanched to loosen skins for easy removal. Vegetables for salads are sometimes blanched to set color and taste. Also, a preliminary step to freezing vegetables.

Blend   To mix two or more ingredients until smooth.

Boil   To cook food in a liquid at the temperature when bubbles are formed in the liquid and rise in a steady pattern, breaking the surface.

Bone   To remove the bones from meat, fish, or poultry. This is usually done to make eating, carving, or stuffing easier.

Bouillon   A clear stock made from poultry, beef, or veal, plus vegetables, and seasoning and liquid.

Braise   To brown in fat, then cook, covered, in a small amount of liquid.

Bread   To coat with bread crumbs, usually after dipping in beaten egg or milk.

Broil   To cook under a broiler or on a grill by direct dry heat.

Broth   A clear stock made from meat, fish, poultry, or vegetables, seasonings and liquid.

Brush   To spread with melted butter or margarine, beaten egg, water, or other liquid, using a small brush.

Candy   To cook fruit, fruit peel, or ginger in a heavy syrup until transparent, then drain and dry. Also, to cook vegetables, such as carrots or sweet potatoes, in sugar or syrup.

Caramelize   To melt sugar in a skillet over low heat until it becomes golden brown.

Charcoal-starter chimney   A device used to light charcoal, composed of a metal cylinder with a handle and air holes on the side, often with a grate three-quarters of the way down. Charcoal is placed on the top of crumpled paper inside the cylinder and the paper is lit. Air directs heat up the chimney to light the charcoal. The chimney can then be lifted and the hot charcoal spread into the grill bed.

Chop   To cut into small pieces.

Coat   To cover with flour, crumbs, or other dry mixture before frying.

Coat the spoon   A term used to describe egg-thickened sauces when cooked to perfection; when a custard coats a metal spoon, it leaves a thin, somewhat jellylike film.

Combine   To mix together two or more ingredients.

Cream   To beat softened (not melted) butter, margarine, or shortening, alone or with sugar, until smooth, creamy, and light.

Crimp   To press the edges of a piecrust together with the tines of a fork or your fingertips.

Crumb   To coat food with bread or cracker crumbs. The food is first dipped in milk or beaten egg so the crumbs will stick.

Crumble   To break between the fingers into small, irregular pieces.

Crush   To pulverize food with a rolling pin or whirl in a blender until it is granular or powdered.

Cube   To cut into cubes.

Cut in   To work shortening or other solid fat into a flour mixture with a pastry blender or two knives until the texture resembles coarse meal.

Dash   A very small amount—less than $\frac{1}{16}$ teaspoon.

Deep-fry   To cook in hot, deep, temperature-controlled fat.

Defat   To remove the fat or grease from soup or stock. This can be done easily by refrigerating the soup and letting the fat rise to the top and solidify.

Deglaze   To loosen the browned bits in a skillet or roasting pan by adding liquid while stirring and heating. The resulting glaze is used as a flavor base for sauces and gravies.

Devil   To season with mustard, pepper, and other spicy condiments.

Dice   To cut into small, uniform pieces.

Dissolve   To stir a powder or solid ingredient into a liquid to make a solution.

Dot   To scatter bits of butter or margarine or other seasoning over the surface of a food to be cooked.

Dough   A mixture of flour, liquid, and other ingredients stiff enough to knead.

Drain   To pour off liquid. Also, to place fried foods on paper toweling to soak up the excess fat.

Dredge   To coat with flour prior to frying.

Drizzle   To pour melted butter or margarine, marinade, or other liquid over food in a thin stream.

Dust   To cover lightly with flour, 10X (confectioners') sugar, or other dry ingredient.

Entrée   A French term for the third course in a full French dinner. Americans use the term to designate the main dish of a meal.

Fillo   See "Phyllo."

Flake   To break up food (salmon or tuna, for example) into smaller pieces with a fork.

Flambé   French word meaning "flaming." In the culinary sense, the verb *flamber* means to pour warm brandy over a food and to set it afire.

Flour   To coat with flour.

Flute   To form a fluted design with the fingers around a piecrust edging.

Fold in   To mix a light, fluffy ingredient, such as beaten egg white, into a thicker mixture, using a gentle under-and-over motion.

Freezer burn   The dehydration that results from improperly storing frozen foods. Freezer burn occurs when air left in the storage container draws moisture from the food, forming frost inside the package. It can be avoided by removing as much air as possible from a container before freezing.

Fricassee   To simmer a chicken, covered in water, with vegetables and often wine. The chicken may be browned in butter first. A gravy is made from the broth and served with the chicken.

Garnish   To decorate with colorful and/or fancily cut pieces of food, flowers, or herbs.

Glaze   To coat food with honey, syrup, or other liquid so it glistens.

Grate   To shred into small pieces with a grater.

Grease   To rub food or a container with butter, margarine, or other fat.

Grill   To cook on a grill, usually over charcoal.

Grind   To put food through a food grinder.

Hull   To remove caps and stems from berries and the outer layers of nuts, seeds, and grains.

Ice   To cover with icing (usually baked goods). Also, a frozen, water-based, fruit-flavored dessert.

Jigger   A bartender's measure of 1½ fluid ounces.

Julienne   To cut food into uniformly long, thin slivers (1½ by ¼ inches).

Knead   To work dough with the hands until it is smooth and springy. Yeast breads must be kneaded to develop the gluten necessary to give them framework and volume.

Line   To cover the bottom, and sometimes sides, of a pan with paper or thin slices of food.

Macerate   To let food, principally fruits, steep in wine or spirits (usually kirsch or rum).

Marinade   The liquid in which food is marinated.

Marinate   To let food, principally meat, steep in a piquant sauce prior to cooking. The marinade serves to tenderize and add flavor.

Mash   To reduce to a pulp.

Mask   To coat with sauce or aspic.

Melt   To heat a solid, such as chocolate or butter, until liquid.

Meringue   A stiffly beaten mixture of sugar and raw egg white.

Mesquite   A thorny shrub found in Mexico and the southwestern United States. Wood chips from the plant can be added to or used alone as coals to give barbecued food a smoked, sweet flavor. Mesquite is best used with beef, poultry, pork, duck, and lamb.

Mince   To cut into fine pieces.

Mix   To stir together.

Mocha   A flavoring for desserts, usually made from coffee or a mixture of coffee and chocolate.

Mold   To shape in a mold.

Mull   To heat a liquid, such as wine or cider, with whole spices.

Oil   To rub a pan or mold with cooking oil.

Panbroil   To cook in a skillet in a small amount of fat; drippings are poured off as they accumulate.

Parboil   To cook in water until about half done; vegetables to be cooked in a casserole are usually parboiled.

Pare   To remove the skin of a fruit or vegetable with a swivel-blade vegetable peeler.

Pastry   A stiff dough, made from flour, water, and butter or shortening. It is used for piecrusts, turnovers, and other dishes. Also a rich cookie-type dough used for desserts.

Phyllo   Greek term for a flaky, tissue paper-thin pastry used in many Greek dishes. (Also spelled "fillo.")

Pinch   The amount of a dry ingredient that can be taken up between the thumb and index finger—less than ¼ teaspoon.

Pipe   To press frosting, whipped cream, mashed potatoes, or other soft mixtures through a pastry bag fitted with a decorative tip to make a fancy garnish or edging.

Plank   A well-seasoned (oiled) hardwood plank used to serve a broiled steak or chop, usually edged with Duchesse potatoes.

Plump   To soak raisins or other dried fruits in liquid until they are softened and almost returned to their natural state.

Poach   To cook in barely simmering liquid usually such foods as fish or poultry.

Pound   To flatten by pounding.

Preheat   To bring an oven or broiler to the correct temperature before cooking food.

Proof   To let a yeast mixture bubble and rise, as a test for activeness of yeast.

Puree   To whirl food in an electric blender or press through a sieve or food grinder to a smooth, velvety texture. Also, the food so prepared.

Reduce   To boil a liquid, uncovered, until the quantity is concentrated.

Render   To melt solid fat.

Rice   To press food through a container with small holes. The food then resembles rice.

Rising   The increase in size of bread dough before it is baked.

Roast   To cook meat or poultry in the oven by dry heat.

Roll   To press and shape dough or pastry with a rolling pin.

Roux   A cooked, fat-flour mixture used to thicken sauces and gravies.

Sauté   To cook food quickly in a small amount of hot fat in a skillet.

Scald   To heat a liquid just until bubbles form around the edge of the pan but the liquid does not boil.

Scallop   To bake small pieces of food in a casserole, usually in a cream sauce. Also a thin, boneless slice of meat, such as veal.

Score   To make shallow, crisscross cuts over the surface of a food with a knife.

Scramble   To stir eggs or an egg mixture while cooking until the mixture sets.

Scrape   To remove fruit or vegetable skin by scraping with a knife.

Shirr   To bake whole eggs in ramekins with cream and crumbs.

Short   An adjective used to describe a bread, cake, or pastry that has a high proportion of fat and is ultratender or crisp.

Shortening   A solid fat, usually of vegetable origin, used to add tenderness to pastry, bread, or cookies.

Shred   To cut in small, thin slivers by rubbing food, such as Cheddar cheese, over the holes in a shredder-grater.

Sift   To put flour or another dry ingredient through a sifter.

Simmer   To cook in liquid at or just below the boiling point.

Skewer   To thread food on a long wooden or metal pin before cooking. Also, the pin itself.

Skim   To remove fat or film from the surface of a liquid or sauce.

Sliver   To cut in long, thin strips.

Soak   To let stand in liquid.

Spit   To thread food on a long rod and roast over glowing coals or under a broiler. Also, the rod itself.

Steam   To cook, covered, on a trivet or in a specially made steamer over a small amount of boiling water.

Steep   To let food soak in liquid until the liquid absorbs its flavor, such as steeping tea in hot water.

Stew   To cook, covered, in simmering liquid.

Stir   To mix with a spoon using a circular motion.

Stir-fry   To cook in a small amount of oil in a wok or skillet over high heat, stirring or tossing constantly, for a short period of time.

Stock   A liquid flavor base of soups and sauces made by long, slow cooking of meat, poultry, or fish with their bones. Stock may be brown or white, depending on whether the meat and bones are browned first.

Streusel   A crumb topping made from flour, butter, sugar, and cinnamon, often used on coffee cakes.

Stud   To press whole cloves, slivers of garlic, or other seasoning into the surface of a food to be cooked.

Thicken   To make a liquid thicker, usually by adding flour, cornstarch, or beaten egg, then cooking the mixture.

Thin   To lighten a liquid mixture by adding more liquid.

Toss   To mix, as a salad, by gently turning ingredients over and over in a bowl, either with the hands or with a large fork and spoon.

Truss   To tie meat into a compact shape before roasting.

Whip   To beat until frothy or stiff with an eggbeater or an electric mixer.

Whisk   To beat with a looped-wire whisk until well mixed.

Zest   The oily, aromatic, colored part of the rind of citrus fruits.

Knife Techniques

Almost every meal preparation begins with some slicing, dicing, peeling, or boning. Some of this can be done in a food processor (see page 144). Often it is just as fast and convenient to use a knife. Select the best knives you can afford (see pages 135–142) and keep them sharp.

KNIFE SHARPENING

Sharpen those blades! If you have a tapered knife that is making progressively duller cuts, chances are that its edge has microscopically curled over. A few swipes on a straightening steel will restore the edge. But if the knife drags as it cuts, there are probably small nicks and the blade should be sharpened with a sharpening stone.

Maintaining a sharp edge. A good knife will hold its edge with a regular honing on a straightening steel. Grip the knife handle in one hand and the steel handle in the other, pointing the shaft away from your body. Keep the knife blade at a 20-degree angle to the steel and draw the blade down and diagonally across, from heel to tip, in one stroke. Ten strokes—five per side—should do the trick. Try to remember to straighten your knives after every fifteen minutes of use.

Sharpening a dull knife. Nothing is more frustrating—not to mention dangerous—than trying to work with a dull knife. To restore a knife's edge, use a sharpening stone. Place the stone on a damp cloth on a hard, flat surface, and place five to six drops of mineral oil down its length. Set the knife blade heel at a 20-degree angle to the stone's coarse grit side—edge leading—then diagonally draw the blade, heel to tip, toward you; guide it with your free hand lightly pressed across the blade side. Do this ten times per side, then flip the stone to its fine grit side, oil it, and repeat the process. Take the blade to a steel, and draw it down each side a few times. Then wash, dry, and store the knife properly.

Your knives will stay sharp if you do this two to four times a year (or as necessary) to remove any burrs or minute nicks that develop along cutting edges through general use.

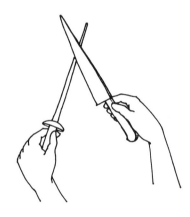

Using a straightening steel.

KNIFE TECHNIQUES FOR FRUITS AND VEGETABLES

Chop. When a recipe tells you to chop the ingredients, the pieces should be cut into small pieces, all about the same size. How small to make the pieces depends on the food and on whether the recipe says to chop fine or coarse.

▶ **Sharpening tools, 135–142**

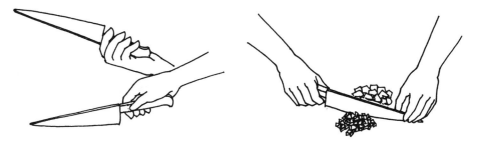

Proper knife grip.   **Chopping/mincing.**

To chop, grip the handle of your chef's knife close to the blade with your thumb and forefinger. Use the other hand to press the knife tip down against the chopping board. Chop with a rocking motion, pivoting the knife back and forth across the food.

Mince. Mincing is the same as chopping, but the resulting pieces should be very small.

Dice. When you dice an ingredient, you end up with small, uniform square pieces. First, slice the food lengthwise with several parallel, evenly spaced horizontal or vertical cuts, holding the food together in its original shape. The spacing between cuts will depend on how large or how small you want the pieces. Then cut crosswise, and the slices will fall into diced pieces.

Cube. When you cube an ingredient, you cut it into uniform cubes. The size will vary, depending on the recipe. The cubes may be bite size, if you are preparing meat for a stew, or smaller, if you are chopping fruit or vegetables for a salad.

Slice. To slice long, round, or oval vegetables, such as carrots, onions, or potatoes, cut the vegetable in half and lay it cut side down

Mincing Garlic

To mince garlic, using a knife, remove the peel from the garlic by smacking the clove against the cutting board with the flat side of a large knife. Then slide off the peel and cut the root end from the clove. Discard the peel and root. Smack the garlic once more with the flat side of the knife. (This flattens and breaks up the garlic for easier chopping.) Holding the knife handle in one hand and placing the fingers of your other hand on the top edge of the blade near the tip of the knife, use a quick rocking motion to chop. Or, you can use a garlic press (see page 144), and squeeze the garlic through the tiny holes to end up with minced garlic.

⟩ Garlic, 30

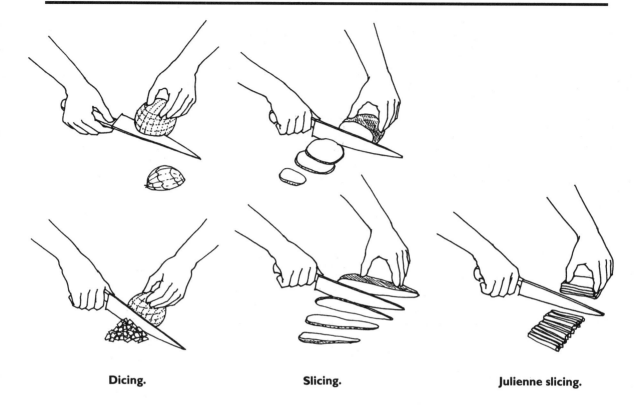

Dicing.   **Slicing.**   **Julienne slicing.**

Peeling Peaches and Apricots

To peel fresh apricots and peaches, drop in boiling water for about 30 seconds, then rinse in cold water, and peel. The fruit will brown from exposure to air, so brush exposed surfaces with a little lemon juice or hold in water to which a few tablespoons of lemon juice have been added.

on a chopping board. Grip the top and sides of the vegetable with your fingertips tucked under. Use your thumb as a pusher. With the middle section of your fingers acting as a guide, "slide" the knife up and down at a right angle to the board.

Julienne. To cut vegetables and meat into matchstick-size strips, first cut the food into 2- or 3-inch lengths. Cut each length into slices 1/8- to 1/4-inch thick. Stack several slices and cut into strips 1/4- to 1/8-inch thick. To cut julienne strips of zest from oranges and other citrus fruits, remove the colored part of the rind with a vegetable peeler, leaving the white pith behind. Stack several strips on top of one another and cut lengthwise into very thin strips. Blanch the strips before using.

Pare or peel. This simply means removing the outer layer or skin of a fruit or vegetable. A vegetable peeler will remove less than a paring knife, though either can be used. Peels are rich in nutrients and fiber so leave them on when you can. But do wash thoroughly when leaving a fruit or vegetable unpeeled.

Roll cut. This is used with long, narrow vegetables, such as asparagus and carrots, to expose as many surfaces as possible for stir-frying. To roll cut, place the vegetable on a cutting board, make a diagonal cut

Sectioning Citrus Fruits

Oranges and grapefruits make delicious and juicy additions to fruit salads. You will want to add the fruit without the bitter pith or tough membranes that separate the sections. Here's how:

Use a sharp paring knife to cut a slice from the top of the fruit to reveal the flesh. As if you were peeling an apple, remove the peel, including the pith, in a strip. Cut deep enough to go right down to the flesh. When the fruit is completely peeled, remove each section by cutting close to and along the membrane that separates the sections. Cut right down to the core of the fruit and carefully remove each section.

Peeling and Seeding Tomatoes

To peel tomatoes, drop them into boiling water for 30 to 60 seconds. Remove from the water and lift off the skin with the tip of a knife. To seed tomatoes, cut in half horizontally and squeeze gently over a cup to catch the seeds, which can then be discarded.

at the end, then roll it a quarter turn and make a diagonal cut again. The resulting pieces will be triangular in shape. Turn and cut in the same manner until the vegetable is entirely cut into triangle-shaped pieces.

Preparing Fish, Shellfish, Poultry, and Meats for Cooking

It's great when the butcher or fishmonger can give you exactly what you need for a dish, but sometimes a little work on your part is unavoidable. Here are the techniques you'll need for filleting fish, deboning chicken, and more.

FILLETING FISH

Of course, it's easier to buy your fish filleted, but when your favorite fisherman brings a gift of a freshly caught fish, it's nice to know how to prepare it. There are two slightly different techniques for filleting fish, based on whether the fish has a round shape, like a salmon, or is flat, like sole.

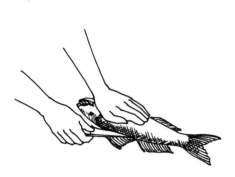

2 Cut along the length of the fish

3 Remove the fillet

1 Make diagonal cut to the backbone

4 Skin the fillet

Filleting a round fish.

Round fish. Begin with a scaled and gutted fish. Rinse thoroughly under cold running water to clean the abdominal cavity.

1. Arrange the fish on a cutting board with the head pointing toward you. With a fish filleting knife or flexible boning knife, make a diagonal cut behind the head of the fish, cutting down to the backbone but not through it.

2. Beginning at the tail, cut a line just above the ridge of the spine from tail to head. With the blade of the knife resting against the backbone, cut along the length of the fish, following the first cut from the tail to the head and cutting about ½ inch deep.

3. With the knife, remove the fillet from the bone by cutting parallel to the bone, peeling back the flesh with your other hand as you go, until the fillet comes away from the bone in a strip. Turn the fish over and repeat the procedure.

4. To skin the fillet, place it skin side down on a cutting board, tail facing you. Scrape ¼ inch of flesh from the tail with the knife and, holding on to the skin, slide the knife, angled down toward the cutting board, between the flesh and the skin to separate the fillet.

Flat fish. Begin with a scaled and gutted fish. Rinse thoroughly under cold running water to clean the abdominal cavity.

♦ **Fish, 82–86**
♦ **Fish fillet knife, 137**

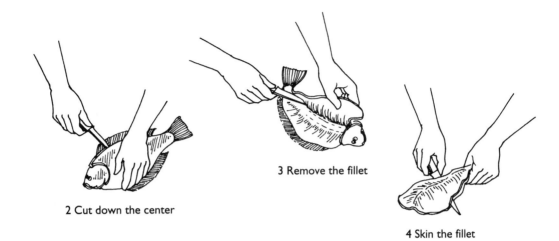

3 Remove the fillet

2 Cut down the center

4 Skin the fillet

1 Make V-shaped cut
behind the head

Filleting a flat fish.

1. With a fish filleting knife or flexible boning knife, make a V-shaped incision behind the head of the fish, cutting down to the backbone but not through it.

2. Arrange the fish on a cutting board with its back facing you. Position the knife at the point of the V. Cut a straight line down the center of the fish from the neck to the tail, following the backbone.

3. Remove the fillet by inserting the knife into the cut and making parallel cuts along the length of the fillet, peeling back the flesh as you go until it comes away in a strip. Rotate the fish and fillet the other side. Turn the fish over and fillet the back.

4. To skin the fillet, proceed as for a round fish.

PREPARING SHELLFISH FOR COOKING

Shrimp. Cooking shrimp with the shell on will give you a more flavorful shrimp, but most recipes call for peeling first. The peels can be saved and cooked in simmering water to cover for about forty-five minutes. This makes a flavorful shrimp stock to use in gumbo, cioppino, or any recipe calling for fish stock.

SHELLING SHRIMP To shell shrimp, use your fingers to open the shell down the length of the body. Then peel away the shell, starting at the head end. Gently pull on the tail portion of the shell to remove it from the tail, making sure to keep the tail meat intact.

DEVEINING SHRIMP Hold the shrimp with the tail and curve away from you. With a small sharp knife make a shallow cut along the back of the shrimp to expose the vein. Rinse the shrimp under cold running water, using your fingertips to remove the black or green vein along the slight incision. (The vein is harmless, but many find the shrimp is more appealing without it.)

♦ **Shrimp, 89–90**

Lobsters. Whole lobsters are most often boiled in the shell, though they can be steamed or broiled. If possible, cook lobsters on the same day you buy them. If that is not possible, place them on a tray and cover with a damp towel; refrigerate for no more than a day and use the freshly cooked lobster meat within 2 days.

To remove the meat for use in a recipe, first split the cooked lobster using a kitchen shears or heavy knife. Place the lobster on its back and cut the body in half lengthwise, starting at the head and working toward the tail. Do not cut all the way through to the back shell.

Spread the halves apart with your hands. Cut away the black vein running through the tail and the small sand sac near the head of the lobster.

Spoon out the green tomalley (liver) and coral roe (eggs found only in females), which can be used in stuffings and sauces.

Twist the large claws away from the body of the lobster. Break open the claws with a nutcracker. Use a seafood fork to remove the meat from the claws, tail, and body.

To remove lobster meat from the shell at the table, first remove the meat from the tail. Then twist off the large claws and crack open with a nutcracker. Pick out the meat and eat. Next break off the legs and carefully suck the meat and juices from them. Finally, remove and eat any meat from the body, as well as the tomalley and roe.

Crabs. Hard-shell crabs are most often boiled or steamed, while soft-shell crabs are most often pan-fried or grilled.

HARD-SHELL CRABS 1. To remove the meat from a cooked crab, turn the crab on its back. With your thumb, pry up the apron, or tail flap. Twist it off and discard.

2. Then hold the crab with the top shell in one hand and grasp the bottom shell at the point where the apron was pulled off. Pull the top shell away from the body of the crab and discard. Using a small knife, remove the spongy gills ("devil's fingers") from each side of the top of the crab. Discard the internal organs, the mouth, and the small

Cleaning a hard-shell crab.

1 (Bottom up) Pry up the apron or tail flap

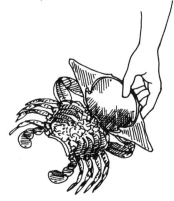

2 (Top up) Pull away the top shell

appendages at the front of the crab. Finally, to remove the meat, twist off the legs and claws with your fingers. Using a nutcracker, crack each joint, then pick out the meat. Break the body in half to remove the remaining meat.

SOFT-SHELL CRABS Just before cooking, clean soft-shell crabs by removing the inedible parts. Turn the crab underside up and use the tip of a knife to lift up the apron, or tail flap. Remove and discard the apron. Lift the shell on each side and use a knife to remove the gills; discard them. Using kitchen shears, snip across the face of the crab; remove and discard the eyes and mouth. Lift the shell where the face was and, using a small spoon, scoop out and discard the innards. The crab is now ready for cooking.

Crayfish. Crayfish is often sold cooked. To remove the meat, squeeze the sides of the tail until the shell cracks. Then remove the tail shell by pulling the sides apart with the thumbs and forefingers; extract the flesh. Remove the tail meat from the shell. Devein as you would shrimp (see page 189). Save the heads and claws for stock.

Clams. Farmed clams are relatively grit-free, but those harvested from the sea may be quite gritty (steam one to test). If you have a batch of these, place them in a large bowl of salted water (⅓ cup salt to each gallon water). Add a handful of cornmeal, then the clams. Leave for 2 hours; the clams will purge themselves of grit.

HARD-SHELL CLAMS First discard any clams that remain open when you tap the shell with your fingers. Use a metal brush to vigorously scrub the shells of the remaining clams under cold running water to remove all particles of sand.

1. Use a clam knife or some other sturdy, short-bladed knife and place a towel in your hand to protect yourself from a slip of the blade. Hold the clam in the palm of your hand. With your other hand, insert the knife between the two shell sections near the hinge and run it between the shells. With a twisting motion of the knife, pry the shells apart. Remove the top part of the shell.

2. Taking care not to pierce the flesh, insert a knife under the meat to loosen it from the shell. Remove and discard any broken shell.

SOFT-SHELL CLAMS Pull the sections apart; slit the tough neck and pull it off.

Oysters. Before shucking, tap those shells that have opened during storage. Discard any that don't close quickly.

1. Use an oyster knife or some other sturdy, short-bladed knife and place a towel in your hand to protect yourself from a slip of the blade. Place the oyster on a work surface with its flat side facing up. Grip the oyster so that the hinged side is exposed and push the point of the oyster knife into or near the hinge. Slide the knife along the seam between the shells until reaching the opposite end. Twist the blade to pry open the shell, keeping the shell level so no liquid spills out.

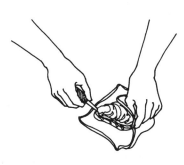

Opening an oyster.

♦ Squid, 92

2. Scrape the blade of the knife along the inside of the top shell; sever the muscle and discard the upper shell. Taking care not to pierce the flesh, slide the blade under the oyster to free it from the bottom muscle, retaining as much of the liquor as possible. Remove and discard any broken shell.

Squid. 1. To prepare squid for cooking, hold the squid with one hand while you reach inside the body with the other and pull the head and tentacles away. Pull off and discard the mottled skin. Feel inside the body for the transparent cartilage (it looks and feels like plastic); draw it out and discard it. Then wash the body inside and out under cold running water.

2. Separate the two flaps from the body; they pull away easily. Locate the ink sac, which is attached to the head; remove and save (for risotto, perhaps) or discard it.

3. Cut the tentacles from the head. Cut the body into thick rings, slice the flaps into strips, and cut the tentacles to an easily forked size.

Cutting up a chicken.

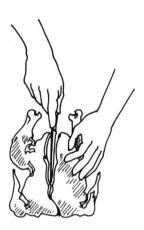

I Cut the chicken in half

2 Cut through the bone from the tail to the neck

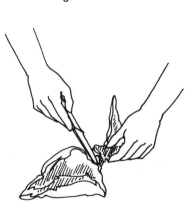

3 Cut through the backbone

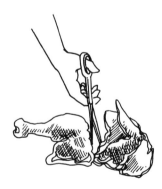

4 Cut into quarters

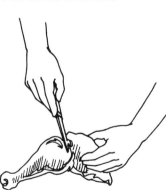

5 Cut through joint between the leg and thigh

6 Remove the wings

POULTRY

Cutting up a chicken. Use poultry shears and a sharp boning knife for this.

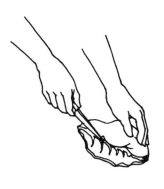

Deboning poultry.

1. First, cut the chicken in half. Use the boning knife to cut through the skin and flesh to prevent tears, cutting from the neck to the tail along the breast.

2. Then use the poultry shears to cut through the bones, from the tail to the neck.

3. Open up the bird like a book, and use the poultry shears to cut through the backbones.

4. Cut into quarters to separate the breast from the leg and thigh. Using poultry shears, cut from the shoulder toward the tail between the joints.

5. To separate the thighs and drumsticks, locate the knee joint by bending the thigh and drumstick together. Cut through the joints of each leg with the boning knife.

6. To remove the wings, place the breast quarter on its back. Cut down through the skin at the base of the wing and through the joint, using the boning knife.

Boning and skinning a chicken or turkey breast. For easy handling begin with a very cold bird.

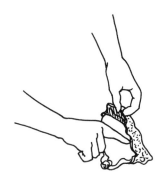

Removing the skin from poultry.

1. Insert a sharp boning knife parallel and close to the large end of the rib bone. Make short, quick strokes to scrape the meat away from the bone. Use your fingers as a guide and keep the knife angled toward the bone. Repeat on the other side of the breast.

2. To skin the breasts, slip your fingertips between the skin and meat and carefully remove the skin and membrane in one piece by pulling it off with your fingers. Cut out and discard the white tendon. Slice the breast in half, if desired.

MEAT FOR STIR-FRIES

Begin with very cold or partially frozen meat or poultry (chicken breast) for easy handling. For more tender meat, slice it against the grain. Make uniform, bite-size slices that will cook evenly.

Carving Techniques

If you aren't comfortable wielding a knife in front of a crowd, do your carving in the kitchen and arrange the meat on a platter. You'll probably find carving in the kitchen less stressful and less messy.

HOW TO CARVE A TURKEY

1. Once roasted, remove the bird from the roasting pan and let it rest for 20 to 30 minutes. Remove the trussing string and any stuffing and carve one side of the bird at a time.

2. Arrange the bird on a cutting board, breast side up. Hold the bird in place with the back of a carving fork, if possible, to avoid sticking the tines into the meat so the juices are not released. With a carving knife, cut through the skin between the breast and the thigh. Gently move the leg to find the joint and cut through the joint to remove the leg.

3. Gently stretch apart the drumstick and the thigh to find the joint and, with a firm downward movement of the knife, cut through the joint.

4. Hold your knife parallel to the bone and cut slices from the thigh.

5. To remove the wing, cut through the skin at the corner of the breast around the wing. Gently move the wing to find the joint, and cut through the joint to remove the wing with a piece of the breast.

6. Beginning on the outside of the breast, cut down diagonally to produce thin slices. Use the back of the carving fork to avoid sticking the meat with the tines. Carve the other side of the bird in the same manner.

HOW TO CARVE A CHICKEN

1. Once roasted, remove the bird from the roasting pan and let it rest for 15 minutes. Remove and discard the trussing string.

2. Arrange the bird breast side up on a cutting board. With a carving knife, cut through the skin between the breast and thigh. Move the leg to find the joint and cut through the joint to remove the leg.

3. Separate the drumstick from the thigh by cutting through the knee joint.

4. To remove the wing, cut through the skin at the corner of the breast around the wing. Move the wing to find the joint. Cut through the joint to remove the wing with a piece of the breast.

5. Begin slicing the breast meat by angling your knife parallel to the bone and slicing from the front of the breast. Carve the other side of the bird in the same manner.

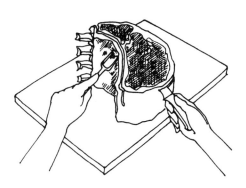

Carving a rib roast.

Carving a rack of lamb.

HOW TO CARVE ROAST PRIME RIBS OF BEEF

1. Remove the beef from the roasting pan and let it rest for 20 minutes before carving.

2. Arrange the roast on its side. With a paring knife make an incision about 2 inches deep following the ribs.

3. Hold the beef in place with a carving fork. With a carving knife, cut horizontally—straight across the "face" of the beef toward the rib bone—cutting the meat into thin slices.

HOW TO CARVE A RACK OF LAMB

1. Remove the lamb from the roasting pan and let it rest for 10 to 15 minutes.

2. Arrange the lamb on a cutting board meat side up. With a carving knife and holding the meat in place with a carving fork, separate into chops by cutting between the ribs.

HOW TO CARVE A LEG OF LAMB

1. Remove the lamb from the roasting pan and let it rest for 15 to 20 minutes.

2. With a dish towel or napkin, hold the shank end of the lamb in your hand and lift it off the cutting board so that it is at a slight angle. With a sharp carving knife held almost parallel to the surface of the lamb, begin cutting long, thin slices starting at the thickest part of the leg. Arrange the slices on a platter as you go and continue slicing the leg in the same manner. Turn the leg over and carve the other side in the same manner.

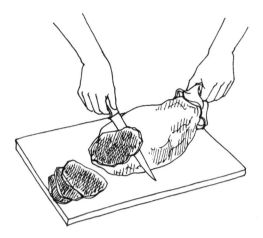

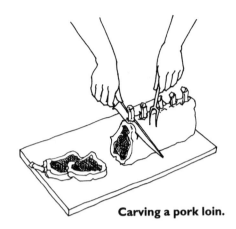

Carving a pork loin.

Carving a leg of lamb.

HOW TO CARVE A LOIN OF PORK ROAST

1. Remove the pork from the roasting pan and let it rest for 15 to 20 minutes.

2. With a sharp carving knife, remove the backbone. Arrange the roast on a cutting board with the rib side facing you. Hold the pork roast steady by inserting the tines of a fork in the top of the roast, and slice the roast by cutting close to the rib bone on each side. One slice will contain a rib and the next will be boneless. Arrange the slices on a serving plate as you go.

HOW TO CARVE A HAM

1. Arrange the ham on a cutting board with the shank end to the left and the cushion portion of the ham on top. With a sharp carving knife, cut along the top of the bone and remove the cushion portion.

2. Put the cushion portion on the cutting board cut side down. Cut the ham crosswise into slices.

3. With the tip of a small knife, cut around the leg bone to remove the meat from the bone. Arrange this meat on the cutting board so that the thick side is down. Cut into slices.

4. Arrange the remaining section on the cutting board with the "face" down and cut along the bone to remove the meaty section. (This may be on either the right or the left, depending on whether it came from a right leg or a left leg.) Cut this section into slices across the grain.

5. Holding the last section steady with a fork, cut across the meat toward the aitchbone. Separate the cut slices from the bone by cutting with the point of a small knife and transfer to a platter.

easuring Techniques

There is a difference between liquid and dry measuring cups, and they should not be used interchangeably. The graduated measuring cups (usually in plastic or metal) are dry measures; liquid measures are usually a heatproof cup with a pouring spout.

Flour. Spoon the flour from the canister or bag into a dry measuring cup, heaping slightly. Hold the cup of flour over the canister or bag and run the flat side of a long knife across the top to level off the cup.

Granulated sugar. Measure as you would flour.

Brown sugar. Pack it into a dry measuring cup, using the back of a spoon. Then level it off with the flat side of a knife.

Solid shortening. Measure solid vegetable shortening by scooping it with a rubber scraper into a dry measuring cup; run the flat blade of a long knife over the top, then scoop out of cup with rubber scraper into the mixing bowl.

Liquids. Put the liquid measuring cup on a flat surface and stoop so you are at eye level with it; pour the liquid to the desired measure printed on the side of the cup. (*Note:* When measuring a syrup, such as molasses or honey, it will pour out of the measuring cup easily if you first lightly grease the cup with butter, oil, or margarine.)

tovetop Cooking

Here's a rundown on basic cooking methods for the stove.

BLANCHING

When you want to set the bright color of green vegetables and herbs, or loosen the skins of nuts, fruits, and tomatoes, you can blanch them. You can also blanch foods to remove salt (as with salt cod) and other strong flavors. Vegetables are blanched before they are frozen.

To blanch, briefly immerse the food in rapidly boiling water to cover, drain, and refresh under cold running water to stop the cooking process. Tomatoes are blanched for 30 to 60 seconds before they are peeled; homegrown green beans are blanched for about 3 minutes before they are frozen. Most vegetables, such as zucchini or carrots, are blanched for 30 to 60 seconds to set the color and enhance the flavor for use in salads.

BOILING

Cooking in boiling liquid is one of the oldest known cooking methods. The liquid is usually water or broth.

Vegetables. When cooking *green vegetables,* add them to rapidly boiling water and cook, uncovered, as fast as possible to retain their color and flavor. To cook *root vegetables*, such as potatoes, carrots, and turnips, add the vegetables to cold water, and allow the water to come to a boil. Then reduce the heat and gently boil the vegetables, covered, until tender.

Lobster. Fill an extra-large pot with sea water or salted fresh water (2 teaspoons salt for each quart of water). There should be enough water to completely cover the lobsters. Plunge the lobsters, head first, into the boiling water. Cover; return to boil. Count from the time that the water returns to a boil. Cook until a head antenna comes out easily and the shell is vibrant red. For regular-size lobsters, allow 5 to 6 minutes per pound (8 to 9 minutes for 1½-pound lobster; 10 to 12 minutes for 2-pound lobster). For jumbo lobsters, cook for 5 minutes for the first pound, 4 minutes for each additional pound.

Shrimp. Use 1 quart water for each pound of shrimp; add 1 tablespoon of salt for shelled shrimp, 2 tablespoons for unshelled shrimp. When the water boils, add the shrimp. Cover. Simmer just until shrimp turn pink, 3 to 5 minutes.

BRAISING

When a large piece of meat is browned, flavored with seasonings, and left to simmer slowly in broth with seasonings and vegetables, it is braised. This can be done on top of the stove or in a slow oven. Choose less tender cuts of meat—the shoulder, neck, or leg—for braising.

Brown the meat slowly on all sides in a heavy kettle or casserole, in oil if needed to prevent meat from sticking. Add a small amount of stock, wine, water, and/or vegetable juice. Bring to a simmer over moderate heat. Lower the heat; cover the pan. Simmer on top of the stove or in a 300°F. to 325°F. oven, adding vegetables toward the end of cooking, if desired, as well as more liquid if necessary, until the meat is tender.

DEEP-FRYING

You probably won't do much deep frying because it isn't as healthful a cooking method as steaming or roasting (or even oven frying—see page 201). Still, when a hankering for Southern fried chicken hits, nothing else will do. Deep frying *is* tricky, because if it isn't done right, the food is greasy. But done properly, deep-fried food is crisp on the outside and moist and flavorful within.

▶ **Dutch oven, 163**
▶ **Deep-fryer, 159**

(continued on page 201)

Braising Beef, Lamb, Pork, and Veal

Brown the meat, then add a small amount of cooking liquid and bring to a simmer
on top of the stove or in a moderate oven. Given below are simmering times.

CUT	METHOD	SIMMERING TIME
Beef		
Beef Flank Steaks (1 1/2 to 2 pounds)	Follow general directions above.	1 1/2 to 2 1/2 hours
Pot Roast (3 to 5 pounds)	Follow general directions above.	2 1/2 to 3 1/2 hours
Round Steaks (3/4- to 1-inch thick)	Follow general directions above.	1 to 1 1/2 hours
Short Ribs	Cut into 2- by 2- by 4-inch pieces. Follow general directions above.	1 1/2 to 2 1/2 hours
Stewing Beef	Follow general directions above.	1-inch cubes: 1 to 1 1/2 hours, 2-inch cubes: 1 1/2 to 2 1/2 hours
Lamb		
Chops, Arm, Blade, Leg, and Shoulder (1-inch thick)	Follow general directions above. Use about 1/2 cup cooking liquid per 4 chops.	3/4 to 1 hour, or until tender
Leg of Lamb, half (4 pounds)	Follow general directions above, using about 1 cup liquid. Cover. Baste two or three times during cooking.	1 1/2 to 2 hours, or until tender
Shanks, cracked into 3 pieces each	Follow general directions above, using about 1/2 cup liquid per 2 shanks. Turn once or twice during cooking.	1 1/2 hours, or until tender
Shoulder of Lamb, boned and rolled (3 pounds)	Follow general directions above, using about 3 1/2 cups liquid. Baste two or three times during cooking.	2 1/2 hours, or until tender
Pork		
Chops and Steaks	Follow general directions above, browning in oil for about 3 minutes per side. Add flavorings and about 1/3 cup liquid for each 4 chops or 2 steaks.	1 hour, or until tender
Tenderloin, whole (about 1 1/2 pounds)	Follow general directions above, using about 1 1/3 cups liquid.	1 hour, or until tender
Fresh Ham (5 to 7 pounds)	Follow general directions above, using about 1/4 cup liquid.	3 1/2 to 4 hours, or until tender
Ham Steaks and Slices, uncooked (1-inch thick)	Brown on both sides in lightly greased, large, heavy skillet over moderately high heat. Pour off drippings, then add 1 cup of liquid. Cover; reduce heat. Turn halfway into cooking time.	20 minutes
Ham Steaks and Slices, ready to eat (1-inch thick)	Brown on both sides in lightly greased, large, heavy skillet over moderately high heat. Pour off drippings, then add 1 cup of liquid. Cover; reduce heat. Turn halfway into cooking time.	10 minutes

(table continues)

Braising Beef, Lamb, Pork, and Veal (continued)

CUT	METHOD	SIMMERING TIME
Veal		
Breast, stuffed (3 to 4 pounds) or boneless (2 to 3 pounds)	Follow general directions above, using about 2 cups liquid.	1½ to 2½ hours
Chops (½-inch to 1-inch)	Follow general directions above, using about ½ cup liquid per 4 chops.	½ to ¾ hour, or until tender
Steaks (½-inch to 1-inch)	Follow general directions above, using about ½ cup liquid per 4 steaks.	¾ to 1 hour, or until tender
Riblets	Follow general directions above, using 1 to 2 inches of liquid.	2 to 3 hours
Shoulder or Rump, boned and rolled (4 to 5 pounds)	Follow general directions above, using about 3½ cups liquid.	2½ hours, or until tender
Stewing Meat, cut into 1-inch to 2-inch cubes	Follow general directions above, using about 2 inches of liquid.	¾ to 1 hour

Low-Fat Braising

Although braising is useful for tenderizing tough cuts of meat, those cuts are usually fatty. Be sure to trim them well before cooking. For maximum fat removal, cook ahead when braising so the food will have a day or several hours to chill. The fat will solidify on top of the juices and can be easily removed.

FIVE STEPS TO A PERFECT LOW-FAT BRAISE

1. In a Dutch oven, brown meat for braising using nonstick cooking spray for less fat.

2. Remove the meat from the pan. In the drippings, brown a mixture of chopped onions, carrots, and celeriac or turnips.

3. Place the meat on the vegetable bed, add enough water or fat-free, low-sodium beef broth to cover the vegetables, and cover. Cook gently in the oven or on the stovetop until the meat is tender.

4. Spoon off the fat from the top of the liquid. In a small saucepan, make a paste of 1½ tablespoons unbleached flour and a little of the braising liquid. Gradually whisk in one cup of braising liquid, and bring to a boil, whisking constantly. Boil for about 2 minutes or until the sauce thickens.

5. Mash the vegetable mixture. Serve the meat and vegetable mixture with the thickened braising liquid.

The secret to deep frying is to keep the oil at the right temperature. If you fry at too low a temperature, the food becomes soggy. If you fry at too high a temperature, the food burns on the outside but remains uncooked inside. Correct temperatures for the fat can range between 350°F. and 400°F. Larger pieces of food fry at lower temperatures so that the outside does not burn before the inside is cooked. If you don't have a deep fryer with thermostatically controlled heat, use a deep-fat thermometer to monitor the temperature of the fat and select a heavy pan to help maintain a constant temperature.

Oven Frying: Deep-Fried Taste Without All That Fat!

Breaded chicken and fish can be baked in the oven for that good old-fashioned flavor without the fuss of frying—and without the calories of all that extra oil.

To make *oven-fried chicken*, preheat the oven to 375°F. Remove the skin from the chicken pieces, if desired. Dip the pieces into milk seasoned with prepared mustard and spices. Then roll in fine dry bread crumbs, cornmeal, cracker crumbs, or cornflake crumbs. Place in a well-greased shallow baking dish; lightly drizzle with melted butter, margarine, or oil. Bake until the coating is golden brown and interior is cooked through.

BAKING TIMES:

Split breasts	15 to 25 minutes
Boneless breasts	10 to 20 minutes
Thighs	20 to 30 minutes
Drumsticks	15 to 25 minutes
Wings	10 to 20 minutes

To make *oven-fried fish* using fillets, steaks, or small whole fish, preheat the oven to 500°F. Dip the fish in milk, then in fine dry bread crumbs, cornmeal, cracker crumbs, or cornflake crumbs. Place in well-greased shallow baking dish; lightly drizzle with melted butter, margarine, or oil. Bake until fish *just* flakes with a fork, 10 to 15 minutes; do not turn the fish.

To make *oven-fried scallops,* preheat the oven to 500°F. Dip the scallops in seasoned milk, then in seasoned dry bread crumbs. Place in a single layer in a buttered shallow baking pan; lightly drizzle with melted butter, margarine, or oil. Bake until golden brown, 7 to 9 minutes; do not turn.

To make *oven-fried french fries,* cut the potatoes into ¼-inch strips. Place in water to cover and add 1 tablespoon white vinegar for every four large potatoes. Soak for 1 hour. Drain well and pat dry. Coat the potatoes with oil, using about ½ cup oil for four large potatoes. Drain again. Preheat the oven to 400°F. Arrange the potatoes on baking sheets and bake for 20 minutes, then flip and continue baking for another 20 minutes, until golden. Drain on paper towels and sprinkle with coarse salt.

Use vegetable oils and shortenings for deep frying. To reuse the fat, strain the fat through cheesecloth, a clean paper coffee filter, or a fine sieve to remove any food particles. Then let cool and chill, covered. (When frying fish, reuse the fat only for fish.)

Never fill your pan with more than one-third fat to minimize the risk of overflow or spilling.

Coat foods to be fried with flour, egg, and bread crumbs, or dip them in a batter. This coating offers protection against the high heat. A light batter of eggs, milk, and flour is ideal for fruit, vegetables, and fish, while some foods may require no more than a light dredging in flour.

A few points to remember when deep frying:

☐ Be sure the temperature is low enough to cook the inside in the same amount of time it takes to brown the outside.

☐ Cut the food into even-size pieces so that all the pieces cook at the same rate.

☐ Deep frying is not suitable for large pieces of food (pieces thicker than 1½ inches) since the exterior will brown before the interior is cooked. When in doubt, cook one piece and test for doneness in the interior before proceeding with the entire batch.

☐ Be sure to coat food thoroughly.

☐ Fry foods in small batches and do not overcrowd in the pan. If you are using a frying basket, arrange only enough food in the basket to cover the bottom. Do not use a basket for foods dipped in batter because they will stick to the basket.

☐ Reheat the fat to the correct temperature in between frying batches of food.

PANBROILING

Panbroiling is a way to cook meat on top of the stove in a skillet or frying pan without any added fat. As the meat renders its fat, pour it off. This makes panbroiling a low-fat cooking method. Its advantage over oven broiling is that it does not heat up the entire oven.

PARBOILING

Parboiling is cooking food in boiling water until it is about half done. It is a good idea to parboil vegetables, especially potatoes, before adding them to a casserole. Use the same method as for boiling (page 198), but drain the food before it is completely cooked.

Panbroiling Beef, Lamb, and Pork

Beef

Hamburger Gently shape 1 pound of refrigerated ground beef into 3 thick or 4 thin patties. Lightly oil a large, heavy skillet or sprinkle the skillet with salt. Heat over moderate heat for 1 minute. Add the patties to the hot skillet and panbroil. Season with salt and pepper after broiling. Time given is for thick patties. Reduce the time by 1 minute per side for thin patties.

DONENESS	TIME IN MINUTES
Rare	4 per side
Medium	5 per side
Well done	6 per side

1-inch Steaks (Club or Delmonico) Make cuts into the fat all around at 1-inch intervals. Heat pan over high heat; reduce to moderately high when meat is added to pan. Turn often.

DONENESS	TIME IN MINUTES
Very rare	6 total
Rare	8 to 10 total
Medium rare	11 to 12 total
Medium	13 to 14 total
Well done	15 to 16 total

1-inch Steaks (Top and Eye Round, Tip and Boneless Blade, plus all other tender steaks except large Sirloins)

DONENESS	TIME IN MINUTES
Very rare	6 to 7 total
Rare	8 to 10 total
Medium rare	11 to 12 total
Medium	13 to 14 total
Well done	15 to 16 total

1½-inch Steaks (Top and Eye Round, Tip and Boneless Blade, plus all other tender steaks except large Sirloins)

DONENESS	TIME IN MINUTES
Very rare	8 to 10 total
Rare	11 to 12 total
Medium rare	13 to 14 total
Medium	15 to 17 total
Well done	18 to 20 total

(table continues)

Panbroiling Beef, Lamb, and Pork (*continued*)

Beef (continued)

2-inch Steaks (Top and Eye Round, Tip and Boneless Blade, plus all other tender steaks except large Sirloins)

DONENESS	TIME IN MINUTES
Very rare	13 to 14 total
Rare	16 to 17 total
Medium rare	18 to 19 total
Medium	20 to 22 total
Well done	25 to 30 total

Lamb

1-inch Lamb Chops

DONENESS	TIME IN MINUTES
Rare	5 to 7 total
Medium rare	8 to 9 total
Medium	10 to 12 total
Well done	12 to 14 total

1½-inch Lamb Chops

DONENESS	TIME IN MINUTES
Rare	7 to 8 total
Medium rare	9 to 10 total
Medium	12 to 13 total
Well done	14 to 16 total

POACHING

Cooking food in a simmering liquid is called poaching. The liquid should not actually bubble, but you can see the surface of the liquid quiver. What you are looking for is a constant slow simmer—195°F. to 205°F. Poaching is excellent for delicate foods such as fish fillets, chicken breasts, and fruits. Poaching whole chicken and large pieces of meat for several hours brings out and concentrates their flavor to the fullest.

If you blanch meat before poaching, you will end up with a clearer cooking liquid. Put the meat in a pan with cold water, bring the water to a boil, drain, and refresh under cold running water. Whether poach-

Panbroiling Beef, Lamb, and Pork (*continued*)

Lamb (*continued*)

2-inch Lamb Chops

DONENESS	TIME IN MINUTES
Rare	8 to 9 total
Medium rare	10 to 12 total
Medium	13 to 15 total
Well done	16 to 18 total

Pork

Bacon, Sliced (not Canadian-style) Place cold bacon slices into unheated skillet. Cook over moderate heat, turning often. Drain.

DONENESS	TIME IN MINUTES
Crisp	6 to 8

Ham Steaks and Slices, ready to eat If meat is very lean, add a light coating of oil or salt to a large heavy skillet; heat the skillet for 1 minute, then add ham steak or slice.

DONENESS		TIME IN MINUTES
Heated	1/4-inch thick	1 1/2 per side
	1/2-inch thick	2 to 3 per side
	3/4-inch thick	3 per side

Ham Steaks, uncooked If meat is very lean, add a light coating of oil or salt to a large heavy skillet; heat the skillet for 1 minute, then add ham steak or slice.

DONENESS		TIME IN MINUTES
Heated	1/4-inch thick	3 per side
	1/2-inch thick	4 per side
	3/4-inch thick	6 per side

ing meat, fish, or poultry, be sure to skim frequently during poaching so that the liquid remains clear.

Poaching fish and shellfish. When poaching a *whole fish,* always start with a cooled liquid—flavored broth, fish stock, wine, or water flavored with lemon juice and herbs. The traditional liquid in which to poach fish is called a court bouillon. This is just a broth made from fish heads and tails, wine, and vinegar. Whatever you use, be sure it is cooled before the fish is added. Adding fish to hot liquid will make the flesh contract, preventing even cooking. *Shellfish,* however, *can* be added to simmering water.

Poaching Times for Chicken and Fish

FOOD	POACHING TIME IN MINUTES
Chicken (2½ to 4 pounds parts)	
Split breasts	20 to 25 total
Boneless breasts	15 to 20 total
Thighs	30 to 35 total
Drumsticks	25 to 30 total
Wings	15 to 20 total
Fish	
Chunks	6 to 8 per pound
Whole fish and large chunks	6 to 8 per pound
Steaks	5 to 10 total
Fillets	5 to 20 total
Scallops	3 to 4 total

Whole fish should be wrapped in a double layer of cheesecloth and placed on a rack in a large casserole or kettle. This will help it retain its shape.

Fish and shellfish overcook easily and require a watchful eye. As a general rule, cook fish 10 minutes for every 1 inch of thickness. The fish should change from a translucent color, usually white, to a solid opaque color, usually white, and the flesh should flake when lightly touched with a fork.

Poaching chicken. You can use the same method for poaching a whole bird as you do for chicken parts, but truss the whole bird (see page 230), so it cooks more evenly.

Immerse the chicken in boiling broth, stock, wine, and/or water flavored with onion, celery, carrots, and herbs. Reduce the heat to simmer and cover the pan. Simmer breasts for about 20 minutes, whole chickens for an hour or two, or just until the chicken is tender. Turn off the heat and allow the chicken to cool in the broth until it is a comfortable temperature to handle. Strain the broth and use to finish the recipe, or pour into a jar and refrigerate. Use the broth within three days, or freeze for longer storage.

Poaching fruits. Poached fruit served on a bed of pureed raspberries makes an easy, elegant dessert. Pears, fresh figs, peaches, and plums are all delicious poached in a syrup of water or wine, sugar, and a flavoring—such as a split vanilla bean and lemon zest and spices.

Low-Fat Poaching

Simmer your favorite meats, poultry, and fish in a bath of low-sodium, fat-free broth flavored with chopped onion, your favorite herbs, and a splash of wine or fresh lemon juice. You can even use low-sodium vegetable juice! All the nutrients—even those water-soluble ones—are put to use if you turn the poaching liquid into a sauce. Here's how it's done.

1. Remove the fatty skin from fish or chicken before poaching so the fat won't melt into the poaching liquid. Be sure to immerse the food totally in the liquid to prevent it from drying out, even though the pan is covered with a lid.

2. For a poaching liquid, select fat-free, low-sodium broths or leftover liquids from cooking vegetables, such as carrots and potatoes.

3. To make the poaching liquid into a sauce, combine a little of it with cornstarch, then add it to more broth. (Use 1 tablespoon of cornstarch for each cup of poaching liquid.) Bring to a boil, whisking constantly until the sauce thickens; add a dash of low-sodium soy sauce or hot pepper sauce.

4. Stir some pureed vegetables, such as carrots or potatoes, into the poaching liquid to make a sauce that's thick enough to veil the poached food.

□ Use leftover poaching liquid for soups.

□ Use herbs, spices, onions, and garlic in the poaching liquid. Strain them out before serving if using whole pieces.

REDUCING

More and more recipes these days require reducing cooking liquids to concentrate flavors. To do this, you simply boil the cooking liquid uncovered until the volume is reduced. Reduced pan juices have a nice, syrupy consistency and make an instant gravy.

SAUTÉING (PAN-FRYING)

To sauté is to cook food quickly in a small amount of hot oil or butter. The French word means to "leap" or "jump" from the pan. Foods prepared in this way are crisp, golden brown, and moist.

Because sautés cook quickly, select tender cuts of meat, firm-fleshed fish fillets or steaks, and small, tender pieces of chicken. Other suitable foods for sautéing are chicken cutlets, veal cutlets and center cuts, pork or lamb chops, and vegetables.

For even cooking, cut the food to be sautéed to uniform size. Foods to be sautéed must be perfectly dry before they are added to the pan or they will not brown properly.

Be sure the pan you use is large enough to accommodate the foods without overcrowding, which would cause the food to steam rather than brown.

◗ **Sauté pan, 158**

(continued on page 211)

Sautéing Times for Beef and Pork

Beef

Fillet Steaks If desired, wrap the edge of each steak with a bacon strip. Sauté in combination of butter and oil (about 2 tablespoons butter to 1 tablespoon oil for every 4 steaks) in large heavy skillet.

DONENESS	SAUTÉING TIMES (MINUTES PER SIDE)
Very rare	3 to 4
Rare	5 to 6
Medium rare	7 to 8

Liver, Calf's Sauté in butter in large, heavy skillet over moderately high heat.

THICKNESS OF CUT	DONENESS	SAUTÉING TIMES (MINUTES PER SIDE)
½-inch thick	Rare	2 to 3
	Medium	3 to 3½

Steak (Boneless Blade, Eye Round, Skirt Fillet, Tip, Top Round (1-inch thick)

DONENESS	SAUTÉING TIMES (MINUTES PER SIDE)
Very rare	3
Rare	4
Medium rare	5

Steak (Cube, Minute, Petite)

DONENESS	SAUTÉING TIMES (MINUTES PER SIDE)
Medium	1 to 2

Pork

Canadian Bacon Slices Cook bacon slices in lightly greased heavy skillet over moderately low heat until lightly browned.

DONENESS	SAUTÉING TIMES (MINUTES PER SIDE)
Medium	4 to 5

Ham Steaks and Slices, ready to eat Brown steaks in oil in large, heavy skillet.

THICKNESS OF CUT	DONENESS	SAUTÉING TIMES (MINUTES PER SIDE)
¼-inch	Heated	1½
½-inch	Heated	2 to 3
¾-inch	Heated	3

Sautéing Times for Beef and Pork (*continued*)

Pork (*continued*)

Ham Steaks and Slices, uncooked Brown steaks in oil in large, heavy skillet.

THICKNESS OF CUT	DONENESS	SAUTÉING TIMES (MINUTES PER SIDE)
¼-inch	Medium	3
½-inch	Medium	4
¾-inch	Medium	6

Loin or Rib Chops, trimmed of excess fat Brown chops in a little oil in large, heavy saucepan or flameproof casserole over moderate heat, about 3 minutes per side. Reduce heat. Continue cooking, uncovered, until chops are no longer pink inside, usually 10 to 15 minutes.

THICKNESS OF CUT	DONENESS	SAUTÉING TIMES (MINUTES PER SIDE)
½-inch	No longer pink inside	13 to 18

Sausage Brown sausages in 1 to 2 tablespoons of fat in a heavy skillet over moderate heat until brown, turning frequently.

DONENESS	SAUTÉING TIMES (MINUTES PER SIDE)
Medium	3 to 5

Sautéing Chicken

Brown the chicken over moderately high heat. Then reduce the heat and simmer, covered, over moderately low heat until cooked through.

PART	BROWNING TIME IN MINUTES	SIMMERING TIME IN MINUTES
Split breasts	6 to 8	15 to 25
Boneless breasts	2 per side	6 to 12
Thighs	6 to 8	30 to 40
Drumsticks	6 to 8	25 to 35
Wings	6 to 8	20 to 30

Sautéing Fish

This method is best for fillets, steaks, and small whole fish. Make sure fish is very dry before it's sautéed. Season fish with salt and pepper, then lightly dredge in flour.

TYPE	MINUTES PER SIDE
Thick fillets and steaks	4 to 5
Thin fillets and steaks	2 to 3
Whole fish	3 to 5

Low-Fat Frying, Stir-Frying, or Sautéing

You can return the skillet to its place of glory with fat-conscious frying.

☐ Nonstick cooking spray is ideal for low-heat sautéing, especially when combined with a nonstick frying pan.

☐ Use broth instead of oil or butter to sauté and stir-fry foods. They won't brown, but the juices will be sealed in the food. Make a coating sauce by adding cornstarch and fat-free broth to the pan juices.

☐ "Brown" ground meats in a little broth in a nonstick frying pan, and drain them through a sieve after browning to remove the fat.

Smoke-Free Sautéing

For smoke-free sautéing, use equal parts of butter or margarine and vegetable oil or olive oil. While butter adds great flavor, the addition of the oil increases the smoking temperature of the butter, allowing you to cook the foods at a higher temperature.

Sautéing Shellfish

TYPE	METHOD	TIME IN MINUTES
Clams and Oysters	Pat dry, then dust with lightly seasoned flour. Sauté in butter in a large, heavy skillet over moderate heat until lightly browned.	3
Crabs, Soft-Shell	Clean crabs (see page 191). Dust cleaned crabs with seasoned flour. Sauté, 3 or 4 at a time, in melted butter, margarine, or oil over moderate heat until crisp and golden.	3 per side
Scallops, Sea	Dip in milk and dust with lightly seasoned flour, if desired. (Or just pat dry.) Sauté in butter in a large, heavy skillet over moderately high heat until lightly browned.	4 to 5
Shrimp	Sauté shelled and deveined shrimp in butter, margarine, or oil just until pink and opaque.	3 to 5

Cooking in Paper: Super Healthy and Flavorful

Steam cutlets and fish fillets "en papillote"—in a parchment paper case—to retain all the flavorful juices. For each serving, place a single cutlet or fillet on a round of parchment, top the meat or fish with herbs and julienned vegetables, place it on a plate, and steam it until tender—about 5 minutes for a ½-inch-thick cutlet or fillet.

Heat the butter or oil in the pan so that it is hot before you add your meat or vegetables. The outside of the food must form a crust to seal in its juices. Use just enough fat to coat the bottom of the pan—too much fat will cause the food to deep-fry.

To finish a sautéed meat, you can add a small amount of wine or stock to the pan along with seasonings for flavor. Then simmer the meat, covered, for a short period of time. Remove the meat from the pan. Boil the pan juices, uncovered, until they are reduced to a light syrupy consistency.

SCALDING

Scalding is to heat a liquid until small bubbles form around the edges of the pan but the liquid never comes to a boil.

SIMMERING

When you simmer, you cook food in a liquid that is just below its boiling point.

STEAMING

Instead of poaching or boiling, you can steam vegetables, fish, and some meats by placing the food on a steamer rack and cooking it over boiling water or an aromatic liquid. Steaming food helps it to retain its natural vitamins without adding calories.

Steamers come in various shapes and sizes (see pages 156–157). A tight-fitting cover is essential to keep all the steam inside the pan and reduce the cooking time. Regardless of the steamer used, the cooking liquid must be contained *under* the food being cooked and never touch it.

You can steam right on a heat-safe dinner plate if you use a wide steamer or a bamboo steamer or wire rack (or two crossed chopsticks) in a wok. Since steamed foods cool quickly, it's an advantage to have a warm plate.

Since water can condense on the dish in a steamer, plan to serve rice or a vegetable puree with the main course to absorb the flavorful juices.

Steam some extra vegetables for later use in a frittata or omelet. Steamed chicken is delicious in salads or any recipe that calls for cooked chicken.

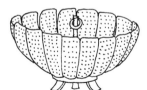

▸ **Parchment paper, 175**
▸ **Steamers, 156–157**

Steaming Fish, Shellfish, Poultry, and Sausage

FOOD	METHOD	TIME
Fish		
	Wrap whole fish or large chunks in double layer of cheesecloth. Use thick fillets or roll up thin fillets.	Fillets: 5 to 10 minutes total Steaks: 5 to 10 minutes total Chunks: 6 to 8 minutes per pound Whole fish: 6 to 8 minutes per pound
Shellfish		
Clams	For best results, use steamers or soft clams. Scrub shells well but do not shuck. Place in large deep kettle with ⅔ cup boiling water. Cover. Steam over moderately high heat until shells open. Discard any clams that do not open.	5 minutes
Crabs, blue and rock	Scrub crab shells. Place crabs on rack in large, deep kettle with enough boiling water to fill kettle 1½ inches (do not immerse crabs in water). Cover. Steam over moderately high heat until crabs turn bright red.	25 to 30 minutes
Lobster	Bring 1-inch of sea water or salted fresh water to a boil in a large, heavy kettle over moderately high heat. Add lobsters, head end first. Cover.	15 minutes
Mussels	Place in big kettle; add 1 cup boiling water. Cover; steam over moderate heat until shells open. Discard any that don't open. Strain liquid before using to remove any sand and debris.	3 minutes
Oysters	Scrub shells well but do not shuck. Place in large, deep kettle with ⅔ cup boiling water. Cover. Steam over moderate heat until shells open. Discard any that don't open.	10 to 12 minutes
Poultry		
Chickens and Capons	Use young birds. Place in a single layer on a rack over a saucepan or in a steamer. Place over simmering water.	Cut up: ¾ hour Whole: 1 to 1½ hours
Sausages		
	Place in a single layer on a rack over a saucepan or in a steamer over moderate heat. Place over simmering water or beer.	8 minutes

STEWING

When you are faced with a less tender cut of meat or poultry, stewing is ideal. Stewing is much like braising, but more liquid is used. It can be done with large or small pieces of meat. Cuts of meat suitable for stewing are from the shoulder, neck, leg, and breast. Mature chickens and turkeys are ideal for stewing, as are aged game, such as duck, pheasant, and hare.

To make a great stew, be sure the meat is dry before you brown it. Coat the meat with seasoned flour, if desired. Brown the meat a few pieces at a time to prevent it from steaming in its own juices. Once all the meat is browned, add onion or other vegetables to the pan together with herbs. Then cover the meat with liquid, such as stock or water or a marinade. If you are not using homemade stock, take care in choosing a canned broth. Most of them are salty, but you can dilute them with water. During the cooking time the liquid will reduce and concentrate, making the sauce even saltier.

Stewing Beef, Lamb, Pork, and Veal

CUT	SIMMERING TIME (HOURS)
Beef	
Roasts, corned or fresh (4 to 6 pounds)	3½ to 4½
Shank Cross Cuts (¾ to 1¼ pounds)	2½ to 3
Beef for stew (1½-inch cubes)	2½ to 3½
Lamb	
Lamb for stew (1½-inch cubes)	1½ to 2
Pork	
Ham, smoked (old-style and country cured)	
Half (5 to 8 pounds)	3 to 4
Small (10 to 12 pounds)	4½ to 5
Large (12 to 16 pounds)	4½ to 5
Hocks, fresh	2½ to 3
Hocks, smoked	2 to 2½
Ribs, country-style and spare	2 to 2½
Shoulder roll, smoked (2 to 4 pounds)	1½ to 2
Veal	
Veal for stew (1½-inch cubes)	2 to 3

♦ **Dutch oven, 163**

Bring to a simmer over moderate heat. Lower the heat; cover the pan. Simmer on top of the stove or in a 300°F. to 325°F. oven, adding vegetables toward the end of cooking, if desired, as well as more liquid, if necessary, until the meat is tender. All stews should be covered tightly to lock in the natural juices and flavors of the food. Stir occasionally to prevent sticking.

Stews improve with age. They can be prepared days in advance and kept covered and chilled. They are also suitable for freezing. Before reheating, remove the fat layer that will form at the top of the chilled stew. If the meat is to be served the next day, or cooled and served, let it cool in the cooking liquid for most succulent results.

STIR-FRYING

Frying food in a small amount of fat over high heat while continually tossing the ingredients is stir-frying. It is an Asian technique and a basic method of Chinese cooking.

A wok is the pan of choice for stir-frying, but if you don't have a wok, a well-seasoned skillet will do. You may want to briefly marinate the meat in soy sauce, sherry, sugar, and other seasonings before cooking to enhance flavor.

Place the wok over high heat, add oil, and heat until hot. Then add the seasonings—green onion, garlic, ginger, and/or other spices. Then add the main ingredient, cut into small uniform pieces. To prevent the food from burning, keep it in continual motion by quickly tossing with a spatula or long-handled spoon and by gently shaking the pan. The temperature of the oil must remain constant. After searing the meat and/or vegetables, you can add a small amount of liquid, then cover the mixture and allow it to steam. Finally, thicken the sauce by blending in dissolved cornstarch and bringing to a boil.

You will be able to create wonderful dishes with no fuss if you have all ingredients prepared and at hand before you start cooking. The ingredients should be premeasured, precut to a uniform size, and ready to be cooked so that there will be no interruption of the cooking process once it begins.

‣ **Cutting meat for stir-fries,** 193
‣ **Woks,** 159

Guide to Preparing and Cooking Vegetables

VEGETABLE (1 POUND)	EQUIVALENTS	PREPARATION	COOKING METHODS
Artichoke	1 globe	Wash, trim bottom. Snip off tips of leaves, brush with lemon juice.	Steam, boil, microwave.
Asparagus	20 large spears, 3½ to 4 cups chopped or sliced	Wash, snap off woody ends. Leave whole, chop, or slice into 1-inch pieces.	Steam, blanch, stir-fry, roast, microwave.
Avocados	2½ cups cubed	Peel, remove seed. Brush cut surfaces with lemon juice to prevent browning.	Serve uncooked.
Dried beans	2¼ to 2½ cups uncooked, 5 to 6 cups cooked	Rinse. Soak overnight or use quick-soak method (see page 218).	Simmer.
Snap beans	2½ to 3 cups snapped in 1-inch pieces	Wash. Snap off tops, leave tails.	Steam, blanch, stir-fry, microwave.
Beets	2½ to 3 cups raw or cooked, diced or sliced	Wash. Peel and trim off tops and roots after cooking.	Boil, steam, roast, bake, microwave.
Broccoli	5 to 6 cups flowerets and sliced stems, 5 cups chopped	Wash. Trim off woody bottom of stem. If necessary, peel off fibrous outer layer. Slice into spears, or slice stems and cut tops into flowerets.	Steam, blanch, stir-fry, microwave.
Brussels Sprouts	3½ cups halved, 4 cups whole	Wash, trim off loose outer leaves. Cut X into bottom of stem end or cut in half for even cooking.	Steam, blanch, stir-fry, microwave.
Cabbage	4 to 4½ cups shredded, 4 serving wedges cut 1½ inches thick	Remove tough outer leaves. Remove white core.	Steam, blanch, stir-fry, microwave.
Carrots	2½ to 3 cups sliced or diced, 2½ cups grated	Wash. Scrub or pare. Slice, dice, or grate.	Steam, blanch, stir-fry, microwave.

(table continues)

Guide to Preparing and Cooking Vegetables (*continued*)

VEGETABLE (1 POUND)	EQUIVALENTS	PREPARATION	COOKING METHODS
Cauli-flower	1 medium-size head, 1½ cups pieces	Wash. Trim away outer leaves. Cut or break off flowerets from tough stem.	Steam, blanch, microwave.
Celery	4 cups chopped, diced, or sliced	Wash. Cut away white ends of stalks if woody. Remove strings from outside ribs by slicing under the surface of the stalk at the base; then pull away along stalk and the strings will pull off.	Stir-fry, braise, sauté, microwave.
Corn on the Cob	5 to 6 ears, 3 cups kernels	Husk, remove silks. If roasting or grilling, soak ears in water for at least 1 hour first.	Steam, blanch, roast, microwave.
Cucum-bers	4 cups sliced	Wash. Pare if waxed.	Serve uncooked.
Eggplant	12 to 16 slices, 5 to 6 cups sliced, 5 cups diced, 2 cups baked and pureed	Pare, if desired.	Sauté, pan-fry, bake, broil, grill, microwave.
Greens (for cook-ing)	12 to 16 cups chopped, 1½ to 2 cups cooked	Wash in several changes of water. Strip leaves from central rib if old and woody. Chop.	Steam, blanch, sauté, microwave.
Greens (for salad)	12 to 16 cups torn	Wash in several changes of water. Strip off stems if old and woody. Tear by hand—do not chop.	Serve uncooked.
Okra	8 cups whole, 4 cups sliced	Wash. Trim off stem end, slice or leave whole.	Steam, blanch, sauté, fry, microwave.
Onions	3 large, 3 cups diced or chopped	Peel. Slice or dice.	Blanch, stir-fry, bake, roast.
Parsnips	4 medium, 3 cups sliced or diced	Trim off tops and roots. Pare.	Steam, sauté, roast, microwave.

Guide to Preparing and Cooking Vegetables (*continued*)

VEGETABLE (I POUND)	EQUIVALENTS	PREPARATION	COOKING METHODS
Peas (in pod)	1½ cups shelled, 4 to 5 cups in pod	Regular peas: shell. Snap peas: snap off stem end and pull the thread from both seams. Snow peas: pull off stem and blossom tassel.	Steam, blanch, stir-fry, microwave.
Peppers	3½ cups diced	*Sweet peppers:* wash, split open, remove seeds and white membrane. Then dice or slice. *Hot peppers:* handle carefully, wear gloves. Avoid touching skin and eyes with hands that have been in contact with peppers. Wash, remove stem. Leave whole or chop. To reduce the heat, remove seeds and white membranes.	Roast, grill, stir-fry, sauté, bake.
Potatoes	3 cups grated or diced, 4 cups sliced or chopped, 1¾ cups cooked and mashed	Wash well. Pare if desired. Chop or slice. Prep just before cooking or hold potatoes in ice water for up to 30 minutes to avoid browning.	Boil, bake, sauté, pan-fry, deep-fry, grill, roast.
Radishes	3 cups whole, 3½ cups sliced	Wash, trim away roots and black spots. Slice or leave whole.	Serve uncooked.
Rutabagas	4 cups sliced or chopped, 2 cups cooked and pureed	Trim off long tap roots and tops. Pare.	Blanch, steam, sauté, stir-fry, roast, microwave.
Summer Squash	4 cups sliced or diced, 3½ cups grated	Wash, trim off stem end and blossom end. Slice, dice, grate.	Steam, blanch, sauté, stir-fry, deep-fry, roast, microwave.

(table continues)

Guide to Preparing and Cooking Vegetables (*continued*)

VEGETABLE (I POUND)	EQUIVALENTS	PREPARATION	COOKING METHODS
Winter Squash	4 cups cubed, 2 cups cooked and pureed	Cut in half. Scrape out fibers and seeds.	Steam, bake, blanch, sauté, roast, microwave.
Tomatoes	3 cups sliced, 1¾ cups diced, 1¼ cups puree	Wash, remove stem end and blossom end. See page 187 for peeling and seeding instructions.	Simmer, sauté, bake.
Turnips	4 cups sliced or chopped, 2 cups cooked and pureed	Trim off long tap roots and tops. Pare older turnips.	Blanch, steam, sauté, stir-fry, microwave.

Cooking Beans, Grains, and Pasta

Foods that contain complex carbohydrates are important components of a healthy diet. If these foods aren't already in your diet, here's some information on how to cook them.

BEGINNING WITH BEANS

Beans require long, slow cooking. They do best with an overnight soaking in water to cover. (Lentils are very fast cooking and do not require presoaking.)

First rinse the beans and discard any stones or shriveled beans. Then soak the beans. Use 8 cups of cold water for each pound of beans. Let the beans soak overnight, or use the *quick-soak method:* After rinsing, combine the beans and water in a heavy saucepan. Bring to a boil, then reduce the heat and simmer for 2 minutes. Remove from the heat and let stand for 1 hour.

Cook the beans in fresh water. You can simmer slowly in a slow cooker for 10 to 12 hours at low heat or for 5 to 6 hours at high heat. If you have a pressure cooker, you can have tender beans in 10 to 35 minutes at 15 pounds of pressure. (Because beans expand so much as they cook, do not fill the pressure cooker more than half full.) On top of the stove, simmer in a heavy-bottomed saucepan for 1 to 3 hours.

Beans need plenty of liquid to cook. If it becomes necessary to add more liquid, heat it first. Adding cold liquid will toughen the beans. Tomatoes and vinegar will slow the cooking process and should be added near the end of the cooking time. Salt toughens beans and should only be added near the end of the cooking time.

Beans are done when they feel soft all the way through.

For a description of various beans and their cooking times, see the table on page 21.

Beans combine very well with strong seasonings. For some simple dishes, try combining kidney beans with chili powder and tomatoes, black beans with cumin, pinto beans with salsa, and lentils with curry powder. Any of these combinations make a delicious complete-protein vegetarian meal when paired with rice.

GREAT GRAINS!

If you can cook rice, you can cook any grain. And eating a variety of grains with small portions of meat puts you on a good road to healthful eating.

A wonderful flavor enhancer is to cook whole grains in chicken, beef, or vegetable stock, or in tomato juice. The heavier the pan, the less likely the grains will scorch or stick to the pan. After cooking, fluff the grains with a fork. Allow between ½ cup and ¾ cup of cooked grain per serving.

♦ **Grains, 59–61**

Guide to Cooking Whole Grains

I CUP UNCOOKED GRAIN	AMOUNT SALTED WATER	COOKING DIRECTIONS	YIELD
Pearl Barley	3 cups	Simmer, covered, for 45 to 60 minutes.	3½ cups
Buckwheat Groats (Kasha)	2 cups	Mix with beaten egg, then toast in pan until quite dry. Add boiling water and simmer, covered, for 12 to 15 minutes.	2½ to 3 cups
Bulgur	2 cups	Add to boiling water. Cover and remove from heat. Stand for about 15 minutes. Drain off any excess water.	2½ cups
Couscous (instant)	I cup	Combine with boiling water, remove from the heat, cover, and let stand for 10 minutes.	1½ cups
Millet	3 cups	Add to boiling water. Return to boiling, then reduce heat and simmer, covered, for 30 to 45 minutes.	3½ cups
Oats, rolled	3 cups	Combine with cold water and bring to a boil. Reduce the heat and simmer until thick, 5 to 7 minutes. Let stand, covered, for 3 minutes.	5¼ cups
Quinoa	2 cups	Rinse first. Combine with boiling water. Simmer, covered, for 12 to 15 minutes.	3 cups
Rice	2 cups	Combine with boiling water. Return to boil, then reduce heat. Cover and simmer white rice for 18 to 20 minutes, brown rice for 35.	3 cups
Wild Rice	3 cups	Rinse in standing water. Discard any debris that float to the top. Drain. Combine with boiling water. Return to a boil, then reduce heat and simmer, covered, until most of the grains have burst open—about 45 minutes.	4 cups

Leftover grains can be reheated by steaming over boiling water or covering and heating in the microwave (moisten with a little water or broth if dry). Or add the cooked grains to soup.

PERFECT PASTA!

Pasta and sauce, pasta and vegetables, pasta salad! You can eat pasta every day of the year and not repeat a single recipe. To cook pasta, select a large pot to allow plenty of room. Fill with at least 16 cups of water (4 quarts) for 1 pound of pasta. Do not cook more than a pound of pasta at a time. Too much pasta cooked in one pot tends to clump together; if there is too little water, the pasta will be gluey.

Salt the water for best flavor. You can also add a little oil to the water to prevent sticking. Let the water come to a full boil before adding the salt.

When the water is at a full, rolling boil, add the pasta, a few handfuls at a time, and stir to keep it from sticking. Adjust the heat to maintain a rolling boil.

Boil rapidly, uncovered, until the pasta is tender but still firm. If you cut a strand in half, you should not be able to see any white starch in the center. Fresh pasta may take as little as 2 minutes to cook. Dry pasta can take anywhere from 3 to 15 minutes.

Drain at once in a large colander. Rinsing is not necessary.

Toss with a little olive oil or sauce to keep the strands separate. Pasta is best served immediately after cooking.

Oven Cooking Methods

BRAISING

Braising can be done on top of the stove or in the oven; it is discussed on page 198.

BROILING

Long favored by dieters for cooking meats without adding extra fat to them, broiling meat under the direct heat of a broiler is easy and quick. It is best done with tender cuts of meat, such as steaks, lamb and pork chops, sliced ham, and ground beef, veal or lamb patties. Steaks and chops should be at least ¾ inch thick and sliced ham should be at least 1 inch thick. Ideally, meat for broiling should be no more than 2 inches thick.

Low-Fat Broiling Tips

☐ **Use a rack in a broiler pan so meats cook above their fat. Baste with broth or heart-healthy olive oil instead of the rendered fat.**

☐ **Broil eggplant and squash instead of frying it for vegetable lasagna or eggplant parmigiana.**

☐ **For low-fat garlic bread or croutons, grease the baking sheet and bread slices with nonstick cooking spray before toasting the bread.**

Hamburger Heaven

Hamburgers, an easy-to-make favorite! Next to charcoal broiling, oven broiling is the best method for making juicy burgers. Gently shape 1 pound of ground beef into three thick or four thin patties. Place the patties on a lightly greased broiler rack. Broil 3 inches from the preheated broiler, 4 to 5 minutes per side for rare, 5 to 6 minutes per side for medium, and 6 to 8 minutes per side for well done. Reduce broiling time by one minute each side for thin patties. Season with salt and pepper after broiling.

The broiler is maintained at a constant rate of high heat, and you control the rate of cooking by adjusting the position of the rack. Arrange the meat on the rack of a broiler pan 2 to 5 inches from the heat, depending upon the thickness of the meat. Meat cut ¾ to 1 inch thick should be placed 2 to 3 inches from the heat and thicker cuts should be placed 3 to 5 inches from the heat. When positioning the broiling rack, measure the distance from the heat source to the top of the food.

Sear beef and lamb quickly on both sides so the juices are retained and flavors are concentrated inside the food. If longer cooking is required, move the rack away from the heat source. Cook pork, veal, chicken, and fish more slowly and further away from the heat.

Broil the meat until its top is browned. Season the cooked side of the meat and turn the meat to brown the other side. It is best to add salt after the surface of the meat is browned since salt tends to draw out moisture and delay browning. Seasoning beforehand with freshly ground pepper and herbs will not affect the browning process.

You may want to marinate meat and fish beforehand for additional flavor. Chicken, lean pork, veal, and fish benefit from a liberal brushing with olive oil or butter before broiling. Basting is essential to these otherwise lean foods.

Broiling chicken. Preheat the broiler for 10 minutes. Season the chicken with your favorite herbs and melted butter, margarine, vegetable oil, bottled salad dressing, or homemade sauce. Place the chicken on a lightly oiled rack of the broiler pan and broil, 4 to 7 inches from the heat, turning and basting with the fat frequently, until it is tender.

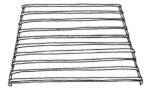

Broiling Beef, Lamb, and Pork

To broil, place the food on an unheated broiler pan. Unless otherwise specified, broil cuts less than 1¼ inches thick 3 inches from the heat. Broil thicker cuts 4 to 5 inches from the heat. Broil on each side for the time specified in this chart, turning once.

Beef

¾-inch Flank Steaks (2½ to 3 pounds), trimmed Score both sides of the meat with crisscross marks, about ⅛ inch deep and 1 inch apart. Place on oiled rack. To serve, slice against the grain ⅛ inch to ¼ inch thick.

DONENESS	TIME IN MINUTES PER SIDE
Rare	4
Medium	5 to 6

¾-inch Hamburger

DONENESS	TIME IN MINUTES PER SIDE
Rare	4 to 5
Medium	5 to 6
Well	6 to 8

1-inch Steaks (Top and Eye Round, Tip and Rump, Chuck and Boneless Blade, plus all other tender steaks except bone-in Sirloin) Broil 2 inches from heat.

DONENESS	TIME IN MINUTES PER SIDE
Very rare	3
Rare	4
Medium rare	5
Medium	6
Well done	7

1½-inch Steaks (Top and Eye Round, Tip and Rump, Chuck and Boneless Blade, plus all other tender steaks except bone-in Sirloin) Broil 3 inches from heat.

DONENESS	TIME IN MINUTES PER SIDE
Very rare	6
Rare	7
Medium rare	8
Medium	9
Well done	10 to 12

Broiling Beef, Lamb, and Pork (*continued*)

Beef (*continued*)

2-inch Steaks (Top and Eye Round, Tip and Rump, Chuck and Boneless Blade, plus all other tender steaks except bone-in Sirloin) Broil 4 inches from heat.

DONENESS	TIME IN MINUTES PER SIDE
Very rare	14
Rare	15
Medium rare	16
Medium	17
Well done	18 to 19

1-inch Steaks (Pinbone, Wedge Bone, Flat Bone Sirloin)

DONENESS	TIME IN MINUTES PER SIDE
Very rare	7
Rare	8
Medium rare	9
Medium	10
Well done	11 to 13

1½-inch Steaks (Pinbone, Wedge Bone, Flat Bone Sirloin)

DONENESS	TIME IN MINUTES PER SIDE
Very rare	10
Rare	11
Medium rare	12
Medium	13
Well done	14 to 15

2-inch Steaks (Pinbone, Wedge Bone, Flat Bone Sirloin) Broil 5 inches from heat.

DONENESS	TIME IN MINUTES PER SIDE
Very rare	18
Rare	19
Medium rare	20
Medium	21
Well done	22 to 24

1- to 2-inch Filet Steaks and Filets Mignons Broil 3 inches from heat.

DONENESS	TIME IN MINUTES PER SIDE
Very rare	4 to 5
Rare	6 to 7
Medium rare	7 to 8

(table continues)

Broiling Beef, Lamb, and Pork (*continued*)

Lamb

¾-inch Arm and Blade Chops, Leg Steaks

DONENESS	TIME IN MINUTES PER SIDE
Medium	5
Well done	6 to 7

1-inch Arm and Blade Chops, Leg Steaks

DONENESS	TIME IN MINUTES PER SIDE
Medium	6
Well done	8 to 10

1-inch Loin, English, Rib, and Sirloin Chops Broil 2 inches from heat.

DONENESS	TIME IN MINUTES PER SIDE
Rare	4 to 5
Medium	6
Well done	7

1½-inch Loin, English, Rib, and Sirloin Chops Broil 2 inches from heat.

DONENESS	TIME IN MINUTES PER SIDE
Rare	6
Medium	7
Well done	8

2-inch Loin, English, Rib, and Sirloin Chops Broil 3 inches from heat.

DONENESS	TIME IN MINUTES PER SIDE
Rare	8
Medium	9
Well done	10 to 12

Pork

Bacon, sliced (not Canadian-style) Place cold bacon slices, slightly overlapping, onto broiler rack of preheated broiler. Broil 4 inches from heat. Drain after cooking.

DONENESS	TIME IN MINUTES PER SIDE
Crisp	2 to 3

Broiling Beef, Lamb, and Pork (*continued*)

Pork (*continued*)

Chops and Steaks Broiling is not recommended.

½-inch Ham Steaks, uncooked Place ham with fat toward back of broiler to minimize splattering.

DONENESS	TIME IN MINUTES PER SIDE
Medium	4

¾-inch Ham Steaks, uncooked Place ham with fat toward back of broiler to minimize splattering.

DONENESS	TIME IN MINUTES PER SIDE
Medium	7

1-inch Ham Steaks, uncooked Place ham with fat toward back of broiler to minimize splattering. Broil 4 inches from heat.

DONENESS	TIME IN MINUTES PER SIDE
Medium	9

1½-inch Ham Steaks, uncooked Place ham with fat toward back of broiler to minimize splattering. Broil 4 inches from heat.

DONENESS	TIME IN MINUTES PER SIDE
Medium	10 to 12

½-inch Ham Steaks, ready to eat Place ham with fat toward back of broiler to minimize splattering. Avoid broiling ham steaks thicker than 1-inch.

DONENESS	TIME IN MINUTES PER SIDE
Heated	3 to 5 total time; do not turn

¾-inch Ham Steaks, ready to eat Place ham with fat toward back of broiler to minimize splattering. Avoid broiling ham steaks thicker than 1 inch.

DONENESS	TIME IN MINUTES PER SIDE
Heated	3

1-inch Ham Steaks, ready to eat Place ham with fat toward back of broiler to minimize splattering. Avoid broiling ham steaks thicker than 1 inch. Broil 4 inches from heat.

DONENESS	TIME IN MINUTES PER SIDE
Heated	5

Sausages Lightly grease broiler rack to prevent sticking. Turn frequently during broiling. Broil 3 inches from heat.

DONENESS	TIME IN MINUTES PER SIDE
Medium to well	3 to 4 total time

Enhance Meats and Fish with Marinades

Marinades not only impart flavor to food, they can also act to tenderize and moisten tough cuts of meat. Oil-based sauces help foods retain internal juices and seal the surface. Olive oil is best. The addition of an acid—wine, vinegar, or citrus juice—breaks down the tough fibers of meat and tenderizes food. A *dry rub* of chopped herbs and spices performs the same function as a marinade, but it does not moisten the meat.

Marinate small cuts of meat for about 1 hour before cooking. Marinate larger cuts of meat for several hours or overnight. Firm-fleshed fish should be marinated for about 30 minutes.

Broiling Chicken Parts

Chicken parts are particularly well suited to broiling. Broil the meat 5 to 6 inches from the heat.

PART	MINUTES PER SIDE
Split breasts	7½ to 12½
Boneless breasts	5 to 10
Thighs	10 to 15
Drumsticks	7½ to 12½
Wings	7½ to 12½

Broiling Fish

Lean steaks should be basted with melted butter, margarine, or oil once during broiling. All fillets, split fish, and whole fish should be basted at least once; very lean twice (very lean whole fish at least three times). Place split fish and fillets that still have skin on the broiler rack skin side down.

TYPE OF FISH	DISTANCE FROM HEAT	TIME IN MINUTES
¼- to ½-inch Fillets	2 inches	4 to 5; do not turn
¾- to 1-inch Fillets	2 inches	7 to 10; do not turn
½-inch Steaks	2 inches	3 on first side; 3 to 5 on second side
1-inch Steaks	2 inches	3 to 5 on first side; 4 to 5 on second side
Small whole fish (1 to 2 pounds)	3 inches	3 to 5 on first side; 5 to 6 on second side
Medium whole fish (3 to 5 pounds)	5 to 6 inches	5 to 7 on first side; 7 to 10 on second side
Flat whole fish (e.g., flounder)	3 inches	8 to 10; do not turn
Whole fish, split in halves, split ½ inch to 1 inch thick	3 inches	7 to 10; do not turn
Whole fish, split in halves, split 1 inch to 1½ inches thick	3 inches	10 to 14; do not turn

Broiling Shellfish

TYPE SHELLFISH	COMMENTS	DISTANCE FROM HEAT	BROILING TIME IN MINUTES
Crabs, Soft Shell	Clean crabs (see page 191). Bread or lightly dust with seasoned flour. Arrange, backs down, on lightly greased broiler rack. Lightly drizzle with seasoned melted butter; broil until golden brown; turn, lightly drizzle with more butter and broil.	4 to 5 inches	3 per side
Lobster	Split and clean lobster. Arrange, cut side up, on broiler pan lined with aluminum foil. Lightly brush with melted butter or margarine before and during broiling.	4 inches	12 to 15; do not turn
Scallops	Pat scallops dry, then dip in melted butter, margarine or oil. Place in a single layer in a shallow baking pan. Broil until lightly browned.	4 inches	5 to 7; do not turn
Shrimp	Shell and devein large shrimp. Place on aluminum-foil–lined broiler pan or shallow baking pan. Brush lightly with melted butter, margarine, or mixture of butter and wine, sherry, or lemon juice before and during broiling.	3 inches	3 to 5 per side

ROASTING

Who can resist a moist, rich Sunday roast, be it chicken, beef, pork, or lamb? Add roasted potatoes and vegetables, and you have a delicious and easy meal.

When foods are dry cooked in the oven or on a rotisserie, they are said to be roasted. Large, tender pieces of meat, poultry, and game are suitable for roasting, as are whole fish, fish steaks, and some vegetables.

An accurate oven temperature is as important in roasting as it is in baking. Use an oven thermometer to test the accuracy of your thermostat, and adjust accordingly. Preheat the oven at least 15 minutes before roasting or until the thermostat has reached the desired temperature.

Meat for roasting should be at room temperature. If there is no outer layer of fat on the food, brush it with oil and season it with salt and pepper. Arrange the food fat side up on a rack in a roasting pan just

♦ **Oven thermometer, 134**
♦ **Roasting pans, 162–163**
♦ **Roasting rack, 162–163**

Stuffing Sense

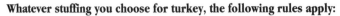

Whatever stuffing you choose for turkey, the following rules apply:

☐ Allow ¾ cup of stuffing per pound of turkey for birds weighing more than 10 pounds, ½ cup of stuffing per pound of turkey for smaller birds.

☐ Since stuffing expands as it bakes, don't tightly pack it into the turkey or else it might explode. Loosely stuff the body and neck cavities. If there's stuffing left over, place it in a lightly greased baking dish and bake it in the oven during the last 30 minutes of the turkey's roasting time.

☐ Never stuff a raw turkey ahead of roasting time. You run the risk of food poisoning. As a time-saver, prepare the stuffing in advance and refrigerate it separately from the bird. Then, when you're ready to roast, the actual stuffing of the bird will take little time.

☐ Never refrigerate a cooked bird with the stuffing still inside of it, since the stuffing will take a long time to cool and bacteria may develop. Instead, remove all of the stuffing from the bird after it's roasted, wrap both separately, and refrigerate or freeze them.

large enough to accommodate the food. (Using a rack increases the circulation of heat around the food and prevents it from sitting in the fat and drippings during cooking.) Several cuts of meat, such as pork loin roasts and rib roasts, have their own natural racks, so you don't have to use a metal rack with them.

Insert a meat thermometer in the center of the largest muscle, being sure it does not touch the bone or rest in fat. Do not add water to the pan or cover the meat, otherwise the meat will steam rather than roast. An exception to this rule is roasting turkey, when it is loosely covered with foil to prevent the skin from burning.

Two methods of roasting. With slow oven roasting, the food is roasted in a slow oven (300°F. to 325°F.). An alternative method to slow roasting is searing the food at a high temperature (450°F.) until browned—about 20 minutes—and then continuing to roast at a low temperature (300°F. to 325°F.). Devotees of this method believe the searing acts to "lock" in the juices of the meat and prevent their loss. Although this method produces a beautifully browned roast, it does result in a higher degree of shrinkage.

Whichever method you use, when the thermometer reaches 5°F. below the desired degree of doneness (see page 233), remove the roast from the oven and let it stand for 15 minutes before carving.

Roasting poultry. The best poultry for roasting are whole broiler-fryers, roasters and capons, young turkeys, Rock Cornish game hens, pheasants, and ducklings. To ready the birds for the roasting pan,

Pan Juices and Gravy

While the meat is resting before carving, you can prepare your pan juices or gravy.

To make *jus*, skim the fat from the roasting pan and *deglaze* the pan with wine, stock, or water. To deglaze, put the baking pan over medium heat, add the wine, stock, or water, and simmer, scraping up any brown bits that cling to the bottom of the pan. Correct the seasoning, adding Worcestershire sauce or other seasonings and salt and pepper to taste; strain into a sauceboat.

To make gravy, simply spoon off all but 2 to 3 tablespoons of fat from the pan, add an equal amount of flour, and cook over low heat, stirring, until golden. Add stock, water, or the deglazed pan juices to the pan and seasonings and simmer for 10 minutes. Strain into a sauceboat and serve with the roast. Cooked mushrooms, chopped giblets, and other additions can embellish the gravy, if desired.

remove the neck and giblets from the body cavities (save these for use in stocks and stuffings), remove any loose fat, thoroughly rinse the bird, and pat dry. To make carving the breast meat easier, cut out the wishbone from inside the neck cavity.

To roast a turkey, brush the turkey with vegetable oil and arrange it on a rack in a roasting pan. Once the turkey is brown, cover the breast loosely with a tent of aluminum foil to prevent further browning. Use a pan no deeper than 2 inches so that it doesn't shield the heat from the drumstick area and increase the roasting time.

To test for doneness, insert a meat thermometer in the thickest part of the thigh next to the body, but not touching the bone. The turkey is done when the thermometer registers between 180°F. to 185°F. If the turkey is stuffed, insert the thermometer in the stuffing. It should read between 160°F. and 165°F. The juices should run clear when the thigh is pricked with a fork and the drumsticks should move up and down easily.

Low-Fat Roasting Tips

☐ **Place roasts on a rack in the roasting pan; add enough water to the pan to cover the bottom. The fat will land in the water and won't smoke.**

☐ **Crush herbs and peppercorns or use a salt-free herb-and spice blend to coat well-trimmed roasts and skinned poultry before baking. Cover loosely with an aluminum-foil tent, and bake. The flavorful crust will keep the meat from drying out.**

▶ **Carving poultry, 194**
▶ **Meat thermometers, 135–136**

How to Truss a Chicken

Your chicken will roast more evenly if it is trussed before it is placed in the roasting pan. (This same method of trussing can be used for birds that are to be poached or barbecued.)

1. Arrange the chicken on a cutting board, breast side up. Bend the wing tip up and back toward the neck until it reaches behind the shoulder. Bend the other wing in the same manner. Secure with kitchen twine.

2. Cross the drumstick ends under the breast and over the tail. With kitchen twine, make several loops around the ankles of the drumsticks and the tail to hold them in place, and knot the twine.

Trussing a chicken.

1 Bend the wing tips up and back

2 Chicken after trussing

How to Truss a Turkey

Trussing allows for more even cooking, so the thigh meat is done at the same time as the breast meat.

1. Arrange the turkey on a cutting board breast side up. Loosely stuff the neck cavity and bring the neck skin up over the stuffing. With a skewer, secure the neck skin to the backbone.

2. Loosely fill the turkey cavity with stuffing, tuck the drumsticks through the skin flap to hold the legs in place or tie with kitchen twine, making several loops around the ankles of the drumsticks and the tail to hold them in place and knot the twine.

Roasting Chicken, Duck, Geese, and Game Birds

Poultry is cooked when a thermometer inserted in the thickest part of the meat, without touching bone, registers 185°F. to 190°F. (Unstuffed boneless turkey rolls and roasts should register 170°F. to 175°F.) Add 15 minutes to roasting time of small birds if they are stuffed, about 30 to 45 minutes for stuffed turkeys and geese.

Cornish game hens, squab, and pheasant should be basted frequently during roasting for juicy results.

TYPE	OVEN TEMPERATURE	TOTAL ROASTING TIME
Chicken, whole broiler (2 pounds)	375°F.	¾ to 1¼ hours
Chicken, whole broiler (2½ to 4 pounds)	375°F.	1¼ to 2 hours
Chicken, whole roaster (5 to 9 pounds)	325°F.	2¾ to 4¾ hours
Chicken, broiler halves or quarters	400°F.	¾ to 1 hour
Chicken, broiler parts (2½ to 4 pounds)	350°F.	
Split breasts		30 to 40 minutes
Boneless breasts		20 to 30 minutes
Thighs		40 to 50 minutes
Drumsticks		35 to 45 minutes
Wings		25 to 35 minutes (or longer for crisper skin)
Cornish game hen and squab (12 to 24 ounces)	350°F.	50 to 65 minutes (unstuffed)
Pheasant, farm-raised (2 to 4 pounds)	350°F.	1¼ to 2 hours (unstuffed)
Duck, whole (4 to 5½ pounds)*	350°F.	2 to 2½ hours (unstuffed)
Duck, halves and quarters	450°F. for ½ hour, then reduce to 350°F.	2 hours
Goose, unstuffed*	325°F.	2½ to 2¾ hours (4 to 6 pounds)
		2¾ to 3¼ hours (6 to 8 pounds)
		3¼ to 4¼ hours (8 to 12 pounds)
		4¼ to 4¾ hours (12 to 14 pounds)

*Note: For crisp results, prick skin often with a fork during roasting time (avoid pricking meat to conserve juices), draining off drippings as they accumulate. Brush with honey at end of roasting and raise oven temperature to 450°F. during last few minutes.

Roasting Turkey

Your turkey is cooked when a meat thermometer inserted in the meatiest part of the thigh without touching the bone reads 180°F. to 185°F.; in the thickest part of the breast, it reads 170°F.; in the center of the stuffing, it reads 160°F. to 165°F. The turkey juices should run clear and the drumsticks should move up and down easily.

Let the turkey stand at room temperature for 20 minutes before carving.

Turkey is roasted at 325°F. as a rule, but roast unstuffed turkey breasts at 350°F.

When preparing turkey parts for the oven, wipe pieces and pat dry with paper towels. Skewer skin to meat to prevent shrinking. Place pieces, skin side up, on rack over aluminum-foil–lined roasting pan.

WEIGHT (POUNDS)	ROASTING TIME IN HOURS (UNSTUFFED)	ROASTING TIME IN HOURS (STUFFED)
Whole Turkeys		
6 to 8	3 to 3½	2½ to 3½
8 to 12	3½ to 4½	3 to 4
12 to 16	4 to 5	3½ to 4½
16 to 20	4½ to 5½	4 to 5
20 to 24	5 to 6½	4½ to 5½
Halves or Quarters		
5 to 8 pounds	2½ to 3	
8 to 10 pounds	3 to 3½	
10 to 12 pounds	3½ to 4	
Boneless Turkey Rolls and Roasts		
3 to 4 pounds	2½ to 3	
4 to 5 pounds	3 to 3½	
Turkey Breasts		
2 to 4 pounds	1 to 1¾	
4 to 6 pounds	1¾ to 2¼	
6 to 8 pounds	2¼ to 2¾	
8 to 10 pounds	2¾ to 3¼	
10 to 12 pounds	3¼ to 3¾	

Roasting beef, lamb, and pork. The most suitable cuts of meat for roasting are beef rib roasts, tenderloin, and boneless rump; veal leg, loin, rib, and boneless shoulder; pork loin, shoulder, tenderloin, ribs, and leg (fresh ham); and rack of lamb, leg, crown roast, and shoulder.

Internal Temperatures for Roast Meats

MEAT/DONENESS	INTERNAL TEMPERATURE
Beef	
Rare	140°F.
Medium rare	150°F.
Medium	160°F.
Well	170°F.
Ground	160°F. to 170°F.
Lamb	
Rare	140°F.
Medium	160°F.
Well	170°F.
Pork	
Fresh Ham	160°F. to 170°F.*
Loin of Pork	160°F. to 170°F.*
Poultry	
Chicken, without stuffing	180°F.
Turkey, without stuffing	180°F. to 185°F.**
Turkey Breast, with bone	170°F. to 180°F.
Turkey Roast, boneless	170°F. to 175°F.
Chicken, Turkey, Cornish Hen, stuffed	160°F. to 165°F.†
Veal	
Medium	160°F.
Well	170°F.
Leg of Venison (rare)	140°F. to 145°F.

*Trichinae, the parasites that cause trichinosis, are killed at 137°F. to 140°F. At 160°F. the pork will be quite pink. At 170°F. it will no longer be pink, but will still be juicy.

**For unstuffed poultry, insert the meat thermometer into the thickest part of the meat without touching a bone.

†For stuffed poultry, insert the meat thermometer through the meat into the stuffing without touching a bone.

Roasting Beef, Lamb, Pork, and Veal

Beef

To cook a beef roast just right, remove the meat from the oven when a meat thermometer registers 10 degrees below the desired temperature of doneness; the meat will continue to cook upon standing. Let the meat stand for 15 to 20 minutes before carving.

Rib-Eye and Eye-Round Roasts (4 to 6 pounds); Small Roasts (less than 3 pounds) Roast at 350°F.

DONENESS	ROASTING TIME
140°F. rare	18 to 20 minutes per pound
150°F. medium rare	20 to 22 minutes per pound
160°F. medium	22 to 24 minutes per pound
170°F. well done	24 to 26 minutes per pound

Sirloin Tips, boneless (3 to 5 pounds) Use only prime or choice grades for roasting. Roast at 325°F.

DONENESS	ROASTING TIME
140°F. rare	20 to 25 minutes per pound
150°F. medium rare	25 to 28 minutes per pound
160°F. medium	28 to 32 minutes per pound
170°F. well done	34 to 39 minutes per pound

Standing Rib Roasts (6 to 8 pounds) Roast at 325°F.

DONENESS	ROASTING TIME
140°F. rare	23 to 25 minutes per pound
150°F. medium rare	25 to 27 minutes per pound
160°F. medium	27 to 30 minutes per pound
170°F. well done	30 to 32 minutes per pound

Standing Rib Roasts, boned and rolled (4 to 6 pounds) Roast at 325°F.

DONENESS	ROASTING TIME
140°F. rare	26 to 32 minutes per pound
150°F. medium rare	32 to 34 minutes per pound
160°F. medium	34 to 38 minutes per pound
170°F. well done	40 to 42 minutes per pound

Roasting Beef, Lamb, Pork, and Veal (*continued*)

Beef (*continued*)

Standing Rump Roasts, boned and rolled (4 to 6 pounds) Use only prime or choice grades for roasting. Roast at 325°F.

DONENESS	ROASTING TIME
140°F. rare	19 to 21 minutes per pound
150°F. medium rare	21 to 23 minutes per pound
160°F. medium	23 to 25 minutes per pound
170°F. well done	25 to 27 minutes per pound

Tenderloin, whole (4 to 6 pounds) Roasting tenderloin beyond medium rare is not recommended. For best results, wrap with bacon or fatback and rub exposed ends with softened butter before roasting. Place meat on a rack in a roasting pan. Roast at 450°F.

DONENESS	ROASTING TIME
120°F. to 125°F. rare	5 to 6 minutes per pound
130°F. to 140°F. medium rare	7 to 8 minutes per pound

Top Round (3 to 6 pounds) Use only prime or choice grades for roasting. Roast at 300°F.

DONENESS	ROASTING TIME
120°F. to 125°F. rare	28 to 30 minutes per pound
130°F. to 140°F. medium rare	30 to 33 minutes per pound
145°F. to 150°F. medium	34 to 38 minutes per pound
155°F. to 165°F. well done	40 to 45 minutes per pound

Lamb

Let the meat stand for about 15 minutes before carving.

Boneless Cuts, Leg of Lamb, Loin, and Saddle Boneless roasts and small roasts (3 to 4 pounds) need about 3 minutes more per pound to reach the desired degree of doneness. Roast at 325°F.

DONENESS	ROASTING TIME
130°F. to 135°F. rare	12 to 13 minutes per pound
140°F. to 145°F. medium rare	14 to 16 minutes per pound
150°F. to 160°F. medium	18 to 20 minutes per pound
160°F. to 165°F. well done	20 to 25 minutes per pound

(table continues)

Roasting Beef, Lamb, Pork, and Veal (*continued*)

Lamb (*continued*)

All other lamb cuts (slow oven method) Boneless roasts need about 3 minutes more per pound to reach the desired degree of doneness. Roast at 375°F.

DONENESS	ROASTING TIME
130°F. to 135°F. rare	11 to 13 minutes per pound
140°F. to 145°F. medium rare	13 to 15 minutes per pound
150°F. to 160°F. medium	16 to 18 minutes per pound
160°F. to 165°F. well done	18 to 20 minutes per pound

All other cuts of lamb (high heat method) Use roasting times below *in addition to the first 15 minutes at 450°F.* Boneless roasts need about 2 or 3 minutes more per pound to reach the desired degree of doneness. Roast at 450°F. first 15 minutes, then 350°F.

DONENESS	ROASTING TIME
130°F. to 135°F. rare	10 to 12 minutes per pound
140°F. to 145°F. medium rare	12 to 14 minutes per pound
150°F. to 160°F. medium	14 to 16 minutes per pound
160°F. to 165°F. well done	16 to 18 minutes per pound

Pork

Remove roasts from the oven when a meat thermometer registers 10 degrees below the desired temperature of doneness; the meat will continue to cook while standing. Let the meat stand for 15 to 20 minutes before carving.

Bacon, sliced Lay cold bacon strips, slightly overlapping, on cookie rack set over foil-lined roasting pan. Bake without turning, uncovered, until crisp. Roast at 400°F.

DONENESS	ROASTING TIME
Crisp	12 to 15 minutes total

Canadian Bacon Roll (minimum 2 pounds) Remove casing and place bacon roll, fat side up, on rack over foil-lined roasting pan. For extra juiciness, pour 1 cup of liquid into pan before placing in oven. Do not cover during roasting. Roast at 325°F.

DONENESS	ROASTING TIME
160°F.	35 minutes per pound

Crown Roasts (large: 7 to 8 pounds; small: 5 to 6 pounds), stuffed Cover tips of bones with aluminum foil to prevent burning. Add stuffing about halfway into roasting period and cover loosely with aluminum foil. Remove foil during last 15 minutes of roasting. Roast at 325°F.

DONENESS	ROASTING TIME
170°F.	30 to 35 minutes per pound

Roasting Beef, Lamb, Pork, and Veal (*continued*)

Pork (*continued*)

Ham, country cured Prior to roasting, soak ham in cool water for one day, to remove excess salt. Change water several times if very salty, otherwise change it once or twice. Scrub soaked ham with a stiff brush, then rinse with warm water. Place ham on rack in large kettle or casserole; add cool water to cover, cover pan, and bring to a boil, skimming surface. Reduce heat; cover and simmer until fork tender—about 30 minutes per pound. Cool in cooking liquid. Skin ham and trim away all but ½ inch of fat. Place, fat side up, on a rack in a roasting pan; top with glaze. Let rest 15 minutes or longer before carving. Roast at 350°F.

DONENESS	ROASTING TIME
160°F.	45 minutes to 1 hour total

Ham, fresh, half (Butt or Shank: 5 to 7 pounds) Roast at 325°F.

DONENESS	ROASTING TIME
185°F.	30 to 35 minutes per pound

Ham, fresh, whole (10 to 14 pounds) Roast at 325°F.

DONENESS	ROASTING TIME
185°F.	25 minutes per pound

Ham, fresh, whole, boneless (7 to 10 pounds) Let rest 15 minutes before carving. Roast at 325°F.

DONENESS	ROASTING TIME
185°F.	35 minutes per pound

Ham Steaks, ready to eat (1½ inches to 2 inches thick) Place ham on rack in shallow roasting pan. Glaze, if desired. Roast at 325°F.

DONENESS	ROASTING TIME
160°F.	30 to 35 minutes total

Ham Steaks, uncooked (1½ inches to 2 inches thick) Place ham on rack in shallow roasting pan. Glaze, if desired. Roast at 325°F.

DONENESS	ROASTING TIME
160°F.	1½-inch steak: 1 to 1¼ hours total
	2-inch steak: 1½ to 1¾ hours total

Ham, uncooked, whole (12 to 14 pounds) or boneless (7 to 10 pounds) Remove skin and trim all but ½ inch of fat, if necessary. Place ham fat side up on rack in roasting pan. Brush with glaze every 15 to 20 minutes. For a crisp brown glaze, raise heat to 425°F. during last 15 minutes of roasting time. Let rest 15 minutes before carving. Roast at 325°F.

DONENESS	ROASTING TIME
160°F.	18 to 20 minutes per pound

(table continues)

Roasting Beef, Lamb, Pork, and Veal (*continued*)

Pork (continued)

Ham, uncooked, half (6 to 7 pounds) Remove skin and trim all but ½ inch of fat, if necessary. Place ham cut side down on rack in roasting pan. Brush with glaze every 15 to 20 minutes. For a crisp brown glaze, raise heat to 425°F. during last 15 minutes of roasting time. Let rest 15 minutes before carving. Roast at 325°F.

DONENESS	ROASTING TIME
160°F.	22 to 24 minutes per pound

Ham, ready to eat, whole or boneless Brush with glaze every 15 to 20 minutes. For a crisp brown glaze, raise heat to 425°F. during last 15 minutes of roasting time. Let rest 15 minutes before carving. Roast at 325°F.

DONENESS	ROASTING TIME
130°F.	12 to 15 minutes per pound

Ham, ready to eat, half or canned Brush with glaze every 15 to 20 minutes. For a crisp brown glaze, raise heat to 425°F. during last 15 minutes of roasting time. Let rest 15 minutes before carving. Roast at 325°F.

DONENESS	ROASTING TIME
130°F.	18 to 20 minutes per pound

Loin Roasts, center (3 to 5 pounds) Roast at 325°F.

DONENESS	ROASTING TIME
170°F.	30 minutes per pound

Loin Roasts, Sirloin and Blade (3 to 4 pounds) Roast at 325°F.

DONENESS	ROASTING TIME
170°F.	40 minutes per pound

Loin Roasts, half (5 to 7 pounds) Roast at 325°F.

DONENESS	ROASTING TIME
170°F.	35 minutes per pound

Loin Roasts, rolled (3 to 5 pounds) Roast at 325°F.

DONENESS	ROASTING TIME
170°F.	40 to 45 minutes per pound

Shoulder, Arm Roasts (3 to 5 pounds) Roast at 325°F.

DONENESS	ROASTING TIME
185°F.	35 to 40 minutes per pound

Roasting Beef, Lamb, Pork, and Veal (*continued*)

Pork (*continued*)

Shoulder, Butt, smoked (1 to 4 pounds) Prior to roasting, place meat on rack in large casserole or kettle; add cold water to cover. Cover casserole, bring to a boil, then lower heat. Simmer for about 15 minutes per pound. Let cool in liquid for 10 minutes. Instead of glazing, drizzle with honey, maple syrup, or molasses during last 10 minutes of roasting time and raise oven temperature to 425°F. Roast at 325°F., then at 425°F. for last 10 minutes

DONENESS	ROASTING TIME
170°F.	30 to 35 minutes per pound

Spareribs, 3 inches long, cut into pieces Arrange ribs in shallow roasting pan; pour over them desired sauce. Roast, uncovered, until tender. Baste frequently for moist results. Roast at 350°F.

DONENESS	ROASTING TIME
Well done	2 hours total

Tenderloin, whole (1½ pounds) Roast at 325°F.

DONENESS	ROASTING TIME
170°F.	1 hour total

Veal

Leg, rib, loin, and rump veal roasts are the best for roasting, but they require additional fat for juicy, tender results (drape the exterior with strips of bacon or salt pork) and should be basted throughout the roasting period. Place roasts fat side up in roasting pan. Let meat stand for about 15 minutes before carving.

Bone-in cuts Roast at 325°F.

DONENESS	ROASTING TIME
155°F. to 160°F. well done	30 to 35 minutes per pound

Boned and rolled cuts Roast at 325°F.

DONENESS	ROASTING TIME
155°F. to 160°F. well done	40 minutes per pound

Roasting Fish and Shellfish

TYPE	NOTES	OVEN TEMPERA-TURE	ROASTING TIME IN MINUTES
Fish			
Chunks, fillets, steaks	Place fish in single layer, not touching, in shallow pan lined with well-greased aluminum foil. Lightly brush fish with a small amount of melted butter, margarine, or oil. Baste frequently during roasting. Roast until fish flakes easily with a fork.	350°F.	20 to 30 total
Whole, unstuffed	Place fish in single layer, not touching, in shallow pan lined with well-greased aluminum foil. Brush lean fish with melted butter, margarine, or oil (and keep basting during roasting). Measure fish at thickest point. Roast until fish flakes easily with a fork.	400°F.	10 per inch or 10 to 15 per pound
Whole, stuffed	Place loosely stuffed fish in single layer in shallow pan lined with well-greased aluminum foil. Lightly brush fish with melted butter, margarine, or oil (and keep basting during roasting). Roast until fish flakes easily with a fork.	400°F.	12 to 15 per pound (before stuffing)
Shellfish			
Clams	Scrub shells with a stiff brush but do not shuck. Roast, uncovered, in shallow baking pan in preheated oven until shells open. Discard any clams that don't open.	450°F.	12 to 15 total
Lobster	Use split and cleaned freshly killed lobsters. Arrange, cut side up, in large shallow roasting pan. Dot flesh with butter; squeeze lemon juice over all. Do not cover. Bake in preheated oven, basting often.	350°F.	25 to 30 total
Oysters	Scrub shells but do not shuck. Roast, uncovered, in shallow baking pan in preheated oven until shells open. Discard any oysters that don't open.	500°F.	12 to 15 minutes

STEWING

Stewing can be done on top of the stove or in the oven; it is covered on pages 213–214.

GRILLING AND BARBECUING

Cooking foods over a charcoal fire or gas grill has become one of America's favorite pastimes. The same foods suitable for broiling—tender cuts of meat, poultry, and fish—are likewise ideal for grilling and barbecuing, and the same principles of seasoning apply to grilling and barbecuing as they do to broiling (see page 221).

Most of the barbecue cooking we do is on an uncovered grill. This is perfect for burgers, steaks, and chops—foods that require quick searing over a bed of hot coals. The characteristic barbecue flavor is given not by the coals but by the melted fat coming into contact with the coals and producing smoke. Large cuts of meat can be cooked slowly, over indirect heat, in a covered grill.

The indirect method of barbecuing. When you are preparing cuts of meat that require long, slow cooking—whole chickens, roasts, leg of lamb, for example—you will want to cook the meat over indirect heat, with the meat arranged over a drip pan, to save the juices and to prevent flare-ups of the fire. A 13 x 9 x 2-inch baking pan makes an excellent drip pan.

Preheat the grill. When the coals have burned down and turned gray, arrange the coals around a drip pan. Add additional charcoal around the outside edge of the coals for long grilling times. Put the meat or food to be barbecued, fat side up, on the grill directly over the drip pan. Cover the grill and adjust the vents according to the manufacturer's directions. Proceed with the recipe directions for cooking time.

For casseroles, arrange the heated gray coals in a circle around the sides of the barbecue. Put the casserole inside the circle of coals on the grill. Cover the grill and adjust the vents according to the manufacturer's directions; proceed with the recipe directions for cooking times.

Making a grill cover or dome for a barbecue grill. When you want to cover an open-air grill, you can construct your own dome using a wire coat hanger frame and covering it with aluminum foil.

1. Cut the hooks off of several hangers and open them out into straight pieces. Make a ring the exact size of your grill by twisting together the ends of two or three hanger pieces with pliers. To fashion a dome you will need to use five or six more straightened hangers. Twist the ends of the hangers to form the dome around the ring base.

2. Cover the dome with several sheets of overlapping heavy-duty aluminum foil, gathering the foil at the top of the dome and twisting it together to form a topknot for a handle. Cut several flaps for vents near the top.

**♦ Cookware for barbecuing,
165**

Making a grill cover.

Making a drip pan. To prevent fat flare-ups, put a drip pan under the meat you are grilling or roasting on the rotisserie. You can use a baking pan or fashion one out of foil to reduce cleanup chores.

1. Begin with three 24-inch pieces of 18-inch-wide heavy-duty aluminum foil and fold each piece in half to make a double thickness.

2. Turn up the edges 2 inches on each side and press the edges firmly together to form mitered corners.

3. Press the mitered corners inward, toward the pan sides, to make a firm pan. (*Note:* This will give you an 8- by 14-inch drip pan. If this is not the right size for your needs, start with the size pan you will need, add 4 inches to both the length and the width, and then double the measurement of the width.)

Making a drip pan.

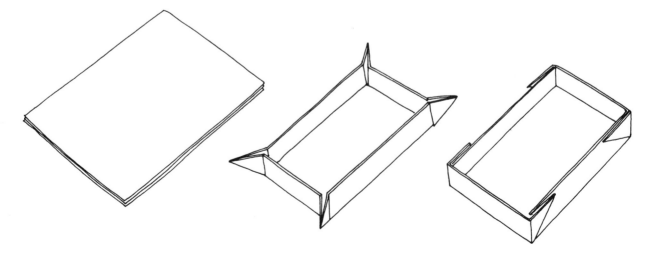

**Cooking chicken on
a rotisserie.**

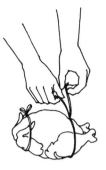

1 Trussing poultry for
the grill

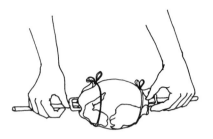

2 Securing chicken on a
rotisserie

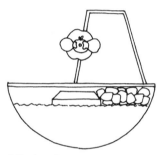

3 Rotisserie setup

4 Grilling poultry over indirect heat

How to use a rotisserie. Roasts, chickens, turkey, and Rock Cornish hens are especially moist and flavorful when cooked over the coals and turned slowly on a rotisserie. The rotisserie consists of a long skewer with a fork at each end to hold the meat securely and a turning mechanism. The roast or poultry must balance evenly on the rotisserie rod for even cooking. Insert the forks securely to prevent the meat from slipping while roasting. Pile the gray coals at the back of the grill with the drip pan directly under the grilling meat or poultry to prevent flare-ups, which give a burnt, rather than a charcoal, taste to foods.

How to Truss Poultry for the Grill

Secure the neck skin with a metal skewer. Push the tail into the cavity and secure with a metal skewer. Press the wings against the side of the breast and wrap a long piece of kitchen twine around the bird twice. Tie securely. Loop a second long piece of twine several times around the drumsticks and tie. If the poultry is stuffed, be sure to close the opening. Insert small metal skewers along the opening and lace it closed with twine.

Wrapping foods in foil for barbecuing. The secret to slow-cooking large pieces of meat is to wrap them in airtight foil packets. This keeps the meat deliciously moist and helps it cook evenly.

Center the food in the middle of a rectangular heavy-duty aluminum foil sheet that is large enough to go around the food and allow for folding at the top and sides. Bring the long sides up and over the food and fold them over about 1 inch. Make a crease the entire length; make two more tight folds to bring the wrapping down to the level of the food surface. Press out the air toward the ends. Fold the ends up and over three times, pressing out the air and shaping to the contours of the food.

Tips for Successful Grilling.

□ Always store the charcoal in its tightly closed package or in a tightly closed plastic or metal container in a cool, dry place. For extra protection, place the package in a plastic or metal container with a tight-fitting lid. If the charcoal gets damp or absorbs a great deal of moisture, it becomes difficult to light.

□ Line the bottom of the barbecue with heavy-duty aluminum foil for easy cleanup.

□ Mound the coals in the center of the barbecue or around a drip pan and set aflame. Or use a special metal "chimney" to light the coals, following the manufacturer's directions. With this device, the coals will be ready in about 15 minutes and no special starting fluid is required.

□ To light the fire, use either charcoal starter fluid or an electric starter. Liquid charcoal starters may impart off flavors in foods, while electric starters will not. If you are using fluid, wait 2 minutes for the starter to soak in before igniting. Paraffin, block, or solid starters are also very good.

□ Light a charcoal fire at least 30 to 40 minutes before you start to cook. This allows the coals time to burn and become covered with a gray ash. The heat will be radiant and will cook the food gradually without burning.

□ Once the coals are hot, spread them into an even layer on the bottom of the grill. For cooking times longer than 45 minutes, add charcoal around the outside edge of the charcoal bed, just touching the hot coals, from time to time.

□ You can scatter fresh herbs (marjoram, rosemary, thyme, or mint) or dried herbs (bay leaf or fennel) soaked in water, over the hot coals to give the grilled meat subtle flavoring. Sprinkling water-soaked wood chips of hickory, apple, cherry, alder, and mesquite on the coals just before grilling will also add flavor.

□ When grilling fish and lean meats, brush the grill with fat or oil or use vegetable cooking spray just before cooking to prevent food from sticking.

☐ When grilling fatty foods, make a drip pan (see page 242) and place it directly under the food to prevent fat flare-ups.

☐ Place the grill in a sheltered place away from drafts to maintain a constant and even temperature. On a windy day, cover the grill with a hood or a tent of foil (see page 242).

☐ When grilling foods that need slow cooking, arrange the grill rack at its highest position and lower it during cooking as the coals cool down.

☐ Use the last glowing embers to keep coffee hot; toast marshmallows or pound cake; heat fudge or butter-pecan sauce for ice cream; warm cookies, rolls, apple pie; or grill orange or pineapple slices.

Barbecuing Safety.

It's always best to be safe with fire! Listed below are guidelines for barbecue safety.

PREPARING FOR A BARBECUE

☐ Read and follow the manufacturer's instructions for your grill carefully.

☐ Check to see if previously used equipment is in good working order—for example, vents open and free from any foreign material. Check to see that there are no leaking connections if you are using a gas grill.

☐ Place the grill so that the cook's back is to the wind.

☐ Situate the grill on a level, noncombustible surface, allowing at least 18 inches of clearance on all sides to maintain sufficient supply and circulation of air.

☐ Always keep a fire extinguisher handy.

☐ Trim meats of excess fat to eliminate the risk of flare-ups.

LIGHTING THE BARBECUE

☐ Gasoline and other highly volatile fuels are very dangerous; do not use them. Use only the manufacturer's recommended starter fuel, and use it in the amounts recommended.

☐ Be sure to reseal starter fluid after use and put it at a safe distance from the grill and all flames.

☐ When lighting the coals or cooking, it is best to refrain from leaning over the grill.

☐ When lighting a gas grill, always be sure the cover remains open until the burner is burning smoothly.

☐ Once coals have been lighted, never add liquid starter.

USING YOUR BARBECUE

☐ When operating a barbecue, never wear loose-fitting clothing, which presents a potential fire hazard.

☐ Adjust hot vents wearing barbecue mitts.

□ Long-handled tongs, forks, and spatulas are best for turning food on the grill.

□ If flare-ups should occur, transfer the food to the side of the grill until the flames have died down.

□ Always be sure young children and all animals are kept away from the grill.

THE END OF A SUCCESSFUL BARBECUE

□ Once the coals have cooled completely they may be disposed of—not before.

□ For gas grills, be sure to check that all burner control valves are switched off and, if applicable, gas supplies discontinued.

□ Clean the grill with a wire brush while it is still hot and store it in a dry place once it has cooled down.

Low-Fat Grilling Techniques.

With an in-house stovetop grill *and* a garden-variety charcoal or gas barbecue, barbecueing can be a low-fat and delicious way to cook year-round.

□ Use fat-free broth or vegetable juice for marinades instead of oil. Baste the food frequently with the marinade while grilling.

□ Instead of grilling large pieces of meat marbled with fat, make satés or kabobs from the meat after it has been well trimmed. This way you can skewer and grill a bounty of low-calorie, nutritious vegetables along with the meat. (Blanch onions and potatoes first to speed up their grilling time to coincide with that of the meat.)

□ Make a delicious meal of flavorful grilled vegetables, including potatoes, eggplant, zucchini, onions, mushrooms, and peppers. Using a hinged grill basket for small pieces of vegetables and fish keeps the foods from slipping into the fire.

□ Be generous with citrus fruit juices and grated peel in marinades. They are nonfat and flavorful!

□ Ripe tomatoes, skinned, seeded, and pureed, make a tenderizing base for marinades.

□ Grease the grill and the food with nonstick cooking oil spray.

□ Grilled red peppers, skinned, seeded, and pureed, make a sweet, flavorful complement to tangy low-fat plain yogurt for dips and sauces.

Grilled Vegetables

Don't confine your grill to meats and fish. Grilled vegetables are delicious. Everyone's favorite: corn on the cob. Soak the ears for at least 1 hour before grilling. Open each ear and remove the silks, then close the husks back over the ear. If you like, you can butter the ear before closing up the husks. Place the corn on the grill and cook for about 20 minutes, turning frequently.

Other good vegetables to try are potatoes (parboiled), zucchini, summer squash, onions, peppers, mushrooms, eggplant, carrots, and asparagus. You'll need a hinged grill basket to prevent the vegetables from slipping into the fire.

Lightly brush the vegetables with a mixture of olive oil and chopped herbs. Then grill till tender, a few minutes per side.

Grilling Meat

Beef

Hamburger Gently shape 1 pound of ground beef into three thick patties. Place the patties on lightly greased grill. Grill 4 inches from moderately hot coals. Season with salt and pepper after grilling.

DONENESS	TIME IN MINUTES
120°F. to 125°F. rare	4 to 5 per side
140°F. to 150°F. medium	5 to 6 per side
160°F. to 170°F. well done	7 to 8 per side

Tenderloin, whole (4 to 6 pounds) Use a spit for even cooking. The tenderloin should be wrapped with suet for moist, juicy results (remove the covering for last 10 minutes of grilling time and brush once or twice with melted butter or flavored oil). Grill 6 inches from hot coals.

DONENESS	TIME IN MINUTES
120°F. to 125°F. rare	25 to 30 total grilling time
130°F. to 140°F. medium rare	35 to 40 total grilling time

Standing Rib, bone in (5 to 8 pounds) Use a spit for even cooking. Set the spit 6 inches from moderately hot coals.

DONENESS	TIME IN MINUTES
125°F. to 130°F. rare	12 to 14 per pound
140°F. to 145°F. medium rare	15 to 17 per pound
155°F. to 160°F. medium	18 to 20 per pound
165°F. to 170°F. well done	21 to 23 per pound

Standing Rib, boned and rolled Rib (4 to 6 pounds) Use a spit for even cooking. Set the spit 6 inches from moderately hot coals.

DONENESS	TIME IN MINUTES
125°F. to 130°F. rare	22 to 24 per pound
140°F. to 145°F. medium rare	25 to 27 per pound
155°F. to 160°F. medium	28 to 30 per pound
165°F. to 170°F. well done	31 to 33 per pound

1-inch Steaks, Tip and Rump, Chuck and Boneless Blade, plus all other tender steaks Grill 4 inches from hot coals.

DONENESS	TIME IN MINUTES
Very rare	3 per side
Rare	4 to 5 per side
Medium rare	6 per side
Medium	7 to 8 per side
Well done	9 to 10 per side

(table continues)

Grilling Meat (*continued*)

Beef (continued)

1½- to 1¾-inch Steaks, Tip and Rump, Chuck and Boneless Blade, plus all other tender steaks Grill 4 inches from hot coals.

DONENESS	TIME IN MINUTES
Very rare	4 per side
Rare	5 to 6 per side
Medium rare	7 to 8 per side
Medium	9 to 10 per side
Well done	12 to 15 per side

2-inch Steaks, Tip and Rump, Chuck and Boneless Blade, plus all other tender steaks Grill 5 inches from hot coals.

DONENESS	TIME IN MINUTES
Very rare	6 to 7 per side
Rare	8 to 9 per side
Medium rare	10 to 12 per side
Medium	13 to 15 per side
Well done	20 to 22 per side

2½-inch Steaks, Tip and Rump, Chuck and Boneless Blade, plus all other tender steaks Grill 5 inches from hot coals.

DONENESS	TIME IN MINUTES
Very rare	10 to 12 per side
Rare	13 to 15 per side
Medium rare	16 to 18 per side
Medium	20 to 22 per side
Well done	23 to 25 per side

Flank Steaks (2½ to 3 pounds) Grill 3 inches from hot coals.

DONENESS	TIME IN MINUTES
Rare	3 to 4 per side

Lamb

¾-inch Arm and Blade Chops, Leg Steaks Grill 4 inches from moderately hot coals.

DONENESS	TIME IN MINUTES
Medium	6 per side
Well done	7 to 8 per side

Grilling Meat (*continued*)

Lamb (*continued*)

1-inch Arm and Blade Chops, Leg Steaks Grill 4 inches from moderately hot coals.

DONENESS	TIME IN MINUTES
Medium	7 per side
Well done	10 per side

1-inch Loin, English, Rib and Sirloin Chops Grill 4 inches from hot coals.

DONENESS	TIME IN MINUTES
Rare	5 to 6 per side
Medium	7 per side
Well done	8 per side

1½-inch Loin, English, Rib and Sirloin Chops Grill 4 inches from hot coals.

DONENESS	TIME IN MINUTES
Rare	7 per side
Medium	8 to 9 per side
Well done	10 per side

2-inch Loin, English, Rib and Sirloin Chops Grill 5 inches from moderately hot coals.

DONENESS	TIME IN MINUTES
Rare	8 to 10 per side
Medium	10 to 12 per side
Well done	12 to 14 per side

Breast of Lamb (about 6 pounds) Use a spit for even cooking. Start with the spit 7 to 8 inches from the moderately hot coals. After 1 hour, bring the spit 1 inch closer to the coals. Baste frequently. Let rest about 15 minutes before carving.

DONENESS	TIME IN MINUTES
Medium	1 hour and 20 to 30 minutes total

Lamb Burgers Gently shape 1 pound of ground lamb into three thick patties. Place patties on lightly greased grill. Grill 4 inches from moderately hot coals. Season with salt and pepper after grilling.

DONENESS	TIME IN MINUTES
Medium	4 to 5 per side
Well done	6 to 7 per side

(table continues)

Grilling Meat (*continued*)

Lamb (*continued*)

Leg of Lamb, boned and cut into 1½-inch cubes for shish kebabs Grill 3 to 4 inches from moderately hot coals. Turn and baste frequently.

DONENESS	TIME IN MINUTES
Rare	15 to 20 total grilling time
Medium	20 to 25 total grilling time
Well done	25 to 30 total grilling time

Riblets Grill 4 to 5 inches from moderately hot coals.

DONENESS	TIME IN MINUTES
Medium	20 total grilling time

Roasts, Double Loin, Leg, Loin, Rack, Rolled Shoulder, Saddle (4 to 5 pounds for all but racks and loins, which weigh around 2½ pounds) Use a spit set 6 to 7 inches from moderately hot coals for even cooking. Let the meat rest about 15 minutes before carving.

DONENESS	TIME IN MINUTES
130°F. to 135°F. rare	7 to 8 per pound
140°F. to 145°F. medium rare	9 to 11 per pound
150°F. to 160°F. medium	13 to 15 per pound
160°F. to 165°F. well done	15 to 20 per pound

Pork

Canadian Bacon Rolls (3 to 4 pounds) Use a spit set 4 to 5 inches from moderately hot coals for even cooking. Baste, if desired, every 15 to 20 minutes.

DONENESS	TIME IN MINUTES
160°F.	25 per pound

½-inch Ham Steaks, uncooked Grill 4 inches from moderately low coals.

DONENESS	TIME IN MINUTES
160°F.	5 per side

¾-inch Ham Steaks, uncooked Grill 4 inches from moderately low coals.

DONENESS	TIME IN MINUTES
160°F.	6 to 8 per side

1-inch Ham Steaks, uncooked Grill 5 inches from moderately low coals.

DONENESS	TIME IN MINUTES
160°F.	10 per side

1½-inch Ham Steaks, uncooked Grill 5 inches from moderately low coals.

DONENESS	TIME IN MINUTES
160°F.	12 per side

Pork (continued)

1½-inch Ham Steaks, uncooked Grill 5 inches from moderately low coals.

DONENESS	TIME IN MINUTES
160°F.	12 per side

½-inch Ham Steaks, ready to eat Grill 4 inches from moderately low coals. Do not turn.

DONENESS	TIME IN MINUTES
Heated	3 to 4 total

¾-inch Ham Steaks, ready to eat Grill 4 inches from moderately low coals. Do not turn.

DONENESS	TIME IN MINUTES
Heated	4 to 5 total

1-inch Ham Steaks, ready to eat Avoid grilling ham steaks thicker than 1 inch. Grill 4 inches from moderately low coals. Do not turn.

DONENESS	TIME IN MINUTES
Heated	5 to 6 total

Ham, ready to eat, skinless and boneless Use a spit set 6 to 7 inches from moderately hot coals for even cooking. Let stand 15 minutes before carving.

DONENESS	TIME IN MINUTES
130°F.	10 to 12 per pound for whole ham roll; 15 to 17 per pound for half ham roll, and 20 per pound for quarter ham roll

Ham, whole (10 to 14 pounds) Use a spit set 7 to 8 inches from moderately hot coals for even cooking. When ham is halfway cooked, lower spit distance to 6 to 7 inches from coals. Let stand 15 minutes before carving.

DONENESS	TIME IN MINUTES
170°F.	25 to 30 per pound

Loin Roasts, bone in (3 to 7 pounds) Use a spit set 7 to 8 inches from moderately hot coals for even cooking. When pork is halfway cooked, lower spit distance to 6 to 7 inches from coals. Let stand 15 minutes before carving.

DONENESS	TIME IN MINUTES
170°F.	25 to 35 per pound

Rolled Loin Roasts (3 to 5 pounds), Whole Boneless Hams (7 to 10 pounds), Half Ham (butt or shank, 5 to 7 pounds) Use a spit set 7 to 8 inches from moderately hot coals for even cooking. When pork is halfway cooked, lower spit distance to 6 to 7 inches from coals. Let stand 15 minutes before carving.

DONENESS	TIME IN MINUTES
170°F.	30 to 35 per pound

(*table continues*)

Grilling Meat (*continued*)

Pork (continued)

Sausages Lightly grease grill to prevent sticking. Place sausages in a single layer 4 to 5 inches from moderately hot coals.

DONENESS	TIME IN MINUTES
Medium	3 to 4 total

Spareribs, 3 inches long, cut into pieces Marinate in barbecue or basting sauce for about 2 hours in refrigerator. Wrap ribs in heavy-duty aluminum foil. Partially bake in 350°F. oven for 1½ hours. Carefully remove from foil, discarding drippings. Grill 4 inches from moderately hot coals, basting with sauce and turning frequently.

DONENESS	TIME IN MINUTES
Medium	20 total

Grilling Poultry

There are some rules of thumb for calculating grilling times for chicken: Cook dark meat parts 30 minutes, white meat parts 15 minutes, basting and turning about every 5 minutes. Grill halves skin side down for 5 minutes; turn skin side up, cover and grill 35 to 40 minutes. Grill wings 10 minutes per side. Grill whole chickens (about 3½ pounds) 1¼ to 1½ hours in a covered grill, 1½ to 2 hours on a rotisserie.

Chicken, whole Lightly grease grill to prevent sticking. Grill 6 to 8 inches from moderately hot coals. Turn frequently.

WEIGHT OR PART	GRILLING TIME
2½ to 4 pounds	50 to 60 minutes

Chicken, whole, using spit Place a drip pan below bird. Set spit 5 inches from moderately hot coals.

WEIGHT OR PART	GRILLING TIME
2 to 3 pounds	1¼ to 1¾ hours
4 to 5 pounds	1¾ to 2½ hours
6 to 8 pounds	2¾ to 3¾ hours

Chicken, broiler (2½ to 4 pounds), parts

WEIGHT OR PART	GRILLING TIME
Split breasts	7½ to 12½ minutes per side
Boneless breasts	5 to 10 minutes per side
Thighs	10 to 15 minutes per side
Drumsticks	7½ to 10 minutes per side
Wings	7½ to 12½ minutes per side

Grilling Poultry (*continued*)

Cornish Game Hens and Squab, using spit Place a drip pan below bird. Set spit 5 inches from moderately hot coals.

WEIGHT OR PART	GRILLING TIME
12 to 24 ounces	1 to 1¼ hours

Duck, whole Prick duck skin, but not meat, all over with a sharp fork and continue pricking during grilling. Grill 6 to 8 inches from moderately hot coals. Watch for flare-ups. Turn frequently.

WEIGHT OR PART	GRILLING TIME
3 to 5 pounds	1 to 1½ hours

Duck, whole, using spit Prick duck skin all over with a sharp fork and continue pricking during grilling. Set spit 5 inches from moderately hot coals. Watch for flare-ups. Turn frequently.

WEIGHT OR PART	GRILLING TIME
3 to 5 pounds	1¾ to 3 hours

Goose, whole, using spit Prick skin all over with a sharp fork and continue pricking during grilling. Set spit 5 inches from moderately hot coals. Watch for flare-ups. Turn frequently.

WEIGHT OR PART	GRILLING TIME
7 to 10 pounds	2¼ to 3½ hours

Turkey, whole, using spit Place a drip pan below bird. Set spit 5 inches from moderately hot coals.

WEIGHT OR PART	GRILLING TIME
4 to 6 pounds	2¼ to 3½ hours
6 to 8 pounds	3¼ to 4 hours
8 to 10 pounds	3¾ to 4½ hours
10 to 12 pounds	4¼ to 5½ hours

Turkey Breast, with bone, using spit Place a drip pan below bird. Set spit 5 inches from moderately hot coals.

WEIGHT OR PART	GRILLING TIME
2 to 4 pounds	1¾ to 2½ hours
4 to 6 pounds	2¼ to 3 hours
6 to 8 pounds	2¾ to 3½ hours
8 to 10 pounds	3¼ to 4 hours

Turkey Breast, boneless, using spit Place a drip pan below bird. Set spit 5 inches from moderately hot coals.

WEIGHT OR PART	GRILLING TIME
3 to 4 pounds	2¼ to 3½ hours
4 to 5 pounds	3¼ to 4 hours

Grilling Fish

It is best to use fillets that are at least 1 inch thick, small to medium whole or split fish. For easy turning, use a well-greased, hinged wire fish grill. Grill 4 inches from moderately hot coals for 5 to 8 minutes per side.

Grilling Shellfish

Grill shellfish 4 inches from moderately hot coals.

Clams and Oysters Scrub shells but do not shuck. Place clams or oysters, 4 to 6 at a time, in heavy-duty aluminum foil packets. Place foil packets directly on coals. Grill until shells open. Discard any that do not open.

GRILLING TIME IN MINUTES   4 to 6; do not turn

Scallops, Sea Thread onto skewers.

GRILLING TIME IN MINUTES   5 to 6 per side

Shrimp Use shelled and deveined large shrimp. Thread onto skewers or place in well-greased, hinged wire grill basket. Grill just until shrimp turn pink and tinged with light brown.

GRILLING TIME IN MINUTES   5 per side

Microwave Techniques

Think of microwave ovens as incredibly versatile kitchen assistants. At their most basic they cook frozen dinners in minutes, defrost food in no time, and make instant snacks. But that's just a start. They can help you cook fish that comes out moist and tender and vegetables that not only taste fresh, but also retain more of their flavor. They make melting chocolate foolproof, and reheating leftovers has never been easier. What microwaves don't do well is bake, roast, or sauté—leave those recipes to your oven or stovetop.

BASICS OF MICROWAVE COOKING

The more you use your microwave, the more you will understand how it works. Below are some of the different factors affecting how foods cook.

Food composition. Foods with a high content of water, fat, and/or sugar attract more microwave energy, so they cook faster than other foods. The high moisture content of many vegetables makes them cook quickly in the microwave oven with a minimal amount of liquid added.

Food density. Dense foods, such as meats, absorb microwaves more slowly than porous foods, such as vegetables and breads. They need longer cooking times and often require more stirring or rearranging during cooking.

Quantity of food. The larger the amount of food, the longer the cooking time. This is because a microwave oven always produces the same number of microwaves no matter how much food is in the oven. For example, if you cook one potato, all the microwaves concentrate on it. If you cook four potatoes, that same number of microwaves is divided among them, so they cook more slowly.

Shape and size of food. Uniformly shaped pieces of food cook more evenly than irregularly shaped pieces. Also, the thicker parts and tougher stem ends of a food cook more slowly, which is why you place the meaty end of a chicken drumstick or broccoli stem end facing the outer edge of the cooking dish. This is where microwaves penetrate best.

Small pieces of food cook more quickly than large ones. When you cut up vegetables or form meatballs, make the pieces even in size so they will all be done at the same time.

Shape of dish. Round dishes allow foods to cook more evenly than square or rectangular dishes. Corners in square dishes receive more microwaves than the sides, so food in the corners tends to be cooked sooner.

Standing time. Foods continue to cook even after you remove them from the microwave oven as heat continues to penetrate to the center. Many recipes, especially those for casseroles and meats, require a standing time for the dish to completely cook. Place the dish on a solid surface for the time indicated.

How Does the Microwave Oven Work?

A magnetron tube inside the microwave oven produces high-frequency waves similar to radio waves. A metal stirrer, or fan, directs these waves to all areas of the oven. Some waves go directly into the food to a depth of 1½ to 2 inches. Others are deflected off the walls and floor of the oven to the surfaces of the food.

Microwaves cause heat by friction, somewhat like the heat produced when you rub your hands together. Microwave energy causes the molecules in food to vibrate very rapidly next to each other, thus producing friction, which in turn produces heat in the food. Because heat is only in the food itself, your oven and kitchen remain cool.

Wattage. The higher the wattage, the more energy produced and the faster the cooking time. Six hundred watts or more is a high-power oven. Five hundred watts or less is a low-power oven. You can find the wattage of your oven in your owner's manual or on the oven door.

Or you can do this test: Pour 1 cup of ice-cold water into a 2-cup microwave-safe measuring cup. Microwave uncovered at high (100 percent) for 3½ minutes. If the water boils in less time, your oven produces 600 to 700 watts. If the water takes more than 3½ minutes to boil, your oven is low power. Most recipes are tested in 600- to 700-watt ovens. If your oven is less powerful, you should cook food longer. Increase cooking times in small increments and check food carefully for doneness.

A microwave oven has power settings ranging from 10 (100 percent) to 1 (10 percent). These figures may be followed with a defining term such as high, medium, and low. These power designations are not referring to the quantity of microwaves produced but to the percentage of time they are being produced. For example, at a power setting of 5 (50 percent), the microwave oven is generating power 50 percent of the time. Recipes for the microwave oven usually indicate the level of power to be used. Although food cooks faster at 100 percent than at 50 percent power, high power isn't necessarily better. Eggs, cheese, and baked goods cook better when microwaves penetrate more slowly and evenly at a lower power.

Microwave-safe cookware. Many of the dishes and utensils you already own can be used in your microwave oven. Heat-resistant, dishwasher-safe plastic, sturdy ceramic, and china are all suitable materials because microwaves will pass through all of them to heat food.

Do not use metal. Microwaves cannot pass through metal and properly cook food. More important, metal—even the silver or gold trim on a dinner plate—can cause sparks, or "arcing," which can cause damage to the oven.

If cookware is not marked "microwave safe," test it before using it. Place cookware in your microwave oven next to (but not touching) ½ cup cool water in a microwave-safe measuring cup. Microwave uncovered at 100 percent power for 1 minute. If the cookware is cool or just slightly warm, it's microwave safe. If it's hot, do not use it.

Coverings. In microwave cooking, you can cover food with microwave-safe glass or plastic lids, plastic wrap, waxed paper, or paper toweling.

Microwave-safe plastic container lids and microwave plastic wrap provide tight covers. Do not allow plastic wrap to touch the food. Always turn back a corner of the wrap to allow steam to escape during cooking and prevent a vacuum seal from forming. To prevent steam burns when uncovering cookware, remove the wrap or lid *away* from your face and hands.

Quick Tricks

Use your microwave oven to speed up cooking chores. A few examples:

☐ *Boil water*. A cup of water boils in 2 to 3 minutes at 100 percent power.

☐ *Cook bacon*. Place slices side by side between paper towels on a paper or china plate. Cook: 2 slices for 1½ to 2 minutes; 4 slices for 3 to 3½ minutes; 6 slices for 4½ to 5 minutes.

☐ *Melt butter or margarine*. Place in a glass measuring cup or small bowl. Cover with a paper towel. Heat at 100 percent power: 15 seconds for 1 tablespoon, 45 seconds for ¼ cup.

☐ *Warm maple or pancake syrup*. Place ½ cup syrup in bottle or pitcher. Heat, uncovered, for 45 to 60 seconds at 100 percent power.

☐ *Toast coconut*. Place ¼ cup coconut on plate. Cook, uncovered, for 1 minute at 100 percent power, stirring once.

☐ *Toast nuts*. Place ½ cups nuts in a glass pie plate. Heat, uncovered, for 2½ to 3 minutes at 100 percent power, stirring twice.

☐ *Melt chocolate*. Place 1 cup semisweet chocolate pieces in a small bowl. Heat, uncovered, for 2 to 3 minutes at 50 percent power.

☐ *Soften cream cheese*. Heat on an uncovered plate at 50 percent power: 40 to 45 seconds for 3 ounces, 1 to 1½ minutes for 8 ounces.

☐ *Soften raisins*. Combine 1 cup raisins with 1 teaspoon water in a small bowl. Cover and heat for 1 minute at 100 percent power.

☐ *Soften brown sugar*. Leave in its original package. Add a slice of apple or bread and close box tightly. Heat at 100 percent power, checking every 40 seconds.

☐ *Thin honey or corn syrup for easy pouring*. Remove metal lid. Heat opened jar at 100 percent power at 10-second increments until honey or syrup is thin enough.

☐ *Warm oranges, lemons, and limes for easier juicing, more juice*. Heat for 15 to 45 seconds at 100 percent power.

☐ *Warm tortillas*. Place 4 medium-size tortillas between paper towels. Heat for 45 to 60 seconds at 100 percent power.

☐ *Defrost frozen English muffins*. Wrap 1 English muffin in a paper towel. Defrost at 30 percent power for 30 seconds.

☐ *Cook frankfurters*. Pierce 1 frankfurter with a fork; loosely wrap in paper toweling, place on plate and cook for 30 to 45 seconds at 100 percent power; cook 2 frankfurters for 45 to 50 seconds; cook 4 frankfurters for 1½ to 2½ minutes.

☐ *Bake an apple*. Core apple, then peel the top third. Sprinkle sugar in the center. Cook in a large, covered custard cup for 1½ to 3 minutes, depending on the variety and size of the apple.

Waxed paper provides a loose cover that allows some steam evaporation for crisper results. A lid set slightly askew on a casserole dish has the same effect.

Paper toweling soaks up excess moisture and grease. It prevents baked goods from becoming soggy and absorbs fat from bacon.

DEFROSTING IN THE MICROWAVE OVEN

Not only is the microwave oven excellent for defrosting food, it's also especially helpful for last-minute defrosting. Some ovens are programmed for automatic defrosting and others may indicate the power level to be used for defrosting. Power levels set at 30 percent will usually cycle the microwave on and off to allow heat to equalize throughout the food. Check food often during the defrosting process. A part that has thawed will start to cook—even though the rest of the food is still thawing.

For best results:

□ Remove food from Styrofoam packages and metal containers before placing in microwave oven.

□ Cover food with waxed paper to retain moisture and promote more even heating.

□ Flex or bend packaged food, such as vegetables, in its wrapping to break the frozen food mass into smaller pieces for better heat distribution.

□ Stir or break food apart while defrosting.

REHEATING IN THE MICROWAVE

Foods reheated in the microwave oven keep their flavor, color, and texture. Cover the dish to retain moisture and speed reheating time.

Here are some guidelines. Any times given are approximate, based on high-wattage, variable-power microwave ovens. To reheat:

□ *A plate of mixed leftover foods:* Spread food out on the plate with the thicker, denser food toward the edge and the more tender, light food in the center. Cover with an inverted pie plate or plastic wrap and heat at 100 percent power for 2 to 3 minutes.

□ *A casserole:* Cover tightly for quickest heating. Stir or rotate several times. Dense casseroles, such as stew or lasagna, benefit by reheating at 70 percent to 80 percent power with a standing time.

□ *Meat and poultry:* Cut or slice into evenly sized pieces and cover loosely with a lid set askew. You can heat small amounts at 100 percent power, but larger amounts do better at 50 percent to 70 percent power for an even temperature throughout.

□ *Vegetables:* Cover tightly and microwave at 100 percent power. Stir or shake the dish once or twice.

(continued on page 263)

Microwave Cooking Times

Times are based on cooking at 100 percent power. Always wash and trim vegetables before cooking.

VEGETABLE OR MEAT	AMOUNT AND PREPARATION	TIME IN MINUTES
Fresh Vegetables		
Wash and trim vegetables before cooking.		
Globe Artichokes	1 medium: Place in 1-quart casserole with 2 tablespoons water and 1 teaspoon lemon juice. Cover with a lid or plastic wrap.	5 to 7
	4 medium: Place in 3-quart casserole with ¾ cup water and 1 teaspoon lemon juice. Cover with a lid or plastic wrap.	14 to 18
Asparagus	¼ pound: Place in 9-inch pie plate, tips toward center; with 1 tablespoon water. Cover with plastic wrap. Rotate dish halfway through cooking time.	2½ to 3½
	1½ pounds: Place in 10-inch pie plate, tips toward center, with 2 tablespoons water. Cover with plastic wrap. Rotate dish halfway through cooking time.	6 to 8
Green Beans and Wax Beans	1 pound: Place in 1½-quart casserole with ⅓ cup water. Cover with a lid or plastic wrap. Stir halfway through cooking time.	10 to 12
Beets	3 medium (¾ pound): Do not peel. Place in 1-quart casserole with ⅓ cup water. Cover with a lid or plastic wrap. Slip off skins *after* cooking.	10 to 15
	6 medium (1½ pounds): Do not peel. Place in 2½-quart casserole with ½ cup water. Cover with a lid or plastic wrap. Rearrange halfway through cooking time. Slip off skins *after* cooking.	16 to 22
Broccoli	1 pound: Cut stalks lengthwise through flowerets into slender spears. Arrange in rectangular dish with flowerets toward center. Add 2 tablespoons water. Cover with plastic wrap. Rotate halfway through cooking time.	8 to 11
Brussels Sprouts	Cut an × into base of sprouts. Place in 1½-quart casserole with 2 tablespoons water. Cover with a lid or plastic wrap. Stir halfway through cooking time.	7 to 10

(table continues)

Microwave Cooking Times (*continued*)

VEGETABLE OR MEAT	AMOUNT AND PREPARATION	TIME IN MINUTES
Cabbage	1 pound (4 wedges): Place in 10-inch pie plate with core ends toward outer edge of dish. Add 1/4 cup water. Cover with plastic wrap. Rotate dish halfway through cooking time.	8 to 10
	1 pound (shredded): Place in 1-quart casserole with 1/4 cup water. Cover with a lid or plastic wrap. Stir halfway through cooking time.	7 to 9
Carrots	1 pound (sliced or diced): Place in 1-quart casserole with 1/4 cup water. Cover with a lid or plastic wrap. Stir halfway through cooking time.	6 to 8
Cauliflower	1 head, whole (1 1/2 pounds): Place in 1 1/2-quart casserole with 1/4 cup water. Cover with a lid or plastic wrap. Rotate dish halfway through cooking time.	9 to 12
	1 1/2 pounds flowerets: Place in 2-quart casserole with 1/4 cup water. Cover with a lid or plastic wrap. Stir halfway through cooking time.	11 to 13
Corn on the Cob	1 ear: Place on plate. Sprinkle with water. Cover with waxed paper.	3 to 4
	4 ears: Place in 9- by 9-inch dish with 1/4 cup water. Cover with waxed paper. Rearrange ears halfway through cooking time.	9 to 14
Mushrooms	1/4 pound (sliced): Place in 8-inch pie plate. Cover with plastic wrap.	1 1/2
	1 pound (sliced): Place in 1 1/2-quart casserole. Cover with a lid or plastic wrap. Stir halfway through cooking time.	4 to 6
Peas (Snow and Sugar Snap)	1 pound: Place in 1 1/2-quart casserole with 1/4 cup water. Cover with a lid or plastic wrap. Stir halfway through cooking time.	6 to 10

Microwave Cooking Times (*continued*)

VEGETABLE OR MEAT	AMOUNT AND PREPARATION	TIME IN MINUTES
Potatoes, white For baking	4 (8 ounces): Prick several times with fork. Place spoke-style on paper towel. Rearrange and turn halfway through cooking time.	12 to 15
For boiling	4 medium (1½) pounds: Cut in 1-inch cubes. Place in 1½-quart casserole with ½ cup water. Cover with a lid or plastic wrap. Stir halfway through cooking time.	8 to 10
Potatoes, sweet For baking	1 (6 ounces): Prick several times with fork. Place on paper towel.	3 to 4
	4 (6 ounces each): Prick several times with fork. Place spoke-style on paper towel. Rearrange and turn over halfway through cooking time.	8 to 12
Spinach	10 to 16 ounces: Do not shake off water after washing. Place in 2-quart casserole. Cover with a lid or plastic wrap.	5 to 7
Squash, Summer (zucchini and yellow)	1½ pounds (sliced or cubed): Place in 1½-quart casserole with ¼ cup water. Cover with a lid or plastic wrap. Stir halfway through cooking time.	6 to 8
Squash, Acorn	1 pound: Pierce several times with fork. Cook in 9- by 9-inch dish for 3 minutes. Halve and seed. Place halves cut side down in dish to finish cooking.	7 to 10
Beef		
Ground	1 pound: Crumble into 1½-quart casserole. Cover with waxed paper. Stir halfway through cooking time. Cook until no longer pink.	5 to 7
Meatballs	1 pound (8 meatballs): Arrange around edge of 10-inch pie plate. Cover with waxed paper. Rotate dish halfway through cooking time. Drain.	6 to 8
Patties	1 pound (4 patties): Place in 9- by 9-inch dish. Cover with waxed paper. Rotate dish halfway through cooking time.	5 to 7

(table continues)

VEGETABLE OR MEAT	AMOUNT AND PREPARATION	TIME IN MINUTES

Pork

Ham steak (fully cooked)	I pound: Place in pie plate with ¼ cup water. Cover with waxed paper.	6 to 8
Sausage links	I pound (8 links): Pierce several times with fork. Place in 11- by 7-inch dish. Cover with waxed paper. Rearrange halfway through cooking time.	6 to 7

Chicken

Boneless breast cutlet	I cutlet (4 ounces): Place on plate, cover with inverted pie plate.	2 to 3
	2 cutlets (4 ounces each): Place in 9-inch pie plate with thicker sides toward edge of plate. Cover with inverted pie plate.	3½ to 4½
Breast half with bones	I breast half (6 to 7 ounces): Place on plate. Cover with inverted pie plate.	3½ to 4½
	2 breast halves (6 to 7 ounces each): Place in pie plate with thicker sides facing edge of plate. Cover with inverted pie plate. Rotate dish halfway through cooking time.	5 to 6

Fish and Shellfish

Fish fillets	I pound (½ to ¾ inch thick): Turn under thin end of fillets to even out thickness. Place in dish in single layer, but not touching. Cover with lid. Rotate dish halfway through cooking time.	4 to 6
Fish steak	I pound (1 inch thick): Place in pie plate, with thinnest part toward center of plate. Cover with plastic wrap. Rotate dish halfway through cooking time.	4½ to 6½
Shrimp, in shell	I pound: Arrange shrimp around edge of 10-inch pie plate with tails toward center. Rotate dish halfway through cooking time.	4 to 6 (or until shells are bright pink)
Shrimp, shelled	I pound: Arrange shrimp around edge of 10-inch pie plate with tails toward the center. Cover with plastic wrap. Rotate dish halfway through cooking time.	3 to 5
Clams, littleneck	I pound: Arrange on 10-inch pie plate with shell hinges toward edge of plate. Halfway through cooking time, rotate dish. Discard any clams that have not opened.	3 to 4

☐ *Grains and pasta*: Cover tightly and microwave at 100 percent power, stirring once.

☐ *Baked goods:* Wrap desired amount in paper toweling and heat at 50 percent power. Overheating causes baked goods to toughen, so check frequently: for one muffin or roll, check after 15 seconds.

ADAPTING STANDARD RECIPES FOR MICROWAVE COOKING

You can prepare many conventional oven recipes in your microwave oven, but they will need adjustment. Look at a similar recipe in a microwave cookbook, and compare amounts and proportions of ingredients, adjusting your recipe as necessary. Use the microwave recipe directions for cooking techniques, power levels, times, cookware, and coverings.

Here are some general rules for adapting standard recipes to your microwave oven:

☐ Use about half the liquid called for in a conventional recipe, since microwave cooking causes less evaporation.

☐ Reduce amounts of herbs, spices, and salt—generally by half. Add salt *after* cooking.

☐ Reduce the amount of fat or eliminate it entirely. Since fat attracts microwaves, it can increase cooking time for your recipe.

☐ Reduce cooking time to about one-fourth when microwaving at high power, to one-half at medium power.

☐ Substitute quick-cooking or instant-cooking ingredients for those that may take longer than other components of the dish. For example, substitute instant rice for regular rice in a casserole or soup.

☐ Rearrange ingredients if some parts cook faster than others. Stir often if your conventional oven recipe calls for constant stirring.

*B*asic Methods of Baking

Good baking technique starts with reading your recipe from beginning to end, preheating the oven, assembling and preparing your baking pans, then preparing your batter or dough. With the exception of butter or shortening used in pastry doughs, all ingredients should be at room temperature before you start.

PREPARING TO BAKE

Preheating. Always preheat the oven for at least 15 minutes, or until it reaches the required temperature, before baking. If the oven temperature is too low, the resulting product may be heavy and soggy.

♦ **Baking sheets and pans,** **169–173**

Preparing the Pan. For cakes, generously coat your pans with vegetable shortening (unless otherwise directed) and dust with flour, shaking out the excess. The flour aids in developing an even golden crust. A sheet of parchment paper in the bottom of the pan will ensure that the cake releases from the pan.

Cookie sheets are sometimes greased, sometimes not, depending on how much fat there is in the dough.

You can eliminate cleanup with muffin pans by using paper liners. However, if you plan to serve the muffins hot from the oven, grease the cups instead. Hot muffins do not always separate well from paper liners.

Sometimes you just don't have the exact pan that a recipe calls for. Often you can substitute another pan of the same volume and still get good results. You can use a standard baking dish, a piece of pottery, or even a casserole dish. If the dish is ovenproof, and if it holds the same volume, it is probably fine, with some adjustment of the recipe.

To measure the volume of dishes and pans, pour in water, cup by cup. Permanently mark volumes on bottoms of dishes and pans with nail polish.

Can I Use This Baking Pan for My Recipe?

The table below lists pans and the amount of batter they can comfortably hold without overflowing.

ROUND PANS	AMOUNT OF BATTER
6-inch pan	1¼ cups
8-inch pan	2¼ cups
9-inch pan	2½ cups
10-inch pan	3⅔ cups
11-inch pan	4¼ cups
12-inch pan	5¾ cups

SQUARE PANS	VOLUME
8-inch pan	3½ cups
10-inch pan	6 cups
12-inch pan	9 cups

TUBE PANS	VOLUME
9-inch pan	5 cups
10-inch angel cake tube pan	10 cups
10-inch fluted tube pan	8 cups
12-inch angel cake tube pan	16 cups
12-inch fluted tube pan	12 cups

◗ **Parchment paper, 175**
◗ **Baking pan substitutes, 168**

To adapt baking recipes to pans of varied sizes, use those with the same volume. (See page 168 for more baking pan equivalents.)

For baking cakes and pies in pans other than those specified in a recipe, baking temperature and time probably will need adjusting. *Larger, deeper pans usually require longer baking at a slower temperature,* so that the interior batter can cook through before the exterior overbakes.

Remember to fill baking pans only one-half to two-thirds full, to allow for rising in the oven without overflowing or uneven baking.

READYING THE INGREDIENTS

See pages 267–268 for tips on working with eggs, page 268 for tips on working with chocolate, and page 197 for measuring techniques.

Sifting flour. If a recipe calls for sifted flour, sift directly over and onto a piece of waxed paper, spoon into a measuring cup and level off excess flour with the straight edge of a knife or spatula.

Some recipes call for flour to be sifted directly into a measuring cup, then leveled off.

Sifting sugar. Sift granulated sugar only if it is lumpy. Confectioners' powdered sugar (10X) is best sifted before using. It sometimes cakes if the package has been left open for a while.

Softening butter or cream cheese. Butter and cream cheese will soften if left to stand at room temperature for at least 20 minutes. They should be soft enough to have a slight give all over. (For softening in a microwave, see page 257.)

Toasting nuts. To toast a small quantity of nuts, cook in a dry skillet over medium heat for 5 to 7 minutes (3 to 5 minutes for pine nuts), stirring often, until golden. Watch closely to avoid scorching. Or place the nuts on a baking sheet and toast in a 350°F. oven for 5 to 10 minutes, stirring occasionally. (For microwave directions, see page 257.)

To roast chestnuts, cut an X on the flat side of the chestnut. Place on a baking tray and roast in a 400°F. oven for about 15 minutes, shaking the tray occasionally. Peel the chestnuts while they are still warm.

For blanching instructions, look under specific nuts on pages 39–43.

Adding dried fruits and nuts to batters. To prevent dried fruits and nuts from sticking to one another or sinking to the bottom of a cake batter, toss the fruits and nuts with a small amount of reserved flour until lightly coated and then add to the batter. This applies only to thick batters. Fruits and nuts invariably fall to the bottom when a thin batter is used.

Whipping cream. Before whipping heavy cream, chill the beaters and bowl in the refrigerator for about an hour or in the freezer for a

▸ **Microwave shortcuts, 257**

half hour. You can use a whisk, a rotary eggbeater, a portable electric beater, or a free standing electric beater for the job. In very warm weather, also place the cream in the freezer until it is very cold—a few ice crystals will not affect it.

Begin by beating the cream at low speed and increase the speed as the cream gains in volume, adding any sweetener, liqueur, or flavoring, such as vanilla extract, after the cream has lightly thickened. To flavor, you may choose 2 tablespoons of confectioners' sugar for 1 cup of heavy cream, or anywhere from ½ teaspoon of extract to 2 tablespoons of liqueur.

Continue to beat the cream until soft peaks form. But if you are using a mixer, watch the cream carefully. Overbeating will turn the whipped cream into butter.

MIXING TECHNIQUES

Beating. When you beat a batter, not only do you mix the ingredients, you also incorporate air into the mixture to increase its volume and make it lighter. You can use a fork, a wooden spoon, a wire whisk, a portable hand mixer, or a freestanding mixer to do the job. Scrape the sides of the bowl frequently to be sure all of the mixture is being beaten.

Check your recipe to see just how much beating is required; it should say something like "beat until smooth" or "beat until thick" or "beat for 2 minutes."

Creaming. Creaming is the technique you use when a recipe tells you to combine a fat—butter, oil, or shortening—with a dry ingredient, usually sugar. Always start with your butter or shortening at room temperature. Using a wooden spoon, whisk, or electric beater, soften the butter first. Gradually add the sugar, continuing to beat as you add. Beat for another 2 to 3 minutes after all the sugar has been incorporated. Stop to scrape the sides of the bowl every so often to make sure *all* the ingredients are being creamed.

Cutting in. When you make pastry dough, you just want to blend the shortening coarsely with the flour so the texture remains crumbly. This process of mixing is called *cutting in.* Use a pastry cutter or two knives in a crisscrossing motion, and cut the fat into the flour until the fat is about the size of peas.

Folding. Folding is a very gentle way of mixing ingredients. Usually you fold beaten egg whites into yolks (for a soufflé, for example), or the dry ingredients into the beaten wet ingredients (when you fold nuts or chips into a cake batter, for example). The trick is not to deflate the mixture by rough handling.

Use a large, deep bowl. Add the ingredients you are about to fold in

◗ **Mixing and beating tools,**
  146–148
◗ **Pastry blender, 148**

by dropping in a single pile on the top of the batter. To fold, you can use a spatula or a flat wooden spoon. Slide the spoon from the side of the bowl to the bottom of the bowl and lift the batter up from underneath with a strong sweeping motion to turn it over completely. Rotate the bowl a quarter turn, slide the spoon to the bottom of the bowl, and lift and turn again. Use as few strokes as possible, just until the ingredients are barely mixed. The batter will not be completely smooth.

WORKING WITH EGGS

Unless a recipe states otherwise, use large eggs. Eggs are easiest to separate when they are chilled, but they should be at room temperature for beating. Separate the eggs as soon as you take them out of the refrigerator, then let them come to room temperature before you proceed with the recipe.

Egg whites.

BEATING To beat egg whites properly, they must be completely free of any trace of yolk. Likewise, the mixing bowl and beater should be absolutely clean and free of any grease. Use vinegar to wipe your bowls and beaters clean, then rinse and dry.

Add the egg whites to the clean bowl. If the whites are cold, set the bowl in a larger bowl of hot water until the whites are at room temperature. Room temperature egg whites will absorb more air than chilled ones, and that means you get more volume.

Cream of tartar helps increase the stability and volume of beaten whites. Add it as soon as the whites appear foamy.

It is best to beat egg whites with a heavy-duty electric beater. Begin beating slowly and very gradually increase the speed. When the whites have formed soft peaks, start adding the sugar, if used, a little at a time. Continue beating the whites until all the sugar is incorporated and the whites are firm but not dry.

FOLDING Beat your egg whites and fold them in as a last step, so the batter doesn't have a chance to deflate before the cake goes into the oven.

The process is described above, under Folding.

When whites are added to batters or denser mixtures, gently stir about one-fourth of the whites into the mixture to lighten it before you fold in the remaining whites.

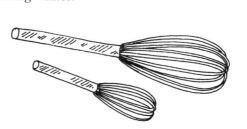

♦ **Meringues, 281–282**

Egg yolks and whole eggs.

BEATING Beaten egg yolks and whole eggs do not multiply in volume the way whites do, but you can incorporate plenty of air into them. This plays a large role in leavening many cakes, quick breads, and muffins, so do not underbeat.

Often a recipe will tell you to beat the eggs and sugar together until they *ribbon*. This means to beat until the mixture is very pale and thick. When you lift your beater, you will see the batter drip slowly back into the bowl in a ribbonlike pattern, which will then very slowly sink into the batter in the bowl.

CUSTARDS To prevent custards and custard sauces from curdling, *temper the eggs* before adding them to the hot liquid: Beat a little of the hot liquid into the eggs, adding it bit by bit and stirring the eggs constantly. Then slowly beat in the remaining hot liquid.

Custards are often cooked just until they *coat the spoon*. This means that if you dip a clean metal spoon into the custard, the custard should evenly coat it. When it does, wipe your finger across the back of the spoon. Your finger should be able to leave a clean path and the remaining custard should hold its shape and not flow into the wiped path.

WORKING WITH CHOCOLATE

Melting chocolate can be tricky, although using a microwave oven eliminates most pitfalls. Place up to 1 cup of chocolate pieces or 2 ounces of chocolate in a small microwave-safe container and cook at 100 percent power for 1½ to 2 minutes, checking every 30 seconds. The chocolate will look solid, but will stir into a liquid.

To melt on top of the stove, use a double boiler set over hot, but not boiling, water. No moisture should come in contact with the chocolate or it may "seize." When chocolate seizes, it becomes stiff, grainy, and lumpy. Seized chocolate can sometimes be saved by stirring in a little vegetable oil, a teaspoon at a time, until the mixture is smooth again.

You can skip the double boiler and just use a heavy saucepan if you can melt the chocolate with the butter, margarine, or oil in the recipe. Melt over low heat and stir frequently to prevent scorching. It is best to break the chocolate into small pieces before you begin to melt it.

CAKES FOR ALL OCCASIONS

Cakes fall into two basic categories—those made with fat (butter cakes) and those made without (foam cakes). Cakes made with butter, margarine, or shortening include layer cakes, rolled cakes, sheet cakes, loaf

▶ Chocolate, 44–45
▶ Cake pans, 169–170

and pound cakes, and fruitcakes. Most of these cakes depend upon baking powder or baking soda for leavening. The addition of fat adds weight and density to the finished cake and results in a deliciously moist crumb. Cakes made without fat are lighter in texture and density. These include angel food cake and some sponge cakes.

There are several exceptions to these general rules. A *génoise cake* is a sponge cake made with whole eggs and the addition of melted butter. It combines the characteristics of both a butter cake and a foam cake. *Chiffon cake* is another exception. Like a génoise it combines the characteristics of both types of cake; however, vegetable oil rather than butter is added to the batter. These cakes have the lightness of angel food and the richness of a cake made with shortening.

Decorating cakes. Once the cake has cooled, it can be filled and decorated with a frosting or glaze.

SPLITTING CAKE LAYERS With a long, sharp serrated knife, draw a line around the side of the cake at the point where it needs to be cut. Continue cutting deeper into the cake, revolving the cake against the knife and keeping the knife parallel to the work surface. Or, as an alternate: Measure the height of the cake and mark cutting lines around the outside of the cake with wooden picks. Gently saw through the cake with the knife.

FROSTING CAKE LAYERS Gently brush off all loose crumbs from the cake before frosting. If you have a cake-decorating stand, arrange the cake on top. If you have a lazy Susan, you can place cake plate on it for ease in frosting.

To prevent drips and frosting smears on the cake serving plate, put three to four strips of waxed paper just slightly under the edge of the layer all the way around.

Put a cake layer, rounded side down, on a cake plate; use a spatula to spread with a generous layer of frosting. Place the second layer, rounded side up, over the frosted bottom layer. Repeat frosting as with the bottom layer.

Top with a generous amount of frosting and spread it in a swirling motion up the side to the top of the cake to cover and make a decorative edge to the cake. Spread the remaining frosting over the top of the cake, making swirling motions with the spatula for a decorative finish. Gently remove the waxed paper strips.

How to store cakes. To keep cake moist, cover cut surfaces with plastic wrap or waxed paper. Store in a cake keeper or with a large bowl inverted over the cake on a serving plate. This will keep for several days.

Cakes with a cream frosting or filling should be refrigerated with plastic wrap or waxed paper covering the cut part, as above.

▶ **Cake-decorating tools, 174**
▶ **Metal spatula, 148**

Tips for Cake Baking

☐ Generously coat your pans with vegetable shortening (unless otherwise directed) and dust with flour, shaking out the excess. Pans for foam cakes are never greased. The light, airy batter must be able to cling to the sides of the pan as it expands.

☐ If you want your cake to have the best possible texture, shape, and volume, follow the recipe carefully and use only the ingredients, measurements, and pan size specified.

☐ Always preheat the oven.

☐ Never fill cake pans more than ⅔ full; the batter may overflow.

☐ When placing pans in the oven, place one layer or an oblong pan on the center rack. If you are baking two layers, use two racks. Place the racks in the center third of the oven and arrange the pans in opposite corners. When baking three or four layers, use two racks in center third of oven. Stagger the pans in opposite corners of both racks so they do not block the heat circulation in the oven. When baking a tube cake, place the oven rack in the bottom third of the oven and arrange the pan in the center of the rack.

☐ If a cake is browning too quickly during baking, loosely cover its top with a sheet of aluminum foil.

☐ The cake may fall if the door to the oven is opened too soon, or if the oven is too hot, or if there is not enough flour in the batter.

☐ Three ways to tell if cakes are done:

When they shrink slightly from the sides of the pan.

When the top springs back if lightly pressed with a fingertip.

When a cake tester or wooden pick inserted near the center of the cake comes out clean, with no batter or moist particles clinging to it.

☐ Cool butter cakes thoroughly before frosting. Remove the cakes from the oven and place the pans on wire racks to allow air circulation around the hot pan. When the cake shrinks from the pan, after about five minutes, turn the cake out onto a wire rack to finish cooling.

☐ Cool foam cakes—angel food cakes and chiffon cakes—upside down until cold. The pans should have little attachments on the rim that enable you to rest the pans upside down. If not, take a glass soda bottle. Invert the cake over the soda bottle, placing the neck of the soda bottle up through the center hole of the cake pan. Balance the cake pan on the upright bottle. This keeps the cake high and light until the walls of the cake are cool enough to support its weight.

Unfrosted cakes may be stored in the freezer for up to four months. Wrap cakes in plastic wrap, plastic freezer bags, or aluminum foil. They will thaw in about 1 hour at room temperature or more slowly in the refrigerator.

Frosted cakes can be frozen. Freeze on a piece of cardboard or a cookie sheet until firm and then wrap as above. Store in the freezer for up to three months. Thaw at room temperature for about 2 hours or more slowly in the refrigerator.

Fruitcakes mellow and improve in flavor with age. If desired, sprinkle the cake with brandy or rum and wrap in heavy foil. For best flavor, store at room temperature for at least one week; in the refrigerator for one month; or in the freezer for three months. Glaze and garnish cake the day you wish to use it.

Frosting a cake.

(continued on page 274)

1 Spread first layer with frosting

2 Add top layer

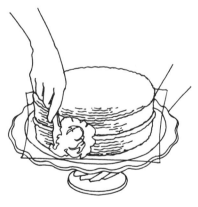

3 Frost up the sides with swirling motion

4 Swirl icing on top to finish

Finishing Touches for Frosted Cakes

Here are some finishing touches you can apply to a frosted cake to add extra appeal.

1. *Feather Top*. Drizzle melted chocolate across the frosting, in straight lines about 1 inch apart. Draw the edge of a spatula or table knife across the lines.

2. *Plaid Design*. Pull a table fork across the cake and make lines at right angles to these.

3. *Crisscross Pattern*. With a knife or spatula, draw parallel lines in the frosting about 1 inch apart. Turn the cake and draw lines at an angle to the first series.

4. *Shadow Design*. Drip melted chocolate from a spoon around the edge of the cake, letting the chocolate run down the sides.

Special effects.

1 Feather top

2 Plaid design

3 Crisscross pattern

4 Shadow design

Rolling a Cake Roll

1. Invert the cake onto a clean towel that has been sprinkled with confectioners' (10X) sugar or cocoa; slice off the crisp edges with a long, thin serrated knife.

2. Gently roll the warm cake and towel along the length of the cake. Place the cake and towel on a wire rack to cool for about 1 hour. Cooling for too long seems to result in cakes that crack easily.

3. Gently unroll the cake and spread with the filling.

4. Reroll the cake and filling without the towel.

Rolling a cake roll.

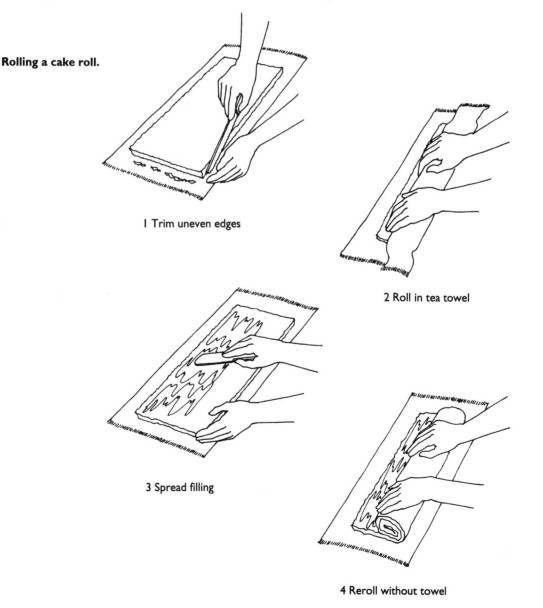

1 Trim uneven edges

2 Roll in tea towel

3 Spread filling

4 Reroll without towel

FAST AND EASY QUICK BREADS AND MUFFINS

Are quick breads quick? Yes! Generally a quick bread can be mixed together in less than 15 minutes. Baking times vary from 15 minutes for muffins to about 1 hour for large loaves.

Quick breads rely on baking powder, baking soda, and eggs for leavening instead of yeast. Steam, air, and a combination of baking soda and an acid liquid, such as buttermilk or sour milk, also can cause the leavening action during baking. There is no waiting for yeast to proof or dough to rise and no kneading is required.

Quick breads include muffins, scones, biscuits, doughnuts, loaves, dumplings, waffles, popovers, pancakes, and spoon breads.

When you prepare a quick bread, mix the dry and liquid ingredients separately. Combine them just before baking. Mix the batter thoroughly but gently with a wooden spoon, just until the ingredients are moistened. Fifteen strokes should be enough. The batter will be lumpy.

Allow the baked breads to cool in their pans on wire racks for 10 minutes. Then finish cooling the breads on wire racks out of the pan.

If you try to slice a quick bread fresh out of the oven, it will crumble. It is better when served completely cooled. Store the cooled bread at room temperature wrapped in plastic wrap or aluminum foil.

You can freeze quick breads for up to six months. To thaw, leave the loaf in its foil wrapper and heat in a slow oven (300°F.) until heated through, about 25 minutes.

STOCKING UP ON COOKIES

A few simple rules apply to all cookie making whether you choose dropped, rolled, refrigerator, pressed, bar, or molded cookies. Closely follow the directions of the recipe and use only the ingredients specified.

Preparing cookie sheets and molds. Follow your recipe and prepare the baking sheet or mold accordingly. Generally vegetable shortening or butter is used to grease the sheets or molds. You can also use nonstick cooking oil spray.

Cookies that bake on greased sheets tend to spread more and are thinner than those baked on ungreased sheets. Using parchment, foil, or a flour coating on the sheet retards the spreading and the resulting cookies will not be as thin.

It should not be necessary to regrease the sheets between bakings. Use paper towels to wipe off any crumbs.

Baking Cookies. The difference between a soft, chewy cookie and a hard one is dependent on the length of time it is baked, so timing is critical. Start with a preheated oven. Carefully watch the cookies; some take less and others more time to bake, depending on how full the oven is, the weight of your cookie sheets, and the type of metal they are made of, as well as the accuracy of your oven thermostat.

Cooling Cookies. Follow specific recipe directions as to whether to transfer immediately or allow to cool for several minutes before transferring to racks to cool completely.

Storing Cookies. Store in airtight containers with tight-fitting lids. To keep crisp cookies crisp, or delicate cookies from breaking, layer the cookies in the containers with waxed paper, plastic wrap, or foil. Bar cookies can remain in their baking pan tightly covered with plastic wrap or foil.

Freezing cookie dough and cookies. Unbaked dough and baked cookies may be frozen and stored for two to four months. Store uncooked dough wrapped in plastic wrap or foil.

Freeze baked cookies in a sturdy box lined with plastic wrap or foil, separating the layers with more plastic wrap or foil. Thaw cookies at room temperature for 10 minutes.

Freeze rolled cookies after they have been shaped. To bake, arrange them, still frozen, on cookie sheets.

Freeze bar cookie dough in the pan in which it is to be baked. Cover with plastic wrap and foil.

Both drop cookie dough and refrigerator cookie rolls should be thawed until just soft enough to slice and use.

PLEASING PIES

There is nothing quite so wonderful as a freshly baked pie straight from the oven. The crust should be flaky and tender, acting as the perfect accompaniment to whatever filling is chosen.

A flaky crust is created by combining flour and little pieces of fat. As the fat melts in the pastry during baking, it creates the flaky texture that is so prized by bakers.

Flaky pastry should be handled as little as possible to insure a light, tender crust. Be sure your butter and water are very cold, and work quickly. Following the simple steps listed below should enable you to make perfect pie pastry every time.

Nine steps to perfect pie pastry.

1. Cut the cold vegetable shortening or butter into the flour and salt in a large bowl with a pastry blender or two knives. Continue to cut in the shortening until the mixture is crumbly and the shortening is evenly distributed.

2. Add the ice water, stirring with a fork, 1 tablespoon at a time, adding just enough water to moisten the mixture.

3. Continue mixing the dough with a fork, just until the pastry forms a ball that leaves the side of the mixing bowl clean. If you are prepar-

♦ **Pastry tools, 168–169**

ing enough dough for two crusts, divide the dough in half. Avoid overworking the dough; pastry dough that is handled too much will become tough. (At this point the dough may be wrapped in plastic wrap and chilled for 30 minutes or overnight. If the dough has chilled overnight, let it soften slightly before rolling. The dough can be held three days in the refrigerator or up to two months in the freezer.)

4. Lightly sprinkle flour on a pastry cloth or other work surface and rolling pin to coat both evenly. To shape the bottom crust, put the ball of dough on the pastry cloth and roll it into a 1-inch-thick round. Beginning at the center and using light pressure, roll to the outside edge, working your way around the entire dough so the pastry will retain its circular shape, to the desired diameter. Turn the dough gently to prevent it from sticking as you roll it out. A pie plate is a good size guide; roll the dough at least 2 inches larger than the diameter of the pie plate. Invert it onto the rolled dough and check to see if additional rolling is needed.

5. Lift and fold the rolled-out pastry at the center of the circle over the rolling pin and transfer the pastry to the pie plate, being careful not to tear the dough.

6. Carefully unroll the pastry over the pie plate and fit it loosely into the pie plate. Try to avoid stretching the dough, which could cause it to shrink during the baking.

7. Trim the edge of the pastry to a 1-inch overhang.

Baking Tips for Pies

☐ **If the pastry edge is browning too quickly, cover it with strips of aluminum foil or loosely rest a sheet of foil over the pie.**

☐ **To prevent oven mess and smoking, arrange a piece of aluminum foil or a large cookie sheet on the bottom to catch any juices that bubble over the sides of the crust during baking.**

☐ **Don't prick piecrusts baked *with* a filling, or else the liquid from the filling will seep under the crust and lead to a soggy mess.**

☐ **To keep the bottom of filled pastry crusts from becoming soggy, brush the inside with beaten egg white and/or sprinkle with a layer of bread crumbs or nuts before adding the filling. For baked crusts filled after baking, an even brushing of strained melted preserves or melted chocolate will prevent sogginess.**

☐ **For tender crusts, keep pastry doughs, work surfaces, and rolling pins well chilled.**

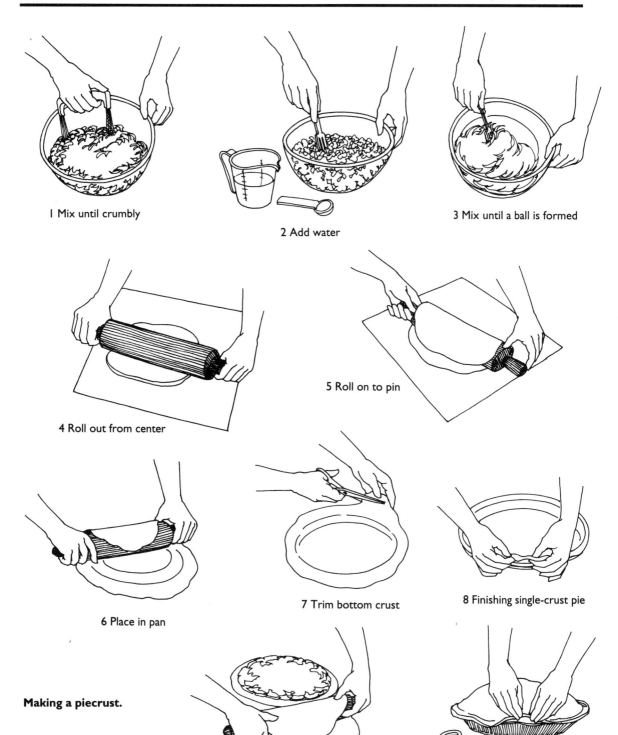

1 Mix until crumbly

2 Add water

3 Mix until a ball is formed

4 Roll out from center

5 Roll on to pin

6 Place in pan

7 Trim bottom crust

8 Finishing single-crust pie

Making a piecrust.

9 Unroll top crust over filling

10 Turning under top crust

Final Touches for Fabulous Pies

Here are some different methods of edging a crust to give your pie a professional look.

1. *Scalloped Edge*. Place your left thumb and forefinger on the outside of the pie rim. With a teaspoon, press the inside of the rim between your fingers, forming a large rounded scallop. Repeat the scallops about every inch around the pastry rim.

2. *Rope Edge*. Press the pie rim firmly between the thumb and forefinger of your right hand, pressing down toward the right with thumb. Continue pressing, turning pie clockwise as you do, until entire rim is finished. *Note:* Left-handed people should reverse hands and turn the pie counterclockwise.

3. *Braided Edge*. Carefully roll out leftover pastry dough into a rectangle and cut lengthwise strips from it. Using three strips at a time, form into a braid; piece enough together to go around the pie rim. Brush the pastry rim with water and press braid on top.

4. *Double Scallop*. Press the point of a teaspoon into the pastry rim in two even rows, one close to the edge of the pie plate and the other a little further in.

5. *Sawtooth One-Crust Pie Edge*. Line the pie pan with the pastry, leaving an overhang of 1½ inches. Spoon the filling into the pie shell, smoothing the top into an even layer. With scissors, snip even sawtooth cuts all around and fold the edge of the pastry over the filling toward the center.

6. *Lattice Top*. Roll the remaining pastry into a rectangle 12 inches by 8 inches. Cut lengthwise into ½-inch strips. Weave the strips into a lattice over the pie filling. Trim the overhand even with the bottom crust. Pinch to seal edge. Turn the sealed edge under. Pinch again to make stand-up edge; flute. Note: You may find it easier to weave the lattice on a piece of waxed paper or heavy-duty aluminum foil, and then place it over the filling. Also, using a pastry wheel will make pretty, unusually shaped lattice strips.

8. With your fingertips, roll the overhang to make a smooth edge. To fix tears or thin spots, or places where you need to extend the dough, brush the pastry with a little cold water and patch with dough trimmings, pressing them into place.

9. If you are preparing a two-crust pie, roll out the remaining dough in the same manner, making sure it is 1 inch larger in diameter than the pie plate. Fill the pastry-lined pie plate with the filling and brush the rim of the bottom crust with water. Using the pastry cloth, lift and fold the rolled-out pastry at the center of the circle over the rolling pin and transfer the pastry to the pie plate. Carefully unroll the pastry over the filling.

10. Trim the dough all around so that there is a ½-inch overhang and press the edges of the two crusts together. Turn the overhang

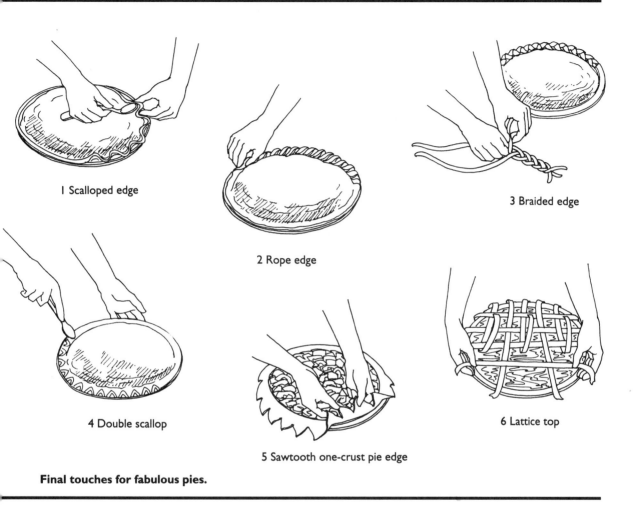

1 Scalloped edge

2 Rope edge

3 Braided edge

4 Double scallop

5 Sawtooth one-crust pie edge

6 Lattice top

Final touches for fabulous pies.

under itself and press to seal. Crimp the edges (see box) to add the finishing touch.

Prebaking empty pie shells. Prebaking—partially or completely—is often called baking pastry blind. *To bake blind,* line the pan with dough; prick generously with a fork all over to prevent air bubbles in case the dough was stretched when it was placed in the pan. Line the pastry with waxed paper or parchment paper. Fill the shell with dried beans or rice to weight down the dough. (Beans should be kept specifically for this purpose and can be reused.) Bake the dough in a preheated 375°F. oven for 15 minutes, or until it sets and no longer has a raw, shiny appearance. Remove the paper and beans and continue to bake until the pastry is dry and golden.

Tempting Tarts

Open-faced tarts are surprisingly easy to make—and they are perfect for showing off the fresh fruits of the season.

Tart pastry is a blended dough—similar to a sugar cookie dough—delicate, short, and crumbly. The pastry is sturdy, so it can be prepared in a food processor. Once baked, a tart shell is unmolded and stands on its own without the need of a pan.

To prevent a soggy bottom crust, brush blind-baked tart shells with an egg wash (one egg yolk mixed with one to two tablespoons milk or water). The egg wash acts as a sealant.

Tart pastry can be prepared ahead and chilled, wrapped in plastic, for up to three days. Or it may be frozen for about a month. Formed unbaked tart shells may also be kept in the refrigerator or freezer.

Seven steps to terrific tarts.

1. Tart pastry is a combination of butter or margarine, flour, water, and salt. In some instances you can add an egg or egg yolk. Blend the ingredients together until the mixture is crumbly, just as for pie pastry.

2. Turn out the dough onto a lightly floured surface and knead it with the heel of your hand to distribute the fat evenly and fully incorporate the ingredients. This gives you uniformly blended, firm-textured dough.

3. Gather the dough into a ball, wrap it in plastic, and chill for 30 minutes before rolling.

4. Roll out the dough as described for pie pastry (see page 276).

5. To line a tart pan, roll the circle of dough onto the rolling pin and lay it loosely over the pan. With floured fingertips, carefully press the dough into the pan, being sure to press the dough against the sides of the pan. Fold back some of the excess dough around the sides of the pan to reinforce them and make them sturdier. Roll the rolling pin across the pan or pans to cut off the excess dough.

6. With your finger and thumb press up the edge all around so that it extends slightly above the rim. (Some shrinkage is expected during baking and this acts to counteract that.)

7. Chill the dough in the refrigerator to firm and relax it. At this point, the tart shell may be "blind baked" (see page 279) or filled and baked.

♦ **Pastry tools,** 168–169
♦ **Tart pan,** 172

MARVELOUS LOW-FAT MERINGUES

In these days of counting calories from fat, knowing how to make a meringue is a wonderful skill to have in your repertoire, because meringues are made without any fat—just egg whites, sugar, and, sometimes, flavoring.

When sugar is folded into beaten egg whites, the mixture becomes a simple Swiss meringue. This is the type of meringue that is the traditional topping for a lemon meringue pie. Because there is some concern about salmonella poisoning from raw or undercooked eggs, if you are going to top a pie with this soft meringue, apply the meringue only on top of a *hot* cream pie filling and bake for *at least* 15 minutes at 350°F.

An alternative to the Swiss meringue is the Italian meringue—drizzling a hot sugar syrup into beaten whites and whipping until cool. This is the basis for 7-minute frosting. For flavor, add vanilla or almond extract and/or a liqueur or freshly grated citrus rind.

Meringues make wonderful low-fat cookies when mixed with nuts, chocolate, coconut, or other ingredients and piped or spooned onto baking sheets. Or you can shape a meringue to make pie and tart or tartlet shells. Here are a few tips to guide you:

□ Humid weather is the worst for making meringues. The humidity will prevent the meringue from hardening and, once baked, the

Meringues Made with Hot Sugar Syrups— Safe and Easy!

Use this soft meringue as a billowy topping for a creamy pie or as a frosting for a layer cake. A candy thermometer is helpful but not necessary for this recipe.

Combine 3 egg whites and a pinch of salt in a bowl and beat until the whites are stiff but not dry. Set aside.

In a small, heavy-bottomed saucepan, combine 1 cup of sugar with ½ cup of water. Heat until the mixture begins to boil; do not stir. Cover for 3 minutes and continue boiling. Remove the lid. Boil the mixture without stirring until it reaches 234°F. to 240°F. on a candy thermometer, or until it reaches the "soft ball" stage. If you don't have a candy thermometer, drop a ½ teaspoon of the syrup into a cup of cold water and knead it with your fingers. If you can make it into a soft ball that flattens out when you hold it, you have reached the proper stage. (If the ball holds it shape, you have cooked the syrup for too long; throw it out and start again.)

Very slowly drizzle the hot syrup over the beaten egg whites while beating again, until the meringue has cooled to room temperature. If you like, beat in vanilla or other flavoring.

▶ **Candy thermometer,**
134–135
▶ **Working with egg whites,**
267

meringue may absorb moisture from the air. Try a different dessert instead!

□ When baking meringues, line baking sheets with parchment paper or grease and flour the baking sheets to prevent the meringue from sticking to them.

□ Bake meringues in a slow oven (200°F. to 250°F.). A well-cooked meringue is completely dry and not browned. Baking times will vary depending on the texture you desire. The shorter the baking time, the softer and chewier the inside will be. The longer the meringue is baked and allowed to dry, the drier and crisper the center will be.

□ Meringues can be stored in airtight containers for up to one week. If a meringue should loose its crispness, bake in a slow oven (225°F.) for 15 to 20 minutes to dry it.

MAKING YEAST BREADS

There are two types of yeast breads: those made from kneaded doughs and those made from batters. Both are made with assorted flours and grains. Kneaded doughs may be formed into various shapes and sizes, baked in pans or baked free-form on a baking sheet or unglazed tiles. Batter breads, however, rely upon a mold for their shape.

Making the dough. The most simple yeast dough is made with a combination of yeast, water, a little sugar, flour, and salt. Begin by proofing the yeast by combining it with a small amount of warm water (110°F. to 115°F.) and a pinch of sugar. Under the proper temperature conditions, the yeast will grow and multiply. During this process it produces carbon dioxide. It is this gas that causes dough to rise.

Next add more liquid to the yeast mixture. Then stir in the flour, one cup at a time, until a soft, slightly sticky dough is formed. Since it is difficult to calculate exactly how much flour will be needed to form the dough, it is best to add it gradually. Then knead the dough to develop the gluten and transform the dough from a wet, sticky mass to a beautifully smooth and elastic dough.

Resting the dough allows the flour to absorb more of the liquid in the mixture, making further kneading easier.

Kneading and shaping bread. Transfer the dough to a lightly

Interrupting a Yeast Bread on the Rise

If you're interrupted while preparing a yeast dough, cover the bowl tightly with plastic wrap and refrigerate it without punching it down. The dough will remain fresh for up to 18 hours. If the dough has risen and you must leave it before it's formed, punch it down, cover tightly with plastic wrap and refrigerate.

♦ Bread flour, 59
♦ Yeast, 64

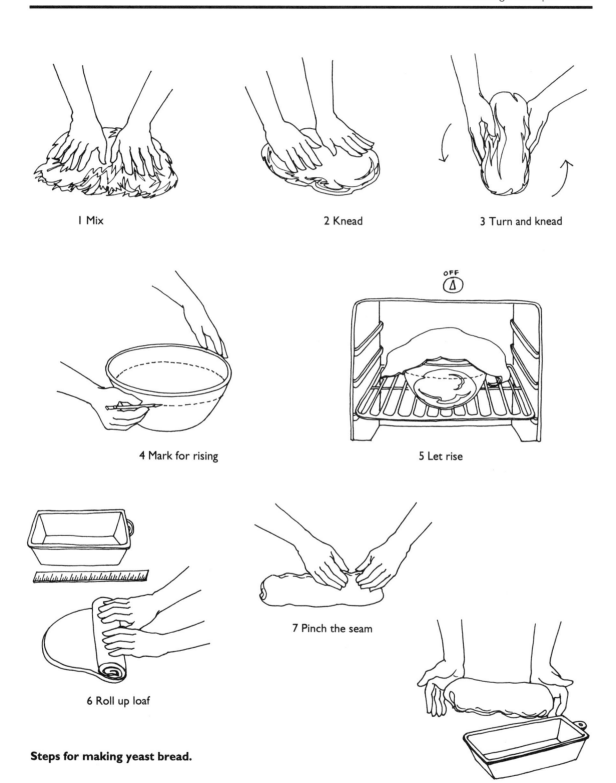

1 Mix

2 Knead

3 Turn and knead

4 Mark for rising

OFF

5 Let rise

6 Roll up loaf

7 Pinch the seam

8 Place in pan

Steps for making yeast bread.

floured board. (Place a dampened tea towel or dampened paper towels under the board to prevent it from moving.) With lightly floured hands, flatten the dough. Using your fingertips, pick up the edge of the dough and fold it over itself toward you.

With the heels of your hands, push the dough away from you. If the dough is sticky, lightly sprinkle it with additional flour and use a dough scraper or metal spatula to lift the dough from the board and keep it clean.

Give the dough a quarter turn and continue to fold, push, and turn until the dough is elastic, smooth, and satiny—usually 8 to 10 minutes. Test the dough's elasticity by pressing your finger into the dough. If the dough springs back when you remove your finger, it has been kneaded enough.

Letting the dough rise. The recipe will tell you to let the dough rise until it has doubled in size. But how will you gauge that? Try this: Transfer the dough to a bowl. Flatten the dough in the bowl, draw a line on the outside of the bowl to measure its level, and remove the dough. Add enough water to the bowl to measure double the level of

Substituting Fast-Rising Yeast for Regular Yeast

Would you like to enjoy the old-fashioned flavor of homemade yeast bread in a lot less time? Simply follow the steps below for using fast-rising yeast in your favorite recipes.

☐ Always include water in the ingredients even if your recipe calls for all milk or another liquid. Decrease the amount of liquid by ¼ cup per envelope of fast-rising yeast and substitute ¼ cup of water. For example, if your recipe calls for two envelopes of yeast and 1 cup milk, use two envelopes fast-rising yeast, ½ cup water and ½ cup milk.

☐ It is not necessary to dissolve the yeast in a liquid first. Simply combine the yeast with about two-thirds of the flour and the other dry ingredients in a large bowl and proceed with the recipe.

☐ Liquids and solid or liquid fats (do not include eggs) should be heated until hot to the touch—about 130°F. This is hotter than the 110°F. to 115°F. usually required if the yeast is first dissolved in a liquid.

☐ Add the hot liquids to the dry ingredients, stirring to combine. Add the eggs, if using, and blend at low speed with an electric mixer. Continue beating at medium speed for 3 minutes, adding enough remaining flour to make a soft dough.

☐ Proceed with the recipe directions for kneading and rising, but reduce the rising time by one-half to one-third. Begin checking the dough halfway through the suggested rising time in a recipe that calls for regular yeast.

the first mark and again draw a line to measure the second level. Rinse the bowl in warm water and dry and oil it. Add the dough to the bowl and turn it to coat it with the oil. This prevents the dough from forming a crust.

Cover the bowl with plastic wrap and let it rise in a warm, draft-free place. An oven is an ideal place to let the dough rise. If you are using an electric oven, preheat to 200°F., turn the oven off, and let it cool for 5 minutes. The pilot light in a gas oven will keep the dough warm. If the oven is warmer than 85°F., leave the oven door ajar.

Shaping the dough into loaves. When using a bread pan for baking, roll the dough out into a rectangle with the short side the same size as the length of the pan. Beginning with the short side nearest you roll up the dough jelly-roll fashion.

Once the loaf is shaped, be sure it is even at both ends. With your fingertips pinch a seam along the dough to secure the dough together. Use the sides of your hands to gently press the dough down on each end, tucking the thin strips formed under the loaf. Transfer the loaf to the pan without stretching it.

To shape a freestanding loaf, shape the dough as for a loaf in a pan. Then, with the palms of your hands, roll the loaf back and forth to taper the ends.

Baking the bread. Bake breads in a preheated oven. Use the exact pan size called for in the recipe. A pan too large will result in a flat bread, too small will cause the dough to overflow. The material of the pan will affect the baking time. Uncoated metal needs longer baking; glass and enamel need lower oven temperatures—reduce the oven temperature by 25 degrees.

Brush the top of the loaf with an egg beaten with a little water for a shiny crust. Rub with softened butter or margarine once removed from the oven for a soft crust.

Check breads for doneness near the end of the suggested baking time. They are done when nicely browned and sound hollow when lightly tapped with your fingertips. Remove the loaves from the pans and cool completely on wire racks.

Storing bread. There's no question that yeast breads taste best fresh out of the oven, but most will keep for a few days, especially those made with milk or containing lots of butter. When thoroughly cooled, store bread in plastic bags or wrapped in foil, in the refrigerator or at room temperature.

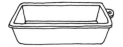

Six Shapes for Dinner Rolls

Dinner rolls are made from the same dough as bread. The second rising will be quicker, and you should shorten the baking time to about 20 minutes.

Pan Rolls. Divide the dough into three equal parts and form each part into a rope about 12 inches long. Cut each roll into slices 1 inch thick. Form the slices into balls and arrange ¼ inch apart in greased 9-inch cake pans.

House Rolls. Divide the dough into three equal parts. Roll each part, one at a time, on a lightly floured surface into a circle about 9 inches in diameter. With a 2½-inch round cutter, stamp out circles. Brush the circles with softened butter or margarine and make a crease across each, slightly to one side of the center. Fold the smaller half over the larger, forming half-moons and put on greased baking sheets about 1 inch apart. Lightly pinch the edges to seal.

Cloverleaf Rolls. Divide the dough into four equal parts. Working with one part at a time, pinch off small pieces of dough about the size of marbles and form into balls. Arrange three balls of dough into each cup of the greased muffin pans, forming "three-leaf clovers."

Quick Cloverleaf Rolls. Pinch off pieces of dough slightly larger than golf balls and form into balls. Place one ball in each greased muffin pan cup. With kitchen shears, snip a cross into the top of each roll, forming "four-leaf clovers."

Pinwheels. Divide the dough into three equal parts. On a lightly floured surface, roll each part, one at a time, into an 8-inch by 16-inch rectangle. Spread the rectangle with softened butter or margarine, sprinkle with cinnamon-sugar, jam, or other filling, if desired, and roll up from the long side, jelly-roll fashion. Cut into slices 1 inch thick and arrange, cut sides up, in greased muffin pan cups.

Fan-tans. Divide the dough into three equal parts. On a lightly floured surface, roll each part into a 9-inch by 15-inch rectangle. Cut the rectangle crosswise into strips 1½ inches wide, then stack them by piling six strips on top of one another. Cut the stack crosswise into squares and place, cut side down, in greased muffin pan cups.

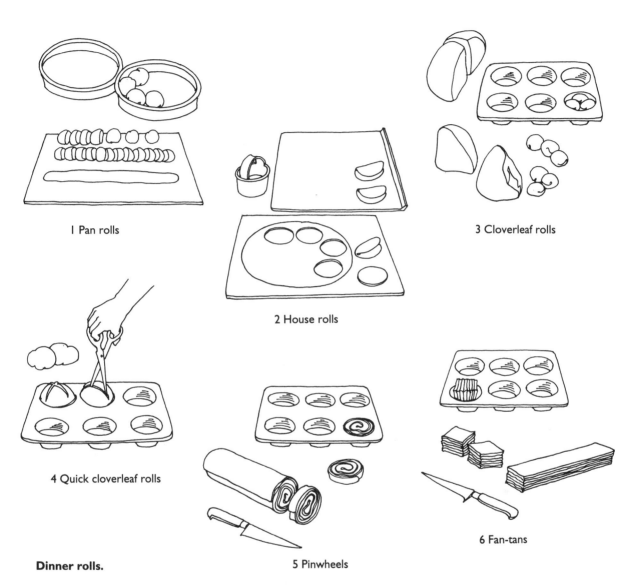

1 Pan rolls

2 House rolls

3 Cloverleaf rolls

4 Quick cloverleaf rolls

5 Pinwheels

6 Fan-tans

Dinner rolls.

Figuring Out Baking Quantities

Who needs recipes when you know how much flour to use to make a single crust or how much frosting to whip up for a layer cake? You can whip up some foods without consulting a recipe, as long as you know how much to make. Here are some basic baking quantities to help you plan your work in the kitchen.

INGREDIENT AMOUNT	YIELDS
Pie Pastry Dough made from	
1¼ cups sifted flour	1 single crust (8, 9 or 10-inch pie)
2 cups sifted flour	1 double crust (8 or 9-inch pie)
2 cups sifted flour	6 turnovers (from 6-inch squares of dough)
Cream Puff Dough made from	
1 cup water, ½ cup butter, 1 cup sifted flour, and 4 eggs	1 dozen cream puffs or éclairs or 4½ to 5 dozen profiteroles or 1 croquembouche
Puff Pastry made from	
4 cups sifted flour and 1 pound butter	1 dozen small patty shells or 1 large vol-au-vent (large patty shell) or 12 napoleons or 5 dozen small palmiers (elephant ear cookies) or 2½ dozen cream horn shells
Crumb Crusts made from	
1½ cups crumbs (graham crackers, vanilla or chocolate wafers, gingersnaps)	1 single crust (8 or 9-inch pie)
Meringue made from	
2 egg whites	Topping for 8-inch pie
3 egg whites	Topping for 9-inch pie or enough to make a 9-inch pie shell
4 egg whites	Topping for 10-inch pie or enough to make two 9-inch or three 7-inch meringue discs
6 egg whites	2 dozen 2½-inch meringues
Pie Fillings made from	
6 apples	9-inch double-crust pie
12 apples	9x9x2–inch deep-dish pie
2 cups diced and peeled apples	6 turnovers (6-inch squares of dough)
1 quart berries or sliced, pitted, and peeled fruit	9-inch double-crust pie
2 pounds rhubarb, trimmed	9-inch double-crust pie
1 jar (28 ounces) mincemeat	9-inch double-crust pie
Custard from 4 eggs and 2½ cups milk	8 or 9-inch pie

Figuring Out Baking Quantities (*continued*)

INGREDIENT AMOUNT	YIELDS
Streusel Topping made from	
½ cup sugar, ½ cup flour, and ⅓ cup butter or margarine	8 or 9-inch pie
Small Cakes made from batter for	
9- by 13-inch cake	4 dozen 1½-inch petits fours
Two 8-inch layers	1½ to 2 dozen cupcakes
Two 9-inch layers	2½ dozen cupcakes
9- by 5- by 3-inch cake	2 dozen cupcakes
Frostings and Fillings	
For an 8 or 9-inch two-layer cake	Frosts 24 cupcakes
Buttercream from ⅓ cup butter and 1 pound confectioners' powdered sugar	Frosts and fills an 8 or 9-inch two-layer cake or 24 cupcakes
3¾ to 4¾ cups buttercream	Frosts and fills 9-inch two-layer (each layer 1½ inches deep) cake or a 9-inch three-layer (each layer 1 inch deep) cake
3 cups buttercream frosting	Frosts and fills 8-inch two-layer (each layer 1½ inches deep) cake or a 9-inch two-layer (each layer 1 inch deep) cake
Cream cheese frosting from 6 ounces cream cheese and 1 pound confectioners' powdered sugar	Frosts and fills 8 or 9-inch two-layer cake or 24 cupcakes
1 large egg white	¾ cup royal icing
Royal icing made from 3 egg whites and 1 pound confectioners' powdered sugar	Decorates an 8, 9, or 10-inch cake, or 24 cupcakes
2 cups glaze	Topping for 9-inch cake
Glaze made from 3 cups sifted confectioners' powdered sugar	Coats 16 petits fours
Glaze made from 1 cup sifted confectioners' powdered sugar and 2 to 3 tablespoons liquid	Tops a tube cake, loaf cake, 24 cupcakes, 8 or 9-inch cake or 6 to 8 éclairs.
1 cup pastry cream (made from ¾ cup milk, 1 egg yolk, and ⅓ cup sugar)	Fills an 8 or 9-inch layer cake
1 cup jelly or preserves	Fills one jelly roll
2 cups whipped cream (made from 1 cup heavy cream)	Fills one cake roll

Freezing Techniques

A good freezer will more than prove its worth in the kitchen. Not only will you be able make and store all manner of frozen desserts, you can stock up on inexpensive seasonal produce, take advantage of bargains at the meat market, and store leftovers and extra foods for long periods of time without spoiling. Freezers also store infrequently used foods well, such as whole-grain flours, pine nuts, and herbs—all of which deteriorate rapidly at room temperature.

A freestanding freezer—either the upright style or the chest style—should keep foods at about 0°F. The freezer compartment of your refrigerator keeps food at 10°F. to 25°F., which is not cold enough for long-term storage of foods.

PACKAGING FOODS FOR THE FREEZER

How well frozen food keeps in the freezer depends on how well it is packaged. Exposure to air during freezing causes "freezer burn," where the food dries out and develops a tough, dry surface. Use plastic containers with tight-fitting lids, or several layers of plastic wrap or foil, or heavy-duty freezer paper for packaging foods. Resealable heavy-weight plastic bags are excellent for the freezer; squeeze out as much air as possible before sealing.

Remember that liquids expand as they freeze. Leave plenty of head space—½ inch in plastic pint containers, 1 inch in plastic quart containers, 1 inch in glass pint containers, and 1½ inches in glass quart containers.

Defrosting the Freezer

Plan to clean out your freezer once a year—or as soon as there is a buildup of ½ to ¾ inch of frost on the shelves and sides of the freezer.

Unplug the freezer and remove all the food. The food should be transferred to a refrigerator or wrapped in blankets or layers of newspaper to insulate it. Discard any packages of food that you can't identify. Throw out any packages that have been stored over a year.

To speed up the defrosting process, you can place pans of hot water in the freezer. Never chip away at the ice or frost with a knife or other tool; you could damage the freezer. Wipe out the defrosted freezer with a solution of 1 tablespoon baking soda to 1 quart lukewarm water. Thoroughly dry the freezer with a clean cloth or a hair dryer. Run the freezer for about 30 minutes before returning the food to it.

When freezing items such as cookies or meat patties, stack the foods with pieces of waxed paper between the layers for ease in separating when frozen.

Wrapping bulky foods. To wrap bulky foods, such as large roasts or cakes, place the food on the center of a large piece of heavy-duty foil or freezer paper. Bring the ends together over the food and fold down until the packaging lies tight against the food. Pleat fold one open end, then the other, making an extra fold before pressing the folded ends against the package. Seal the package with masking tape, not cellophane tape, which won't hold at cold temperatures.

Labeling. Don't rely on your memory to tell you what a package in the freezer contains. Label everything. Include the date the food was purchased or made, and be sure to use it in a timely fashion (see pages 117–119 for maximum storage times). Ordinary pens and felt-tip markers will smudge and fade in the freezer, so use a pencil or special marking pen for labeling frozen foods, and record the information on masking tape rather than directly on the container (which you may want to reuse).

THAWING AND USING FROZEN FOODS

Many foods can go right from the freezer to the stove or oven. Labels on commercially frozen foods will tell you whether thawing is necessary or not. Home-frozen vegetables do not require thawing before cooking. Precooked casseroles, soups, and stews can also go from freezer to oven.

To reheat frozen casseroles, soups, and stews, slip them out of their freezer packaging and into pots or casseroles. Figure that a 2-quart frozen casserole will take about 1½ hours to reheat at 350°F. Soups and stews can be reheated on top of a stove over low heat as long as they are stirred frequently. Microwave ovens can be used to reheat frozen entrées as long as you rotate the dish and stir once or twice.

Other foods, including meat and poultry, require thawing first. The very best way to thaw frozen foods is slowly, wrapped in its original packaging, in the refrigerator. This provides time for the food to reabsorb any juices it may have lost, as well as prevent any bacteria from multiplying in the food. When you must defrost food quickly, make sure the food is in an airtight container or wrapper, then immerse the food in ice water that is kept cold. A microwave oven can also be used to speed up the thawing. Consult the manual that came with your oven for settings.

Baked goods are the only foods that can be safely defrosted at room temperature. Most will take 2 to 3 hours and should be left wrapped. Unbaked pies can go directly into the oven. Bake at 450°F. on the lowest shelf of the oven for 15 to 20 minutes. Then reduce the heat to 350°F. and bake for 1 hour.

♦ **Microwave defrosting and reheating, 258**

Power Breaks

A storm hits and the power goes out. Your freezer is off for hours. What should you do?

If the freezer is full and without power for one or two days, there is no problem. Chances are the food will remain frozen—as long as you don't open the freezer door. If the power will be out for a while, see if you can get a 50-pound block of dry ice for your freezer. This will prevent defrosting for two or three days. Handle dry ice with gloves to prevent burns!

Without the dry ice, the food will begin to thaw after a day or so. Any food that still has ice crystals in it may be refrozen when the power is restored. If in doubt, particularly with uncooked meat, poultry, or fish, cook the food immediately. It can be refrozen safely as a cooked dish.

Previously frozen foods are vulnerable to bacterial growth if left at room temperature, especially foods with gravies, sauces, and stuffings. Reheat quickly and serve promptly.

Since flavors change in the freezer, taste and adjust seasonings as required in reheated foods. More salt may be needed. Some foods will be watery and should be heated for a few minutes without a cover to evaporate excess moisture; other foods will become dry and should be basted with a little water or stock.

It is safe to use defrosted frozen (raw) meat, poultry, or fish in dishes that will then go back into the freezer. However, cooked meats, fish, and poultry should never be refrozen.

FREEZING FRUITS

There is no best way to freeze fruit; each fruit can be treated in a variety of ways—dry packed or tray frozen, packed in a sugar syrup, or simply sprinkled with sugar. Most fruits will have good flavor after freezing, but expect that the fruit will be much softer.

Making Sugar Syrups for Freezing Fruit

Combine the water and sugar and heat just until the sugar dissolves.

SYRUP	SUGAR	WATER	YIELD
Thin Syrup (30 percent sugar)	2 cups	4 cups	5 cups
Medium Syrup (50 percent sugar)	3 cups	4 cups	5½ cups
Heavy Syrup (50 percent sugar)	4 cups	4 cups	6½ cups

Freezing Fruits

FRUIT	PREPARATION	DRY PACK	WET PACK WITH SUGAR (AMOUNT SUGAR PER PINT)	SYRUP PACK	PACK IN JUICE	ASCORBIC ACID*
Apples	Pare, core, slice. Steam for 2 to 3 minutes over	Yes	1/4 cup	Medium	No	Yes
Apricots	Halve and pit; pare. Slice if desired.	No	1/4 cup	Medium	Yes	Yes
Berries (except Straw-berries)	Remove leaves and stems.	Yes	6 tablespoons	Medium	Yes	No
Cherries, sour	Pit.	No	6 tablespoons	Heavy	No	Yes
Cherries, sweet	Pit.	No	6 tablespoons	Thin or medium	No	Yes
Cranberries	Place package in freezer.	No	No	No	No	No
Currants	Remove stems.	Yes	6 tablespoons	Heavy	No	No
Gooseberries	Remove stems and ends.	Yes	6 tablespoons	Heavy	No	No
Grapes	Stem; leave seedless grapes whole, halve and pit seeded grapes.	Yes	No	Medium	No	No
Melon	Pare, seed, cut in cubes or balls.	No	No	Light	No	No
Nectarines	Halve, pit, pare; slice if desired.	No	1/3 cup	Medium	Yes	Yes
Peaches	Halve, pit, pare; slice if desired.	No	1/3 cup	Medium	Yes	Yes
Pears	Pare, core; slice. Add to boiling medium syrup and cook for 1 to 2 minutes.	No	No	Medium	No	Yes
Pineapple	Pare; cube or crush.	Yes	No	Light	Yes	No
Plums	Halve and pit.	Yes	6 tablespoons	Medium	No	Yes
Rhubarb	Cut stalks in 1-inch pieces; discard leaves. Blanch for 1 minute (optional).	Yes	1/2 cup	Medium or heavy	No	No
Strawberries	Hull; leave whole or slice.	Yes	6 tablespoons	Heavy	Yes	No

*1/2 teaspoon dissolved in 3 tablespoons water, mixed with fruit as it is sliced

Foods Affected by Freezing

Many foods change in taste or texture in the freezer. If a prepared dish contains any of the ingredients below, expect some changes—how concentrated these ingredients are in the dish will affect whether the dish should be frozen or not. For example, garlic tends to get stronger in the freezer—but stronger garlic flavor in a casserole is still acceptable.

☐ Garlic and sweet green peppers taste stronger once frozen.

☐ Onions lose flavor in the freezer.

☐ Salad greens, radishes, celery, and scallions become unpleasantly mushy when frozen.

☐ Many spices are affected by freezing, becoming stronger or weaker in flavor. Basil, oregano, and thyme lose flavor. Sage becomes bitter, as do some peppers. Cloves get decidedly stronger. Avoid freezing spice cakes.

☐ Fried foods taste stale after freezing.

☐ Hard-cooked eggs become rubbery.

☐ Cheddar cheese becomes crumbly, but can still be used in cooked dishes.

☐ Cooked pasta becomes soggy.

☐ Potatoes become grainy and soft.

☐ Boiled icings become sticky (butter-based icings do not).

If you want to serve the fruit thawed, without further preparation, freeze the fruit in a sugar syrup. If you plan to use the fruit in a baked dessert, such as pie or cobbler, it should be tray frozen or packed with sugar. Tray freezing works best with berries.

To prevent the fruit from darkening. Fruit that darkens when cut (apples, apricots, peaches, pears, etc.) should be treated by steam-blanching or mixing with ascorbic acid (vitamin C) before it is frozen. Unlike lemon juice and citric acid, ascorbic acid will not affect the flavor of frozen foods. It is available as crystals or tablets. It is found in most supermarkets (look for it where preserving and canning supplies are sold) and drugstores.

Allow ¼ teaspoon ascorbic acid dissolved in 3 tablespoons cold water for each pint of sugar syrup (see page 292) or prepared fruit (for wet pack with sugar). If you are substituting vitamin C tablets for crystalline ascorbic acid, figure that 3000 mg of vitamin C equals 1 teaspoon of ascorbic acid in crystal form.

Dry pack and tray-freezing (no sugar method). The easiest way to freeze fruit is to put whole or cut-up fruits in containers and freeze.

This works best for firm fruits, such as cranberries, blueberries, currants, figs, gooseberries, and rhubarb. It also works for raspberries and blackberries. If you like, you can first tray freeze the fruits, spreading them out in a single layer on a shallow tray, then bagging once the fruit is frozen. This way the fruit will not stick together. For best results, make sure the fruit is dry before it is frozen.

Wet pack. For the best flavor and texture, pack any fruit (except cranberries) in a sugar syrup before freezing. Whether to use a thin syrup (30 percent sugar), a medium syrup (40 percent sugar), or a heavy syrup (50 percent sugar) depends on your own taste and the fruit—the milder the fruit, the lighter the syrup. See page 292 for water-to-sugar ratios and plan to use ⅓ to ½ cup syrup for every pint of fruit.

You can also sprinkle sugar directly on fruit and toss gently until the fruit's own juice is drawn out and the sugar is dissolved. Then pack and freeze. This is a good method for fruit that is to be cooked or added to fruit salads or compotes.

If you prefer a sugarless treatment, substitute unsweetened fruit juice for the sugar syrup. You can extract the juice from the less-perfect fruits (cook the fruit in a little water until very soft, then strain through a double thickness of cheesecloth to separate the juice from the pulp) or use a commercial unsweetened fruit juice.

FREEZING VEGETABLES

Freezing is an excellent way to preserve vegetables from your garden or local farm stand. The vegetables should be blanched first to preserve flavor and color and to destroy enzymes that cause the vegetable to age.

To blanch, heat a large pot of water to boiling. You will need a gallon of water for each pound or quart of vegetables to be blanched. Wash and slice or chop the vegetable. Then plunge into boiling water and begin counting the blanching time (see the table on page 296). If the water doesn't return to a boil within 1 minute of adding the vegetables, you are trying to blanch too much at a time. Boil for the specified length of time. Immediately plunge the vegetables into a large bowl of ice water to stop the cooking process. When cool, drain, then pat dry.

You can pack most vegetables in serving-size portions into freezer bags or plastic containers. If desired, you can tray freeze the vegetables first so they don't stick together, then freeze in large plastic bags. To tray freeze, spread the blanched, cooled, and drained vegetables in a single layer on large shallow pans. Freeze for 1 to 2 hours, then pack into bags, squeeze out the excess air, label, and return to the freezer.

Freezing Vegetables

VEGETABLE	PREPARATION	BLANCHING TIME IN MINUTES
Asparagus	Trim off woody ends. Peel stalks with vegetable peeler. Leave whole or cut into 2-inch lengths.	2 to 4, depending on thickness of stalk
Beans, Green and Wax	Trim off ends. Leave whole, cut into 1- to 2-inch lengths, or cut into strips for "French-style" beans.	3
Beans, Lima and other shell beans	Remove from shells and sort by size.	2 to 4, depending on size
Broccoli	Remove large leaves, trim woody ends, peel stalks. (If homegrown, soak in a saltwater solution of 4 teaspoons salt to 4 quarts water for 30 minutes to remove insects.) Cut stems lengthwise so flowerets are about 1 ½ inches across.	3
Brussels Sprouts	Remove outer leaves. (If homegrown, soak in a saltwater solution of 4 teaspoons salt to 4 quarts water for 30 minutes to remove insects.) Sort by size.	3 to 5, depending on size
Carrots	Scrub or pare as needed. Cut into ¼-inch cubes or slices.	3
Cauliflower	Trim and break into 1-inch flowerets. (If homegrown, soak in a salt water solution of 4 teaspoons salt to 4 quarts water for 30 minutes to remove insects.)	3
Corn	On the cob: Remove husks, silks. Sort by size and blanch similar size cobs together. Whole kernel: Remove husks, silks. Scrape kernels from cob after cob is blanched.	3 to 6
Greens	Trim tough stems and ribs. Cut as desired.	2 (3 for collard greens)
Okra	Remove stem end. Sort by size. Leave whole or slice crosswise after blanching.	3 to 4, depending on size
Onions	Peel and chop. Do not blanch.	
Peas	Shell.	2
Squash, Winter	Cook and puree as for fresh use. Freeze in plastic containers.	

Tips for Freezing and Using Specific Foods

☐ Freeze casseroles in baking dishes or aluminum foil pans that can go straight from the freezer to the oven. If you line a casserole dish with foil before freezing, you will be able to remove the frozen casserole from the dish, wrap it in foil, and return to the freezer. This enables you to use your casserole dish for other meals. When you are ready to reheat it, slip the foil-wrapped casserole back into its original dish.

☐ Casseroles made with rice are preferable to casseroles made with pasta because rice retains its texture better.

☐ Freeze small amounts of gravies, sauces, stock, pesto, tomato paste, and other liquids used for seasonings in ice cube trays. Once frozen, turn into plastic bags. Remove as many cubes of seasoning as needed at a time, and reseal the bag.

☐ Most soups freeze well, but those with potatoes will become watery. If possible, remove the potatoes before freezing and add freshly cooked potatoes before serving.

☐ Freeze store-bought meat and poultry in its original packaging, whenever possible. If you must transfer poultry, remember there is a chance of salmonella when handling raw poultry, so wash hands, surfaces and utensils with warm soapy water when through.

☐ Do not thaw frozen vegetables before cooking.

☐ Freeze dry-packed berries in resealable plastic bags. Remove as much as you need at a time and reseal.

☐ Freeze frosted cakes unwrapped so the frosting doesn't stick to the wrapping. As soon as they are frozen, wrap in foil, plastic, or freezer paper. Thaw, still wrapped, in a covered cake dish at room temperature for several hours before serving.

CHAPTER 4

Recipe Savers, Time Savers, and Money Savers

CAN THIS RECIPE BE SAVED? Can I substitute the ingredients I have on hand for the ones called for in a recipe? Can I juggle my busy schedule and still create fine, affordable, nutritious meals for me and my family? The answer is yes!

Recipe Savers

Sometimes things just don't go as planned, especially in the kitchen. But often there's a quick fix that will remedy your mistakes and keep dinner on track.

FOOD FIXERS

Don't lose heart if something goes wrong during cooking. Food from most culinary mishaps can be salvaged—and enjoyed.

☐ *Dish too sweet?* As long as the dish isn't milk-based and in danger of curdling, add a dash of vinegar or lemon juice.

☐ *Gelatin set before you folded in the solid ingredients?* Remelt the gelatin by heating it gently in the top of a double boiler placed over boiling water. Once it is completely melted, remove it from the heat and place in the refrigerator. Let it set again, just until it is as thick as unbeaten egg whites. Quickly add the dry ingredients, pour the mixture into a mold or other container; refrigerate until completely set.

☐ *Cheese overripe?* Cut out any dried spots. Grate or mash the remainder; mix with softened butter or cream cheese and season to taste; serve with crackers as spread.

☐ *Stew or soup too salty?* Add a cut-up potato or two to the simmering mixture; it will absorb some of the saltiness.

☐ *Soup too thin?* Thicken it with a paste made of equal parts softened butter and flour; add to the simmering soup; cook and stir vigorously with a wire whisk until the flour is cooked and the soup is thickened. Or puree some of the vegetables from the soup; return to the soup.

☐ *Soufflé fall?* Serve a savory soufflé in individual portions. Spoon the mixture into au gratin dishes, top with buttered bread crumbs and cheese, and broil until bubbly. Serve the soufflé with a cheese, vegetable, or tomato sauce.

☐ *Roast chicken or turkey fall apart?* Slice in the kitchen and serve already sliced. (This is always good advice for the nervous carver!)

☐ *Meatloaf fall apart?* Crumble the whole thing into a pot of tomato sauce and serve over pasta. Or use as a base for moussaka or other casserole dish.

Emergency Ingredient Substitutions

Don't panic if you're out of an ingredient called for in a recipe.

WHEN THE RECIPE CALLS FOR:	YOU MAY SUBSTITUTE:
I square unsweetened chocolate	3 tablespoons unsweetened cocoa powder and I tablespoon butter, margarine, or vegetable shortening
I cup sifted cake flour	I cup less 2 tablespoons all-purpose flour
2 tablespoons flour (for thickening)	I tablespoon cornstarch
I teaspoon baking powder	1/4 teaspoon baking soda plus 1/2 teaspoon cream of tartar
I cup corn syrup	I cup sugar and 1/4 cup additional liquid of the same kind used in recipe
I cup honey	1 1/4 cups sugar and 1/4 cup additional liquid of the same kind used in recipe
I cup sweet milk	1/2 cup evaporated milk plus 1/2 cup water
I cup buttermilk	I tablespoon vinegar or lemon juice plus enough milk to make I cup
I cup sour cream (in baking)	7/8 cup buttermilk plus 3 tablespoons butter or I cup yogurt
I cup firmly packed brown sugar	I cup granulated sugar or I cup sugar and 2 tablespoons molasses
I teaspoon lemon juice	1/4 teaspoon vinegar
1/4 cup chopped onion	I tablespoon instant minced onion
I clove garlic	1/8 teaspoon garlic powder
I cup tomato juice	1/2 cup tomato sauce and 1/2 cup water
2 cups tomato sauce	3/4 cup tomato paste and I cup water
I tablespoon fresh snipped herbs	I teaspoon dried herbs
I tablespoon prepared mustard	I teaspoon dry mustard
1/2 cup (I stick) butter or margarine	8 tablespoons (1/2 cup) vegetable shortening

◗ **More chocolate substitutes, 301**

□ *Fruit too ripe to serve?* Puree and sweeten to make a fresh-tasting sauce.

□ *Vegetables overcooked?* Puree them into a side dish, adding a bit of cream, buttermilk, or plain yogurt. Or use the puree as the base for a soup or sauce.

□ *Gravy lumpy?* Give it a whirl in the food processor or blender. Or force it through an extra-fine sieve.

Avoid Last-Minute Dessert Disasters

□ **If you don't have a toothpick to test a cake you're baking, use a strand of uncooked spaghetti.**

□ **To unmold gelatin onto the center of a platter with ease, lightly moisten the platter with cold water just before unmolding the gelatin; you'll be able to slide the mold into place.**

□ *Hollandaise sauce curdle?* Heat a small amount of the sauce in a clean pan, whisking in a fresh egg until the mixture is smooth. Slowly whisk in the curdled mixture, a little at a time, beating after each addition, until incorporated. Heat very gently for 1 minute longer, beating constantly.

□ *Custard curdle?* Strain out the curdled part using a fine sieve. Cover the top of the strained mixture with plastic wrap to prevent a skin from forming.

□ *Poached eggs misshapen?* Place in toast-lined casserole. Top with cheese sauce, white sauce with herbs and mushrooms, or tomato sauce, and bake until bubbly.

□ *Dessert soufflé fall?* Sweet dessert soufflés can be served in individual portions too. Top each portion with whatever accompaniment you had planned for the soufflé—a dollop of whipped cream, chocolate sauce, or softened ice cream or frozen yogurt.

□ *Cake crumble?* Make a delicious trifle by moistening the pieces with a bit of melted jam and liqueur, topping with custard and/or fruit.

□ *Cookies crumble?* Crush the pieces into crumbs. Use the crumbs for crumb crusts for dessert pies instead of graham cracker crumbs. Or moisten with liqueur and roll into balls for no-bake truffles. Use the crumbs sprinkled on ice cream, yogurt, and puddings.

□ *Ice cream melted?* Use it as a sauce for cut-up fruit or a topping for crumbled cake or cookies. Or make ice cream shakes and malteds.

□ *Cake sink in the center?* Cover the top with whipped cream, frosting, or fruit.

□ *Cake frosting too thin?* Refrigerate until it firms up.

Time Savers

RECIPE ROSTER

Always read a recipe from beginning to end before you start cooking or baking.

□ Get out the ingredients called for, noting any that require special preparation, such as chopping, marinating, or bringing to room temperature.

□ Use your microwave to soften butter, melt chocolate, precook foods for grilling (see Microwave Techniques, page 254).

□ Use the correct size and shape container for mixing, cooking, and, most important, baking. (See Emergency Baking Dish and Pan Substitutes on page 168.)

□ For best baking results, preheat the oven for about 15 minutes before using it, or as directed.

KITCHEN ORGANIZATION

You can make your kitchen ultraefficient for fast meal preparation and cleanup.

☐ Label spices and other perishables with the date of purchase. (After six to twelve months, most spices lose flavor and need to be replaced.) Arrange them in alphabetical order for easy retrieval.

☐ Store utensils needed for each work station (stove, sink, counters) within arm's reach, leaving counters clear. Store pots and pans near cooking area, dishes near dishwasher and sink.

☐ Reserve the cupboards under the counters for stashing cutting boards, colanders, and other bulky items. Store cleaning supplies in a nearby utility closet.

☐ Create a tray with ready-to-go table-setting supplies: silverware caddy, napkins, placemats, salt, pepper, condiments, everything necessary for one-trip-only table setting.

☐ When you empty the dishwasher, wrap a flatware place setting in a napkin for each family member. You or your kids will be able to set the table with ease.

☐ Assign priority shelf space to equipment and foods you use most often; track items that need replacing with a pad and pencil kept near cabinets.

☐ Use wall racks and ceiling racks to keep often-used pots, pans, and utensils within easy sight and instant reach.

USE YOUR REFRIGERATOR AND FREEZER

☐ Make multiple batches of food whenever possible, preparing extra for the refrigerator or freezer (see pages 117–123 for storage times). Doubling or even tripling most recipes doesn't require much more work than preparing the regular yield. Rice, for example, can be frozen, then heated over boiling water or in the microwave when you need it. Don't double recipes for baked goods, because the outcome of those recipes is very much dependent on pan size and baking times.

☐ The following dishes reheat beautifully and even improve in flavor: soups and stews without potatoes; osso buco (braised Italian veal

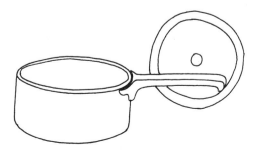

shanks); meat or vegetable chili; stuffed shells; lasagna; meatballs; marinara and other tomato-based pasta sauces; chicken curry; moussaka.

☐ Refrigerate small amounts of leftovers in a muffin pan covered with plastic wrap. Everything will be easy to see and retrieve.

☐ Before placing hard-cooked eggs in the refrigerator, write the date they were cooked on the shells. Cover the eggs. Plan to eat them within four days. Do not store cooked eggs with uncooked eggs.

☐ To keep uncooked bacon fresh, spread the slices on a long sheet of waxed paper. Roll up the paper lengthwise, jelly-roll style, then wrap the roll in plastic wrap and freeze. At cooking time, unroll just as much bacon as you need; return the remainder to the freezer.

☐ For fast retrieval and thawing from the freezer, store items in serving-size amounts. A slice of frozen bread thaws in seconds in the microwave, just a matter of minutes in the toaster. A slice of frozen meatloaf can be removed to make an impromptu hot sandwich supper or crumbled into spaghetti sauce.

☐ Shape ground meat into patties; store with waxed paper between them in a container in the freezer.

☐ Halve English muffins with a fork, bagels with a knife, before freezing them, to save work later on and speed up thawing.

☐ To store semisolid items, such as tomato paste, in recipe-size amounts, freeze them by the spoonful on a piece of waxed paper; thin mixtures such as broth, pesto, and juice can be frozen in ice cube trays, then unmolded. Once frozen solid, these items can be stored in an airtight container or plastic bag. When you need flavoring for a soup or sauce, just remove as many spoonfuls as you need.

☐ Line casseroles with aluminum foil before filling. Freeze, then remove foil-wrapped food, label, and return to freezer. At reheating time, place foil-wrapped food back in casserole.

☐ Seal freezer containers well to keep out flavor-diminishing air.

☐ Always label and date everything you put in the freezer. To be superorganized, keep a list of the dishes you've frozen. This eliminates hunting and guessing later on.

BECOME A MENU PLANNER

Work out a week's dinners in advance, jotting down your shopping list at the same time.

☐ Use your computer or a copy machine to make multiple copies of a personal shopping form: List those ingredients you're apt to buy often and leave blank spaces for special items. At shopping time, check off the regular purchases and fill in the unusual items.

☐ Select meals that use the same ingredients in different ways, to save both shopping and cooking time.

Staples Make Speedy Work

Keep the following basic items on hand and you won't need to waste time running to the store at the last minute.

Pantry Staples

Rice
Pasta
Flour
Cornstarch
Gelatin
Cornmeal
Oatmeal
Bread crumbs
Sugar: granulated, brown, 10X confectioners'
Corn syrup
Maple syrup
Honey
Baking powder
Baking soda
Cream of tartar
Unsweetened chocolate
Cocoa
Evaporated and condensed milk
Dry milk powder
Chicken broth
Beef broth
Canned soups
Vegetable oil
Olive oil
Vinegar
Salt
Pepper
Onions

Garlic
Dried fruit
Vanilla extract
Pizza/pasta sauce
Canned whole plum tomatoes
Canned stewed tomatoes
Canned meats and fish
Canned and bottled fruit and vegetable juice
Peanut butter
Jams and jellies
Condiments and sauces (soy sauce, relishes, etc.)

Refrigerator

Milk
Butter
Eggs
Margarine
Grated Parmesan cheese
Worcestershire sauce
Liquid red-pepper seasoning
Mayonnaise
Mustard
Catsup
Salad dressing
Lemon juice or lemons

Herbs and Spices

Allspice
Anise seed
Basil
Bay leaf
Caraway seed
Cardamom
Celery seed
Chili powder
Cinnamon: ground and sticks
Cloves
Coriander
Cumin
Curry powder
Dill
Fennel seed
Ginger
Marjoram
Nutmeg
Oregano
Paprika
Ground hot pepper
Peppercorns
Poppy seed
Rosemary
Sage
Tarragon
Thyme
Turmeric

□ If your schedule permits, devote a block of time on the weekend to prepare the next week's meals.

□ Limit menus to two or three simple courses.

□ Expand your definition of a meal: Hearty soups, substantial appetizers, salads, and sandwiches can be combined with satisfying results.

□ Expand your existing repertoire by varying familiar recipes. Preparing new recipes usually takes more time.

SHOPPING SAVVY

□ Plan a once-a-week shopping trip for perishable items—meat, dairy products, fruits, and vegetables. Shop for nonperishable items less often and buy them in sizes that are economical and reasonable for your needs—as much as you can afford and can store.

□ Delegate some of the shopping to other family members, detailing brand names and sizes on clearly written lists.

□ Group items on shopping lists according to the aisles where they are located in the supermarket.

□ Divide shopping responsibilities with a friend.

□ Patronize stores that deliver and/or take orders over the phone.

□ Patronize stores that have extended shopping hours. Stop at off-peak times to avoid crowds in the aisles and at checkout counters.

CUT INGREDIENT PREP TIME

□ If you're pressed for time, buy meat that's already deboned or cut up, grated cheeses, and sliced and chopped vegetables from the salad bar.

□ Use top-quality produce and well-trimmed meats so you don't waste time removing brown spots and fat.

□ Stock up on frozen vegetables; they're already chopped, cleaned, and ready to go.

□ If your budget allows, stock up on condiments and specialty items

Ingredient Time Savers

Save on time by using prepared ingredients in recipes.

INSTEAD OF:	USE:
Cucumbers with seeds removed	European seedless cucumber
Cooked dried beans	Drained and rinsed canned beans
1/4 cup chopped fresh onion	1 tablespoon instant minced onion or 1/4 cup frozen chopped onion
Cooked, boneless, skinless chicken	Deli-roasted chicken

such as sun-dried tomatoes, good-quality grated Parmesan cheese, pesto, oil-cured olives, preserves, mustards, oils, and vinegars. They're great to have on hand for adding instant flair to food.

☐ Scissor-snip fresh herbs, pizza, and chicken for speedy cutting.

☐ To cut up sticky dried fruit, spray kitchen scissors or chopping knife with nonstick vegetable cooking spray before using. Or dredge the fruit in flour before cutting. Or dip scissors or knife frequently in a cup of water.

☐ Before sifting flour or measuring out other dry ingredients onto a piece of waxed paper, crease the paper in the center to create an efficient pouring spout.

☐ Place semisoft cheeses and meats for stir-fry in the freezer 15 minutes before shredding or slivering them; they'll be easier to handle.

☐ Smash garlic cloves with the side of a heavy chef's knife; the skin will separate from the garlic, making it easy to remove. Or soak the garlic cloves in water for an hour or two; the skins will slip right off.

☐ Use canned soups and soup mixes for last-minute sauces.

☐ Split baking potatoes lengthwise; they'll be done in less time.

☐ To reduce cooking time, shape meatloaf mixture into tiny loaves for baking; bake them in muffin pans or small loaf pans, or shape them free-form and bake them on a foil-lined jelly-roll pan. Or make meatloaf patties or meatballs and sauté or broil them.

☐ To easily retrieve whole spices from stews and soups, place them in a metal tea ball and hang it from the rim of the pot.

☐ Remove the skin and bones from cooked poultry you'll be using for salads and casseroles while the poultry is still warm; the meat will be much easier to separate.

☐ Meals that don't require a recipe are fast. Broil meat, poultry, or fish, steam a vegetable and toss with lemon butter or balsamic vinegar. For dessert, serve frozen yogurt with a splash of liqueur.

USE THOSE UTENSILS

Utensils can be great time savers. The following tips prove that one utensil can be used for a variety of tasks.

☐ Slice bananas with a pastry blender. Mash them with a potato masher.

☐ Core halved apples and pears with a melon ball cutter.

☐ Use a hard-cooked egg slicer to make uniform slices of cooked potatoes, mushrooms, and other foods that will fit into the egg-sized mold.

☐ Use a swivel-bladed vegetable peeler to remove the zest in strips from oranges and lemons, peel skin from apples, pears, and other firm fruits and vegetables, and strings from celery.

□ Use the tip of a potato peeler to pit cherries.

□ Instead of a vegetable brush, use a nylon scouring pad to scrub vegetables that are cooked in their skins, such as potatoes and carrots.

□ Use a serrated grapefruit spoon to scoop out tomatoes for stuffing.

□ Use a clean soft toothbrush to clean fresh mushrooms.

COMPUTE THE REWARDS!

Use your home personal computer to help plan family meals.

□ File the recipes you use most often; they'll be easily retrieved when you need them. Include your favorite variations, what foods they go well with, when you served them, and to whom.

□ Keep an inventory of the contents of your pantry and freezer.

□ Use the computer to print out shopping lists.

TWO-FOR-ONE COOKING

Prepare dishes in larger amounts than you'll need for one meal, so that they can be used a second or third time around.

□ Pureed soups make great sauces for poached chicken or fish, vegetables, and pasta. If necessary, simmer the soup to reduce it to a saucelike consistency.

□ Serve tomato sauce over pasta one night, then use it as a simmering base for chicken cacciatore.

□ Prepare large oatmeal cookies and use them to make homemade ice cream sandwiches. Crush the remainder and layer the crumbs with applesauce and vanilla yogurt.

□ Prepare corned beef with steamed potatoes and cabbage. Use the corned beef and cooked potatoes for corned beef hash. Shred any remaining raw cabbage, sauté it with apple slices, and serve with the hash.

□ Serve whole poached pears for dessert one night. Chop and core the remaining pears; reduce the poaching syrup, add the chopped pears, and heat briefly to make a topping for French toast or vanilla ice cream.

□ Serve hard-cooked eggs for breakfast. Use the remainder for egg salad sandwiches.

□ Serve steamed rice, vegetables, and meat or fish for dinner. Use whatever's left over to make fried rice the next night.

□ Serve steamed rice as a side dish. Use the remainder to make rice pudding.

□ Prepare ratatouille or another vegetable medley. Serve it as a side dish one night. Another night, add chopped cooked meat or chick-peas and serve over rice as a main dish.

□ Bake or broil tomatoes to accompany a simple meat, fish, or poultry entrée. Puree the remainder along with its liquid; season with herbs and serve as a hot or chilled soup.

□ Serve a stew or casserole for dinner. Chop any leftover meat or vegetables; add broth to make a hearty soup.

□ Prepare sausage and peppers for hero sandwiches. Slice the remainder and use in a frittata.

□ Cook twice as much potatoes, pasta, or rice as you'll need. Use the remainder to make potato, pasta, or rice salad.

□ Remove the inside of leftover baked potatoes; mash with butter, a bit of milk, cheese, minced onion or green onion and your favorite herbs. Pile the mixture back into the potato shells and bake until the filling is hot and golden brown.

BREAKFAST IS A BREEZE

Cereal.

□ Prepare oatmeal in batches and refrigerate in individual serving-size microwave-proof containers. Remove as many portions as needed and reheat in the microwave.

Yogurt.

□ Yogurt shakes blend in an instant, go down fast. Combine ¾ cup low-fat yogurt, ¼ cup skim milk, your choice of fruit, such as banana, berries, ripe peeled peaches, or nectarines, and 3 ice cubes in a blender container; add a scant teaspoon of sugar or honey if desired. Cover and blend until thick and creamy.

□ Low-fat yogurt, with or without fresh fruit, is a soothing way to start the day. Accompany it with a bran muffin or piece of toast for energy to keep you going all morning long.

Hearty breakfast every day!

□ Since most kids love pancakes and French toast, make them on the weekend and wrap individual servings in aluminum foil and freeze. Unwrap and reheat in the toaster oven or in the microwave.

Top of the Morning

Nutritious toast toppers turn a slice of bread into a meal. Try the following:

□ **Peanut butter with sliced banana.**

□ **Low-fat yogurt topped with fresh fruit or raisins and wheat germ.**

□ **Sugar-free fruit preserves and low-fat cottage cheese.**

□ **Low-fat ricotta cheese blended with raisins and cinnamon, or finely chopped fresh vegetables, such as green pepper, green onion, radishes, and carrots.**

HORS D'OEUVRES IN A HURRY

☐ Buy prepared pastry cups. Fill with prepared seafood or chicken salad, finely chopped if necessary. Garnish with a sprig of a fresh herb or a strip of red pepper.

☐ Wrap prosciutto around bread sticks.

☐ Slice cooked new potatoes in half. Garnish each half with a dollop of sour cream and a tiny spoonful of caviar.

☐ Roll goat cheese logs in finely chopped nuts and paprika. Serve with crackers.

☐ Fill mushroom caps with garlic and herb cheese spread. Place on a well-greased pan and broil until the cheese is bubbly hot, about 4 minutes.

☐ Prepare a tray of assorted sausages, mustards, and pretzels.

☐ In a small bowl, combine equal parts sour cream or plain yogurt and mayonnaise. Use as a base for dips, adding onion soup mix, curry powder and chopped chutney, pesto sauce, etc.

LAST-MINUTE FIRST COURSES

☐ Heat canned broth with sliced mushrooms. Place a tablespoon of dry sherry and a few snips of chives into individual soup bowls; add the broth mixture.

☐ Buy an assortment of Italian-style cold cuts and cheeses, as well as two or three prepared vegetable condiments, such as marinated artichoke hearts and olives. Serve as antipasto.

☐ Broil or microwave cubes of goat cheese until bubbly. Toss into a green salad and serve at once.

☐ Sauté a mixture of sliced mushrooms in butter. Add dry sherry or vermouth toward the end of cooking time. Spoon over toast triangles spread with prepared chicken liver pâté.

☐ Heat canned chicken broth. In a small bowl, beat together an egg with grated Parmesan cheese; beat into the hot soup along with sprigs of Italian parsley and cook just until the egg is set.

ENTRÉES IN A HURRY

Boneless, skinned chicken or turkey breasts, pork tenderloin, and fish fillets are the best for quick preparation and cooking. *Or* use frozen and packaged foods, deli-counter preparations, and salad bar ingredients to make almost instant entrées.

☐ *Skillet Rice Dinner.* Prepare packaged brown and wild rice mix. Toss in sliced fresh mushrooms, frozen peas or peas and carrots, and slivered smoked turkey or ham. Serve warm.

☐ *Great-Tasting Beans.* Stock up on a variety of canned beans for instant entrées. Drain and rinse, to reduce sodium, before using. Favorite combinations: canned tuna, cannelloni beans, and red onion;

sautéed chick-peas, chopped onions, sweet peppers, and tomatoes flavored with curry powder; kidney beans with dill and green onion; black-eyed peas, cooked ham cubes, and rice.

☐ *Stir-Fry Dinner.* Stir-fry frozen Oriental-style vegetables with firm tofu and soy sauce.

☐ *Pasta Plus.* Jazz up prepared pasta sauce with vegetables, sautéed onion and garlic, cubed or shredded cooked meat, canned clams or peeled cooked shrimp.

☐ *Tasty Tacos.* Fill taco shells with shredded chicken, cheese, black beans, sour cream, salsa, and sprouts. Or buy canned chili or refried beans and use as the filling.

Chicken.

☐ *Speedy BBQ Chicken.* Coat quartered deli-roasted chicken with prepared barbecue sauce; glaze under the broiler.

☐ *Instant Chicken Valencia.* Heat equal amounts of orange juice and brown sugar; add vinegar and Dijon mustard to taste. Brush mixture on quartered deli-roasted chicken. Glaze under the broiler. Serve with packaged herbed or wild rice mix.

☐ *Healthy Chicken.* Toss sliced, roasted take-out chicken with an assortment of salad bar vegetables. Toss with oil and vinegar.

☐ *Chicken Parmesan.* Top prebreaded fresh or frozen chicken cutlets with prepared tomato sauce, packaged shredded mozzarella, and grated Parmesan cheeses in a shallow casserole. Bake until bubbly.

☐ *Chicken 'n' Biscuits.* Add cooked chicken pieces or canned chicken chunks and frozen peas to canned chicken gravy and cook gently until heated through. Serve over split prepared biscuits or toast points.

Soup.

☐ *Soup Meals.* Add ingredients to canned soups to make them a meal-in-a-bowl: Slice franks or chop kielbasa into pea soup; add leftover cooked vegetables and pasta or rice to minestrone; simmer chicken soup, then whisk in a lightly beaten egg and chopped parsley or spinach; combine potato soup with canned or frozen corn and crumbled crisply cooked bacon.

☐ *Hearty Lentil Soup.* Heat canned lentil soup and pour over a tablespoon of grated Swiss cheese in individual soup bowls. Top with additional cheese; serve with purchased garlic bread.

Salads.

☐ *Seafood Pasta Salad.* Chop up prepared shrimp in cocktail sauce; add to prepared pasta salad along with sliced ripe olives, sliced red onion, and chopped celery. Toss gently. Serve on lettuce leaves.

☐ *Meal-in-One Potato Salad.* Toss diced cooked deli ham, prosciutto or provolone with deli potato salad. Garnish with strips of pimiento, chopped green onion.

☐ *Timely Tuna*. Arrange canned water-packed tuna and anchovies on top of assorted salad bar greens. Garnish with hard-cooked eggs, oil-cured olives, and packaged croutons. Toss with bottled vinaigrette dressing.

Sandwiches.

☐ *Fantastic Fish Sandwich*. Cook a package of frozen fish sticks, following the package directions. Place in toasted hot-dog rolls; top with Russian dressing. Serve with prepared coleslaw, if desired.

LAST-MINUTE SIDE DISHES

Pasta.

☐ Use tiny pasta, such as stars, alphabets, and pastina, as a pilaf-like side dish. Toss with butter, currants, and toasted pine nuts.

Potatoes.

☐ Oven-bake frozen french fries, following package directions, and add a generous sprinkle of grated Parmesan cheese toward the end of baking time.

☐ Bake sweet potatoes. Serve with dollops of lemon yogurt or honey blended into softened butter.

Rice and couscous.

☐ Sauté leftover rice with green onions and sweet red pepper strips in a bit of olive oil or butter in a large skillet over medium heat. Toss in a package of frozen peas and heat a minute longer.

☐ Make couscous pilaf from instant couscous: Sauté a small onion, chopped, in butter in a medium-size saucepan until translucent. In the saucepan with the onion, make the coucous following package directions, substituting chicken broth for all of the water.

Vegetables.

☐ Top steamed broccoli with toasted sesame seeds or chopped nuts, a few drops of Oriental sesame oil, and a splash or two of soy sauce.

☐ Cook sliced carrots in a mixture of apple, orange, or apricot juice and sweet sherry. Toward the end of cooking time, add a little butter or margarine, raisins, and ground cinnamon.

☐ Shred zucchini and/or carrots. Sauté for a scant minute in butter, margarine, or vegetable oil in a skillet over medium heat. For the zucchini, add dried dillweed to the skillet while sautéing. For the carrots, add a splash of orange juice and a generous sprinkling of ground nutmeg or cinnamon.

☐ Hollow tomatoes; fill with thawed frozen spinach soufflé. Bake until the soufflé is cooked through.

☐ Hull cherry tomatoes. Sauté with chopped onion in olive oil in a large skillet, just until the tomatoes soften but still retain their shape.

□ Cut off the top third from firm, ripe tomatoes (save for another use). Place tomatoes in a single layer in a broilerproof container. Sprinkle generously with grated Parmesan cheese and Italian bread crumbs. Drizzle with olive oil. Broil until bubbly.

□ Bake halved winter squash in the microwave. Fill with prepared cranberry relish and chopped apples toward the end of cooking.

□ Sauté slivered or sliced almonds in butter until both the nuts and the butter are golden brown. Pour over just-steamed green beans or asparagus spears.

□ Add frozen chopped green pepper and onion to frozen corn as you cook it.

□ Prepare frozen chopped spinach, following package directions. Stir in a small package (3 ounces) of cream cheese, cubed, and 2 tablespoons dried chives. Season to taste.

LAST-MINUTE HOT AND COLD SAUCES AND GLAZES

For meals.

□ Puree cooked vegetables. Heat gently, adding cream or chicken broth to make a sauce consistency. Serve with poached chicken or vegetables.

□ Serve cold poached fish or chicken with prepared guacamole and salsa.

□ Finely chop pimiento-stuffed olives. Stir into a mixture of equal parts plain yogurt or sour cream and mayonnaise seasoned with lemon juice, salt, and pepper. Delicious on fish fillets.

□ Puree drained canned water-packed tuna with equal parts plain yogurt or sour cream and mayonnaise seasoned with a dab of anchovy paste (optional), capers, and lemon juice. Good on sautéed fish fillets, turkey, or veal cutlets.

□ Mix together equal parts prepared horseradish and applesauce. Serve with pork or ham.

□ Glaze a ham with a mixture of equal parts apricot preserves and mustard.

For desserts.

□ *Orange-Cranberry Dessert Sauce.* Puree prepared cranberry-orange relish. Warm in a glass measuring cup in the microwave on 50 percent power or simmer in a heavy-bottomed saucepan over medium heat on top of the stove. Stir in a tablespoon or two of orange-flavored liqueur. Serve over cheesecake or bread pudding.

□ *Valencia Sauce.* In a small saucepan over moderate heat, cook 1 cup orange juice and 1 cup sugar until the sugar dissolves. Lower the heat and simmer the mixture for 5 minutes, or until it forms a light syrup. Remove from the heat; stir in ⅓ cup orange or apricot liqueur.

Serve over toasted pound cake with tiny scoops of orange sherbet and frozen vanilla yogurt.

□ *Pourable Preserves.* Stir 1 or 2 tablespoons of liqueur into a jar of preserves. Heat in a saucepan, stirring constantly, until the mixture melts and forms a saucelike consistency. Serve over crêpes filled with yogurt and fresh berries.

□ *Peach-Almond Sauce.* Heat store-bought or homemade peach preserves, adding a squeeze of lemon juice, if desired. Remove from the heat; stir in a handful of slivered almonds, toasted if desired, and a generous splash of Amaretto liqueur. Serve over French toast or waffles. Add some sliced fresh peaches, if desired.

□ *Caramel-Nut Sauce.* Melt caramel candies in a glass measuring cup in the microwave at 25 percent power. Or simmer in a heavy-bottomed saucepan over low heat on top of the stove. Thin the mixture with a little water, milk, cream, or coffee, if necessary, then stir in chopped nuts. Serve over pound cake and/or ice cream.

□ *Mocha Sauce.* Melt semisweet chocolate pieces with double-strength coffee in a small heavy saucepan over low heat. Add a splash of coffee and/or chocolate liqueur, if desired. Layer with vanilla, chocolate, and coffee ice cream in parfait glasses.

□ *Fruit Sauce.* Use baby-food fruit purees as simple sauces for sautéed or baked fruit such as bananas, apples, and pears.

DESSERTS IN A HURRY

Fruits.

□ Freeze drained canned fruits; just before serving, process into a sorbetlike treat in a blender or food processor.

□ Melt chocolate in the microwave. Dip bananas in the melted chocolate, then roll in chopped nuts or coconut, if desired. Freeze on a sheet of waxed paper or aluminum foil until dessert time.

□ Puree drained prepared cooked prunes, adding enough of their liquid along with a squeeze or two of orange juice to make a soft puree. Layer with vanilla yogurt and graham cracker crumbs.

Frozen desserts.

□ A splash of liqueur turns ice cream, frozen yogurt, or sorbet into an elegant dessert. Serve in stemmed glasses or crystal bowls set on doily-lined plates.

Cakes.

□ To reduce cake baking time, make cupcakes. Or prepare a jelly-roll cake; most bake in less than 15 minutes.

Pies.

□ Fast: Pastry dough can be refrigerated or frozen. Shape dough into a round disk, wrap tightly in a double layer of plastic wrap, and refrigerate for up to three days. Or overwrap the plastic wrap with a layer of aluminum foil and freeze for up to two months; thaw in the refrigerator overnight before shaping and baking.

☐ Faster: Roll out pastry dough and fit into pie pans; crimp the edges. Freeze until solid, then cover tightly with plastic wrap, and return to freezer. Bake while still frozen.

☐ Fastest: Use ready-made crusts, crimping around the edge to add a homemade look.

☐ For extra-quick cleanup, keep your rolling pin and work surface clean by rolling the dough between sheets of plastic wrap or waxed paper.

☐ Crumb crusts are fast to prepare and need no chilling before using. Ten minutes in a 350°F. oven brings out their crispy goodness.

☐ To speed up apple pie preparation, microwave the apples, sugar, and spices in a microwaveproof bowl until the apples are almost soft. Pour the filling into a piecrust and bake the pie in a conventional oven until golden and bubbly.

Start dessert with mixes.

Add your own touches to cake mixes for homemade flavor.

☐ Add chopped apples or pears to gingerbread mix.

☐ Add chopped candied or crystallized ginger to date-nut bread mix.

☐ Spoon prepared cake or muffin batter into paper-lined muffin pan cups to cover the bottoms. Add a generous teaspoon of jam or preserves, then top with the remaining batter, and bake as directed.

☐ Top prepared cheesecake with best-quality berry preserves.

☐ *Mock Cassata.* Combine ricotta cheese with sugar to taste, semisweet chocolate pieces, dried fruit, such as raisins and apricots, and apricot or orange liqueur in food processor. Pulse-process. Use as a filling for thawed frozen pound cake that you've split in two or three layers. If desired, top with 1 cup melted semisweet chocolate pieces blended with ⅓ cup sour cream.

FOOD GIFTS IN A HURRY

Sweet.

☐ *No-Cook Mint Julep Balls:* Crush enough vanilla wafers to make 2½ cups of crumbs. In a large bowl, combine the crumbs with 1 cup sifted 10X (confectioners') sugar, 1 cup finely chopped walnuts or pecans, 3 tablespoons light corn syrup, 3 tablespoons bourbon, and 1 tablespoon white crème de menthe. Mix until well blended. Use two spoons to shape into balls and drop into miniature (1¾-inch) muffin pan liner cups. Top with another teaspoonful of mixture. Let mellow at room temperature for twenty-four hours. Store in airtight containers.

☐ *Peanut Butter "Truffles."* In a medium-size bowl, combine 1¼ cups graham cracker crumbs, 1 cup unsifted 10X (confectioners') sugar, 1 cup smooth or chunky peanut butter, and ¼ cup (½ stick) butter or margarine, softened. Beat with a wooden spoon until well blended. Roll into walnut-size balls between palms, then roll in 1 cup chopped peanuts or chocolate jimmies (sprinkles). Store in airtight containers. Makes about 3 dozen.

☐ *Chocolate-Covered Pretzels.* Melt one 6-ounce package semisweet chocolate pieces with 1 tablespoon vegetable shortening in a small heatproof bowl over simmering water in a saucepan. Remove the saucepan from the heat, but keep the bowl over the hot water. Drop small pretzels, one at a time, into chocolate. Lift out with a fork, lightly tapping your fork against side of the bowl so excess chocolate drips back into bowl. Place the dipped pretzels on wire rack over waxed-paper–lined cookie sheet. Allow to dry before packing between layers of waxed paper in a container. Makes about 2 dozen.

☐ *Raspberry Butter.* In a small bowl, blend ½ cup (1 stick) unsalted butter with ⅓ cup raspberry preserves and 2 teaspoons lemon juice. Place in a crock. Cover and refrigerate or freeze. To freeze, shape into a ball or bar on waxed paper or plastic wrap. Wrap the paper or plastic wrap around the butter, then rewrap in aluminum foil, sealing well. Makes about ¾ cup.

Savory.

☐ *Herb Vinegars.* Heat red or white wine vinegar slightly in a nonreactive saucepan over low heat. Pour over a handful of cleaned and dried fresh herbs packed in a decorative jar or cruet. Let stand, covered, for at least two weeks, shaking gently every day.

☐ *Herb-Marinated Goat Cheese.* Place small, round goat cheeses in wide-mouthed canning jars. Julienne hot red and green pickled peppers, scatter over the tops, then sprinkle with cracked pepper and thyme. Place a peeled garlic clove in each jar, then pour in enough extra-virgin olive oil to cover the cheese completely. Seal each jar well. Let stand in the refrigerator overnight; it will keep for up to two weeks.

☐ *Fresh Cranberry Sauce.* In a medium-size saucepan, combine 2 cups fresh or frozen cranberries with 1 cup each sugar and orange juice. Cook over low heat until the sugar dissolves. Cover; bring to a boil; lower the heat. Continue cooking until the berries pop, about 10 minutes. Remove from the heat; cool. Refrigerate in decorative glass jars.

CUT DOWN ON CLEANUP

☐ When using the food processor, process all of the dry ingredients first, then the moist ones. This will greatly reduce, in some cases eliminate, the need for rinsing the workbowl out before each use.

☐ To make pancake batter in a flash *and* do away with messy mixing bowls, put all the ingredients into a cleaned, empty milk carton. Stir the eggs before adding. Close tightly and shake to blend. Pour the batter directly from carton to griddle.

☐ Line muffin pans with paper liners before adding batter for muffins or cupcakes. You save time preparing the pans, removing the muffins or cupcakes, *and* cleaning up.

☐ Cleanup's a snap when you line broiler and roasting pans with aluminum foil.

☐ To reduce cleanup time, spray sauté pans, casseroles, and broiler pans with nonstick vegetable cooking spray before you start to cook.

*M*oney Savers

If grocery bills are taking too big a chunk of your weekly budget, it's time to look at the way you are spending. Here are some useful ideas for reducing food costs.

WHEN IS IT A BARGAIN?

Nothing is a bargain if most of it gets thrown out or wasted.

☐ Only buy foods in bulk if you have room for them in your kitchen or pantry. Remember that most foods have a definite storage limit (see pages 117–125). Don't buy more than you can use in a timely fashion.

☐ If possible, try out a smaller size of a product before purchasing a larger quantity or size. That way you can determine how your family likes it.

☐ To avoid waste, only buy as much of a perishable item as you'll be able to use within a reasonable amount of time.

☐ Buy items according to their use. Soft bananas are great for baking. Day-old bread makes great toast, stratas, French toast, and bread crumbs. Slightly soft sweet peppers can be used for stuffing or roasting. Small eggs can be used for scrambled eggs and omelets. Small sizes of fruit are great snacks for kids with small appetites.

☐ Preserve the fresh herbs of summer by processing them with a little water and freezing the mixture in ice cube trays. Come winter, use the herb cubes to impart the flavor and color of summer to soups, spaghetti sauces, and stews.

MAKE YOUR OWN CONVENIENCE FOODS

You pay for convenience when you buy time-saving products, so make some of them yourself and you'll save money.

☐ Chop onions, divide into recipe-size amounts, pack in freezer-proof bags, and freeze.

Processed Foods Cost More

The more processed the food is, the more expensive it is, so buy as much minimally processed food as possible. Frozen vegetables, for example, are at their cheapest when they're plain rather than sauced. Unsweetened cereals such as rolled oats and plain shredded wheat squares are noticeably less expensive than sugared varieties. (To reduce cereal costs—and sugar content—mix a low-sugar cereal with an already sweetened one.)

☐ Blend together the dry ingredients and shortening, butter, and/or margarine called for in a muffin, biscuit, or scone recipe. Keep in a tightly closed container in the refrigerator for up to two weeks. At baking time, add the liquid called for in the recipe. (If only solid shortening is used, the mix can be kept in a cool, dark place for up to three months.)

☐ *Pancake Mix.* In a very large bowl, combine 12 cups all-purpose flour, 3 cups instant nonfat dry milk, ½ cup sugar, ⅓ cup baking powder, and 2 tablespoons salt. To vary the mix, substitute whole-wheat flour and/or cornmeal for 3 cups of the all-purpose flour; add wheat germ or bran; add spices such as ground cinnamon. Store the mix in airtight containers in a cool, dry place for up to six months. (Refrigerate in warmer weather or if you've added wheat germ or whole-wheat flour.) For each 1½ cups of the mix (enough to make about 10 pancakes), add 1 egg, 1 cup water and/or juice, and 2 to 3 tablespoons oil or melted butter. Beat together until blended; let stand a few minutes before using.

☐ *Spring Onion Dip Mix.* Combine 1 tablespoon freeze-dried chives, 2 teaspoons instant minced onion, 1 teaspoon dried dillweed, ½ teaspoon regular, celery, or garlic salt (optional), and ½ teaspoon paprika. Store in a small airtight container in a cool, dry place for up to six months. To use, combine the mix with 1 cup *each* mayonnaise and sour cream or plain yogurt.

GETTING THE MOST FROM LEFTOVERS

Even the tiniest bit of leftover food can be used in creative ways.

☐ Add leftover rice, potatoes, noodles, or vegetables to soup.

☐ Make savory pancakes from leftover pasta or rice: Season with chopped onion, herbs, and/or grated cheese. Beat in an egg and enough flour and/or bread crumbs to form a mixture that will hold its shape when dropped from a spoon.

☐ Use leftover cooked meat as the base for stuffed vegetable or crêpe fillings.

□ Add a cup of cooked rice to muffin batter; the muffins will be moist and chewy.

□ Just a tablespoon of grated Parmesan cheese, nuts, or wheat germ will enhance bread coatings for cutlets and fish fillets.

□ Puree a cup of leftover cooked meat, fish, or poultry with seasonings, yogurt or sour cream, and mayonnaise to make a satisfying dip or spread.

□ Save extra pan juices from roasting beef: Chill to solidify fat for removal, then place the defatted mixture in ice cube trays. When solid, wrap in aluminum foil. Return to the freezer. Add to sauces, soups, and gravies for an extra flavor boost.

□ Just a tablespoon or two of jelly or jam makes a great glaze for poultry or ham. If you've got a bit of prepared mustard left, mix that into the glaze, too.

□ Small amounts of cooked vegetables can be chopped together and tossed with a light cream dressing to form a salad. Serve in dollops on lettuce-lined plates. Or use to fill hollowed tomatoes.

When Life Gives You Lemons

□ **Bring oranges, lemons, and limes to room temperature or microwave them for 20 seconds before squeezing them; they'll yield more juice and you won't need to squeeze as many.**

□ **To squeeze just a bit of lemon juice, soften the lemon by rolling it on a hard surface or microwaving it for 20 seconds, then pierce it twice near one end with an ice pick. Squeeze the lemon and allow the juice to drip out of the holes.**

□ **The easiest, fastest way to grate lemon and orange zest is with the help of your food processor. Remove strips of zest (colored part of skin with no white pith attached) with a swivel-bladed vegetable peeler; add to food processor along with part of the sugar called for in a recipe. Pulse-chop until the zest is very finely ground.**

*E*arth Savers

These ideas will save you money, as well as help you save the environment.

□ Use cloth napkins and towels instead of paper whenever possible.

□ Buy biodegradable cleaning supplies.

□ Buy foods in bulk to avoid excess packaging. Buy cheese in blocks instead of individually wrapped slices. Buy grains, flour, beans, and pasta from bulk bins at natural food stores. When you get these items home, remove them from the paper bags and store in airtight glass jars.

□ Use regular plates and cutlery instead of paper and plastic.

□ Find out what materials can be recycled in your area. Many communities will recycle glass, aluminum, tin, newspaper, office paper, and plastic products. You will find it easier to recycle if you establish a convenient storage area in your kitchen or mudroom or utility closet for the temporary storage of recyclable materials.

□ Only use your dishwasher when it is full. Air-dry dishes instead of using the drying cycle.

□ Consider using nonmeat food scraps for a compost heap. The compost pile can be kept out of sight near the kitchen or garden, where the food scraps, along with garden wastes and leaf and grass clippings, can biodegrade into rich soil. Your county extension service (a division of the USDA) will have information on establishing a compost pile.

□ Ask for paper bags instead of plastic at the supermarket.

□ Reuse plastic bags and pieces of plastic wrap and aluminum foil.

□ Coordinate cooking so that you use the oven to prepare several items at one time. For example, serve baked potatoes with meatloaf; tuck a batch of muffins into the oven while dinner is baking.

□ Use your toaster oven when you don't have a large amount of food to bake or heat up.

□ Stir-frying and other superquick cooking techniques save on fuel as well as your precious time.

□ Wipe up as many kitchen spills as possible with a damp cloth or a sponge rather than paper towels. When you *do* use paper towels, try to reuse them if they're not too soiled.

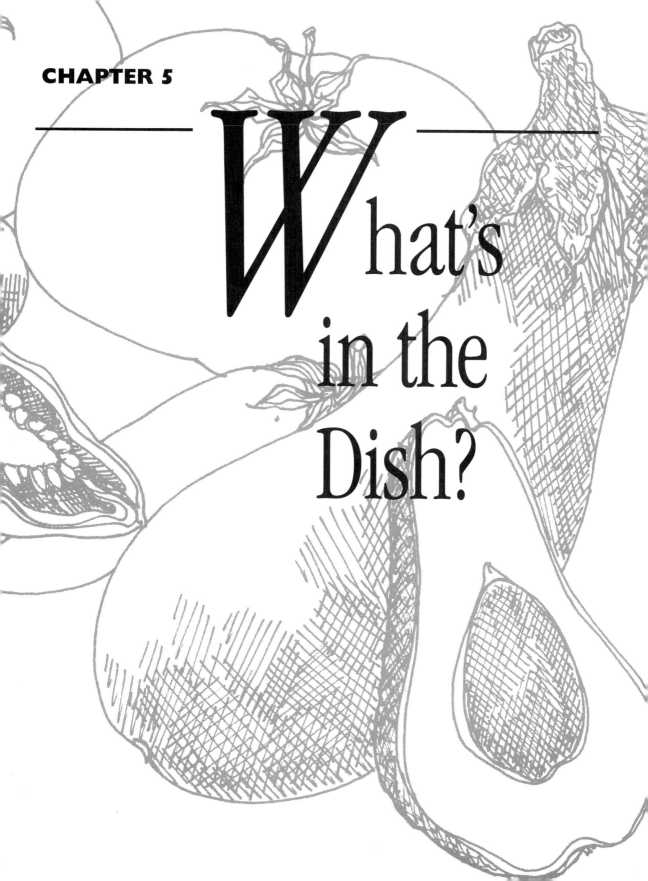

CHAPTER 5

What's in the Dish?

YOU DON'T HAVE TO TRAVEL FAR AT ALL to encounter foods of foreign lands. Most every city has a few restaurants that feature the cuisines of other countries and various ethnic groups. Sometimes the food is prepared by recent immigrants who bring with them the rich memories of their homeland. Other times the dishes are prepared by adventurous American-born chefs.

But no matter who is in the kitchen, it's nice to know what is in the dish.

Not all the foods listed here are particularly healthy choices for your diet. Some we even recommend you avoid, such as steak tartare, which is made with raw beef. However, these listings should help you decide which dishes to try when you are dining out and when you are making your own culinary travels in the kitchen.

☐ A

Abruzzese   A pasta sauce from the Abruzzi region in Italy; with oil, garlic, and sweet peppers.

Acarje   Fritters made from black-eyed beans and dried shrimp; fried, and served in Brazil as an appetizer, often with a spicy shrimp sauce.

Acciughe   An Italian pasta sauce with mashed anchovies, garlic, olive oil, and parsley; with or without tomatoes.

Accra lamori   Fried small salt cod cakes prepared on St. Lucia in the Caribbean.

Achar   A pickled and highly spiced relish or salad served in India.

Ackee and saltfish   The national breakfast dish of Jamaica. Ackee is a bright red tropical fruit, which bursts open when ripe and exposes three large black seeds and creamy white flesh. It has a delicate flavor, and when cooked together with salt cod, it looks and tastes like scrambled eggs. (Unripe ackee and its seeds are poisonous.)

Adeece howeed   A dish of lentils and spinach of Lebanese origin.

Adobo   The Philippine national dish of braised chicken, pork, or fish containing pepper, soy sauce, garlic, vinegar, and sometimes coconut milk. Also, a Mexican sauce made with vinegar and chilies.

Aebleskiver   A light Danish cake with apple filling, made in a pan of the same name.

Aglio e olio   A simple Italian sauce for pasta that consists of olive oil in which garlic has been simmered, then topped with parsley and grated Parmesan.

Agrodolce sauce   An Italian sweet and sour sauce first made in ancient times. The sweet flavor comes from brown sugar, the sour from vinegar; it is also flavored with raisins, garlic, bay leaves, capers, chocolate, and the juice of the meat it is to accompany. The sauce is used with rabbit, hare, wild boar, venison, and other braised meat.

Aioli   From the Provence region of southern France, aioli is mayonnaise made with olive oil and copiously flavored with fresh, crushed garlic. Served with vegetables, beef, or salt cod as a sauce or dip.

Ajiaco   A thick Colombian vegetable, chicken, and sausage soup garnished with cream and sliced hard-cooked egg.

Aji de gallina   Chicken with spicy walnut sauce, native to Chile and Peru.

À la   In the manner of, as in *à la maison:* "in the style of the house"—the house specialty.

Albondigas   Albondigas are spicy meatballs served, often in a tomato sauce, in Mexican, Brazilian, and Spanish recipes.

Amaretti   Italian meringue cookies made with sweet and bitter almonds.

Amatriciana   An Italian tomato sauce flavored with salt pork or bacon, tomatoes, hot red peppers, and onions. Served combined with spaghetti and alongside meat or poultry dishes.

Ameijoas a bulhao pato   A classic Portuguese dish of clams cooked with garlic and cilantro.

Anadama bread   An early American yeast bread flavored with cornmeal and molasses.

Anchoyade   A spicy anchovy and garlic spread from Provence in southern France.

Antipasto   An Italian word meaning "before the meal." Antipasto is a selection of hors d'oeuvres, such as salami, marinated mushrooms, tuna, or anchovies.

Apple amber pudding   A British specialty, made from a short pastry crust that is filled with apple puree, topped with meringue, and baked.

Arepas   Savory cornmeal cakes from Colombia and Venezuela. Crisp on the outside and soft on the inside, they make a great snack.

Arrabbiata   A spicy tomato-based Italian pasta sauce with hot pepper, and often spicy sausage and bacon.

Arroz con pollo   A Hispanic dish of chicken and rice.

Au gratin   Covered with bread crumbs and/or cheese and browned in the oven or broiler—often, but not always, vegetables.

Au naturel   A French phrase referring to foods that are cooked simply or served in their natural state.

Avgolemono   An egg (avgo) and lemon (lemono) soup or sauce of Greek origin. The sauce contains egg yolk and lemon juice, and the delicate soup contains those ingredients as well as chicken stock and rice. The sauce is great on fish, chicken, or vegetables. Once cooked, the sauce or soup can be served hot or cold.

□ **B**

Baba au rhum   A light yeast-raised Polish cake, similar to brioche, containing raisins or currants and soaked in rum. It can be baked in a tall round mold, or in small individual molds. If it is baked in a ring mold, it is known as a savarin.

Baba ghanoush   Puree of eggplant, tahini (sesame paste), olive oil, garlic, and lemon juice of Middle Eastern origin. Used as a dip for Middle Eastern flat bread, such as pita.

Babi lemak   A pork stew made with coconut milk that's popular in Singapore.

Babka   Polish sweet yeast bread containing nuts, raisins, and orange peel.

Backhendl   Chicken coated with flour, beaten egg, and bread crumbs, and fried in lard or oil. Served in Austria, garnished with lemon and parsley and served with boiled potatoes.

Badaam kheer   A favorite in the south of India, this is a pudding made of almonds, milk, sugar, saffron, and farina.

Bagno caldo   A pot of hot olive oil, butter, garlic, and mashed anchovies, this is a specialty of the Piedmont region in Italy and literally means "hot bath." Usually a winter dish, it is served warm as a dip for raw vegetables such as celery, bell peppers, cauliflower, and fennel. Cream, Barbera red wine, and/or white truffles may be added. Bagno caldo is often accompanied by bread and cheese.

Baguette   The long, slender everyday bread of France. It has a crisp brown crust and chewy interior.

Baklava   Popular in Greece and the Middle East, this very sweet dessert is made from alternating many layers of phyllo pastry with melted butter, spices, and chopped walnuts. A spiced honey syrup is poured over the pastry after it's baked and allowed to soak into the layers. Served cut into diamonds.

Bamye   A Turkish stew of minced lamb, okra, tomato, onion, and green pepper, flavored with lemon juice and seasonings. Served with pilaf.

Bananas Foster   Created at Brennan's restaurant in New Orleans in the 1950s and named for one of their regular customers, it consists of bananas sautéed in butter and brown sugar, flambéed with rum and banana liqueur, and served over vanilla ice cream.

Bangers and mash   A British term for a meal of sausage and mashed potatoes.

Bannock   This traditional Scottish cake is baked on a griddle or in an open hearth. It contains barley meal and oatmeal, occasionally wheat, and sometimes almonds and orange peel. Served at breakfast and/or high tea, it slightly resembles a shortcake.

Bansita   From Bulgaria, this is a very thin, figure-eight–shaped, flaky pastry stuffed with cheese, yogurt, and egg.

Baps   Yeast rolls, eaten throughout Scotland.

Bashed neeps   Mashed turnips, from Scotland.

Basoondi   This popular Indian dessert is a cream or milk pudding, studded with pistachios and almonds, and served at room temperature. Often garnished with silver foil.

Béchamel   A standard creamed white sauce of butter, flour, and milk. One of the classic French sauces, it is a basic building block of many other sauces, such as Mornay sauce, a béchamel with cheese.

Beef à la mode   A rich French beef stew. Larded beef is marinated in red wine and brandy and then baked very slowly with vegetables, calf's feet, and pork rind. Garnished with carrots and pearl onions.

Beignet   Light, golden fritters, either savory or sweet. In New Orleans they are a yeast pastry, deep fried and served warm with a sprinkling of powdered sugar, often with the famous New Orleans coffee.

Benne wafers   Crisp cookies made with sesame seeds, pecans, and brown sugar. The recipe is a traditional Southern confection developed by African slaves, who brought the seed to America, where they called them benne seeds.

Bienenstich   A German yeast-raised honey cake containing sliced almonds and topped with more almonds. The name means "bee sting" in German, and it is thought to be derived from the fact that the cake has honey in it.

Bigos   The national dish of Poland, it used to be a favorite there during hunting expeditions. A hearty stew of cabbage, sauerkraut, bacon, chopped lean pork, red wine, sausage, onions, lard, tomato puree, paprika, dried mushrooms, and garlic.

Birchermuesli   A Swiss national dish. Made of uncooked rolled oats, fresh and dried fruits, and nuts; served most frequently at breakfast.

Bird's-nest soup   A favorite in Chinese cookery, the soup literally is made from the nests of certain swifts, along with chicken stock, ham, chicken, and seasonings. The resulting soup is high in protein and gelatinous when cooked.

Biriyani   An elaborate rice dish from India containing saffron or turmeric. Richer than a pilaf because it contains more butter, biriyani also contains twice as much meat or fish as it does rice.

Biscotti   Twice-baked Italian cookies, flavored with nuts, anise, or various other flavorings. The crispy, crunchy texture is perfect for dipping into coffee or dessert wine.

Blancmange   A British pudding made with sweetened corn flour and cooked with milk and sugar, then chilled until set.

Blinis   One of the oldest Slavic dishes, these Russian buckwheat pancakes are made with yeast. They are the traditional accompaniment to caviar, smoked salmon, and/or a glass of vodka.

Blintzes   Related to Russian blinis. Jewish pancakes stuffed with fruit or sweetened cheese and served with sour cream.

Bollito misto   A variety of meats simmered with vegetables, herbs, spices, and seasonings. The broth is often served as a soup with pastini; the meats as a main course with horseradish. An Italian specialty accompanied by different sauces, according to locality.

Bolognese   The classical Italian meat sauce that Americans associate with spaghetti. It is made with ground meat, sometimes bacon, garlic, olive oil, herbs, and finely minced tomato, carrot, and celery.

Bombe   A dish of layered ice creams made in a mold of the same name; invented in France. The original bombe molds were round; any round bowl can be used to made a bombe.

Börek   Turkish or Greek phyllo pastries filled with meat, poultry, vegetables, or cheese. Served hot or cold, they may be fried or baked.

Borscht   It is said that there are as many recipes for borscht as there are Russians. While there is no single authentic recipe for the soup, most will contain beets and other vegetables, and some contain beef. It can be thick or thin, served hot or cold, but should always be served with sour cream.

Boterkoek   A Dutch butter cake very much like Scottish shortbread.

Bouillabaisse   A seafood stew from Marseilles, France. It is made with an assortment of fresh fish and seafood in a tomato and saffron-scented broth.

Bourride   A creamy French fish stew served with aioli.

Brandade   A puree of cooked, dried salt cod blended with olive oil, milk or cream, possibly potatoes, often garlic, lemon juice, and other seasonings. From Provence in France.

Brek   A Tunisian dish of tiny parcels of ground lamb and egg wrapped in phyllo and fried in oil.

Brioche   A classic French yeast-raised bread. Usually circular in shape, with a small round topknot, and baked to a deep brown. Rich with eggs and butter, and often made in fluted tins.

Brodetto   An Italian fish soup made of various fish and/or shellfish, and onions, garlic, herbs, tomatoes, white wine or vinegar, and possibly saffron.

Brunswick stew   Made from squirrel and/or chicken and vegetables, including okra, tomatoes, and corn. From the southern United States, Brunswick County, Virginia, claims credit for its origin.

Bruschetta   Italian bread toasted in the oven, rubbed with garlic and then drizzled with olive oil.

Bubble and squeak   A British dish of meat and greens that first "bubbles" in water, then "squeaks" in the frying pan, and finishes as fried, cold, boiled meat and greens. Cabbage and mashed potatoes are fried in lard to form a crisp cake, then the meat is added, usually the leftovers of Sunday dinner.

Buñuelos   Deep-fried Mexican fritters. Heavily dusted with powdered sugar and cinnamon, they are served hot with coffee or hot chocolate.

Burfi   Called Indian fudge (although it does not contain chocolate), this dessert can be made with coconut, nuts, vegetables, fruits, lentils, flour, and/or milk. The ground ingredients are cooked with sugar until it is reduced to a fudgelike consistency. The "fudge" can then be flavored with spices or flower essences and decorated with silver foil.

Burgoo   An American stew of mixed meats, originally including goat, squirrel, and whatever game had been caught.

Burrida   A thick Italian fish stew with regional variations. In Liguria it is made with a variety of fish cut in pieces and/or shellfish, cooked with onion, garlic, carrots, celery, anchovies, tomatoes, dried mushrooms, pine nuts, and chopped parsley.

Burritos   Flour tortillas filled with chicken, meats, and/or beans, these Mexican favorites are rolled, folded, and sometimes served with salsa.

B'ysteeya   A flaky Moroccan pastry pie stuffed with pigeon or chicken and almonds. Served sprinkled with sugar and cinnamon.

□ **C**

Cacciatore   An Italian hunter's sauce; usually an herbal tomato-meat sauce with mushrooms and white wine. Chicken cacciatore is a popular dish prepared in this style.

Cacciucco   An Italian fish soup made with a variety of fish and seafood, tomatoes, red wine, and served with garlic-flavored croutons. Chili peppers are what distinguish the dish, and it includes at least five different fish—one for each *C* in its name.

Caesar salad   Made of romaine lettuce, croutons, and a dressing that includes anchovies and coddled egg, Caesar salad was first made in Mexico by Caesar Cardini, an Italian immigrant who opened a series of restaurants in Tijuana.

Calas   Fried spiced rice cakes, a specialty of New Orleans.

Caldo verde   A national specialty in Portugal, it's a soup of kale/cabbage, cured loin of pork or garlic sausage, and potatoes. It is eaten for lunch or dinner, often with dark corn bread.

Callaloo   Creole soup of greens. Most authentic Caribbean versions use young taro leaves, but any mild green may be substituted, including spinach or Swiss chard.

Calzone   Deep-fried or baked, these pizza-turnovers are stuffed with meats, cheeses, and/or vegetables. Calzones can be made large and cut up in server pieces or as individual servings.

Cannelloni   A large smooth or ridged tube pasta, stuffed, baked and served with a sauce and cheese. The stuffing is herbs, meat, and/or cheese.

Cannoli   Italian cylindrical pastry cases that are deep fried and then filled with sweetened ricotta cheese mixed with candied fruits, nuts, and/or cocoa. Served as a dessert.

Caponata   A Sicilian dish of diced eggplant, sweet peppers, onions, and tomatoes fried in olive oil, then mixed with herbs, olives, capers, pine nuts, and vinegar. Served as a salad, side dish, or relish, warm or at room temperature.

Carbonara   Hot cooked spaghetti or other pasta is mixed with beaten egg yolks. Italian bacon is added, Parmesan is grated over the pasta, and it is served hot.

Carbonnade   A baked Belgian stew prepared with dark beer, onions, and brown stock.

Carnitas   In Mexico this is succulent pieces of pork cooked over a high heat that sears the outside of the meat to form a crisp brown crust.

Carpaccio   Very thin slices of raw, lean beef served with an olive oil dressing and often topped with shavings of Parmesan from Italy. We do not recommend this dish as raw beef poses a health risk.

Carpetbag steak   A thick steak stuffed with raw oysters. Originated in the United States, it gets its name from its appearance, which is similar to a carpetbag, the traveler's handbag popular in the mid-nineteenth century.

Cassata   An Italian dome-shaped mold containing layers of vanilla ice cream, pistachio ice cream, pound cake soaked in rum, and a mixture of chocolate, uncooked egg white, and cream. It is decorated with candied fruits, orange peel, and whipped cream, and served in slices and wedges. We do not recommend this dish, as uncooked eggs pose the risk of salmonella.

Cassoulet   A homey, robust French stew of white beans baked for hours with fresh or smoked pork, split pig's trotter, other meats, carrots, onions, possibly duck confit, spareribs, lamb, red wine, bread crumbs, and garlic sausage.

Castagnaccio   An Italian cake made of chestnut flour, pine nuts, almonds, raisins, and candied fruits and baked until crusty. Served cold.

Caznela de cordero   A Chilean lamb and vegetable stew, containing pumpkin and thickened with eggs.

Ceviche   A cold dish containing pieces of white fish or scallops that are marinated and "cooked" by the acid in lime and/or lemon juice and seasoned with onions, garlic, chilies, and herbs. Popular in Mexico and the United States, the dish originated in Peru.

Chakchouka   A North African vegetable stew similar to ratatouille.

Champ   An Irish creamed potato and green onion or chive dish, topped with melted butter.

Chantilly   Heavy cream whipped until soft, not stiff; it may or may not be sweetened.

Chapatis   An unleavened bread from India, it is made with whole-wheat flour and water only, and it is baked on a griddle. Pieces of chapati are often broken up and used to scoop up many East Indian dishes.

Charlotte   A mold of biscuits, sponge cake, ladyfingers, or sliced bread filled with custard, cream, and fruit.

Chicharrones   Puffy, crackly, fried pork skins served as a snack in Mexico.

Chilaquiles   A hot Mexican dish, generally eaten for breakfast or brunch, often to accompany eggs. Tortilla pieces are fried until golden, returned to the pan, and cooked together with tomatoes, chilies, and garlic. Topped with onion, epazote, cream, and fresh cheese.

Chiles rellenos   Green chilies stuffed with cheese, dipped in batter and fried. A Mexican favorite.

Chimichanga   From the state of Sonora in Mexico, made from a large flour tortilla that is filled and folded or rolled and fried until crisp. It can be stuffed with any of the ingredients that are stuffed into burritos, including shredded beef, pork, or chicken; beans and rice; and/or grated cheese

Chimichurri   An Argentinian sauce made from oil, vinegar, onions, garlic, cayenne, and other seasonings.

Chlíodnik   A delicious cold summer soup from Poland. Made with beets, cucumbers, green onions, radishes, and dill in sour cream, lemon, beet juice, and vinegar.

Cholent   A Sabbath stew of Jewish origin. Made with beans, brisket of beef, vegetables, and barley. It can be made the day before and kept in a warm oven lighted before the Sabbath, so it doesn't violate the Jewish traditional laws about lighting a fire on that special day.

Choucroute à la alsacienne   An Alsatian dish of sauerkraut, bacon, apples, pork ribs, sausage, and potatoes.

Chupe de camarones   A shrimp soup from Peru that also contains vegetables, herbs, eggs, and cream.

Churrasco   From Brazil, this is grilled skewered pieces of beef, lamb, pork sausage, meatballs, and/or goat served with a tomato and onion sauce.

Churros Spanish fritters coated with sugar and eaten for breakfast.

Chutney Fresh or preserved Indian relishes served as condiments with a meal. They may be made from fruits, herbs, and/or vegetables. There are no rules as to which chutney should be served with what entrée.

Cioppino A tomato-based seafood stew that originated in California.

Cirassian chicken A Turkish dish of shredded chicken in a walnut sauce.

Clafouti A French fruit flan. Traditionally made with cherries, but it can be made with other fruits. Clafouti is a baked pastry made from a creamy batter and served warm, sprinkled with sugar and cream.

Cobbler An American deep-dish fruit pie with a top crust of biscuit dough.

Cock-a-leekie soup A Scottish soup of leeks simmered with prunes in chicken stock.

Coeur à la crème From France, a cream dessert made of curd or cream cheese combined with cream. Drained and chilled in a cheese-cloth-lined heart-shaped mold overnight. The heart is then turned out into a dish and served with crushed, very ripe berries, usually strawberries.

Colcannon From Ireland, this is a stew of chopped cabbage, mashed potatoes, carrots, and turnips.

Confit From southwestern France, confit is made by preserving birds (usually geese or ducks) in their own fat. It can also be made with pork, chicken, or rabbit and will keep for six months to a year.

Cornish pasty An English-style turnover of chopped beef and vegetables baked in a shortcrust pastry. Served hot or cold.

Coulibiac French term for a Russian salmon pie. Salmon sautéed with onion and mushrooms (and traditionally the spinal cord of sturgeon), baked in puff pastry.

Coulis A French term that originally meant juices from cooked meats. Today it means a thick puree of fruit or vegetables used as a sauce.

Couscous The national dish of Morocco. The word refers both to the stew itself and to the durum wheat semolina that is the principle ingredient. The stew is a savory mixture of mutton or chicken, vegetables, chick-peas, and raisins.

Cozido Brazilian version of a boiled dinner, this stew is made of marinated chicken, smoked sausage, pork, cassava, yams, potatoes, cabbage, turnips, pumpkin, green beans, squash, corn, okra, and plantains.

Crema catalana   Spanish version of crème brûlée. It is sometimes flavored with orange or lemon.

Crème brûlée   A rich custard served in a ramekin with caramelized sugar on the top. Many say that it was first served in Cambridge, England; however, the name is French, meaning "burnt cream."

Crème caramel   A chilled French dessert custard that has been baked in a caramel-coated mold. When the custard is turned out of the mold, the top is glazed with caramel. In Spain, this dish is known as flan; in Italy, it's crema caramella.

Croque monsieur   From France, a grilled ham and cheese sandwich, which is usually dipped in a beaten egg before it is grilled.

Crostata   An Italian open-faced fruit or custard tart with various toppings.

Crostini   Small slices of toasted or grilled Italian bread with any type of cheese, ham, chicken, liver paste, anchovies, and/or tomatoes. They can be skewered or toasted in the oven.

Croutons   Small, fried bread cubes.

Crudités   A selection of raw sliced vegetables.

Cuy   A roasted pig, the national dish of Ecuador, also eaten in Peru.

□ **D**

Damper   An unleavened bread cooked in the ashes of a fire, found in Australia and New Zealand.

Dashi   Basic Japanese soup stock that is fish-based, made with a sea vegetable (kombu) and dried fish flakes (bonito). It does not taste fishy, but rather gives a hint of the salty sea.

Daube   A French beef stew made with red wine.

Dhal   An Indian lentil puree served as a side dish. Any type of lentil can be used.

Dim sum   Means "little heart" or "heart's delight." These are various small Cantonese dishes that properly appear only before lunchtime or as snacks at odd times of the day. Many of the dishes are tiny steamed dumplings with various fillings, but there is an almost infinite variety.

Dirty rice   A popular Cajun dish made with chicken livers and gizzards, vegetables, long-grain rice, and lots of pepper. Served as a side dish. It gets its "dirty" appearance from the meat it contains.

Djuveč   A meat, vegetable, and rice casserole that is a national dish of Yugoslavia.

Dobostorte   A Hungarian cake layered with chocolate and caramel.

Dolmas   Small Greek or Turkish parcels of grape leaves containing rice and herbs, sometimes meat or vegetables. From the Arabic word for "something stuffed," they can be made with other vegetables, but vine leaves are the most common.

Donburi   Means "big bowl" in Japanese, this meal-in-a-dish features hot rice topped with various fish, meats, eggs, or vegetables. Very popular for lunch.

Dosa   Rice pancakes from India that are stuffed with various fillings and eaten with chutneys and pickles. They are served at breakfast, for snacks, and at main meals as well.

Duchesse   Mashed potatoes mixed with egg, butter or margarine, and cream, piped around meat, poultry, or fish as a decorative border, then browned in the oven or broiler just before serving.

Dundee cake   A classic Scottish rich fruitcake covered with blanched almonds.

□ E

Empanadas   A Spanish or Central American stuffed turnover of meat, onions, eggs, dried fruit, and/or olives. Served as a first course or snack.

Enchiladas   Rolled corn tortillas from Mexico filled with cheese, beans, vegetables, poultry, and/or meat, then baked with a chili sauce and topped with cheese.

Erwenten soep   The traditional Dutch pea soup. There are many variations, but it is always made with split peas.

Escargots à la bourguignonne   The classic French dish of snails cooked in wine, replaced in their shells, and placed in the oven with a mixture of butter, garlic, shallots, parsley, and bread crumbs.

□ F

Fadge   Fried Irish potato cakes.

Fajitas   A popular dish from the Southwest. Pieces of skirt steak, usually marinated, are grilled, sliced, and wrapped in flour tortillas. Often served with salsa, guacamole, sour cream, grilled vegetables, and/or refried beans. Fajitas also can be made from flank steak, boneless chuck, chicken, or turkey.

Falafel   A mixture of pureed fava beans or chick-peas, parsley, coriander, onions, and garlic shaped into balls and deep-fried. Eaten hot in pita bread with tahini in the Middle East.

Får-i-kål   Lamb and cabbage stew from Norway.

Fattoush   An Arab peasant salad of cucumbers, tomatoes, parsley,and mint.

Feijoada completa   Brazil's national dish. There are many variations, but most usually contain black beans, garlic, onions, several cooked meats, sausage, and salt pork. It is served with fluffy rice, orange slices, cooked greens such as collards, and sprinkled with seasoned cassava meal condiment called farofa.

Finnan haddie   Smoked finnan haddock that is baked, broiled, or stewed in butter and simmered in milk. Served in Scotland, often with a cream sauce.

Flan   Caramel custard (*crème caramel*) served in Spanish countries.

Flauta   Flour tortillas that are filled and rolled very tightly, secured with a toothpick, and fried until crisp and golden. The name of this Mexican dish means "flute" in Spanish.

Florentine   In the style of Florence, Italy, which usually means served on a bed of spinach, topped with a delicate cheese sauce, and browned in the oven. Fish and eggs are often served "Florentine."

Focaccia   An Italian flat bread that is dense and chewy, and somewhat similar to pizza. It is brushed with olive oil and sprinkled with salt and can be topped with herbs, sautéed onions, tomatoes, or even prosciutto. This bread can be eaten as a snack, or with simple meals.

Fondue   Native to Switzerland, this silky concoction of melted cheese, white wine, and kirsch is served in an earthenware crock set over a burner. To eat the fondue, chunks of bread are speared with special, long-handled fondue forks and then twirled in the semiliquid cheese mixture. Fondue Bourguignonne is a convivial Swiss version of a French dish: Cubes of raw steak are speared with fondue forks, fried at the table in a pot of piping hot oil, then dipped into assorted sauces.

Fonduta   An Italian, hot melted cheese mixture containing chunks of Italian fontina or Swiss cheese, milk, egg yolks, and topped with sliced white truffles. Toasted bread is dipped into the mixture or it is served over rice or polenta.

Fool   An English dessert of stewed and pureed fruit combined with sweet cream. Its name may have come from the French *foule*, meaning pureed.

Fra Diavolo   A very spicy Italian sauce with paprika and cayenne pepper. For example, lobster *fra diavolo* means "lobster in devil's sauce."

Frappé   A mushy, frozen dessert. In New England, it is a milkshake; elsewhere, a frozen fruit drink.

Frijoles refritos   Refried beans. Mexican beans, usually pintos, that are mashed and fried after being completely cooked. Found on the table in Mexico at most meals.

Frittata   A kind of flat Italian omelet that consists of beaten eggs combined with cooked, diced vegetables, cheese, ham, herbs, or any combination of these, baked in the oven.

Fritter   A crisp, golden, deep-fried batter bread containing corn or minced fruit or vegetables. Also, pieces of fruit or vegetable batter-dipped and deep-fried.

Fruit crisp   A baked fruit dish—often of apples, rhubarb, peaches, or apricots—with a crisp, crunchy topping.

Fruit crumble   A baked dessert of fruit topped with a crumbly flour-sugar mixture. From England.

Ful Medames   From Egypt, a dish of cooked brown beans seasoned with olive oil, lemon juice, and garlic. Served all day long, they are an important part of the diet in the Middle East.

□ G

Gado-gado   An Indonesian mixed vegetable salad with peanut dressing. It contains Indonesian sweet soy sauce, tofu, and usually eight to ten raw or partially cooked vegetables. Garnished with hard-cooked egg, fried shallots, and shrimp chips.

Gazelle horns   Delicate pastry from Morocco shaped like the horns of the gazelle, flavored with almonds and orange flower water.

Gazpacho   A chilled Spanish soup made with tomatoes, sweet peppers, cucumbers, onions, oil, vinegar, and sometimes bread crumbs and seasonings.

Gefilte fish   One of the classic dishes in Central European Jewish cuisine. A puree of fish and vegetables is mixed with matzoh meal, eggs, and seasonings, then slowly poached in fish stock. Gefilte fish is served hot or cold.

Gelato   Italian ice cream, denser (with less air) than American ice cream.

Génoise   A moist sponge cake from France made of eggs, sugar, butter, and cake flour.

Giunech   A spicy stew, from Bulgaria, of vegetables and meat baked with a top layer of yogurt and eggs.

Gnocchi   A small Italian dumpling usually made of boiled potatoes and flour. It can also be made from semolina flour, cornmeal, or rice. Eggs, spinach, and cheese may also be added.

Golubtsy   Cabbage stuffed with beef, rice, bacon, and seasonings. Served in Russia.

Goulash   A beef or pork stew from Hungary, flavored with paprika. Traditionally it is garnished with sour cream and served over buttered noodles. In Hungary the dish is called *gulyás,* and it may be served as a soup or a stew. The direct translation of *gulyás* is "cowherd," and it was the food of the herdsmen cooked over an open fire after the day's work was done.

Granita (also granité)   A coarsely textured frozen dessert based on water rather than milk or cream.

Gravlax   A Swedish dish of marinated raw salmon. It is more delicate than smoked salmon. The fish is cured in salt, sugar, and dill.

Guacamole   A mixture of mashed avocado, onions, chilies, cilantro, salt, and a bit of chopped tomato; eaten with tortilla chips or used as an accompaniment for other dishes. Best when made in a *molcajete,* a Mexican mortar and pestle.

Guiso de dorado   A freshwater-fish stew served in Paraguay.

Gulab jamon   An Indian dessert of small spheres made from flour, butter, yogurt, and sometimes ground almonds; fried and soaked in rosewater syrup.

Gumbo   There are many varieties of gumbo, but all have a roux base, are thickened with okra or filé, and often contain chopped vegetables. In New Orleans, where it originated, oyster-and-sausage gumbo is very popular. Among the most common ingredients are duck, crab, shrimp, chicken, sausage, and game.

Gyro   Molded spiced ground lamb from Greece by way of the Middle East. Cooked on a vertical spit and sliced off a rack.

□ **H**

Haggis   The minced innards of an animal (usually lamb) cooked with oatmeal, onions, seasonings, and suet. Traditionally, a meat pudding or sausage was made and then boiled in the cleaned stomach of a sheep. Served very hot with rutabaga and potatoes. Traditional Scottish specialty.

Halaszle   A fiery Hungarian fish stew. Carp and other freshwater fish are poached slowly with onion, peppers, tomatoes, and whole cherry paprika peppers.

Halva   A sweet dish or candy made from ground sesame seeds and honey, and possibly dried fruit and nuts. Near Eastern in origin. Sold in slices, cut from blocks.

Hamantaschen   A pastry served for the Jewish holiday Purim. Small and triangular in shape, they can be filled with apricots, poppy seed, or prune mixtures.

Harrira   A thick meat, bean, and vegetable soup from Morocco. Served to break the fast of Ramadan, a Moslem month of fasting.

Hasenpfeffer   German rabbit stew, often served with noodles or dumplings and sour cream.

Hermit   Spicy, chewy cookie native to the United States. It usually contains dried fruits and nuts.

Hoecake   An American cornmeal bread originally cooked on a hoe over an open fire. See also Johnny Cake.

Hopping John   Black-eyed peas cooked with salt pork and seasonings and served with rice. From the southern United States. There are two possible explanations for the unusual name of this traditional New Year's dish. One is that hosts encourage guests to stop in and eat it with a "Hop in, John." The other comes from the ritual of making children hop once around the table before eating the dish.

Horiatiki   The classic Greek salad. Contains feta cheese, cucumbers, tomatoes, bell peppers, olives, and onions, and is dressed with olive oil and vinegar.

Hors d'oeuvres   Bite-size appetizers often served with cocktails.

Hot and sour soup   A soup from Beijing containing pork and vegetables and seasoned with hot pepper and vinegar.

Huevos rancheros   A breakfast dish from Mexico that contains tortillas, eggs, salsa, chilies, and cheese.

Hummus   A dip of mashed chick-peas mixed with sesame paste (tahini), garlic, lemon juice, and olive oil. Eaten with pita bread as an appetizer.

Hundred-year-old eggs   A Chinese delicacy, these are raw eggs preserved by wrapping in combinations of ashes, tea, lime, and salt, covered with rice husks and buried for up to two months. Also known as thousand-year-old eggs and Ming dynasty eggs. They emerge from the aging process dark and with a pungent flavor.

Hush puppies   A traditional dish of the southern United States made of fried cornmeal batter. The term is said to have originated at a southern fish fry where the cook, who had fried extra batter, gave it to the noisy dogs to "hush the puppies."

Hutspot   A Dutch national dish, which is a casserole of beef and vegetables. In France and Belgium, the dish is referred to as *hochepot* and contains pig's ears and feet. The same dish in England is called hot pot and contains mutton, oysters, and potatoes.

□ **I**

I'a lawalu   Fish baked in taro leaves, a specialty in Hawaii.

Iman bayildi   Means "swooning priest." The name comes from the story of a gourmet Muslim priest who was so overcome by the fragrance of the dish that he fainted. Some say it was not the delicious smell but the overpowering smell of garlic that caused him to faint. It is a refreshing dish for the hot days of a Turkish summer, made with eggplant, lots of garlic, tomatoes, onions, olive oil, lemon, raisins, and hazelnuts.

Indian pudding   A spicy cornmeal and molasses staple of early American colonists, the pudding varied with each day and according to the condiments available in the cook's larder. It was even popular in France in the seventeenth century.

Ingera na wat   A spongy, crêpelike unleavened bread served in Ethiopia.

Inlagd gurka   Swedish salad made with cucumbers marinated in vinegar, sugar, and dill or parsley.

Inlagd sill   Swedish pickled herring.

Italienne, à la   Served Italian style, with a garnish of pasta.

□ **J**

Jambalaya   A Creole rice dish, created in New Orleans by Spanish settlers around the year 1700. The name is derived from *jamón*, the Spanish word for ham. There are many variations of this dish, and it is often named according to what it contains—shrimp, sausage, ham, chicken, etc. It almost always contains sweet peppers, onions, garlic, long-grain rice, and tomatoes.

Jerk   A Jamaican cooking method in which pork or chicken is marinated in a liquid marinade or dry rub of allspice, thyme, green onions, garlic, hot peppers, ginger, lemon or lime juice, clove, and bay leaves. Once marinated, the meat is cooked and lightly smoked outside over a fire.

Johnnycake   From New England, a cornbread or griddle cake that is unique because the meal is water ground and made from sweet white corn. Also called hoecake.

Junket   Milk that has been thickened with rennet, sweetened, and is served as a dessert pudding in England.

□ **K**

Kabak dolmasi   Baked squash (often zucchini) stuffed with raisins, pine nuts, onions, herbs, and seasonings. Served cool throughout the Middle East.

Kabob (also kebab)   Grilled chunks of meat, fish, and/or vegetables, usually threaded on a skewer and broiled over charcoal. Served throughout the Middle East and the United States.

Kahve   Strong Turkish coffee, often made with cardamom and a large amount of sugar.

Kai yang   Grilled chicken, from the northeast of Thailand, that is marinated in spices before cooking and served with sticky rice.

Kakavia   A Greek fish stew or soup.

Kalbee   From Korea, these are grilled marinated beef spareribs served with a sesame seed sauce.

Kåldolmar   Swedish cabbage stuffed with beef, beets, rice, and seasonings. The gravy is thickened with sour cream.

Kalua puaa Highly seasoned shredded pork cooked in taro leaves. Served in Hawaii.

Kartoffelpuffer German potato pancakes, often served with apple sauce.

Kasha Hulled, crushed kernels of buckwheat groats, they are cooked and served as a side dish, similar to rice. Used in Jewish cooking.

Kedgeree An English breakfast dish brought from India and made from fish, curry powder, rice, and hard-cooked eggs.

Kefta Ground meat, chopped onions, and parsley mixed with spices and grilled on skewers. Popular all over the Middle East.

Keftedes From Greece, these aromatic croquettes of meat, chicken, fish, or vegetables can be fried, grilled, or poached and are served with sauces.

Keskül A Middle Eastern milk pudding flavored with almonds. Served garnished with pistachios and coconut.

Khichri Rice and lentils cooked together. Served in India.

Kibbeh A popular Middle Eastern specialty with many variations and a general term for Middle Eastern dishes that contain bulgar. Cracked wheat, ground wheat, onions, and spices are wrapped around a mixture of cooked ground meat, chopped onions, and pine nuts, and deep-fried. May also be eaten raw.

Kim chee One of Korea's national dishes, it is pickled cabbage, served as a condiment with almost every meal. With as many recipes as there are cooks, kim chee is spicy, hot, very pungent, almost always cabbage based, and contains chilies. Served with almost every meal.

Kippers An English preparation of herring split open, lightly cured, and smoked.

Kissel The traditional Russian fruit pudding, it can be as thin as soup or as thick as molded jelly. Served hot or cold, often topped with cream or a custard sauce.

Knishes Jewish pastry filled with cheese, potato, kasha, or sauerkraut. Served as a side dish or an appetizer.

Koeksisters African doughnuts served cold in a spiced syrup.

Kofta A meatball popular in the Balkans and the Middle and Far East. Made with ground meat, and after being broiled or fried, they are simmered in rich sauces.

Kolacky An Eastern European tart made of yeast dough, filled with plum jam, cheese, or almond paste.

Kourabiedes Special occasion Greek cookies that contain lots of butter, possibly nuts, and are very thickly coated with powdered sugar.

Kreplach Jewish noodle dumplings, stuffed with meat, served as part of a soup.

Kugel A Jewish baked pudding, usually made of noodles or potatoes. Served as a side dish, although a sweetened noodle kugel may be served as a snack or dessert.

Kugelhopf   Traditional Austrian cake with a hole in the center, made with raisins, almonds, rum, butter, flour, and yeast to make it tall and light.

Kulich   A traditional Russian Easter cake. Made of sweet bread dough and candied fruit, baked tall and round like the headgear of a Russian Orthodox priest. Traditionally served with *pashka*.

□ **L**

Lamingtons   Australian cake with chocolate frosting and coconut cut into small pieces.

Langues du chat   Means "cat's tongues" in French. These are dry, crisp, sweet, and flat biscuits that are long, slender, and slightly waisted in the middle.

Lassi   A refreshing drink from India, made with yogurt, sometimes spices, rosewater, and sugar. There is also a salty lassi, which often includes cumin. It is foamy, frothy, very tasty.

Lebkuchen   A traditional German cakelike cookie that's a specialty at Christmas. These frosted cookies feature honey, ginger, and a variety of spices, citron, and almonds.

Leckerle   Chewy honey or almond cookie from Switzerland.

Lekvar   Usually prune or apricot, this is a soft spread used in Hungary for filling pastries.

Lescó   A vegetable side dish served often in Hungary. It usually contains sweet peppers, bacon, onions, and tomatoes, and is seasoned with paprika.

Limpa   Swedish yeasted dark rye bread flavored with anise or fennel, and sometimes orange.

Linzertorte   A hazelnut tart with a lattice top filled with raspberry jam. Made famous in Vienna.

Liptauer cheese spread   A Hungarian cheese spread flavored with paprika, capers, anchovies, onions, butter, and caraway seeds.

Locro   A potato soup often served in Ecuador and garnished with avocado.

Lohikeitto   Salmon, leek, and potato soup from Finland.

Lumpia   A stuffed, fried egg roll from the Philippines.

Lyonnaise   Seasoned in the style of Lyons, France, meaning with parsley and onions.

□ **M**

Macque choux   A Cajun Christmas dish of tomatoes, corn, hominy, sweet peppers, celery, and seasonings.

Madeleine   A small shell-shaped, light sponge cake baked in a mold. Eaten like a cookie, and often dipped in tea or coffee. French.

Maître d'hôtel   Simply cooked dishes seasoned with parsley, butter, and lemon. *Maître d'hôtel* butter is a mixture of butter (or margarine), parsley, lemon juice, and salt. It is most often used to season fish, grilled steaks or chops, or boiled carrots.

Malloreddus   The Sardinian name for Italian gnocchi, these are tiny dumplings flavored with saffron and served with meat sauce and grated cheese.

Mămăligă   A national dish of Romania, where it is called *Mămăligă de aur* or bread of gold. Made with cornmeal and topped with poached eggs, cheese, and sour cream.

Mandelbrot   A firm German cookie often made with almonds.

Manicotti   A rolled sheet of pasta or a tube stuffed with ricotta, meat, herbs, and baked with tomato sauce. An Italian specialty.

Marinara   An Italian pasta sauce, meaning "in the sailor's style," perhaps because sailors would put their daily catch in a steaming cauldron of the sauce in preparation for dinner. Often a quickly cooked tomato sauce with capers, black olives, garlic, parsley, and olive oil.

Marjolaine   A French pastry of roasted ground almonds and hazelnuts, sugar, flour, and egg whites. The four layers of the baked meringue are sandwiched together with a chocolate cream, a butter cream, and a praline butter cream, and dusted with chocolate and sugar.

Marzipan   A confection made from almond paste, sugar, and egg whites, often colored and shaped into tiny fruit and vegetable forms.

Matelote   French freshwater-fish stew.

Mechouia   A Tunisian salad of assorted vegetables.

Mee krob   Sweet, crisp-fried Thai noodles served as an appetizer. Contains shrimp, pork, tofu, thin rice noodles, garlic, onion, palm sugar, vinegar, fish sauce, soy beans, green onions, and chilies.

Meggyleves   Hungarian sour-cherry soup.

Melitzanos salata   A pureed eggplant salad from Greece. Flavored with lots of garlic, onions, olive oil, vinegar, seasonings, and sometimes tomato. Usually served as an appetizer, sometimes as a side dish.

Menudo   A Mexican tripe soup, which may or may not contain hominy, depending on the region it comes from. Known as a hangover remedy.

Meze   A selection of Middle Eastern or Greek appetizers.

Miso-shiru   Clear Japanese miso soup made with sweet white miso or shiro miso. Miso is a fermented soybean paste.

Moglai biriyani   A very rich pilaf, usually layered with a spicy lamb or chicken mixture, steamed very gently so the flavors blend.

Mole   A sauce of Mexican origin, usually containing chilies, onions, garlic, and other ingredients, especially bitter chocolate. All the ingredients are pounded until finely powdered, so the sauce is smooth. It is usually served over poultry.

Mont Blanc   Sieved cooked chestnuts with sweetened vanilla-flavored whipped cream piled on top to resemble a mount of snow. A classic French dessert.

Mostarda di frutta   A specialty of Cremona, Italy, that consists of various preserved fruits in a mustard sauce, served with cold meats or chicken.

Moulokhiya   An herb used as an ingredient in a dish of the same name. The dish is cooked with lamb or chicken stock, flavored with garlic and coriander, and served on a bed of rice or on chicken or lamb chunks. Served in Lebanon, Egypt, and Jordan.

Moussaka   A traditional dish of the Balkan peninsula, and generally known as Greek. There are many variations, but all are layered casseroles of vegetables and ground meat. The favorite is a combination of eggplant with tomatoes and lamb. Moussaka is often topped with a béchamel sauce before baking.

Mousse   A rich, creamy, frozen or chilled dessert. Also, a velvety hot or cold savory dish, rich with cream, bound with eggs or—if cold—with gelatin.

Mozzarella in carrozza   A slice of mozzarella cheese between two slices of bread, dipped in beaten egg, then bread crumbs, and then fried. A classic Italian appetizer.

Mozzarella spedini   Skewered alternating pieces of cheese and bread, baked in the oven, traditionally served with a melted butter and anchovy sauce.

Muffuletta   Originating in New Orleans, a sandwich made from a hollowed-out loaf of bread stuffed with a combination of cold cuts, salami, cheese, marinated vegetables, and chopped olives.

Mulligatawny   This popular, elegant soup was invented in Madras, India, over two hundred years ago. There are many variations, vegetarian and nonvegetarian. Though its name means "pepper water," it usually includes chicken, eggs, coconut, and cream.

Murgh tikka   Marinated, skewered barbecued chicken from India.

□ **N**

Naan   A puffy leavened bread from India made with white flour and traditionally baked in a tandoori oven.

Nabemono   Literally means "things in a pot" in Japanese. Freshly cut vegetables, tofu, firm whitemeat fish, chicken, and mushrooms—all in a delicious broth—are placed in a cauldron at the center of the table and diners choose their favorite morsels.

Nacho   A Mexican appetizer made with green chilies and cheese melted on a flour tortilla.

Nam prik   Thai chili dip or sauce.

Napoletana   An Italian tomato sauce in the Naples style. Made from olive oil, tomatoes, garlic, and onion, and usually served with grated cheese. One of the most popular meatless sauces.

Nasi goreng   A fried rice dish popular in Singapore, Malaysia, and Indonesia. No two versions are ever the same. Usually contains vegetables, shrimp paste, pork, garlic, chilies, soy sauce. It is garnished with fried egg, tomato, cucumber, green onions, and fried shallots.

Natillas   A Spanish custard flavored with cinnamon and lemon. Served cold.

Navarin   A French lamb stew.

Nesselrode   A mold of frozen custard flavored with candied fruits and chestnut puree. Named for Count Nesselrode, a nineteenth-century Russian diplomat, who inspired the dish.

Niçoise   Prepared in the manner of Nice, France—with black olives, tomatoes, garlic, and olive oil.

Nouvelle cuisine   A French cuisine established by classically trained younger chefs with a new and lighter twist on classic French dishes and preparation techniques. It has been adapted by many other cuisines.

Nuoc cham   The most essential Vietnamese sauce. A dipping sauce made with chilies, vinegar, fish sauce, lime juice, grated carrot, garlic, and sugar.

☐ O

Oeufs à la neige   A French dessert of soft, oval meringues poached in simmering milk and served in a custard sauce. Its name means "snow eggs."

Olla podrida   A national dish of Spain. A thick, spicy soup or stew with assorted meats, poultry, sausages, and vegetables.

Osso buco   A piece of veal shank/shin cut across the bone, horizontally, then braised in white wine, broth, tomato, onions, and garlic. Often served sprinkled with gremolata (grated lemon peel, minced garlic, and minced parsley) before serving. The specialty and the pride of the city of Milan, it is often served with risotto.

☐ P

Pabellón caraqueño   Steak, rice, black beans, and plantains topped with a fried egg; the national dish of Venezuela.

Paczki   Polish rum doughnuts filled with rose jam.

Pad Thai   One of Thailand's most popular noodle dishes. It usually contains shrimp, peanuts, tofu, daikon, shallots, eggs, rice noodles, dried shrimp, green onion, and bean sprouts.

Paella   A one-pot rice dish from Valencia in Spain. There are many recipes and variations, and some say the original contained rabbit. Now the recipes may contain chicken, ham, shellfish, and often sausage, as well as vegetables, garlic, other seasonings, and rice. All the ingredients are cooked together in a large shallow pan with two handles, called a paella pan. Often flavored with saffron.

Paglia e fieno Translated from the Italian, it means "straw and hay." It is a serving of half yellow and half green noodles and can be served with a variety of sauces.

Pakoras Small deep-fried fritters of India. Vegetables, fish, or chicken are spiced with ginger, cumin, chopped onion, and garlic, then blended with chick-pea flour, shaped into small patties; and deep-fried.

Palacsinta Hungarian dessert pancakes. Austrians refer to them as *palatschinke*. Often filled with nuts or pot cheese flavored with lemon, raisins, and sugar. Served with chocolate sauce.

Pan bagna A sandwich sold on the streets of Nice in southern France, the name means "soaked bread." They are often made the night or day before so the flavors can blend and the olive oil can soak into the bread. Possible other ingredients are garlic, a bit of vinegar, tomatoes, anchovy filets or tuna, hardcooked egg, and fresh leaves of basil.

Pan de muertos A Mexican bread made especially for All Saint's and All Soul's Day with a great variety of recipes. Usually contains lots of butter and eggs, and often orange flavor as well.

Pandoro di Verona A very light Italian cake made in a deep, star-shaped mold; served sprinkled with sugar.

Panettone An Italian dome-shaped cake-bread or coffeecake with raisins and candied fruits; made in all sizes. From Milan.

Panforte A hard, disk-shaped fruitcake made with dried fruit, nuts, spices, and honey. Traditional at Christmas. Made since the twelfth or thirteenth century, first in Sienna, Italy.

Panisses "French fries" made from chick-peas that are cooked, pureed, formed into long sticks, and then deep-fried. One of Nice's oldest recipes, panisses are sold each morning in the pasta shops. They are the children's favorite for lunch or snack, and when sprinkled with sugar they make a favorite dessert. They are also good as a side dish, seasoned with lots of black pepper.

Papillote A French term for food sealed in a container of heavy paper and cooked in the oven.

Pappa al pomodoro Italian soup, eaten hot or cold, of tomatoes, bread, garlic. There are many versions of this dish.

Pappadam From Malabar on the west coast of India, these are crunchy, crisp wafers made from lentils, baking soda, and a pinch of salt. Served most often as an appetizer.

Paratha Known for its exquisite flakiness, this is one of the great breads of India. Made with whole-wheat and white flour, it is like a simple version of puff pastry, because each layer is separated by oil. Sometimes stuffed with vegetables, spices, meats, and/or herbs.

Parkin   A dense ginger cake made in England.

Partan bree   Crab and rice soup from Scotland.

Pashka   A traditional Russian Easter cheesecake with nuts and candied fruit made in the form of a pyramid.

Pasta or pastina in brodo   Pasta cooked in and/or served in broth. Italian.

Pastitsio   A baked pasta dish from Greece similar to moussaka with a layer of pasta added.

Pâté   A well-seasoned mixture of finely minced or ground meats and/or liver. *Pâté de foie gras* is made of goose livers and truffles.

Patlican dolmasi   A Turkish dish of eggplant stuffed with beef, rice, seasonings, and vegetables.

Pavlova   A meringue basket filled with cream and fruit such as strawberries, passion fruit, or pineapple. Served in Australia, often with a fruit sauce, it is named after Russian ballerina Anna Pavlova.

Pease pudding   Split green peas cooked as a side dish, served in England. This is the "peas porridge" of nursery-rhyme fame.

Peking duck   In this popular Chinese dish, the duck is first dried in the wind, smeared with honey, dried again, then roasted. Served with slices of cucumber, green onion, hoisin sauce, and little pancakes. Diners roll up the shredded duck and vegetables in the pancake, which they have covered with sauce, and eat it with their fingers.

Pel'meni   Siberian boiled dumplings.

Peperonata   An Italian appetizer similar to ratatouille, it contains sliced sweet peppers, onions, herbs, seasonings, and tomatoes stewed in olive oil and garlic. Served cool.

Pepparkakor   Spiced Swedish Christmas cookies.

Pepper pot   A classic American soup, from Philadelphia. Made with tripe, vegetables, hot peppers, herbs, spices, and cream. Sometimes served with dumplings. Also a West Indian stew made with cassareep (raw cassava), mixed meats, and vegetables.

Pesto   Made in a mortar and pestle and uncooked; this is a sauce from Genoa prepared with fresh basil leaves, garlic, olive oil, grated cheese, pine nuts, and seasonings.

Petit fours   Tiny, fancily frosted cakes.

Pfannkuchen   Austrian pancakes often served with berries.

Pho   Vietnamese noodle soup. There are many varieties, and it is often served for breakfast.

Phulka   A puffy baked whole-wheat bread from India. Baked on a griddle and then cooked directly over a flame. It can be made from chick-pea, whole-wheat, and/or millet flour.

Picadillo   A dish of ground meat or meats cooked with tomatoes, onions, seasonings, and sometimes raisins. Wide variations in this dish occur among Hispanic cuisines. Its name is Spanish for "hash."

Pilaf   Rice cooked in a savory broth, often with small bits of meat or vegetables, herbs, and spices.

Pirozhki   Russian pies, usually pocket-sized and oval, both savory and sweet. The larger ones are called pirogi, and they are usually square or rectangular. They can be made with a variety of doughs, depending on which best suits the chosen filling. The possibilities for stuffings are many; meats, cabbage, mushrooms, and green onion are among the favorites.

Pissaladière   A tart made of bread dough with onions, tomatoes, garlic, anchovies, black olives, and/or other garnishes. A French-style pizza without the cheese.

Pitcaithly bannock   Shortbread with chopped citrus zest and often topped with almonds.

Pizzaiola   An Italian sauce of meat juices, garlic, tomato, olive oil, oregano, and parsley.

Plättar   Swedish pancakes often served with lingonberry preserves or applesauce.

Polenta   A cornmeal porridge popular in Italy. Served warm, freshly made as is. Or it is cooled, sliced or cubed, then baked, grilled, or fried with butter and Parmesan cheese.

Poor boy   A sandwich made from a whole French loaf split down the middle and stuffed with a savory filling, usually fried oysters. A Cajun specialty.

Poori   A deep-fried puffy Indian bread. It has a beautiful sheen and is very flaky. Served on special occasions.

Posole   A hominy stew, from New Mexico, that includes pork, onion, garlic, and chili.

Pot-au-feu   The most traditional of all French dishes, and each French province has its own version. It is usually made with beef (or sometimes chicken, pork, or an assortment of meats), vegetables and herbs, all cooked together in a large stockpot of water. The resulting dish is served as a soup.

Pot stickers   Small Chinese stuffed dumplings that are browned first and then simmered in broth.

Praline   A mixture of crushed caramelized sugar and almonds used as a garnish or ingredient. It is also a candy from Louisiana made with brown sugar and pecans.

Profiteroles   Tiny French cream puffs. Can be filled with sweet or savory mixtures.

Puttanesca   An Italian pasta sauce, literally meaning "a lady of ill repute." It is tomato based, with capers, anchovies, hot peppers, black olives, garlic, and chopped parsley in olive oil.

□ **Q**

Quesadillas Warm flour tortillas topped with melted cheese and your choice of other toppings. A popular snack or appetizer in Mexico.

Quiche Lorraine An open, savory bacon custard tart from Lorraine, France. There are many variations on this peasant dish, but the classic contains bacon, cream, cheese, and eggs.

□ **R**

Raclette A Swiss dish related to fondue. A cheese that melts smoothly and easily is brought to the table melting under or in one of the Raclette stoves used for making the dish. It is served with a boiled potato for each person and side dishes of tiny cocktail onions, dill pickles, and gherkins. Diners scrape the melting portion of the cheese onto a bit of potato, and add a spicy relish to each bite. Raclette is the name of the dish as well as the name of the cheese.

Ragout A thick, rich, well-seasoned French stew made with meat, chicken, or fish, and sometimes vegetables.

Raita An Indian meal is not complete without this condiment/side dish made of raw or cooked vegetables, dumplings, fruits, herbs, chilies, spices, and/or nuts in a yogurt base. The cooling yogurt soothes the palate after a fiery curry.

Ratatouille A southern French dish of sautéed vegetables, usually onion, eggplant, zucchini, garlic, sweet green peppers, and tomatoes, flavored with oregano, rosemary, and/or basil.

Raznjici Meat kabobs, a specialty in Yugoslavia.

Red beans and rice An old New Orleans dish made with a ham bone, baked ham (not country or smoked), kidney beans, onion, green onion, bell pepper, garlic, parsley, pickled pork, rice, and seasonings.

Red cooking A Chinese stewing method. First the ingredient (often chicken) is seared and browned, and then simmered in the red cooking ingredients of soy sauce, star anise or five-spice powder, water, sesame oil, ginger, sherry, and sugar, until richly glazed and colored.

Redeye gravy A traditional southern U.S. gravy made by adding a little water or black coffee to a skillet in which ham has just been fried. It is served with the ham and spooned over biscuits.

Red flannel hash Beef, potatoes, onions, and beets fried together; a speciality of New England.

Ribollita The most famous Tuscan soup, with endless variations. The name comes from "reboiled," and it usually contains cabbage, cannellini beans, and bread arranged in layers.

Rijsttafel Means "rice table" in Dutch. It is a large meal consisting of a vast array of Indonesian dishes with rice at the center.

Rillettes A coarse French pork pâté usually served in a crock.

Risi e bisi   A very thick Italian soup made with rice and peas, often flavored with onion, ham, and celery.

Risotto   An Italian dish traditionally made with arborio (a short-grained rice) browned in fat and cooked with chicken broth until tender but firm. The dish is stirred constantly and the broth is added slowly, which gives the dish its characteristic creamy texture. The dish varies according to region and chosen additions.

Rodgrod med flode   Stewed, thickened, and sweetened summer fruits usually topped with whipped cream. A Danish specialty.

Rogan josh   A mild lamb curry from northern India that derives its characteristic red color from ground red chilies.

Rösti   Fried potato cakes from Switzerland.

Rotkohl   Red cabbage cooked with wine vinegar, sugar, onions, sliced apple, and spices. This German sweet-and-sour dish is often served with roast pork and potato dumplings.

Rouille   A spicy version of aioli, flavored with chilies, which is used primarily to give fire to fish soups. Rather than being made like a mayonnaise, it is made with stale bread soaked in water for a thickener.

Roulade   A slice of meat, most often veal or beef, rolled around any number of fillings. Also, a name for jelly-roll cake.

Ruisleipa   A sour rye bread that is the "staff of life" in Finland. In west Finland, it is baked as a round flat loaf with a hole in the center, and in the east it is a thick round soft loaf.

Rumbledthumps   A mush of mashed potatoes, cabbage, and kale; sometimes sprinkled with cheese and browned. From Scotland.

□ **S**

Sacher torte   A rich and famous Viennese dessert of chocolate cake, layered with apricot filling, with a dark chocolate icing.

Saint Honore   A festive French dessert of caramel-glazed cream puffs circling cream filling. It is named for the patron saint of pastry bakers.

Salamagundy   An English dish of raw and cooked vegetables, fruit, and diced cooked meat or fish mixed with a salad dressing.

Sally Lunn   A sweet yeast-raised bread, rich with butter and eggs. Folklore has it that Sally Lunn lived in Bath, England, in the eighteenth century and baked bread for her entire town.

Salsa   A number of sauces in Mexican and Southwestern cuisines with flavors ranging from very subtle to very spicy. Also, an uncooked, seasoned tomato sauce served as a condiment and used to add flavor to other dishes.

Salsa verde   An Italian green salad dressing of chopped parsley and/or other herbs. It may include capers, anchovies, bread, garlic, onion, vinegar, and olive oil. Served cool or at room temperature.

Saltimbocca   Very thin cutlets of veal with fresh sage leaves, covered with a thin slice of ham and fried in butter. From Italy.

Salzburger nockerlin   An Austrian dumpling.

Sambal ulek   Indonesian hot chili paste, made with red chilies, vinegar and/or tamarind, and salt. Used as a condiment.

Samosas   Probably the best-known Indian snack. Crisp turnovers that are stuffed with ground lamb, peas, and potatoes, or leftovers.

Sashimi   A Japanese dish of raw saltwater fish sliced paper thin and served with such condiments as shredded daikon radish, sliced ginger root, wasabi, and soy sauce. It is eaten as a meal or an appetizer.

Saté   A Thai appetizer and street food that arrived from Indonesia via Malaysia. Marinated in coconut milk, lime leaves, coriander, lemongrass, sugar, and curry powder, satés can be made from pork, beef, or chicken. They are almost always served with marinated cucumbers and a peanut sauce.

Sauerbraten   A marinated beef (top round) dish from Germany; one of the best and most varied recipes in German cuisine. A typical version is pot roast marinated in red wine, vinegar, peppercorns, mustard, juniper berries, bay leaf, thyme, and vegetables. Then the meat is browned in bacon fat and simmered on low heat until tender. The stock is thickened and blended with sour cream. In other versions the beef is marinated in beer or even buttermilk.

Sayyadiya   A Middle Eastern fish stew containing vegetables and rice.

Scaloppine   A boneless thin slice of meat (usually veal), probably the most frequently encountered cut of meat in Italy. It can come from any part of the animal, and there are an infinite number of ways of preparing it.

Schav   A Russian sorrel or spinach soup, served cold.

Schneitz and kneep   A Pennsylvania Dutch dish of apples, ham, and dumplings.

Scone   A soft quick bread from the British Isles. Scones are served hot with butter and jam or clotted cream for tea or breakfast. They can be made in various shapes.

Scotch broth   A lamb, barley, and vegetable soup from Scotland.

Scotch eggs   Hard-cooked eggs wrapped in sausage and fried.

Scotch woodcock   A Scottish dish of anchovies on toast covered with creamy scrambled eggs. Served as an appetizer, an entrée, or at the end of a formal dinner.

Scrapple   A Pennsylvania Dutch loaf of ground pork ("scraps") mixed with onions, spices, herbs, and cornmeal, slowly simmered and then sliced and fried.

Semifreddo   In Italian it means "half cold." Mostly molded desserts that contain combinations of ice cream, custard, gelatin mixtures, whipped cream, candied fruits, and nuts. It is frozen or refrigerated before serving.

Sfogliatelle   Flaky Italian pastry cases filled with sweetened ricotta cheese and candied fruit.

Shabu-shabu   The Japanese version of a Mongolian "fire pot." Paper-thin pieces of beef and vegetables are cooked at the table in broth and then dipped in a sesame sauce. The name comes from the gentle swishing sound made as the food is cooked.

Shashlik   An Eastern European kabob made of skewered lamb, marinated in pomegranate juice, herbs, lemon juice, and garlic.

Shawarma   Sold by street venders in the Middle East. Slices of lamb are marinated overnight and then packed onto a vertical skewer and roasted. The meat is shaved off to serve.

Shepherd's pie   Ground lamb cooked in stock, placed in a pie dish, topped with mashed potatoes and baked. Popular in Britain.

Shinsonro   The Korean "royal casserole." A meat broth with sea vegetables, seafood, vegetables, and eggs cooked at the table.

Shirin polo   A rice and chicken dish from the Middle East, flavored with orange peel, almonds, and saffron.

Shirumono   Japanese soups.

Shish kebab   Skewered meat or seafood and vegetables. It originated in Turkey and is now enjoyed all over the world. It is often made with lamb and is traditionally served with pilaf.

Shoofly pie   A biscuit crumb pie shell filled with a mixture of molasses, sugar, and spices. Probably of Pennsylvania Dutch origin, supposedly named for the fact that it is so sweet, one must "shoo away the flies."

Shortbread   A crumbly cake or cookie made with a large amount of shortening.

Skink   Vegetables and chopped beef stewed in beef stock, served in Scotland.

Skyr   A national dish in Iceland. It is an ancient dish that was brought to Iceland by the Vikings of Norway. Made from skim milk and whipped before serving, skyr probably resembles yogurt more than anything else. Eaten either as dessert or for breakfast, it often has heavy cream poured over it.

Smørrebrød   Literally means bread and butter, but it now refers to Danish open sandwiches. They are rich and imaginative combinations of food, never fewer than three kinds. Seafood, liver pâté, hard-cooked eggs, bacon, mushrooms, tomato, and cheese are often found on these sandwiches.

Soba   Japanese buckwheat noodles.

Socca   Unfilled crêpes made from chick-pea flour sold on the streets of Nice in the morning. Great for snacks and appetizers as well as breakfast.

Sopaipilla   A light and puffy deep-fried pastry that is often served with honey, it is a popular dessert in the southwestern United States. It can also be served as a savory, filled with guacamole or refried beans.

Soufflé   A light, fluffy combination of egg yolk, sauce, puree, and flavoring, with a stiffly beaten egg white folded in. A soufflé may be hot or cold, sweet or savory.

Souvlakia   A Greek dish of marinated meat, speared on skewers, and grilled over charcoal.

Spanakopita   Savory Greek phyllo pastry, usually filled with feta cheese and spinach.

Spatzli   Means "little sparrows." They are tiny German dumplings cooked in boiling water.

Spoon bread   A very soft cornbread baked in a casserole dish. It is served as a side dish and eaten with silverware rather than with the hands.

Spotted dick or dog   A steamed suet pudding with raisins, from Great Britain.

Stamp and go   Served in Jamaica, these are codfish fritters usually served as hors d'oeuvres or with drinks.

Steak and kidney pie   Steak, kidney, and stock steamed in a suet crust. Served in England.

Steak Macfarlane   A Scottish dish of steak rolled in oatmeal and fried.

Steak tartare   A dish of freshly chopped or ground raw beef that is seasoned with salt, pepper, and herbs, and most often served with minced onion, parsley, and capers. It is usually shaped into a mound, and sometimes a raw egg yolk is placed on top. It may have originated in the Baltic provinces of Russia, where meat was shredded with a knife and eaten raw. This dish is not recommended as eating raw beef or raw egg poses a health risk.

Stifatho   Classic Greek veal, beef, poultry, or octopus stew.

Stollen   Yeast bread served on Christmas in Germany. The rich loaf is filled with dried fruit and topped with powdered sugar icing.

Stovies   A Scottish dish of potatoes simmered in water, sometimes with onion.

Stracciatella   A light Italian soup of beef or chicken stock, with eggs and grated cheese worked in.

Strudel   A flaky pastry rolled around a filling, either savory or sweet. Fillings often include apple, cheese, cherry, pineapple, as well as chopped meat.

Suan la tang   A thick hot-and-sour soup of shredded meat, bean curd, vegetables, and mushrooms, with vinegar, pepper, and chilies. Served in China.

Suimono   Clear Japanese soups.

Sukiyaki   A Japanese cooked-at-the-table dish of thinly sliced meat, tofu, and vegetables. It is flavored with soy sauce, sugar, and sake.

Summer pudding   In this traditional British dessert, lightly stewed fresh berries and/or currants are put in a bowl lined with buttered white bread, covered with more bread, and allowed to stand overnight.

Sushi   A Japanese word that means "vinegared rice." The rice is often served with raw or broiled fish and shellfish, vegetables and herbs, and/or Japanese omelets. Often served with wasabi (Japanese horseradish), soy sauce, and pickled ginger.

□ T

Tabbouleh   A Middle Eastern cracked wheat salad with lots of fresh mint, olive oil, lemon juice, onion, tomatoes, and parsley. Eaten with lettuce, cabbage, or vine leaves as scoops; served cool or at room temperature.

Taco   A fried Mexican cornmeal tortilla folded around a filling, such as cheese, beef, chicken, or refried beans.

Tafelspitz   An Austrian dish of short ribs, slowly simmered with vegetables. Served with either an apple-horseradish or chive sauce.

Tamales   A cornhusk spread with cornmeal and filled with chili-seasoned chicken, beef, pork, or cheese, then rolled and steamed.

Tandoori chicken   One of the most popular Indian preparations, the dish takes its name from the *tandoor* or clay oven in which it is cooked. The chicken—or even meat or seafood—is first marinated overnight in a spiced yogurt sauce, then roasted over coals. The traditional orange or red color of cooked tandoori chicken comes from food coloring.

Tangine   A sweet spicy stew from Morocco that contains lamb or poultry, prunes, lemons, chick-peas, olives, and/or almonds. Also the pot in which a *tangine* is cooked.

Tapas   Spanish hors d'oeuvres that traditionally accompany sherry, served in bars and restaurants. The dishes range from very simple preparations, such as cured olives and cubes of cheese, to more elaborate dishes, such as cold omelets or shrimp in garlic sauce.

Tapénade   This black olive, anchovy, garlic, and caper spread is also good served as a dip.

Taramasalata   A spread or dip made of fish roe, lemon juice, olive oil, and bread crumbs; served in Greece.

Tarator   A Bulgarian soup of diced cucumber, yogurt, walnuts, dill, garlic, and oil. Served chilled.

Tempura   A Japanese dish of vegetables and seafood dipped in a very light batter, deep-fried, and served with a sauce. Good tempura is crisp and light, the batter a mere wisp that covers the food.

Teriyaki   A sweet soy sauce glaze that is added in the last stages of grilling, broiling, or pan frying to fish, chicken, beef, or pork. "Teri" literally means glossy or luster, and "yaki" means broiled in Japanese.

Terrine   A type of container used for baking dishes such as pâtés. The prepared dish may also be referred to as a terrine.

Tikka   Small pieces of meat or poultry marinated in yogurt and tandoori spices.

Tilliliha   Lamb stew with dill, popular in Finland.

Timbale   A savory meat, fish, poultry, or vegetable custard, baked in a small mold. Also, pastry shells made on special iron molds— Swedish rosettes, for example.

Tiramisu   The name literally means "pick me up" and this Italian dessert is made with cake soaked in espresso and layered with mascarpone (a sweet creamy cheese) and egg cream flavored with coffee.

Tiropetes   Tiny fried Greek pies filled with feta cheese and herbs.

Toad in the hole   An English name for meat, sausage, or lamb cutlets baked in batter. Also, an egg cooked in a hole cut from the center of a slice of bread.

Tonkatsu   From Japan, these are deep-fried pork cutlets. *Ton* means "pork," and *katsu* is the Japanese pronunciation of "cutlet."

Topfenknodel   Austrian farmer cheese dumplings, sometimes served with plum sauce.

Torte   A very rich multilayered cake made with eggs and often grated nuts. Usually it is filled, but frequently it is not frosted.

Tortilla   A Mexican tortilla is a small rolled pancake made with cornmeal or wheat flour. A Spanish tortilla is an omelet, often made with potatoes.

Tortino   An Italian pie prepared with cooked vegetables, often combined with cheese or ham, added to a beaten egg and milk mixture and poured into a pie pan, which can be lined with a pastry shell or slices of bread.

Tostadas   Fried corn tortillas topped with salad, meat, fish, poultry, salsa, and cheese.

Tostones   A dish popular in many Hispanic countries, this is plantains fried until crisp.

Tourtière   A French Canadian spiced pork pie, traditionally served on Christmas eve.

Trifle   An English sweet pudding made with sponge cake moistened with sherry, topped with jam and almonds, and layered with custard and/or whipped cream. May be decorated with angelica.

Tsatsiki   A Greek salad or condiment made from yogurt, and possibly cucumber, lemon juice, garlic, green onion, and/or fresh mint.

Türlü   A Turkish mixed vegetable stew.

Turnover   A folded pastry usually made by cutting out a dough circle or square, adding a dollop of sweet or savory filling, folding into a semicircle or triangle, then crimping the edges with the tines of a fork. Most turnovers are baked, but some are deep-fried.

Tutti-frutti   A mixture of minced fruits used as a dessert topping.

Tweed kettle   A Scottish dish of salmon with shallots and vinegar.

Tzimmes   Slow-cooked casserole of brisket, carrots, honey, and dried fruit. It is often topped with potatoes and/or dumplings. Traditionally served on the Jewish New Year.

□ **U**

Udon   Japanese white wheat noodles.

□ **V**

Vareniki   Ukranian dumplings.

Västkustsallad   A seafood, vegetable, mayonnaise, and dill salad from Sweden.

Veprova pecene   Pork roasted with caraway seeds. It is served in Czechoslovakia with dumplings and sauerkraut.

Véronique   Any dish garnished with seedless green grapes.

Vichyssoise   An American soup of potatoes, leeks, and cream. It is garnished with chives and served cold.

Vinaigrette   A sauce or dressing, French in origin, made from oil, vinegar, salt, pepper, and herbs; usually served on cold meat, fish, vegetables, or salads.

Vindaloo   Hot Indian curry of beef, pork, lamb, chicken, or fish that is marinated in vinegar. The dish often contains potatoes, herbs, spices, and chilies.

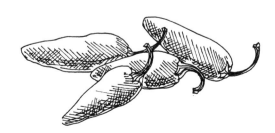

Vitello tonnato   Usually a rolled veal roast braised or pot roasted in white wine, herbs, lemon juice, oil, and water. After cooking, it is sliced and covered with a thick mayonnaise or cream sauce containing mashed canned tuna and anchovies, lemon juice, and stock, and garnished with capers, lemon slices, chopped tomatoes, and black olives.

□ **W**

Waterzooi   A rich Belgian chicken or fish soup or stew made with wine.

Welsh rarebit   A kind of sandwich made with butter, beer or ale, salt, pepper, dry mustard, and Caerphilly or Cheddar cheese mixed together and served on bread, then broiled until the cheese is melted. Tradition has it that rarebit is a corruption of the word "rabbit," which this dish was intended to replace, as Welsh farmers were forbidden by their English landlords to shoot rabbits. True or not, it is a fact that this dish of melted cheese was eaten in Wales as early as the fourteenth century.

Wiener schnitzel   Means "Viennese cutlet" in German. A very thin slice of veal that is dipped in flour, eggs, and bread crumbs, and sautéed, usually served with a slice of lemon.

Wonton   Chinese pasta dumpling filled with minced meat, seafood, and/or vegetables. It is served boiled in soup or deep-fried.

□ **Y**

Yachae tweegim   A Korean vegetable pancake with potatoes, onion, carrot, bell peppers, and zucchini mixed into a batter and fried.

Yakitori   Grilled chicken on a skewer from Japan.

Yorkshire pudding   A popover–like pastry from Britain, cooked in roast beef drippings. It puffs as high as a giant popover and is crusty and savory with the natural gravy of the roast.

Yo-yo   Tunisian doughnuts made with orange juice, deep-fried, and then dipped in a honey syrup.

Yu jr tang   Shark's fin soup, popular in China.

□ **Z**

Zabaglione   A rich, frothy Italian custard made with beaten egg yolks. Flavored with Marsala or white wine and sugar; it is served warm or cold.

Zarzuela   Spanish seafood stew.

Zuccotto   A dome-shaped dessert made of layers of cake soaked in liqueur, with whipped cream, chocolate, fruit, and nuts.

Zuppa inglese   Literally translated from the Italian it means "English soup," but it's not a soup at all. It is an Italian version of the English trifle, made with rum-soaked slices of sponge cake layered with whipped cream or custard and candied fruit and/or toasted almonds.

CHAPTER 6

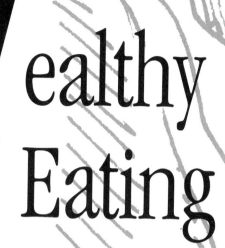

Healthy Eating

WHAT SHOULD YOU EAT—AND NOT EAT? With so much information, *and* new research appearing almost daily, it's difficult to know what's best. This chapter provides you with a basic understanding of nutrition, gives you the current recommendations for healthy food choices, and offers ways you can incorporate this information into your daily life.

Healthy Diets and Healthy Living

These days there is a very important reason to eat sensibly: there is a medically proven relationship between diet and health. Poor diets have been linked to heart disease, stroke, osteoporosis, obesity, diabetes, high blood pressure, and some types of cancer. Although food fads may make it seem so, there is no single wonder food. Take oat bran, for instance. Some years ago it was just an ordinary ingredient that didn't get much attention. Then word got out that it might lower blood cholesterol. Suddenly oat bran was in everything from potato chips to cereals, and people assumed that the more oat bran they ate, the healthier they'd be. If only that were true!

Healthy eating doesn't depend on a single or a few foods for good nutrition. It means choosing a variety of foods to provide your body with all the nutrients it needs.

Of course your diet is not the only factor associated with good health. Your exercise routine, genetic predisposition, age, and weight also affect your physical well-being. Although some of these factors are out of your control, *you can* control your food choices and exercise habits. Keeping up-to-date with nutrition information, eating a variety of healthy foods, and getting regular exercise are the most important things you can do for optimal health.

Nutrition Basics

Complex carbohydrates. Beta carotene. "Good" cholesterol. Nutritional terms like these pop up in articles, television shows, and books every day. But what do they really mean, and what is their importance for you? Here is a guide to the elements of good nutrition.

CALORIES

The word *calorie* is used to describe the measure of energy derived from the foods you eat. This energy is required by your body not only for physical exertion, such as walking or running, but for your vital organs to function and for your body to keep operating.

When the number of calories consumed exceeds the amount needed by your body, the excess calories are stored as body fat (3,500 extra calories equals 1 pound of fat).

For a well-balanced diet, your total calories should come from three sources: 8 to 12 percent from protein, 30 percent or less from fat, and the rest (approximately 60 percent) from carbohydrates.

CARBOHYDRATES

Carbohydrates are the body's fuel. They help you meet your body's energy needs and keep your digestive system functioning properly. They also combine with fat, so it can be used for energy.

All carbohydrates are composed of sugars. *Simple carbohydrates*, such as candy, honey, jelly, maple syrup, and sugar, do not have to be broken down very much by the body to be digested. That's why you experience an instant rise in blood sugar after eating them. Frequently, though, this rise is followed by a rapid drop in your blood sugar, which makes you feel tired, and crave more sweets. Simple carbohydrates also lack other nutrients, so you should eat them in moderation.

Complex carbohydrates are breads, cereals, grains, fruits, and vegetables. Besides energy, they provide a wealth of vitamins, minerals, and fiber. Because complex carbohydrates take longer for the body to break down for use, they provide a steadier source of energy than simple carbohydrates.

PROTEINS

The building blocks of the body, proteins are essential for the growth and repair of cells. They are also vital to the regulation of hormones, the transport of nutrients, and the production of antibodies for disease prevention, and they are an important energy source.

Proteins are made up of amino acids. Most animal and dairy foods contain all the amino acids, so they are referred to as *complete proteins.* Plant sources—vegetables, grains, breads—lack one or more amino acids; they are called *incomplete proteins.* What does this mean in terms of eating nutritiously? In order to get the complete protein benefit from these sources, you eat them in combination, whether they're in the same dish or at the same meal. These food combinations produce complete proteins: rice with beans or dairy products or seeds (or all three); wheat products with beans or dairy products (or both); legumes with grains, seeds or dairy products (or all three); corn with beans or milk; potatoes with milk or cheese (or both).

How much protein do you need? The Recommended Dietary Allowance (RDA) is 0.8 grams per 2.2 pounds of body weight. For

Eat Fatty Fish for Good Health

Although the general rule of good nutrition is to select lean foods, fish is an exception. Scientists have found that certain fatty fish contain substances called omega-3 long-chain fatty acids, and eating these seems to reduce the risk of heart disease. Good sources of omega-3 fatty acids are bluefish, herring, mackerel, rainbow trout, salmon, swordfish, and tuna.

example, a 140-pound person needs about 50 grams of protein daily (140/2.2 × .8 = 50). The bottom line again is variety. Eat a variety of foods in varying combinations and you will get an adequate amount of protein in your diet.

FAT

Although fat generally gets a lot of bad press, it is a fundamental part of the body's structure and operation. It provides energy, helps maintain normal body heat, and assists in the absorption of fat-soluble vitamins A, D, E, and K. The problem is that most of us eat more fat than is good for us and that excess fat in the diet is stored as body fat.

Fat is made up of three types of fatty acids: saturated, polyunsaturated, and monounsaturated. *Saturated fats* are found in animal foods and tropical oils, such as palm oil. They have been shown to decrease the body's ability to break down cholesterol, which increases cholesterol levels in the blood. (The following section explains what cholesterol is and why too much can be a problem.) *Polyunsaturated fats* are found in vegetable oils, such as corn and safflower. They lower cholesterol levels. (*Note:* When buying margarine made from polyunsaturated oils, keep this in mind: When an oil is hydrogenated—converted from liquid to solid—the process also converts some polyunsaturated fats into saturated ones. This is why margarines contain more saturated fats than the oils from which they are made).

Monounsaturated fats are also from plant sources. These fats are very high in olive, canola, and peanut oils, and, like polyunsaturated fats, they decrease cholesterol levels.

How much fat can you safely consume? No more than 30 percent of your total daily calories should be from fat, and in the following proportion:

10 percent monounsaturated
10 percent polyunsaturated
10 percent or less saturated

CHOLESTEROL

Manufactured by the liver, cholesterol is an essential part of cell membranes, is used in building nerve sheaths, and provides the raw material for manufacturing hormones.

Dietary cholesterol comes from animal sources: egg yolks, meats, whole-milk products, butter, and lard. Too much dietary cholesterol and saturated fat may result in high cholesterol levels in the blood (serum cholesterol). These elevated levels increase the risk of hardening of the arteries and heart disease. The American Heart Association

Where's the Cholesterol?

FOOD SOURCE	CHOLES-TEROL
Beef liver, 3 ounces, cooked	331 mg.
Egg, 1 yolk	272 mg.
Beef sirloin, 3 ounces, cooked	76 mg.
Chicken, white meat, skinned and boned, cooked	72 mg.
Shrimp, 3 ounces, steamed	166 mg.
Whole milk, 1 cup	34 mg.
Skim milk, 1 cup	5 mg.

Credit: United States Department of Agriculture/Human Nutrition Information Service.

Beta Carotene

Beta carotene is the pigment that gives many fruits and vegetables a yellow-to-red color. Once eaten, it is converted to vitamin A in the body. Diets rich in beta carotene and vitamin A have been shown to reduce the risk of cancer. Foods rich in beta carotene are apricots, beet greens, broccoli, cantaloupe, carrots, peaches, spinach, and winter squash.

recommends the average healthy adult consume no more than 300 milligrams of cholesterol a day.

There is a link between the fat you eat and your cholesterol level. Cholesterol travels back and forth from the liver to cells in the bloodstream, carried by proteins. HDLs (high-density lipoproteins) safely deliver cholesterol to the liver for processing and excretion. LDLs (low-density lipoproteins) tend to drop cholesterol along the way. This cholesterol forms deposits on arteries, resulting in plaque formation, hardening of the arteries, and a slowing down of blood flow. This increases blood pressure and the risk of heart disease or stroke. Evidence suggests that unsaturated fats may increase the number of HDLs in the blood, while saturated fats may increase the LDLs.

VITAMINS

Vitamins are organic substances found in plant and animal sources. They work with minerals to help proteins, fats, and carbohydrates produce energy, and are necessary for all bodily functions.

There are fat-soluble and water-soluble vitamins. The *fat-soluble* vitamins—A, D, E and K—are usually found in the fats and oils of food, and are stored in the body's fat. The *water-soluble* vitamins—the Bs and C—are found in many foods: eggs, milk and dairy products, grains, nuts, vegetables, and fruits. Those we don't use each day are eliminated in the urine, so water-soluble vitamins have to be eaten every day.

Fat-soluble vitamins can survive extreme heat, such as cooking. Water-soluble vitamins are easily destroyed in high heat and leech into water during cooking. For the maximum benefit from these vitamins, eat their food sources raw. Or, cook them quickly in small amounts of water by blanching or steaming. In addition, cook or eat foods containing water-soluble vitamins as soon as possible after cutting them up. Exposure to the air also destroys these fragile vitamins.

MINERALS

Minerals are inorganic substances found in plants, animals, and the earth. They work with vitamins to ensure proper bodily functions, and they're important to making bone, maintaining fluid in the cells, and transmitting nerve impulses.

Sulphur, one of the minerals, is not included in the table because it is found in proteins, so as long as your diet is adequate in protein you'll get enough sulphur.

Vitamins

VITAMIN	WHAT IT IS	WHAT IT DOES	SOURCES
Vitamin A	Fat-soluble; produced from beta carotene and other carotenoids (the pigments that color yellow and orange vegetables).	Helps form cell membranes and builds bones and teeth; maintains good vision, especially night vision; protects nerves and normal cell growth; makes and maintains skin, hair, mucous membranes, and gums; necessary for reproduction.	Apricots, broccoli, butterfat, cantaloupe, carrots, cheese, egg yolk, fish liver oils, liver, mangoes, fortified milk and margarine, pumpkin, sweet potatoes, and dark leafy green vegetables, such as kale, spinach, and turnip greens.
Vitamin B	Family of eight water-soluble vitamins: thiamin (B_1); riboflavin (B_2); niacin (B_3, nicotinamide, nicotinic acid);Z B_6 (pyridoxine, pyridoxal and pyridoxamine); B_{12} (cobalamin); folacin (folic acid); pantothenic acid; and biotin.	Each vitamin has a specific task, but generally this group helps build new tissue and releases energy to cells by burning calories; keeps the reproductive system, immune system, and brain functioning; helps make hormones, blood, hemoglobin; forms nucleic acid and other genetic material.	Breads, enriched cereals, pasta, whole grains; green vegetables, potatoes; dried peas and beans; brewer's yeast; fish, shellfish; organ meats (such as liver and kidneys), pork, and other meats; poultry; eggs; dairy products.
Vitamin C	Fragile and water-soluble; breaks down in cooking and must be replenished daily in the body.	Fights infections; promotes healing; aids in iron absorption; protects vitamins and fatty acids from destruction; maintains capillaries, bones, and teeth.	Citrus fruits and fruit juices, melons, strawberries; cabbage, dark green vegetables, green peppers, potatoes, tomatoes.
Vitamin D	Fat-soluble.	Helps build bones and teeth; regulates cell division and metabolism.	Vitamin-D enriched milk and other fortified foods; cod-liver oil; egg yolk; fatty fish, such as salmon and tuna; self-synthesis through exposure to sunlight.
Vitamin E	Fat-soluble.	Assists in forming and protecting red blood cells, muscles, and other tissues; protects cell membranes from toxic substances, particularly in the lungs.	Breads, whole grains; dried beans, vegetables; fruits; liver; vegetable oils and margarine, wheat germ oil.
Vitamin K	Fat-soluble.	Helps blood to clot; promotes and maintains bone growth.	Cabbage, cauliflower, leafy green vegetables; cheese; liver; also produced by bacteria in the intestine.

Minerals

MINERAL	WHAT IT DOES	SOURCES
Calcium	Works with phosphorus and magnesium to build bones and teeth, maintain cell fluid levels, contract muscles, and transmit nerve impulses. Also clots blood; regulates hormones; helps absorb vitamin B12.	Broccoli, leafy greens, such as bok choy, kale, mustard, and turnip greens; pinto beans; figs; almonds, Brazil nuts, English walnuts, and pecans; sardines and salmon with bones; milk and dairy products; calcium-enriched milk and calcium-enriched grain products. *Note:* Soft drinks interfere with calcium absorption.
Chloride	Acts with sodium and potassium to maintain cell fluid levels and transmit nerve impulses; necessary for liver function and proper digestion.	Kelp, purified water, table salt.
Copper	Releases iron from the liver; important in formation of hemoglobin and red blood cells, in production of nucleic acids and bone, in muscle formation, and in the protection of nerve fibers and blood vessels; maintains bone, nerves, and heart muscle; helps convert fats and carbohydrates to energy.	Almonds; dried beans and legumes; leafy green vegetables; organ meats; shellfish; whole grains.
Fluoride	Builds and strengthens bone and makes teeth resistant to decay.	Cheese; fluoridated water; meat; seafood; black and green tea.
Iodine	Needed by the thyroid gland to produce hormones that control metabolism and promote physical and mental development and reproduction.	Iodized salt; seafood; seaweed.
Iron	Combines with protein and copper to form hemoglobin, a substance needed to carry oxygen in red blood cells, and myoglobin, needed to carry oxygen in muscle cells. Necessary for muscle contraction; affects physical and mental performance, and the immune system.	Enriched and fortified breads, grains and cereals; dried peas and beans; dried fruits; egg yolk; kidney; liver, especially pork, then calf, beef, and chicken liver; molasses; oysters; leafy green vegetables, potatoes.
Magnesium	Builds bone; makes proteins; releases energy from cells; regulates calcium, phosphorus, sodium, and potassium absorption. Conducts nerve impulses to muscles; regulates body temperature and heart function; helps body use B vitamins and vitamins C and E.	Almonds, cashews, sunflower seeds; apples, figs; corn; milk; oysters; raw leafy green vegetables; seafood; soybeans; whole grains and cereals.
Manganese	Works with copper and zinc to build bone; helps produce milk, urea, protein, fat, carbohydrates, sex hormones, and thyroxin in the thyroid gland; maintains nerves and muscles.	Dairy products; eggs; liver; meat (especially beef); oysters; poultry; whole grains.

(table continues)

Minerals (*continued*)

MINERAL	WHAT IT DOES	SOURCES
Phosphorus	Builds bone and teeth; releases energy from carbohydrates, fat, and protein; forms genetic material, cell membranes, and enzymes.	Dairy products; dried peas and beans; eggs; fish; meats; nuts; poultry; seeds; whole grains and cereals.
Potassium	Works with magnesium to control heart function; maintains cell fluid level and sodium balance, contracts muscles, and transmits nerve impulses; helps release energy from carbohydrates, fat, and protein.	Bananas, dried fruits such as prunes, peaches, apricots, and dates; kiwifruit, orange juice; avocados, potatoes, winter squash; dried peas and beans; almonds, cashews, filberts and peanuts; meats.
Sodium	Functions with potassium to regulate fluid balance, muscle contraction, and transmission of nerve impulses; helps regulate blood pressure; necessary for good digestion.	(Just about everything we eat contains sodium chloride, also known as salt.) Table salt; plant and animal foods, especially processed foods: smoked or cured meats and fish; pickles and relishes; condiments (soy sauce, steak sauce, ketchup, mustard, etc.); snack foods; ready-to-eat cereals.
Zinc	Promotes immunity and rapid healing; essential to growth and development of sexual organs; regulates insulin; promotes absorption of vitamins; necessary in digestion, metabolism, and in protein formation.	Whole grains; dairy products; eggs; liver; meats (especially beef); oysters; poultry.

Calcium and Strong Bones

Do you know that your body replaces its skeleton every seven to ten years? That's why it's important not to restrict calcium intake at any age. Getting enough calcium is especially important for adolescent girls and adult women because calcium helps form dense bones, which lowers the risk of bone loss and bone fracture in later life. Pregnant women need extra calcium so they can meet the demands of the growing baby while protecting their own bones. When the body is not supplied with enough dietary calcium for all its functions, it draws the necessary calcium from its own bones, resulting in calcium depletion. Osteoporosis, a degenerative bone disease caused by calcium depletion, afflicts one out of every three women over sixty-five.

Eating a balanced diet, not smoking, and exercising regularly (which helps bones absorb calcium and puts beneficial stress on them to stimulate thickening) will further reduce the risk of osteoporosis.

Three glasses of milk or four ounces of cheese contain the daily requirement for calcium (800 mg for women age 23 to 50). For other calcium-rich foods, see the table "Bone Builders."

Bone Builders: Good Sources of Calcium

The National Research Council has set the RDA for calcium for women aged 23 to 50 years at 800 mg per day. Here's how much calcium you get from various foods.

FOOD	MGS CALCIUM
Milk Group	
Buttermilk, 1 cup	285
Cheese, American, 1 ounce	174
Cheese, Cheddar, 1 ounce	204
Cheese, ricotta, part skim, ½ cup	337
Cheese, Swiss, 1 ounce	272
Ice cream, vanilla, ½ cup	88
Whole milk, 1 cup	291
Milk, low-fat (2%), 1 cup	297
Milk, skim, 1 cup	302
Yogurt, fruit, low-fat, 1 cup	345
Yogurt, plain, low-fat, 1 cup	415
Meat and Bean Group	
Beans, dried, cooked, 1 cup	90
Oysters, raw, 7 to 9	113
Salmon, canned, with bones, 3 ounces	167
Sardines, with bones, 3 ounces	372
Shrimp, canned, 3 ounces	99
Tofu (bean curd), 4 ounces*	240
Fruit-Vegetable Group	
Beet greens, ½ cup	72
Bok choy ½ cup	126
Broccoli, stalk, ½ cup	68
Collards, from raw, ½ cup	57
Collards, from frozen, ½ cup	179
Kale, from raw, ½ cup	47
Kale, from frozen, ½ cup	90
Mustard greens, from raw, ½ cup	52
Spinach, from raw, ½ cup	122
Grain Group	
Cornbread, 2½ by 2½ by 1½ inches	94
Pancakes, two, 4-inch diameter	116
Waffles, 7-inch diameter	179

*Note: Only tofu processed with calcium sulfate is a source of calcium.

Information courtesy of the National Dairy Council

Recommended Dietary Allowances* (Revised 1989)

AGE (YEARS) & GENDER	WEIGHT KG	LBS	HEIGHT CM	IN	P. G	VIT. A RE	THIAM. MG	RIBO. MG	NIACIN NE	VIT. B₆ MG	FOLACIN μG	VIT. B₁₂ μG
Infants												
0.0–0.5	6	13	60	24	13	375	0.3	0.4	5	0.3	25	0.3
0.5–1.0	9	20	71	28	14	375	0.4	0.5	6	0.6	35	0.5
Children												
1–3	13	29	90	35	16	400	0.7	0.8	9	1.0	50	0.7
4–6	20	44	112	44	24	500	0.9	1.1	12	1.1	75	1.0
7–10	28	62	132	52	28	700	1.0	1.2	13	1.4	100	1.4
Males												
11–14	45	99	157	62	45	1000	1.3	1.5	17	1.7	150	2.0
15–18	66	145	176	69	59	1000	1.5	1.8	20	2.0	200	2.0
19–24	72	160	177	70	58	1000	1.5	1.7	19	2.0	200	2.0
25–50	79	174	176	70	63	1000	1.5	1.7	19	2.0	200	2.0
51+	77	170	173	68	63	1000	1.2	1.4	15	2.0	200	2.0
Females												
11–14	46	101	157	62	46	800	1.1	1.3	15	1.4	150	2.0
15–18	55	120	163	64	44	800	1.1	1.3	15	1.5	180	2.0
19–24	58	128	164	65	46	800	1.1	1.3	15	1.6	180	2.0
25–50	63	138	163	64	50	800	1.1	1.3	15	1.6	180	2.0
51+	65	143	160	63	50	800	1.0	1.2	13	1.6	180	2.0
Pregnant					60	800	1.5	1.6	17	2.2	400	2.2
Lactating												
1st 6 months					65	1300	1.6	1.8	20	2.1	280	2.6
2nd 6 months					62	1200	1.6	1.7	20	2.1	260	2.6

* "Recommended Dietary Allowances," 10th revised edition © 1989, by the National Academy of Sciences, National Academy Press, Washington, D.C.

This table was prepared by the ESHA Research-Nutriton Systems, Salem, Oregon, with permission from the National Academy Press.

Definitions: mcg or μg = micrograms; 1,000 mcg = 1 mg; 1,000 mg = 1 gram. Thiamin = Vit B₁; Riboflavin = Vit. B₂; Niacin = Vit. B₃. RE (Retinol equivalents) = 1 μg Vitamin A from animal sources, or 6 μg of Vitamin A from B-carotene (plant sources). Vitamin D: 10 μg of Vitamin D (as cholecalciferol) = 400 IU (International Units); IUs are an older measure. Vitamin E: 1 mg of d-α-TE = 1α-TE (TE = tocopherol equivalents) Niacin (vit. B₃): NE (niacin equivalent) is 1 mg of niacin or 60 mg of dietary tryptophan. Also referred to as mg-NE.

Recommended Dietary Allowances (*continued*)

VIT. C MG	VIT. D μG	VIT. E ATE	VIT. K μG	CALCIUM MG	IODINE μG	IRON MG	MAGNE-SIUM MG	PHOS-PHORUS MG	SELE-NIUM μG	ZINC MG
Infants										
30	7.5	3	5	400	40	6	40	300	10	5
35	10	4	10	600	50	10	60	500	15	5
Children										
40	10	6	15	800	70	10	80	800	20	10
45	10	7	20	800	90	10	120	800	20	10
45	10	7	30	800	120	10	170	800	30	10
Males										
50	10	10	45	1200	150	12	270	1200	40	15
60	10	10	65	1200	150	12	400	1200	50	15
60	10	10	70	1200	150	10	350	1200	70	15
60	5	10	80	800	150	10	350	800	70	15
60	5	10	80	800	150	10	350	800	70	15
Females										
50	10	8	45	1200	150	15	280	1200	45	12
60	10	8	55	1200	150	15	300	1200	50	12
60	10	8	60	1200	150	15	280	1200	55	12
60	5	8	65	800	150	15	280	800	55	12
60	5	8	65	800	150	10	280	800	55	12
70	10	10	65	1200	175	30	320	1200	65	15
Lactating										
95	10	12	65	1200	200	15	355	1200	75	19
90	10	11	65	1200	200	15	340	1200	75	16

Iron: How to Get What You Need

There are many sources of iron, but it is absorbed by the body more efficiently from some foods than from others. Iron from animal foods (known as "heme" iron) is easily absorbed, but iron from plant sources (called "nonheme" iron) is more difficult to absorb. Rich sources of nonheme iron are dried beans, nuts, grains, and dried fruit.

Keep in mind that your iron absorption should be sufficient if your calcium and vitamin C intakes meet the RDAs. And to enhance the absorption of iron in animal foods, serve them in a meal that also contains plant foods. Cooking in a cast-iron skillet is another absorption booster. This is especially useful for acidic foods like tomatoes.

Note: Tea and coffee contain substances that inhibit iron absorption, so wait at least one hour after eating iron sources to drink these.

The body increases or decreases iron absorption according to its need, and absorbs iron more efficiently during periods of growth. The iron requirement is greatest for children, adolescents, and women of childbearing age.

Guidelines for Good Nutrition

Now let's put all the pieces of the nutrition puzzle together.

USE THE FOOD GUIDE PYRAMID

Until 1991, the United States Department of Agriculture recommended that Americans eat from four basic food groups: 1) breads, cereals, and grains; 2) meat, poultry, and fish; 3) milk and milk products; and 4) fruits and vegetables. In 1991, the USDA changed its recommendations to emphasize the importance of complex carbohydrates—fruits, vegetables, grains—and make them the basis of a healthy diet. You can see this clearly in the USDA's Food Guide Pyramid, which organizes the new food groups with the foods you should eat most at the base—the broadest part of the pyramid, and the foods you should eat least at the top—the smallest part of the pyramid.

Using the Food Guide Pyramid, it's easy to get the right foods in your meals and snacks every day. The pyramid has six components, with the suggested daily servings from each of the food groups. Plan your diet from the bottom up. At the base of the pyramid, the largest section includes the breads, cereals, rice, and pasta group—six to eleven servings a day. The next level is divided into two categories: three to five servings of vegetables and two to four servings of fruit.

**FOOD GUIDE
PYRAMID**

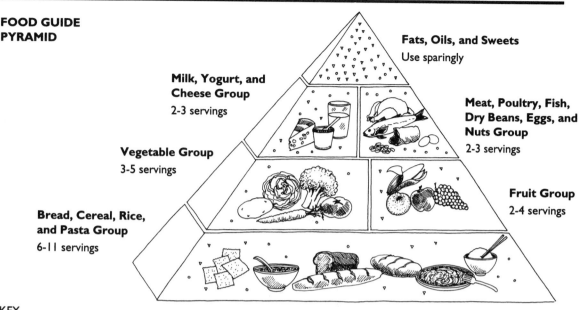

Fats, Oils, and Sweets
Use sparingly

**Milk, Yogurt, and
Cheese Group**
2-3 servings

**Meat, Poultry, Fish,
Dry Beans, Eggs, and
Nuts Group**
2-3 servings

Vegetable Group
3-5 servings

Fruit Group
2-4 servings

**Bread, Cereal, Rice,
and Pasta Group**
6-11 servings

KEY

∘ Fats

▿ Sweets

This ensures that you consume enough vitamins, minerals, and fiber. Your protein needs are met on the next level, also in two categories: two to three servings of milk, yogurt, and cheese, and two to three servings of meat, poultry, fish, dried beans, eggs, and nuts. The smallest level—at the tip of the pyramid—suggests using fat, oils, and sweets sparingly.

A Sample Menu

It's not difficult to get the right amount of servings of good-for-you grains, vegetables, and fruit. Here's a sample menu:

Breakfast	¾ cup orange juice
	1 cup cooked oatmeal topped with sliced peaches
Midmorning snack	1 apple
Lunch	Hummus (chick-pea spread flavored with tahini) or lean grilled chicken breast in a pita pocket, with lettuce, tomato, and cucumber
	1 cup skim milk
	1 banana
Afternoon snack	1 cup flavored yogurt
Dinner	Rice pilaf with shrimp (and peas, onions, red pepper)
	Cooked broccoli
	Green salad
	Dinner roll

Food Guide Pyramid for Adults

When you calculate your daily food intake, remember that serving sizes may vary with the food. For instance, a bagel may count as two servings, and a restaurant portion of pasta often measures 1 ½ cups (three servings). The number of servings you need depends on your daily calorie requirement. If you are trying to lose weight, eat the lesser number of suggested servings.

This chart was created by the United States Department of Agriculture/United States Department of Health and Human Services.

FOOD GROUP	SUGGESTED SERVINGS	SERVING SIZE
Vegetables	3 to 5 servings	1 cup raw leafy vegetables
		½ cup other vegetables, cooked or chopped raw
		¾ cup vegetable juice
Fruits	2 to 4 servings	1 medium apple, banana, orange
		1 cup melon or berries
		½ cup chopped, cooked or canned fruit
		½ to ¾ cup fruit juice
		¼ cup dried fruit
Breads, cereals, rice, and pasta	6 to 11 servings	1 slice bread
		½ cup pasta
		½ cup rice
		½ cup cooked cereal
		¾ cup (1 ounce) ready-to-eat cereal
		4 to 6 crackers
Milk, yogurt, and cheese	2 to 3 servings	1 cup milk or yogurt
		2 ounces processed cheese
		1 ½ ounces cheese: Cheddar, American, etc.
		½ cup cottage cheese
Meats, poultry, and fish	2 to 3 servings	2 to 3 ounces cooked lean meat, fish, dry beans, poultry, or fish (a portion the size of a deck of cards)
		½ cup cooked peas and beans, 1 egg, 1 ounce nuts (2 tablespoons peanut butter counts as 1 ounce of lean meat)

Don't Forget to Drink Enough Water!

Water plays a vital role in maintaining health. It's important for proper digestion, transporting nutrients to cells, and ridding the body of wastes. Drink at least six to eight glasses of water a day to maintain young, healthy-looking skin, improve digestion, and keep all cells functioning properly. If you exercise heavily, work in a dry environment, travel by air, or drink caffeinated beverages, you should drink even more water.

Power Foods

These foods pack a greater nutritional punch than others, so eat them often.

Broccoli. Delicious in everything from pasta salads to Chinese stir-fries, one serving of broccoli supplies 120 percent of the RDA of vitamin C and 35 percent of the RDA for vitamin A. It's also rich in calcium and folacin, and is a source of iron, fiber, and Vitamin E. Frequent consumption of broccoli and other cruciferous vegetables (like Brussels sprouts and cabbage) has been linked to reduced risk of cancer.

Sweet green and red peppers. Surprising, but true—peppers are even richer in vitamin C than oranges. They also supply vitamin A and iron.

Cantaloupe. One serving of cantaloupe provides 50 percent of the RDA for vitamin A and more than 100 percent of the RDA for vitamin C. Cantaloupe also supplies potassium and folic acid.

Kidney beans. You probably already know that beans are a great source of fiber, but did you know that a single serving of kidney beans (as in one cup of chili) also supplies a healthy dose of magnesium, iron, copper, zinc, and folic acid?

Potatoes. Cooked with its skin, the versatile potato provides 50 percent of the RDA for vitamin C, 18 percent of the RDA for iron, 50 percent of the RDA for potassium, and 18 percent of the RDA for niacin.

Nonfat yogurt. Many women find it hard to get enough calcium in their diets. Nonfat yogurt is a rare fat-free dairy source of this important mineral. Yogurt also contains riboflavin and vitamin B_{12}.

MANAGE YOUR WEIGHT WISELY

Being overweight affects more than your appearance. It increases the risk of high blood pressure, diabetes, and heart disease. If you need to lose weight, remember that many fad diets carry risks as well—anemia, vitamin deficiencies, and lack of energy and physical strength. And instead of solving your weight problem, unsound diets put you on a roller coaster of weight loss and gain.

Your best approach for long-term effects is gradual weight loss, achieved by a gradual change in your eating habits and food choices. The best place to start a diet is at your doctor's office. Your physician can weigh you, test your blood cholesterol level, discuss your family history of health problems, and advise you of the desirable weight for your height and age. He or she can also tell you how many calories you should take in each day to maintain or reduce your weight. Your doctor can recommend a suitable exercise program as well.

Then you can begin by cutting back on fat, stepping up your exer-

How to Keep Pounds Off

If you're not overweight, or if you have lost weight and want to avoid gaining it back, use these strategies:

☐ **Don't let more than five hours go between eating. Hunger is likely to lead you to overeat or to binge on high-fat, high-sugar snack foods.**

☐ **Don't save your biggest meal for the evening. Your body needs time and activity to burn off excess calories.**

☐ **Do drink at least six 8-ounce glasses of water a day. A glass before each meal will make you feel full, so you won't be as tempted to overeat.**

Recommended Number of Food Servings Based on Calorie Intake

Generally speaking, your weight is controlled by the number of calories in your diet, and how many calories you need depends on your age, gender, size, and amount of activity. Here are the number of servings from the food pyramid recommended for three different calorie levels.

	APPROX. 1,600	APPROX. 2,200	APPROX. 2,800
	NUMBER OF SERVINGS		
Bread Group	6	9	11
Vegetable Group	3	4	5
Fruit Group	2	3	4
Milk Group	2 to 3*	2 to 3*	2 to 3*
Meat Group (total ounces)	5	6	7
Total Added Sugars (teaspoons)	6	12	18

*Women who are pregnant or breast-feeding, teenagers, and young adults to age 24 need 3 servings.

cise level, and eating a variety of appealing and nutritious foods. The less deprived you feel, the more likely you are to keep to your weight-loss plan and avoid unhealthy binges.

CHOOSE FOODS LOW IN TOTAL FATS

Since fat contains more than twice the number of calories as the same amount of carbohydrates or protein, you can make an impressive dip in your daily calorie count by switching to low-fat or nonfat versions of foods you eat every day.

A healthy diet limits fat to a maximum of 30 percent of your daily calories. To figure the maximum number of grams of fat you should consume in a day, multiply your total calories by .30 (30 percent) and divide by 9 (each gram of fat has 9 calories). For example, 2,200 calories × .30 = 660 calories from fat divided by 9 = 73 grams of fat. If you want to visualize a gram of fat, hold a standard size paper clip—it weighs about 1 gram. Here's another image: a teaspoon of oil. It has 3.5 grams of fat.

Twenty-seven ways to cut the fat.

1. If you eat a lot of high-fat foods at one meal, go fat-free at another meal that same day.

2. Use nonstick cookware and vegetable oil sprays to minimize fat in cooking.

3. Emphasize steaming, roasting, and broiling as cooking methods. Avoid deep frying.

4. Cook more microwave recipes—they require less fat than conventional ones.

5. Do more ethnic cooking. These dishes tend to use smaller amounts of meats, more grains and vegetables.

6. Buy "Select" or "Choice" meat rather than "Prime." Trim all visible fat from meat before cooking.

7. Replace ground beef with ground turkey and chicken in recipes. For further fat savings, buy skinless white meat and have it ground for you.

8. Remove the skin from poultry before cooking, or at least before serving.

9. Make oil-free marinades and save half to use as basting sauce.

10. Select tuna packed in water rather than oil.

11. Simmer vegetables in broth, vegetable juice, and/or wine.

12. Use balsamic vinegar, tomato sauce, or lemon juice to flavor steamed vegetables.

13. Serve and cook with eggs in moderation. Use fat- and cholesterol-free egg substitutes in omelets, baking, and coating. Eggs contain 6 grams of fat each, with 274 mg cholesterol. Look for egg substitutes that contain 0 mg fat and 0 mg cholesterol.

14. Replace each whole egg in baking with 2 egg whites.

15. Remove butter, margarine, and peanut butter from the refrigerator to soften before spreading. You'll use less.

16. Sprinkle popcorn, pasta, or vegetables with a nonfat butter-flavor topping.

17. Use low-fat buttermilk or yogurt instead of sour cream, heavy cream, oil, or mayonnaise to give tang and velvety smoothness to dressings, sauces, and drinks.

18. Stir nonfat dry milk into soups and sauces for extra richness without the fat of cream.

(continued on page 374)

Grams of Fat in Common Foods

FOOD	NUMBER OF SERVINGS	GRAMS OF FAT PER SERVING
Bread, Cereal, Rice, and Pasta Group		
Eat 6 to 11 servings daily		
Bread, 1 slice	1	1
Hamburger roll, bagel, English muffin, 1	2	2
Tortilla, 1	1	3
Rice, pasta, cooked, 1/2 cup	1	Trace
Breakfast cereal, 1 ounce	1	*
Pancakes, 4-inch diameter, 2	2	3
Croissant, 1 large (2 ounces)	2	12
Doughnut, 1 medium (2 ounces)	2	11
Danish, 1 medium (2 ounces)	2	13
Cake, frosted, 1/16 average	1	13
Cookies, 2 medium	1	4
Pie, fruit, 2-crust, 1/6 8-inch pie	2	19
Vegetable Group		
Eat 3 to 5 servings daily		
Vegetables, cooked, 1/2 cup	1	Trace
Vegetables, leafy, raw, 1 cup	1	Trace
Vegetables, nonleafy, raw, chopped, 1/2 cup	1	Trace
Potatoes, scalloped, 1/2 cup	1	4
Potato salad, 1/2 cup	1	8
French fries, 10	1	8
Fruit Group		
Eat 2 to 4 servings daily		
Whole fruit: medium apple, orange, banana	1	Trace
Fruit, raw or canned, 1/2 cup	1	Trace
Fruit juice, unsweetened, 3/4 cup	1	Trace
Avocado, 1/4 whole	1	9
Milk, Yogurt, and Cheese Group		
Eat 2 to 3 servings daily		
Skim milk, 1 cup	1	Trace
Nonfat yogurt, plain, 8 ounces	1	Trace
Low-fat milk, 2 percent, 1 cup	1	5
Whole milk, 1 cup	1	8
Chocolate milk, 2 percent, 1 cup	1	5
Low-fat yogurt, plain, 8 ounces	1	4

FOOD	NUMBER OF SERVINGS	GRAMS OF FAT PER SERVING
Milk, Yogurt, and Cheese Group (*continued*)		
Low-fat yogurt, fruit, 8 ounces	1	3
Natural Cheddar cheese, 1½ ounces	1	14
Processed cheese, 2 ounces	1	18
Mozzarella, part skim, 1½ ounces	1	7
Ricotta, part skim, ½ cup	1	10
Cottage cheese, 4 percent fat, ½ cup	1	20
Ice cream, ½ cup	1	21
Ice milk, ½ cup	1	9
Frozen yogurt, ½ cup	1	4
Meat, Poultry, Fish, Dry Beans, Eggs, and Nuts Group		
Eat 5 to 7 ounces daily		
Lean meat, poultry, fish, cooked, 3 ounces	1	6
Ground beef, lean, cooked, 3 ounces	1	16
Chicken, with skin, fried, 3 ounces	1	13
Bologna, 2 slices, 1 ounce	1	16
Egg, 1, 1 ounce	1	5
Dry beans and peas, cooked, ½ cup, 1 ounce	1	Trace
Peanut butter, 2 tablespoons, 1 ounce	1	16
Nuts, ⅓ cup, 1 ounce	1	22
Fats, Oils, and Sweets		
Use sparingly		
Butter, margarine, 1 teaspoon	1	4
Mayonnaise, 1 tablespoon	1	11
Salad dressing, 1 tablespoon	1	7
Reduced-calorie salad dressing, 1 tablespoon	1	*
Sour cream, 2 tablespoons	1	6
Cream cheese, 1 ounce	1	10
Sugar, jam, jelly, 1 teaspoon	1	0
Cola, 12 fluid ounces	1	0
Fruit drink, ade, 12 fluid ounces	1	0
Chocolate bar, 1 ounce	1	9
Sherbet, ½ cup	1	2
Fruit sorbet, ½ cup	1	0
Gelatin dessert, ½ cup	1	0

*Check product label

Credit: United States Department of Agriculture/United States Department of Health and Human Services

Shopper's Guide to Fat Facts

To take charge of your fat intake, analyze the real fat content of the foods you buy. Remember that you are trying to limit fat intake to 30 percent or less of total calories over a period of time.

☐ **To determine the percentage of calories from fat per serving, look at labels. Multiply the number of grams per serving by 9 (because each gram of fat contains 9 calories) to get the total number of calories from fat per serving. Then divide the fat calories by the total calories to figure the percentage of fat.**

☐ **Don't be misled by label talk. "Light" or "lite" does not necessarily mean "low in fat." The same goes for "% fat-free" or "% less fat." "Light" bologna and turkey bologna marked "82% fat-free" get as much as 77 percent of their calories from fat—which can add up to 11 grams of fat per slice! Turkey franks labeled "40% less fat" still contain 10 grams of fat per serving. Even "2%" milk—though better than whole—gets 35 percent of its calories from fat.**

☐ **"Low-cholesterol" or "cholesterol-free" does not mean low-fat or fat-free. Foods with low or no cholesterol can still be high in dietary fat. Most vegetable oils, for example, are cholesterol-free but contain 100 percent fat. A teaspoon of cholesterol-free olive oil contains 13.5 grams of fat. And low-cholesterol cheese products may get over 70 percent of their calories from fat.**

☐ **Butter and margarine contain the same number of calories per tablespoon. For fewer calories buy diet margarines and whipped margarines and butters.**

19. Use evaporated skim milk in cream-based soups, stews, and salad dressings.

20. Use reduced fat, nonfat, or cholesterol-free mayonnaise and salad dressing for sandwiches and salads. Or, take a tip from Italian cooking: Use a light olive-oil dressing for pasta, tuna, and potato salads instead of mayonnaise.

21. Spoon, don't pour, gravies and sauces on foods.

22. Flavor foods with herbs, spices, vinegars, or fresh lemon juice in place of butter and sour cream.

23. Skim fat off all soup stocks and casseroles. For best results, make food several hours ahead. Refrigerate or freeze until the fat solidifies on the surface. It will be easy to scrape off. To remove fat from canned soups or broths, chill unopened cans and then take off the solidified fat.

24. Replace whole milk with skim milk or low-fat buttermilk in baking recipes.

25. Use reduced-fat cream cheese in cheesecakes or as a spread for bagels.

26. Bake one-crust pies to reduce calories and fat considerably in each slice of pie. For even less fat, make crumb crusts.

27. Make your own low-fat topping for fruit salad or sponge cake. Mix plain low-fat or nonfat yogurt with vanilla extract, spices, pureed fresh fruit, and/or no-sugar preserves. Add a bit of honey or sugar to taste, if desired.

CHOOSE A DIET WITH PLENTY OF VEGETABLES, FRUITS, AND GRAINS

The basis of healthy eating, these complex carbohydrates should make up approximately 60 percent of your diet each day.

Eat foods with adequate starch and fiber for maximum energy, vitamins and minerals, and proper bowel function. (For more on healthy ways to get fiber in your diet, see the section on fiber, below.)

Select fruits and vegetables in a variety of colors—these are your clues to different nutrients. Keep fresh and dried fruit on hand for snacks, but measure or count pieces of dried fruit. They are a concentrated source of calories! Another way to increase fruits in your diet: Add chunky applesauce, homemade pear sauce, or natural fruit juice in place of water when you cook hot cereals.

Remember that vegetables, fruits, and grain products are naturally low in fat, so keep them that way—free of creamy toppings and sauces. And with stews, casseroles, salads, and stir-fries, use grains, pasta, or vegetables as your main ingredient and meat as an accent.

MAKE SURE YOUR DIET IS RICH IN FIBER

"Eat a high-fiber diet" is advice we've been hearing for years. But what is fiber, and how much is enough?

Fiber is a nondigestible complex carbohydrate found in plant foods—fruits, vegetables and grains. It cannot be broken down by human digestive enzymes, and therefore it leaves you with a satisfied, full feeling (great for dieters!).

There are two kinds of dietary fiber, insoluble and soluble. *Insoluble fiber* aids swift and proper elimination and lowers the risk of alimentary and intestinal diseases, including some types of cancer and diverticulosis. Good sources of insoluble fiber are bean sprouts, corn, dried figs, peas, pumpkin, raspberries and wheat bran. *Soluble fiber* may help to reduce the level of cholesterol in the blood. Foods rich in soluble fiber are broccoli, brussels sprouts, carrots, grapefruit, oats, oranges, pears, and prunes.

The National Cancer Institute recommends 20 to 35 grams of fiber a

(continued on page 377)

Eat Your Vegetables

Here's the nutrition lowdown on some of the most popular vegetables. The cooking tips will help you preserve maximum flavor, color, and the all-important nutrients.

FOOD	NUTRITIONAL VALUE	COOKING TIPS
Asparagus	Iron and vitamins A and C; 23 calories per ½ cup.	Steam in a covered skillet over medium heat 5 to 10 minutes, until asparagus bends slightly.
Beans (green and yellow)	Vitamin A; 22 calories per ½ cup.	Steam or stir-fry until crisp-tender.
Beets	Vitamins A and C; 26 calories per ½ cup.	Microwave, grill, steam, or serve raw. Wash first; leave nutrient-packed skin intact; remove skin after cooking.
Bok Choy	Vitamin C and calcium; 15 calories per cup.	Stir-fry, sauté, or serve raw. Separate leaves from stem; stem takes longer to cook.
Broccoli	Vitamins A and C, calcium, fiber; 32 calories per stalk.	Steam, blanch (to crisp-tender), stir-fry, or microwave.
Carrots	Vitamin A; 70 calories per cup, sliced.	Steam, stir-fry, microwave, or serve raw.
Cauliflower	Vitamin C and iron; 30 calories per cup.	Steam, stir-fry, or microwave.
Cucumbers	Trace of vitamins and minerals; 32 calories each.	Best served raw. Scrub skin or peel if waxed.
Lettuce	Darker leaves contain vitamins A, C, and E; about 15 calories a head.	Best served raw.
Mushrooms	Trace of vitamins and minerals; 20 calories per cup.	Best served raw. May be sautéed or steamed.
Onions	Some vitamin C; 40 calories per dry-skinned onion; 9 calories per green onion.	Cook chopped onion, covered, to mellow flavor.
Peas	Protein, iron, vitamins A and C; snow peas: 40 calories per ½ cup; garden peas: 60 calories per ½ cup.	Stir-fry snow peas or blanch in boiling water 1 minute; hold blanched peas under cold running water to stop cooking process. Steam fresh peas.
Peppers (sweet)	Vitamins A and C, phosphorus, iron; one contains 15 calories.	Best raw, unpeeled; scrub if waxed. Also, steam or stir-fry.
Potatoes	Vitamins C and B₁, iron, protein; medium-size potato contains approximately 218 calories.	Best to cook (and serve) potatoes in skin. Bake, boil, or microwave.
Spinach	Vitamins A and C, iron, calcium; 14 calories per cup.	To retain its color, cook in nonaluminum pan. Steam, sauté, or microwave.
Zucchini	Vitamins A and C; 9 calories per ½ cup.	Serve raw, unpeeled. Steam; stir-fry; sauté; or microwave.

day. Unfortunately, most Americans get only about 11 grams daily. But if you eat the recommended three to five servings of vegetables, two to three servings of fruit, and six to eleven servings of bread, cereals, and grains, you'll be well on your way to a diet with sufficient fiber. To translate this into specific foods, here's what you might have on a typical day: a bowl of 100 percent bran cereal, a banana, three slices of high-fiber bread, one serving of Brussels sprouts, one serving of carrots, one serving of corn, one apple, and one serving of brown rice.

If your diet is low in fiber, increase the amount gradually to give your digestive system time to adjust. Too much fiber too quickly may cause blockage in the intestines, interfere with nutrient absorption, or cause bloating and gas.

To increase dietary fiber:

☐ Switch to a cereal with at least 5 grams of fiber per serving.

☐ Make muffins with whole-grain instead of refined flour; add whole-kernel corn to corn muffins.

☐ Use a little whole-wheat flour in recipes instead of all white flour. Start with ⅓ whole-wheat flour and ⅔ white flour. Gradually increase the proportion of whole-wheat to white flour to an amount your family enjoys.

☐ Top baked potatoes with a vegetable-nonfat sour cream blend. Some suggestions: chopped cooked broccoli, onions, or cabbage.

☐ Replace white-bread crumb toppings on casseroles with whole-grain cracker crumbs, toasted rolled oats, or crushed whole-grain cereals, such as shredded wheat.

☐ Add chopped prunes and dates to a side dish of rice pilaf, kasha, wheat berries, or couscous. Sprinkle with a dash of ground cinnamon.

☐ Serve side dishes made with dried peas and beans or lentils at least once a week. Make them Boston baked beans style, sweet with molasses or maple syrup, or give them an Indian accent with toasted spice mixtures. (Toast curry powder, cumin powder and chili powder for 5 minutes in a 350°F. oven or in a dry nonstick pan on top of the stove over low heat.)

USE SUGARS IN MODERATION

Where there's sugar, there's usually butter and cream! So in addition to calories, you're getting saturated fat. If you get a craving for something sweet, reach for a piece of fruit. On those occasions when only candy will do, avoid the kinds made with fats and dairy products. Remember, though, that hard candies promote tooth decay because they remain in the mouth so long. It's best to develop a low-sugar palate and encourage your children to do the same. And always brush your teeth after eating sweets.

To cut down on sugar:

□ Sweeten iced tea with natural fruit juices. Pineapple, grape, and apple juice are only a few of the possibilities.

□ Concoct your own "house blend" punch with natural juices. Keep it in the refrigerator to reduce snacking on sugary soft drinks. For fizz, add no-sodium seltzer just before serving.

□ Make frozen treats from your house punch or unsweetened fruit juices. Pour them into plastic freezer cups.

□ Blend caffeine-free herb teas with apple and citrus juices for a refreshing drink.

□ Buy unsweetened canned or frozen fruits and fruits packed in water or natural juice, not syrup.

□ Use the juice from unsweetened canned fruit for ice cubes.

□ Substitute juice from canned fruits or frozen juice concentrates for part of the liquid in a muffin, quick bread, or cake recipe. You will then need less sugar than called for.

□ Use purees of fresh, frozen, or canned-in-natural-juice fruits for dessert sauces.

USE SALT AND SODIUM IN MODERATION

Your body can't function without sodium. It regulates the balance of water in your tissues, is necessary for muscle contraction, and helps maintain normal blood pressure. However, too much sodium may lead to high blood pressure. How much sodium is acceptable in a healthy diet? The National Research Council recommends no more than 3,300 mg a day.

The best way to cut down on sodium is to limit table salt and high-sodium processed foods.

Other ways to reduce sodium are

□ Gradually accustom yourself and your family to a lower salt level. For starters, switch to a saltshaker with tiny holes. Even if you automatically shake salt on your food before tasting it, less salt will come out. Next, get in the habit of tasting food before you salt it.

□ Substitute freshly ground pepper or no-salt herb-and-spice blends, which use dehydrated herbs, onion, and garlic mixed with pepper and other spices.

□ Use lemon juice, vinegar, and grated citrus peel to enhance the natural flavors in food.

□ Get into the habit of rinsing canned foods, such as shrimp, beans, and corn, with water immediately after opening.

□ Limit consumption of high-sodium foods: pickles, soy sauce, ketchup, relishes, smoked or cured meats, and cheese.

□ Use low-sodium versions of products ordinarily very high in sodi-

Translating Sodium Labels

WHAT IT SAYS:	WHAT IT MEANS
Unsalted	No salt used in processing
Sodium-free	5 mg or less sodium per serving
Very low sodium	35 mg or less sodium per serving
Low sodium	140 mg or less per serving
Reduced sodium	Compared to the food it replaces, the sodium content is reduced by at least 75 percent

um: soy sauce, baking powder, cheese, chicken or beef broth, canned soups, and canned vegetables and vegetable juices.

IF YOU DRINK ALCOHOLIC BEVERAGES, DO SO IN MODERATION

Because alcoholic beverages supply little or no nutrition, they are a source of empty calories. Teenagers, individuals who drive or operate machinery, women who are trying to conceive, and pregnant women should not drink alcohol.

Alcohol can alter the effects of medicines, so don't consume alcohol when you are taking medication. Even aspirin has been shown to enhance the adverse effects of alcohol.

CHOOSE HEALTHY SNACKS

To eat well, you don't have to stop eating between meals. In fact, snacking is recommended by nutritionists and doctors. It's what you eat that counts. A well-chosen snack keeps you right on your healthy track and helps supply you with enough energy to get through the day.

The key to sensible snacking is to plan ahead, so you won't settle for high-fat high-sodium packaged snacks later when hunger strikes. Take food along when you leave the house. Apples and bananas travel well, as do melons cut in cubes, berries, seedless grapes, a peach or plum in a plastic container. A wedge of low-fat cheese with your fruit will add protein and calcium.

Raw vegetables—carrots, celery, green and red peppers, cauliflower, cucumbers—cut up and bagged in plastic are also good for toting. Or keep them in your refrigerator. If munching on plain vegetables doesn't appeal to you, whip up a low-fat dip of cottage cheese and herbs in the blender.

Popcorn makes an excellent snack, without the butter and oil. A cup of plain popcorn contains only 54 calories. For flavorings, use chili powder, curry powder, garlic powder, or low-sodium soy sauce.

When you are in the mood for something hot and soothing, try soup. Low-sodium bouillon is very low in calories and fat (1 cup of chicken bouillon has 22 calories and just a trace of fat) and can be wonderfully satisfying, especially if you add a handful of fresh snow peas, shredded Chinese cabbage, or other greens. You can also pack the soup in a thermos for snacking at work.

Crackers, toasts, and chips are convenient—but frequently too high in fat and sodium. Read labels, and stay clear of foods higher than 30 percent fat. An easy way to do this is to avoid products with more than 3 grams of fat per 100 calories. And don't forget: beware of the "no cholesterol" banner. It's the total *fat content* that counts. Many brands now put out low-fat and low-sodium versions of their popular varieties. You get a slightly better health profile with little or no noticeable change in flavor.

When thinking of "go-withs" for cheeses, spreads, and dips there are many healthful choices to replace high-fat chips. Flat breads and zwieback are low in fat and sodium. Some brands of corn chips now offer baked instead of fried versions. Pretzels, virtually fat-free, are a crunchy base for low-fat cheese. (And if you buy the unsalted pretzels, you save on sodium, too.) Bread sticks can be served with dips. Bagel chips are another alternative, but be careful. Although bagels are low in fat and salt, bagel chips are often laden with them. Again, be sure to check the label.

pecial Nutritional Needs

FOOD ALLERGIES

An allergy is a sensitivity to a particular substance known as an allergen. The allergen may be harmless to most people, but in sensitive people it can cause nausea, abdominal pain, and diarrhea—symptoms that resemble food poisoning. Other symptoms are rashes, itching, nasal congestion, a tight feeling in chest and throat, wheezing resembling an asthmatic attack, migraine headaches, weakness, and tingling.

Common causes of allergic responses are corn, milk and other dairy products, nuts, peanuts, soybeans, and wheat. Monosodium glutamate (MSG), food coloring, eggs, citrus oils in fruit peels, chocolate, beef, chicken, rye, peas, fish, shellfish, and sulfite preservatives used on fresh vegetables, dried fruit, and in wine are other common allergens.

To avoid your allergy triggers, read food labels carefully. Unfortunately, reading labels doesn't guarantee protection. Although labeling laws require manufacturers to list ingredients added directly to foods, chemicals added during processing or packaging do not have to be listed. Nor do ingredients in a standard formula used by many manufacturers—mayonnaise, for example. Another exception: specific information, such as "corn-based" or "wheat-based" on a vinegar label.

What can you do? Consult your physician for advice on brands that don't contain your specific triggers. You can also look in your local health food store. Many carry brands specially labeled for people with allergies.

LACTOSE INTOLERANCE

Lactose intolerance is the inability to digest lactose, or milk sugar. Some people have a genetic inability to make enough of the enzyme lactase, which breaks down milk sugar. For others, an illness—even the flu—can temporarily disrupt lactase production. Many people lose the ability to produce lactase as they age.

The common symptoms of lactose intolerance are gas, diarrhea, and stomach cramps. These can occur after eating or drinking dairy products.

Fortunately, if you are lactose intolerant, you don't have to avoid dairy products, which are such abundant sources of calcium, vitamins A and D, riboflavin, and protein. Low-lactose milk, cottage cheese, and ice cream contain a form of lactase that breaks down the lactose before you eat it. You can also buy the enzyme in liquids and powders, which you add to milk, or in chewable tablets and pills, which you take before consuming milk products. Yogurt and milk with the bacteria acidophilus added may be more easily digested by people with a mild lactose intolerance. The bacteria reduces the effects of lactose in the milk.

Aged cheeses, such as Swiss and Cheddar, have lower lactose levels than other cheeses, and do not usually affect the lactose intolerant.

VEGETARIAN DIETS

From the humble Tex-Mex bean dip and corn chip appetizer to the celebrated vegetable stew and couscous of the Middle East, meatless cooking follows the Food Guide Pyramid's recommended emphasis on vegetables, breads, cereals, and grains.

A major benefit of reducing meat consumption and eating more vegetables and grains is a lower fat intake. And if you include dairy foods in your diet, there is little risk of nutritional deficiencies. In fact, the average vegetarian may be healthier than the average meat eater. Studies show that vegetarians have lower cholesterol levels; fewer incidences of colon, prostate, and breast cancer; lower blood pressure; and lower weight than meat eaters of the same socioeconomic level and age group.

Some vegetarians eliminate meat entirely but eat eggs and/or dairy products; others exclude only "red meat," such as beef, lamb, and pork, but eat poultry and fish. The strict vegans eat no foods of animal origin.

Vegans have special dietary needs, because as discussed in the section "Proteins," plants are not complete proteins. So vegans must combine foods that will create complete proteins that the body can use, such as rice with beans.

Getting enough calcium, iron, B vitamins, vitamin D, and trace nutrients is also a problem, especially for women, who are at risk for calcium and iron deficiencies. If you are considering switching to a vegetarian diet, read up on nutrition first to make certain your food choices will be nutritious. You may also want to consult your doctor or nutritionist.

Healthy Ideas for Meals

These suggestions cover the bases, from breakfast to eating out.

START THE DAY RIGHT

☐ Serve whole, fresh fruit instead of juice. It has more fiber and is more filling.

☐ Have a main-dish fruit salad: combine fresh and canned fruits (packed in natural juices) with chopped-up dried fruit. Add a little nonfat yogurt or cottage cheese.

☐ Make fewer egg yolks go further in an omelet or frittata by using a few extra egg whites and lots of steamed vegetables.

☐ Make your own healthy pancakes and waffles ahead and freeze for quick heating in the microwave. Use whole-grain ingredients and nonstick vegetable cooking spray to grease the griddle or waffle iron. Instead of butter or syrup, use a fruit topping. Make a chunky puree of apples and strawberries in the blender; freeze in small plastic containers. Reheat pancakes and waffles with the topping.

☐ Turn French toast into a crunchy, low-fat, high-fiber treat. Dip whole-grain bread in a mixture of egg substitute and wheat germ. Fry in a skillet greased with nonstick cooking spray. Dust lightly with confectioners' sugar.

MAKE OVER YOUR BROWN-BAG LUNCH

☐ Start making school lunch sandwiches with whole-grain bread. Since kids often resist a change in their sandwich bread, begin by pairing one slice of white with one slice of whole-grain. Or make a couple of fun-to-eat sandwiches with smaller sizes of bread.

☐ For a light lunch that will still satisfy you, carry a package of low-sodium soup mix to reconstitute at work. Serve it with low-fat cheese and unsalted whole-grain crackers.

☐ Keep sandwiches healthy with low-sodium and extra-lean deli meats and cheese, low-fat or cholesterol-free mayonnaise, and sugarless, all-fruit spreads instead of jellies and jams on peanut butter.

☐ Toss a macaroni or tuna salad (made with water-packed tuna) with nonfat plain yogurt instead of mayonnaise. Pack a container of cleaned vegetables, such as radishes, cucumbers, cabbage, zucchini, and red and green peppers, to add for crunch.

☐ Make a cholesterol-free egg salad: Combine chopped cooked egg whites, cholesterol-free mayonnaise, chopped celery and red pepper, a dash of dry mustard, and freshly ground black pepper.

DROP THE FAT OUT OF DINNER

☐ Freeze cooked brown rice and whole-wheat pasta in family-size portions. In the morning, remove a package and place it in the refrigerator to thaw. You now have a perfect base for quick stir-fries and Italian-style sauces. Or make a salad by tossing the rice or pasta with trimmed leftover meat, cold grilled vegetables, and fat-free dressing enhanced with chopped fresh herbs.

☐ Start salads ahead. Shred cabbage and carrots and store in the refrigerator for up to three days in a plastic bag. Toss with fat-free salad dressing or cholesterol-free mayonnaise just before serving.

☐ Try turkey sausage, a tasty alternative to pork sausage, in the family's favorite dishes. For spaghetti sauce, crumble and "brown" sausage in a nonstick skillet, drain off the fat, add a can of unsalted tomato sauce, and season with Italian herbs or chili powder. For chili, stir a can of drained, rinsed pinto or kidney beans into the meat-and-sauce mixture; season with chili powder.

☐ Mix olive oil and lemon juice and brush on fish and chicken before broiling.

□ For a frozen dessert, whirl frozen strawberries and/or banana slices in the blender until thick. Or make a parfait by layering frozen nonfat yogurt with crumbled graham crackers or Fig Newtons.

DINE OUT FOR HEALTH

□ Read through the entire menu before ordering. Stick to dishes that are broiled, grilled, roasted, steamed, or poached. Indicate clearly that you want them cooked and served without butter, and that any sauce should be served on the side.

□ Ask for freshly ground pepper and lemon slices to squeeze on salads and vegetables—even works for corn on the cob!

□ Order fresh fruit for dessert, or, if you have skimped on fat in your other meals, share the most tempting dessert with everyone at the table.

Nutrient Values of Common Foods

FOOD		CALORIES	PROTEIN (G)	FAT (G)	CARBO-HYDRATE (G)	SODIUM (MG)	CHOLES-TEROL (MG)
Fruits							
Apple	fresh, 1 medium	81	Trace	1	21	0	0
Applesauce	unsweetened, 1 cup	105	Trace	Trace	28	5	0
	sweetened, 1 cup	194	Trace	Trace	51	8	0
Apricots	fresh, 3 medium	51	1	Trace	12	1	0
	dried, raw, ½ cup	155	2	Trace	40	7	0
	dried, cooked without sugar, 1 cup	213	3	Trace	55	8	0
	dried, cooked with sugar, 1 cup	306	3	Trace	79	8	0
Banana	fresh, 1 medium	105	1	1	27	1	0
Blackberries	fresh, 1 cup	75	1	1	18	0	0
	frozen, unsweetened, 1 cup	97		1	24	2	0
Blueberries	fresh, 1 cup	82	1	1	20	9	0
	frozen, sweetened, 1 cup	187	1	Trace	50	3	0
Cantaloupe	½ medium	93	2	1	22	24	0
Casaba Melon	1 wedge	43	1	Trace	10	20	0
Cherries	raw, sweet red, 1 cup	104	2	1	24	0	0
	canned, sweet, in light syrup, 1 cup	169	2	Trace	44	8	0
Coconut	fresh, shredded, 1 tablespoon	18	Trace	2	1	1	0
Currants	dried, 1 cup	408	6	Trace	107	12	0
Dates	dried, 4	91	1	Trace	24	1	0
Figs	dried, 1 medium	48	1	Trace	12	2	0
	fresh, 1 medium	37	Trace	Trace	10	1	0
Grapefruit	fresh, ½ medium	38	1	Trace	10	0	0
Grapes	American, fresh, green seedless, Delaware, etc., 1 cup	58	1	Trace	16	2	0
	European, fresh, Thompson, Emperor, etc., 1 cup	114	1	1	28	3	0
Honeydew Melon	1 wedge	45	1	Trace	12	13	0
Kiwifruit	1 medium	46	1	Trace	11	4	0
Lemon	1 medium	22	1	Trace	12	3	0
Lime	1 medium	20	Trace	Trace	7	1	0
Mango	fresh, 1 whole	135	1	1	35	4	0
Nectarine	fresh, 1 medium	67	1	1	16	0	0

(table continues)

Nutrient Values of Common Foods (*continued*)

FOOD		CALORIES	PROTEIN (G)	FAT (G)	CARBO-HYDRATE (G)	SODIUM (MG)	CHOLES-TEROL (MG)
Fruits (*continued*)							
Orange	fresh, peeled, 1 medium	69	1	Trace	17	0	0
Papaya	fresh, 1 medium	119	2	Trace	30	9	0
Peaches	fresh, peeled, 1 medium	56	1	1	15	0	0
	dried, uncooked, 1 cup	382	6	1	98	11	0
	canned, without sugar, 1 cup	59	1	Trace	15	7	0
Pears	fresh, unpeeled,						
	1 medium	98	1	1	25	0	0
	dried, 1 medium	92	1	Trace	24	2	0
Pineapple	fresh, 3½- by ¾-inch slice	41	Trace	Trace	10	1	0
	canned in juice, 1 cup	150	1	Trace	39	3	0
Plum	fresh, 1 medium	36	1	Trace	9	0	0
Pomegranate	fresh, 1 medium	105	1	Trace	26	5	0
Prunes	dried, pitted, 10 medium	201	2	Trace	53	3	0
Raisins	seedless, 1 cup	435	5	1	115	17	0
Raspberries	fresh, 1 cup	60	1	1	14	0	0
Rhubarb	cooked with sugar, 1 cup	278	1	Trace	75	2	0
Strawberries	fresh, whole, 1 cup	48	1	1	11	2	0
	frozen, sweetened, sliced, 1 cup	246	1	Trace	66	8	0
Tangerine	fresh, peeled, 1 medium	37	1	Trace	9	1	0
Watermelon	1 slice	152	3	2	35	10	0
Vegetables							
Alfalfa Sprouts	Raw, 1 cup	10	1	Trace	1	2	0
Artichoke	1 medium	53	3	Trace	12	79	0
Asparagus	fresh, cooked spears,						
	4 medium	15	2	Trace	3	2	0
	frozen, cooked cut and tips, 1 cup	52	6	Trace	10	44	0
Avocado	fresh, ½ medium	162	2	15	7	10	0
Beans, fresh	green, cooked, ½ cup	22	1	Trace	5	2	0
	lima, cooked, ½ cup	105	6	Trace	20	14	0
	sprouted mung, raw, ½ cup	16	2	Trace	3	3	0
	wax, cooked, ½ cup	22	1	Trace	5	2	0
Beans, frozen	green, cooked, 1 cup	35	2	Trace	8	18	0

Nutrient Values of Common Foods (*continued*)

FOOD		CALORIES	PROTEIN (G)	FAT (G)	CARBO-HYDRATE (G)	SODIUM (MG)	CHOLES-TEROL (MG)
Vegetables (continued)							
Beets	canned, diced, 1 cup	53	2	Trace	13	401	0
	fresh, cooked, 1 cup	53	2	Trace	11	83	0
Broccoli	cooked, 1 large stalk	52	5	1	10	20	0
Brussels Sprouts	fresh, cooked, 1 cup	61	4	1	14	33	0
Cabbage	raw, shredded, 1 cup	17	1	Trace	4	13	0
	cooked, 1 cup	32	1	Trace	7	29	0
Carrots	raw, 1 medium	31	1	Trace	7	25	0
	fresh, cooked, sliced, 1 cup	70	2	Trace	16	103	0
Cauliflower	fresh, cooked, 1 cup	30	2	Trace	6	7	0
	frozen, cooked, 1 cup	34	3	Trace	7	32	0
Celery	raw, 1 stalk	6	Trace	Trace	1	35	0
Cilantro	fresh, 1/2 cup	2	Trace	Trace	Trace	2	0
Collards	frozen, cooked, 1 cup	61	5	1	12	85	0
	raw, 1 cup	35	3	Trace	7	52	0
Corn	fresh, cooked, 1 ear	77	3	1	17	14	0
	frozen, cooked, 1 cup	133	5	Trace	34	8	0
Cucumber	raw, 1 medium	31	1	Trace	7	5	
Eggplant	boiled, 1 cup	27	1	Trace	6	3	0
Endive	1 cup	9	1	Trace	2	11	0
Lettuce	Boston or Bibb, 1 cup	10	1	Trace	2	5	0
	iceberg, 1 cup	10	1	Trace	2	5	0
	romaine, 1 cup	9	1	Trace	1	4	0
Mushrooms	canned, 1 cup	37	3	Trace	8	624	0
	fresh, 1 cup	18	1	Trace	3	3	0
Onions	raw, chopped, 1 cup	52	2	Trace	12	3	0
	green, raw, chopped, 1 cup	25	2	Trace	6	4	0
Mint	fresh, 1/2 cup	5	Trace	Trace	10	NA	0
Parsley	10 sprigs	3	Trace	Trace	1	4	0
Parsnips	fresh, cooked, sliced, 1 cup	109	2	Trace	26	13	0
Peas	green, fresh, cooked, 1 cup	134	9	Trace	25	5	0
	green, frozen, cooked, 1 cup	125	8	Trace	23	139	0
Peppers	green, 1 medium	19	1	Trace	4	2	0
	red, 1 medium	19	1	Trace	4	2	0
	hot, chili, green, canned, 1 cup	34	1	Trace	8	830	0

(table continues)

Nutrient Values of Common Foods *(continued)*

FOOD		CALORIES	PROTEIN (G)	FAT (G)	CARBO-HYDRATE (G)	SODIUM (MG)	CHOLES-TEROL (MG)
Vegetables (*continued*)							
Potatoes	baked in skin, I medium	220	5	Trace	51	16	0
	boiled in skin, sliced, I cup	136	3	Trace	31	6	0
Radishes	raw, 10 medium	8	Trace	Trace	2	11	0
Spinach	raw, I cup	12	2	Trace	2	44	0
	frozen, cooked, I cup	53	6	Trace	10	163	0
Squash	summer, fresh, cooked, I cup	36	2	Trace	8	2	0
	winter, baked, I cup	129	4	1	32	2	0
Sweet Potatoes	fresh, baked in skin, 4 ounces	117	2	Trace	28	11	0
Tomatoes	raw, I medium	23	1	Trace	5	10	0
	canned, I cup	48	2	1	10	391	0
	paste, 1/4 cup	55	2	1	12	517	0
	sauce, 1/2 cup	37	2	Trace	9	738	0
Turnips	steamed, cubes, I cup	28	1	Trace	8	78	0
Watercress	I cup	4	1	Trace	Trace	14	0
Legumes, Nuts, and Seeds							
Almonds	whole, shelled, I cup	766	26	68	27	14	0
	slivered, shelled, I cup	795	27	70	28	15	0
Beans, canned	red kidney, I cup, includes liquid	207	13	1	38	888	0
Beans, dry	chick-peas, cooked, I cup	269	15	4	45	11	0
	lentils, cooked, I cup	230	18	1	40	4	0
	lima, cooked, I cup	105	6	Trace	20	14	0
	navy or pea, cooked, 1/2 cup	129	8	1	24	1	0
	red kidney, cooked, 1/2 cup	112	8	1	20	2	0
Cashews	dry-roasted, salted, shelled, I ounce	163	4	13	9	181	0
Filberts	shelled, chopped, I cup	727	15	72	18	3	0
Peanut Butter	I tablespoon, smooth	95	5	8	3	76	0
Peanuts	dry-roasted, salted, shelled 1/4 cup	203	9	18	8	317	0
	dry roasted, unsalted, shelled, 1/4 cup	203	9	18	8	0	0
Pine Nuts	shelled, I ounce	146	7	14	4	1	0
Pumpkin Seeds	with shells, I cup	285	12	12	34	12	0

Nutrient Values of Common Foods (*continued*)

FOOD		CALORIES	PROTEIN (G)	FAT (G)	CARBO-HYDRATE (G)	SODIUM (MG)	CHOLES-TEROL (MG)
Legumes, Nuts, and Seeds (*continued*)							
Tahini (Sesame Paste)	1 tablespoon	89	3	8	3	17	0
Soybean Curd (Tofu)	regular, 1 ounce	22	2	1	1	2	0
	firm, 1 ounce	41	4	2	1	4	0
Sunflower Seeds	hulled, dry-roasted, salted, 1 cup	745	25	64	31	998	0
Walnuts	black, shelled, 1 cup	759	30	71	15	1	0
	regular, shelled, 1 cup	770	17	74	22	12	0
Grains and Grain Products							
Barley	dry, 3 ounces	303	10	1	64	8	0
Bulgur	dry, 1 ounce	102	2	Trace	23	1	0
Breads	bagel, 1 plain, 2 ounces	150	6	1	30	352	NA
	bagel, pumpernickel, 2 ounces	160	6	1	31	369	NA
	French, 1-inch slice	102	3	1	19	203	1
	hoagy, 1 medium 11½ inches	392	12	4	75	783	4
	Italian, ¾-inch slice	83	3	Trace	17	176	Trace
	oatmeal, 1 slice	70	2	2	13	185	NA
	pita, 1 small plain, 2 ounces	174	5	Trace	37	363	NA
	pita, 1 small whole-wheat, 2 ounces	167	6	1	35	364	NA
	pumpernickel, 1 slice	79	3	Trace	17	182	Trace
	raisin, 1 slice	66	2	1	13	91	1
	roll, hard, 1 medium	156	5	2	30	313	2
	rye, 1 slice	61	2	Trace	13	139	Trace
	white, enriched, 1 slice	65	2	1	12	122	1
	whole-wheat, 1 slice	56	2	1	11	121	1
Couscous	dry, 2 ounces	199	7	0	41	NA	0
Crackers	graham, 2	55	1	1	10	95	0
	melba toast, 3	50	2	0	10	NA	NA
Noodles	egg, enriched, cooked, 1 cup	200	7	2	37	3	50
Oats	dry rolled, uncooked, 1 cup	311	13	5	54	3	0
	oat bran, dry, 2 ounces	219	11	5	32	2	0
	oatmeal, cooked, 1 cup	145	6	2	25	2	0

(table continues)

Nutrient Values of Common Foods (*continued*)

FOOD		CALORIES	PROTEIN (G)	FAT (G)	CARBO-HYDRATE (G)	SODIUM (MG)	CHOLES-TEROL (MG)
Grains and Grain Products (*continued*)							
Pasta	enriched, cooked, I cup	155	5	I	32	I	0
Rice	brown, cooked, I cup	232	5	I	50	0	0
	white, cooked, I cup	223	4	Trace	50	0	0
Wheat	wheat bran, unprocessed, ¼ cup	42	2	Trace	7	I	0
	cream of wheat, I cup cooked	133	4	I	28	3	0
	wheat germ, I tablespoon	27	2	I	4	Trace	0
Fats and Oils							
Butter	lightly salted, I tablespoon	102	Trace	12	Trace	117	31
	sweet, I tablespoon	102	Trace	12	Trace	2	31
	whipped, I tablepoon	68	Trace	8	Trace	78	21
Lard	I tablespoon	116	0	13	0	0	12
Margarine	regular, I tablespoon	102	Trace	II	Trace	134	0
Oil, Vegetable	I tablespoon	120	0	14	0	0	0
Vegetable Shortening	solid, I tablespoon	113	0	13	0	0	0
Fish							
Anchovies	drained, 2-ounce can	95	13	4	0	1,651	25
Catfish	raw, 4 ounces	132	21	5	0	71	66
Caviar	black or red, I tablespoon	40	4	3	I	240	94
Clams	raw, shucked, I pint	336	58	4	12	254	154
Cod	broiled fillet, 4 ounces	119	26	I	0	88	62
Crab	canned, blue, I cup	134	28	2	0	450	120
Flounder	baked, 4 ounces	133	27	2	0	119	77
Halibut	broiled, 4 ounces	158	30	3	0	78	46
Lobster	cooked meat, I pound	445	93	3	6	1725	327
Salmon	Atlantic fillet, raw, 4 ounces	161	23	7	0	50	62
Sardines	canned in oil, drained, I ounce	59	7	3	0	143	40
Scallops	bay and sea, raw, 4 ounces	100	19	I	3	183	37
Shrimp	raw, ½ pound	241	46	4	2	336	345
Swordfish	broiled, 4 ounces	176	29	6	0	130	57

Nutrient Values of Common Foods (*continued*)

FOOD		CALORIES	PROTEIN (G)	FAT (G)	CARBO-HYDRATE (G)	SODIUM (MG)	CHOLES-TEROL (MG)
Fish (continued)							
Trout	raw, 4 ounces	168	24	8	0	59	66
Tuna	chunk, canned in oil, drained, 3 ounces	168	25	7	0	301	55
	chunk, canned in water, 3 ounces	111	25	Trace	0	303	36
	fresh, broiled, 4 ounces	208	34	7	0	57	55
Meat and Poultry							
Bacon	cooked, 2 medium slices	73	4	6	Trace	202	11
	Canadian, cooked, 1 ounce	52	7	2	Trace	433	16
Beef, braised, simmered, or pot roasted	chuck, stew meat, 3 ounces	301	23	23	0	50	84
	corned beef, 3 ounces	213	15	16	Trace	964	83
	hamburger, lean, broiled, 3 ounces	231	21	16	0	65	74
	liver, 3 ounces	137	21	4	3	60	331
	rib roast, 3 ounces	306	19	25	0	54	72
	sirloin steak, broiled, 3 ounces	277	20	21	0	51	71
Chicken, cooked	light meat, without skin, 4 ounces	196	35	5	0	87	96
	dark meat, without skin, 4 ounces	232	31	11	0	105	105
	livers, 4 ounces	178	28	6	1	58	716
Frankfurters	1 all-beef, 2 ounces	179	7	16	1	582	35
Lamb, cooked	leg, lean, roasted, 3 ounces	153	24	6	0	56	74
	loin chop, broiled, 3 ounces	183	26	8	0	71	80
	stew meat (shoulder), 3 ounces	287	18	23	0	45	83
Pork, cooked	ham, roasted, 3 ounces	151	19	8	0	1276	50
	boneless center loin chop, trimmed of fat, broiled, 3 ounces	196	27	9	0	66	83
	spareribs, braised (8 ounces as purchased)	351	26	27	0	82	107

(table continues)

Nutrient Values of Common Foods (*continued*)

FOOD		CALORIES	PROTEIN (G)	FAT (G)	CARBO-HYDRATE (G)	SODIUM (MG)	CHOLES-TEROL (MG)
Meat and Poultry (*continued*)							
Turkey, roasted	light meat, 3 ounces	131	25	2	0	58	59
	dark meat, 3 ounces	157	24	6	0	70	75
Veal, cooked	boneless, cutlet, fried, 3 ounces	155	28	4	0	69	112
	loin chop, rib, roasted, 3 ounces	143	22	6	0	87	108
	loin chop, braised, 3 ounces	185	28	7	0	76	138
Dairy							
Buttermilk	1 cup	98	8	2	12	257	10
Cheeses	American, 1 ounce	106	6	9	Trace	405	27
	blue, 1 ounce	100	6	8	1	395	21
	Camembert, 1 ounce	85	6	7	Trace	239	20
	Cheddar, 1 ounce	114	7	9	Trace	176	30
	cottage (4.5% milk fat) creamed, regular, 1 cup	216	26	9	6	851	32
	cottage, low-fat, 1 cup	163	28	2	6	918	9
	cottage, unsalted, dry curd, 1 cup	123	25	1	3	19	10
	cream cheese, 1 tablespoon	49	1	5	Trace	42	16
	Parmesan, grated, 1 tablespoon	23	2	2	Trace	93	4
	ricotta, whole milk, 1 ounce	49	3	4	1	24	14
	ricotta, part skim, 1 ounce	39	3	2	1	35	9
	Swiss, 1 ounce	107	8	8	1	74	26
Cream	half-and-half, 1 tablespoon	20	Trace	2	1	Trace	6
	heavy, 1 tablespoon	51	Trace	6	Trace	6	20
	light, 1 tablespoon	29	Trace	3	1	6	10
Eggs	white, 1 large	16	3	0	Trace	50	0
	yolk, 1 large	63	3	6	Trace	8	272
	whole, 1 large	79	6	6	1	58	272
Ice Cream	regular, 1 cup	269	5	14	32	116	60
	soft frozen, French vanilla, 1 cup	377	7	23	38	153	153
Ice Milk	1 cup	183	5	6	29	105	18
	soft, 1 cup	223	8	5	38	163	13

Nutrient Values of Common Foods (*continued*)

FOOD		CALORIES	PROTEIN (G)	FAT (G)	CARBO-HYDRATE (G)	SODIUM (MG)	CHOLES-TEROL (MG)
Dairy (continued)							
Milk	whole, 1 cup	149	8	8	11	120	34
	skim, 1 cup	86	8	Trace	12	127	5
	low-fat (2% fat), 1 cup	122	8	5	12	122	20
	condensed, sweet, 1 cup	982	24	27	166	389	104
	nonfat instant powder, 1 cup	243	24	Trace	35	373	12
Yogurt	plain, whole, 8 ounces	155	8	7	11	104	29
	plain, low-fat, 8 ounces	143	12	4	16	159	14
	plain, nonfat, 8 ounces	127	13	Trace	17	172	8
Beverages							
Alcohol	80 proof (gin, rum, vodka, whiskey), 1 jigger (1½ oz)	97	0	0	0	0	0
Apple Juice	canned, 1 cup	117	Trace	Trace	29	7	0
Beer	12-ounce can	146	1	0	13	18	0
Coffee	black, 1 cup	5	Trace	0	1	5	0
Cranberry Juice Cocktail	1 cup	144	0	Trace	36	5	0
Grapefruit Juice	fresh, 1 cup	96	1	Trace	23	3	0
	frozen, unsweetened concentrate, diluted, 1 cup	102	1	Trace	24	2	0
Grape Juice	canned or bottled, 1 cup	154	1	Trace	38	8	0
	frozen, sweetened concentrate, diluted, 1 cup	127	Trace	Trace	32	5	0
Lemon Juice	fresh, 1 tablespoon	4	Trace	0	1	Trace	0
	bottled, unsweetened, 1 tablespoon	3	Trace	Trace	1	3	0
Orange Juice	fresh, 1 cup	112	2	1	26	3	0
	canned, unsweetened, 1 cup	105	1	Trace	25	5	0
	frozen concentrate, reconstituted, 1 cup	112	2	Trace	27	2	0
Peach Nectar	canned, 1 cup	124	1	Trace	35	17	0
Pineapple Juice	canned, unsweetened, 1 cup	140	1	Trace	35	3	0
Prune Juice	canned, 1 cup	182	2	Trace	45	10	0
Tea	brewed, 1 cup, unsweetened	2	0	0	1	7	0
Tomato Juice	canned, 1 cup	41	2	Trace	10	881	0

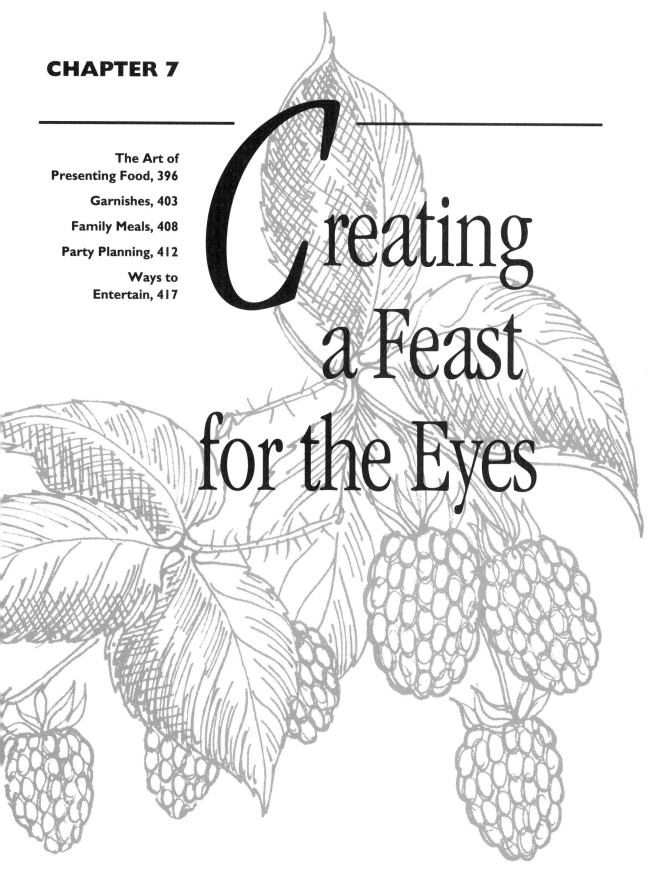

Creating a Feast for the Eyes

THERE'S MORE TO GOOD COOKING than making food that is tasty and nutritious. Food can be a feast for the eyes, too. So whether you are cooking for your family or planning a party for friends, if you take a little extra care, your food will be as beautiful to behold as it is delicious to eat.

The Art of Presenting Food

Food that's as pretty as a picture doesn't have to mean a lot of extra time in the kitchen or any special skills. Often the most effective touches are the easiest. Highlight the natural beauty of each dish. Keep garnishes simple, don't crowd the food on the plate, and use imaginative serving dishes and accessories.

MAKING BEAUTIFUL FOOD

The most important thing to remember when you put together a menu is to choose dishes that contrast in color and texture but complement one another in taste.

Color. "A plate of many colors" is an old axiom for a healthful meal, but it's also true for an eye-appealing meal. Since main dish entrées are frequently "neutral" in color—meat, fish, and poultry all tend to vary from white to beige to brown—try to include at least one vivid side dish on the plate: bright red tomatoes, yellow corn, lightly steamed broccoli. And two bright colors are even better!

VEGETABLES   If you are going to serve two vegetables, choose one green vegetable and either one yellow or one red, for variety in both nutrients and color. Acorn squash and peas will look more appealing on the plate than broccoli and spinach. Zucchini and tomatoes are another appealing combination. Succotash made with yellow corn and green lima beans is a favorite because it looks as good as it tastes.

Other colorful combinations include

☐ Roasted red peppers and corn.

☐ Sautéed zucchini and summer squash.

☐ Grilled onions with red and green pepper strips.

☐ Kabobs of cherry tomatoes, pearl onions, and zucchini chunks, grilled or broiled.

☐ Julienned strips of carrots, parsnips, and beets, sautéed together.

☐ Beets, with just about anything!

POTATOES AND GRAIN   Potatoes, rice, and other grains can be rather plain-looking. But you can make those side dishes more appealing with these simple tips.

☐ Brighten mashed potatoes by mixing in a handful of chopped fresh parsley or chives.

☐ Select tricolored pasta and toss it with butter and Parmesan cheese—or combine it with your vegetable for a side dish of interesting color, flavor, and texture contrasts.

☐ Combine white rice with brown rice or wild rice.

☐ Toss sliced potatoes with red pepper strips before oven roasting for great flavor and color contrast.

☐ Diced red peppers—fresh or roasted—can be tossed into just about any mixture to add color. They look lovely in rice or grain pilafs or risottos; mixed in with corn, peas, or any vegetable sauté; tossed into pasta or potato salads.

☐ Kasha varnishkas is a dish that combines kasha (buckwheat groats) with small pasta bowties. The dark grains and the pale pasta offer contrasts in taste, color, and texture—a winning combination.

☐ Cook peeled, seeded, and chopped tomatoes with rice, or add them uncooked to rice salad.

☐ Sprinkle a pinch of saffron powder into the cooking liquid of white rice for a lovely golden color and wonderful flavor.

☐ Add raisins to rice dishes for slightly sweet flavor.

☐ Many kinds of nuts—pistachios, cashews, almonds, walnuts, pine nuts—look and taste wonderful stirred into rice.

SALADS One of the easiest ways to introduce color into a meal is with a salad. These days salad greens run the gamut from traditional lettuces (in all shades of green) to the red leaf variety (tinged with brownish red on the curly edges) to radicchio (gorgeous purple-red leaves on a white stem). Other salad fixings, including herbs, fruits, vegetables, and edible flowers (see page 407 for a list), give you a wide variety of options—you can virtually paint a salad with any colors you choose, just by picking the appropriate ingredients. Some suggestions:

☐ Mixed-greens salad with radicchio, escarole, Boston lettuce, and snow peas.

☐ Citrus salad with grapefruit and orange sections tossed with endive, red onion, and watercress.

☐ Tomato salad with red and yellow tomatoes drizzled with olive oil and spiked with cracked black pepper and fresh basil.

☐ Three-pepper salad combining slices of various different-colored peppers.

☐ Winter root salad with shredded carrots, parsnips, and leeks mixed with strips of red pepper.

☐ Three-bean salad. The mélange of green, wax, and kidney beans are already colorful; add chopped-up red pepper and celery for even more interest.

□ Warm spinach salad. Rather than adding the traditional hard-boiled eggs, toss with a thinly sliced pear and crumbled bacon.

SAUCES, DRESSINGS AND ACCOMPANIMENTS   Don't forget sauces and dressings as other colorful options. They're great for disguising a plain piece of meat, fish, or poultry, and can also pep up vegetables. For instance:

□ Green sauces, usually herb-based (often dill) and garnished with more herbs, are lovely drizzled over fish. Or try a sauce of pureed spinach and serve with poached chicken breasts.

□ Citrus sauces, orange in color, are nice with "white" entrées, such as poached chicken or fish.

□ Mustard sauces, with their tart taste and yellow-brown tone, work with lamb, ham, chicken, fish, and vegetables.

□ Chutneys—such as strawberry chutney, mango chutney, and pear chutney—are excellent accompaniments to grilled or roasted meats and poultry.

Texture.   Just as you want to provide contrasts in color on the plate, there should be contrasts in texture. First, consider the texture of your entrée or main dish. If it is soft in texture—a soup, a tender stew, or pasta, for example—then match it with a crunchy green salad and a loaf of chewy whole-grain bread. A chewy steak might be matched with smooth mashed potatoes or pureed butternut squash and a crunchy salad. A juicy fruit salad might be the perfect match for roasted chicken (which is somewhat dry). Crispy potato pancakes are always good with braised meats—a nice change from potatoes cooked in the braising liquid.

Sometimes you can offer two textures within one dish. Flavorful rice pilaf garnished with crispy toasted pine nuts is irresistible. Again, the combination of white and wild rice offers pleasing contrasts of textures (smooth with chewy). Oriental stir-fries are wonderful because they combine the crunchy with the smooth: bright, crisp vegetables are tossed with tender morsels of chicken, fish, meat, or tofu. Indian raitas combine crunchy vegetables in smooth yogurt for a mouth-pleasing contrast to fiery curries.

Sizes and Shapes.   If you vary the sizes and shapes of different foods on one plate, you create greater eye appeal. Contrast round slices of beets, for example, with narrow spears of beans or asparagus, or julienned carrots.

Some vegetables have naturally elegant shapes—asparagus, snow peas, and whole green beans—and always look lovely on a plate. These long shapes can be matched with round slices (carrots, beets, potatoes, etc.) or purees (winter squash, spinach, etc.). Other vegetables present interesting shapes when cut. Rounds of okra or beets are usually pleasing and simple to do.

Simple Touches

Sometimes adding a burst of color and texture can be a very simple business. For example:

☐ **A handful of diced sweet red pepper gives a pasta salad added zing.**

☐ **Unskinned red potatoes turn your potato salad into something special.**

☐ **A sprig of fresh thyme or rosemary lends elegance to any dish.**

☐ **A lemon twist or julienned lemon peel sets off grilled fish beautifully.**

☐ **A sprinkle of paprika makes a wonderful garnish for baked or mashed potatoes.**

☐ **Grate fresh nutmeg over a favorite drink—eggnog, hot cocoa, cappuccino, café au lait, coffee with cream liqueur.**

If you have the time, cut meat, fish, and vegetables into unconventional shapes for striking presentations. For instance, roll-cut (see pages 186–187) carrots, asparagus, and turnips or use a channel knife (pages 139–140) to decoratively sculpt cucumbers, lemons, and carrots. Children, in particular, love having their vegetables cut into "fancy" shapes. Your family and guests will think you spent far more time than you actually did.

Serving dishes are important, too. Flea markets and tag sales are excellent places to find unusual baskets, platters and plates, glasses and bowls. You might even be able to find some graceful goblets—perfect for serving ice cream in a special way.

Most serving dishes fall into five general shapes—square, rectangular, round, oval, and faceted—and may be flat, shallow, or deep. Regardless of the shape, a few general guidelines should be remembered.

Choose metal platters with care—some metals react unfavorably with food. In general, it is best to avoid aluminum, copper, and pewter since these metals react with highly acidic or alkaline foods. Silver, too, will tarnish when it comes in contact with egg whites or acidic foods for more than an hour.

If you *must* use a metal serving dish, cushion the bottom with at least one layer of decorative greens, such as kale or lettuce, before the food is placed on top. Naturally, food served in pastry cases or on bread canapés comes with its own buffer to prevent moist fillings from coming in contact with the metal.

China, glass, crystal, lacquerware, and ceramic won't react with acid or alkaline foods. But remember that some pottery or ceramic pieces have lead glazes, so check them for safety before purchasing. When in doubt, don't use glazed pieces for serving or storing food.

When garnishing a platter remember that any food used as a border or part of the design should relate to the dish itself and be complementary to the recipe. For example, you might garnish an orange soufflé with orange slices or julienned orange rind. Whole berries and mint sprigs make an elegant touch for raspberry sherbet.

Framing food in a complete border or even a partial border will give it a larger and more dramatic appearance. The flat rims of platters are ideally suited for fans of lime slices or a row of decoratively cut zucchini.

When serving food in a deep-dished bowl, mound it so that it reaches above the rim and decorate the top with lemon or cucumber slices, sprigs of parsley, or minced fresh herbs. A light dusting of paprika or a sprinkling of chives or dill is always inviting.

Finally, never crowd food on plates and platters or the general effect will be messy rather than appealing.

PRESENTING SPECIFIC FOODS

Sliced cold cuts and cheese. Cold cuts and cheese are favorite quick lunch or supper fare for family or guests. Add marinated mushrooms, artichoke hearts, and roasted peppers from a delicatessen or gourmet shop to create a wonderful antipasto platter. Accompanied by bread sticks or crusty Italian bread, antipasto becomes an instant festive meal.

Arrange the sliced meat and cheese in any pattern you like—straight rows or curving serpentines, spirals, wagon wheels, or sunbursts. Cold cuts can be individually rolled into cylinders or cones, which will take up less space and, in addition, will add height.

Wooden carving boards, lacquerware, and glass platters are good choices for serving dishes.

Fruit and cheese. Fresh fruit and cheese are always a welcome addition to family gatherings and parties. You can serve them as hors d'oeuvres or dessert. Here are a few suggestions for presenting them.

☐ Cheeses should be brought to room temperature before serving.

☐ If the cheese is sliced, arrange in either straight or converging rows, or roll up the slices and arrange them in swirls, serpentines, or circles. Different colored cheeses will create a more vivid pattern.

☐ If the cheeses are served in wedges or rounds, put them on wooden boards, marble slabs, or in lined wicker trays. Try pairing cheeses with contrasting textures, colors, and flavors. For instance, match a hard cheese, such as Jarlsburg or Cheddar, with softer Boursin or St. Andre. Blue-veined cheeses, such as Stilton or Danish Blue, go well with goat cheese, such as Montrachet or Boucheron.

□ Vary the shapes on your cheese tray—wedge, cylinder, ball, and wheel. Some hard cheeses, such as Swiss or Cheddar, can be sliced and then cut into small shapes with a decorative cutter. They can also be served on skewers along with fruit.

□ The fruit itself should be equally attractive. Snip bunches of grapes into small clusters of three or four, then arrange into a large triangular cluster on the platter. Apple and pear slices, brushed with lemon juice, along with figs, kiwis, and assorted berries can be arranged decoratively in spirals and fans.

Crudités. No guest can resist a bright array of crisp fresh vegetables presented in a napkin-lined basket or on a platter. Make the crudité basket the centerpiece on your buffet or cocktail table.

Fill the bottom of a country basket or serving bowl with paper to act as stuffing and cover the paper with a large cloth napkin. Nestle clusters of fresh vegetables in the basket—sweet red pepper, celery, broccoli, and carrots—filling it to overflowing.

Generally, these vegetables are served raw, but a quick blanching of asparagus, broccoli, sugar snaps, and snow peas not only enhances the flavor but also brightens the color. Carrots, sweet pepper strips, radishes, cucumbers, celery, and most other vegetables are fine raw.

For a platter presentation of crudités, arrange them in a quirky geometric pattern.

Finger-size vegetables work best. They can be cut into numerous shapes with the aid of a channel knife, zester, or decorating knife. Store the vegetables, wrapped in plastic, in the refrigerator until ready to serve. Accompany the arrangement with one or two dipping sauces.

Thick dipping sauces—those with a sour cream, yogurt, mayonnaise, or peanut butter base—will cling to the vegetables better than thin sauces—with a buttermilk or soy sauce base, for example. Serve the dips in small bowls or in vegetable containers, such as pepper or squash cases or in hollowed heads of red or green cabbage. If you are using serving bowls, arrange flowers and sprays of fern and herbs around the bowls and set the bowls on bright napkins.

INVENTIVE VEGETABLE AND FRUIT PRESENTATIONS

Vegetable boats. Hollowed-out vegetables make excellent cases for stuffings and add a great deal to buffet tables and hors d'oeuvre trays. Various small squashes (butternut, zucchini, and pattypan), cabbages (green and red), and pumpkins make wonderful holders for other vegetables, dips, and even soups.

Oblong vegetables, such as eggplant, zucchini, and cucumber, can be halved lengthwise and stuffed. Trim a thin slice from the base so the shell will stand firmly. With a spoon or melon ball scoop, hollow out

Vegetable boat.

▶ **Channel knife,** 139
▶ **Decorating knife,** 140
▶ **Melon ball scoop,** 140
▶ **Zester,** 140

the center, leaving a shell sturdy enough to hold the filling. Shells may be left whole for larger presentations or cut into varying lengths and then filled.

Delicious stuffings include assorted vegetable purees, finely minced cooked vegetables, and meat bound with a light sauce or mayonnaise.

Sweet pepper cases.   No other vegetable comes in such as appealing array of colors! Cut off a third of the pepper either from the top or along the length and remove the seeds and ribs. If necessary, trim to flatten the base so that the pepper stands firmly. If trimmed, the bottom of the pepper may be lined with a thin slice of cucumber to make it leakproof. Combinations of cooked grains and pasta with vegetables, chicken, meat, or fish make mouth-watering stuffings.

Watermelon basket.   With the tip of a sharp knife, etch a 2-inch-wide band crosswise along the center of the watermelon, ending about one-third of the way down from the top. This is the handle of the basket.

Make a cardboard pattern for cutting the scalloped edge of the melon. The pattern should be in a half-moon shape large enough to make five or six scallops along each side of the melon and one at either end.

Put the pattern against one side of the melon about one-third of the way down from the top and etch the scallops into the rind until the pattern runs all the way around the melon. Now cut into the etched marks, using them as guides, right through the rind of the melon along the handle and the scalloped edges. Cut away the flesh and hollow out the melon in large pieces.

Cut the interior of the watermelon about 1 inch from the skin so that the walls are straight and cleanly defined. With a spoon, scoop out the excess pulp. (Reserve the melon pulp for the filling in combination with other fruits.)

Use the watermelon basket to hold mixed melon balls or fruit salad.

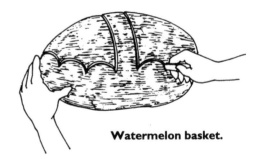

Watermelon basket.

Sweet pepper cases.

▸ **Melon ball scoop, 140**

*G*arnishes

Any dish is more appealing to the eye with the addition of the right garnish, and it doesn't need to be elaborate or difficult to make. Several radish roses added to a salad plate or decorative lemon slices used as a border around a seafood dish make an enticing display. Sometimes all it takes is a fresh herb sprig or a scattering of edible flowers.

TIPS FOR MAKING VEGETABLE GARNISHES

□ Most garnishes can be made two days ahead.

□ Green onions, leeks, cabbage, cauliflower, and mushrooms should be chilled until you are ready to cut them. After cutting, wrap vegetable and fruit garnishes and keep them chilled.

□ Soaking vegetable flowers in cold water causes them to swell, expand, and complete their shape. Prechill the water in the refrigerator. A quick soaking of vegetable flowers for 5 to 10 minutes in cold water will freshen them if they show signs of wilting.

□ If a particular garnish, such as a radish fan, does not want to "sit properly," sprinkling it with salt and letting it stand for several minutes will make it more cooperative. Salting food causes it to exude liquid, making it considerably softer than normal. Rinse off the salt as soon as the radish reaches the desired pliancy.

□ After 1 hour, vegetable flowers may need to be sprayed with a gentle mist of water to keep them looking fresh.

□ If you wish to reuse green onion brushes or radish roses, soak them in cold water for about 30 minutes before wrapping them in plastic and refrigerating them. Properly wrapped, they keep for several days in the refrigerator.

TOMATO GARNISHES

Tomato garnishes give a bright burst of color to meat platters, hors d'oeuvre trays, and salads.

Stuffed cherry tomatoes. Halve cherry tomatoes crosswise or cut off the top third. With a small melon ball cutter, scoop out the pulp and fill as desired. Cherry tomatoes are the ideal size for hors d'oeuvres and are beautiful filled with flavored mayonnaise, seafood or vegetable puree, or finely minced shellfish or chicken.

Stuffed tomato halves. Halve a tomato and with a melon ball cutter or teaspoon scoop out the pulp. Cut a thin slice off the base of each half so it will stand firmly. Fill with couscous and vegetables, diced cooked vegetables, or seafood salad.

*M*ulticolored Tomatoes Make a Big Splash

During the summer months, small yellow and orange baby tomatoes are available. Either variety, or both, look wonderful along with the red cherry tomatoes as an accompaniment to large rounds of cheese or on platters of cold poached seafood and chicken.

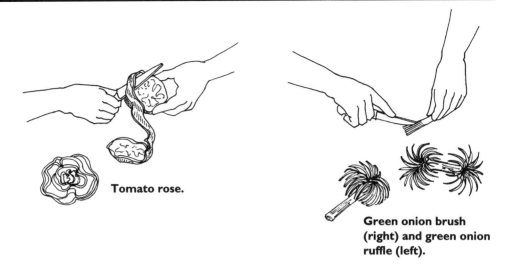

Tomato rose.

Green onion brush
(right) and green onion
ruffle (left).

Tomato rose.   With a small sharp knife, cut a base from the tomato but do not sever it. Continue cutting the skin in a gentle sawing
motion, forming a strip about ¾ inch wide. Leave a small amount of
pulp attached to the skin so that it won't tear, but be sure it is thin
enough to roll into a flower shape. Instead of moving the blade of the
knife, rotate the tomato into the blade and cut in a sawing motion.

Curl the strip of skin onto the base with the pulpy side on the inside
to form a rose.

Tomato crowns.   Tomatoes also may be formed into crowns. Simply follow the directions described on page 406 for orange crowns.

GREEN ONION GARNISHES

Lovely for garnishing meat, seafood, or chicken, as well as most Oriental dishes, edible green onion garnishes add color, shape, and texture
to a plate.

Green onion brushes.   Lay the white part of the onion (about 4
inches in length) on a cutting board and cut ¼ inch from the root end.
Insert the tip of a paring knife about 1½ inches from the root end and
make a straight cut through the root end. Give the onion a quarter turn
and continue to make parallel cuts all the way around the onion. Turn
the onion and make similar cuts along the other end, leaving a ½-inch
section in the center uncut. Soak in cold water until opened. Use to
garnish Oriental dishes and salads.

Green onion ruffles.   Lay the onion on a cutting board and cut ¼
inch from the root end. Using a long, sharp knife, shred the green top
by making lengthwise cuts about 4 inches long. Soak in cold water
until curled. These ruffles are beautiful with cold seafood and meat as
well as salads and may also be included in a crudité basket.

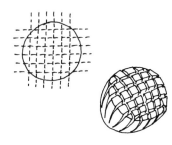

Radish pompon.

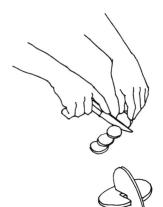

Radish jack.

▸ **Melon ball scoop, 140**
▸ **Radish decorator, 140**

RADISH GARNISHES

Radish garnishes hold up extremely well and can be prepared several days in advance.

Radish pompons. With a paring knife, trim the radish and thinly slice it lengthwise and then crosswise without cutting through to the stem. Soak in cold water until opened into a flower.

Radish jacks. Choose a radish with a nice round shape. With a paring knife, cut the radish crosswise into slices about the thickness of a dime. With the tip of your knife, make a slit from the center of each slice to the outside. Using two cut slices for each jack, hold one slice vertically and the other horizontally with slits facing each other. Gently bend one slice to open its slit and slide the two slices onto one another. These make whimsical additions to an hors d'oeuvres selection.

Radish fan. Make six straight vertical cuts from the top of the radish to within ⅓ inch of the base. Soak in cold water until cuts are opened. Insert a slice of radish in each cut to form a fan.

Radish flower. With a small knife, cut a radish into thin slices, and arrange these slices slightly overlapping one another in a ring to form a flower. Place a carrot cutout in the center of the flower and make the stem and leaves from cucumber peel or blanched leek green.

CUCUMBER GARNISHES

Perfect for salads and seafood dishes!

Cucumber slices. Draw a channel knife along the length of an unpeeled cucumber at ⅛-inch intervals. Cut the cucumber into slices. Use the slices as a base for canapés or halve the slices and arrange them overlapping slightly as an edging on a platter of cold or hot seafood.

Cucumber balls. Peel a cucumber. Cut in half lengthwise and remove the seeds. With a melon ball cutter, cut out balls from the cucumber. Arrange the balls in a cluster to resemble a bunch of grapes. The balls also can be used as a garnish for salads or as part of a filling for stuffed tomatoes and sweet pepper cases.

Cucumber cups. Draw a citrus scorer along the length of an unpeeled cucumber at ⅛-inch intervals. Cut the cucumber crosswise into 3-inch-thick slices. With a melon ball cutter, hollow out the centers of each slice leaving a base about ½ inch thick. Fill with flavored mayonnaise or a seafood spread.

MUSHROOM GARNISHES

To select mushrooms for garnishes, choose smooth white mushrooms with closed caps, and avoid those that are bruised, browned, or have caps that are opened like an umbrella. Store mushrooms, unwashed, in

Scored mushroom.

Lemon twists.

Lemon slice border.

paper bags in the refrigerator. Just before using them, wipe the mushrooms clean with dampened paper towels and sprinkle them with a little lemon juice to keep them white.

Stuffed mushrooms.   Choose mushrooms of the same size. Clean them, sprinkle them with lemon juice, and cut off the stems. If necessary, hollow out a little of the center with a melon ball cutter before filling. After filling with a vegetable puree, sprinkle with grated nutmeg.

Scored mushrooms.   With a channel knife, begin at the center of the mushroom cap and draw the scorer downward six or eight times at even intervals. Sprinkle with lemon juice to keep the mushrooms white.

If the garnish will be on display for several hours, the cut mushrooms can be simmered in salted water acidulated with a teaspoon or 2 of lemon juice for 3 to 5 minutes, or until firm. This will help maintain the mushrooms' white color longer.

CITRUS FRUIT GARNISHES

Garnishes made from citrus fruits are excellent highlights for seafood and chicken dishes and for citrus desserts.

Lemon fan.   Halve several lemon slices and arrange the halves behind one another to form a fan. This garnish is ideal for bordering a platter of smoked salmon or whitefish.

Lemon twist.   Begin with a lemon slice ⅛ inch thick. Slit the slice to the center. Twist the two cut surfaces in opposite directions. A wavy line may be formed by arranging several twists in a row.

Lemon slice border.   Halve several lemon slices and arrange the halves in an alternating pattern, with the cut sides touching, as illustrated. This can be done with orange and lime slices as well.

Lime cone.   Begin with a lime slice ⅛ inch thick. Slit the slice to the center. Arrange the two ends over one another to create a funnel.

Lime wedges.   Cut a lime into quarters or eighths. With a sharp knife, make a 1-inch slit in the skin on one end, but do not remove the skin. Hang the lime by the slit on the edge of a glass.

Decorative orange slices.   This garnish works for lemons and limes, too. With a channel knife, cut vertical grooves in the peel of the fruit at ¼-inch intervals so that when sliced the slices have decorative patterns. If the slices are to decorate drinks or will lie flat as a garnish, cut them ¼ inch thick. For twists and cones, cut them thinner.

Orange cup.   Halve an orange crosswise and cut a thin slice from the base of each half so it will stand firm. With a spoon, remove the pulp and fill each cup as desired. This is a lovely way to serve sherbet or ice cream and also works with diced fruit for brunch.

Orange crown.   With the point of a small sharp knife, make sawtooth cuts to the center of the orange, cutting all the way around the

(continued on page 408)

Edible Flowers

Flowers can be used to decorate and garnish salads, appetizer trays, and desserts. But only use edible ones! And, of course, use flowers from gardens that have not been sprayed with pesticides. Also, do not collect wildflowers from the side of the road. Be sure the scent of the flowers doesn't overpower the dish. Here are a few flowers you may wish to use:

Borage. The small pink and blue flowers of this herb have a mild cucumber taste. A nice addition to salads.

Calendula. Also known as pot marigold. These orange, white, and yellow flowers have a mild peppery taste. Toss the petals in mixed green salads.

Chamomile. Delicate, daisylike flowers in miniature, with a mildly sweet fragrance and sweet, grassy taste. Use with desserts.

Chive blossoms. Lavender-colored globes. Lovely in salads and to garnish platters of appetizers, chicken, or fish. These blossoms taste strongly of onion.

Dandelion flowers. These common yellow flowers can be used sparingly in salads. They have a slightly bitter, grassy taste.

Daylilies. The dried buds of these dramatic orange flowers are stir-fried and served in some classic Oriental dishes, including hot-and-sour soup. They taste mildly of fennel. You can also use the dramatic, sweet-tasting blooms in salads and to decorate cakes.

Elder flowers. The delicate white umbels of the elderberry bush can be used as a garnish or be batter dipped and deep-fried. They taste sweet.

Scented geraniums. Lemon-, rose-, and mint-scented geraniums in pink, red, white, and purple make lovely garnishes for salads and desserts.

Nasturtiums. These peppery-tasting blooms come in a riot of colors and can be used to garnish all manner of salads.

Pansies. Multicolored pansies make a lovely, dramatic garnish for cakes. Their flavor ranges from grape to clover to grassy.

Rose petals. Sprinkle the petals over salads or use the whole blossoms to garnish desserts. They taste just like they smell.

Squash blossoms. Orange-colored squash blossoms can be stuffed, sautéed, or deep-fried, or used as a dramatic garnish. The flavor is bland, like that of zucchini.

Violets. These small blue, purple, white, or yellow blossoms have a sweet taste and make a lovely garnish on cakes or individual dessert plates.

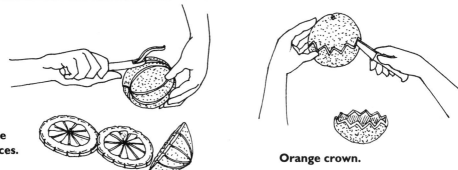

Decorative orange slices.

Orange crown.

fruit. Separate the halves carefully. Cut a thin slice from the base of each half so it stands firmly. With a spoon, remove the pulp. When filled with cranberry sauce, these crowns make a festive garnish for the Thanksgiving turkey.

BUTTER GARNISHES

Butter garnishes can dress up broiled steaks and fish and steamed vegetables.

Butter balls. Dip a melon ball cutter in hot water for a few seconds and press it into a stick of slightly softened butter, turning while pressing. Transfer the ball as it is formed to a bowl of ice water. The balls will not be perfectly round. Store in ice water. Before serving, the butter balls may be rolled in paprika or minced fresh parsley or chives.

Butter molds. There are numerous butter molds available at hardware stores and specialty food shops. Put the mold in cold water for a few minutes while the butter softens. Press the butter into the mold and let it harden in the freezer. To unmold from a metal mold, dip the mold in hot water for a few seconds, invert it onto a plate, and shake it to release the butter. If the butter refuses to slip out of the mold easily, gently ease the butter out with the tip of a small knife. To unmold from a plastic mold, turn the mold upside down and bend it slightly until the butter is released. Store the molded butter in ice water.

*F*amily Meals

In the struggle to juggle the demands of hectic family schedules, family meals have fallen by the wayside. Too rarely do you get a chance to gather with your family for a peaceful, unrushed meal.

So on those all-too-infrequent occasions when schedules coincide and everyone is gathered, it is nice to take a little extra care in your menu presentation. Armed with a few simple garnishes and the principles already discussed, you can easily plan meals that will delight your family.

FAMILY MENU PLANNING

Family meals can be special—particularly because they occur less frequently than they used to. Make them fun for all by choosing dishes you know your children will enjoy eating and perhaps even enjoy helping to prepare. Homemade pizza is a great one to try. Here are a few more ideas.

Chili night.   Chili, which can be prepared ahead of time, is fun to eat and to serve. Brightly colored linens and plates add just the right touch.

Serve the chili in an attractive pot or oven-to-table casserole, and just before serving sprinkle the top with minced fresh cilantro or parsley.

Set the chili in the center of the table and surround it with pretty condiment bowls containing grated cheese, kidney beans, finely chopped onion, and tortilla chips. Let family members help themselves to the chili and then add whichever condiments they like.

For dessert, a store-bought chocolate cake is always a welcome treat. Arrange the cake on a plate lined with a lace doily and serve it with fresh seasonal fruit in a glass bowl. Garnish the fruit with mint sprigs and a sprinkling of toasted pine nuts.

Soup for supper night.   You can either prepare the soup ahead of time and reheat it (soup is always better on the second day) or buy the soup from a local gourmet shop or food store.

Does your china closet include a soup tureen? If so, you can serve at the table. Wherever you serve, garnish the top of each bowl with a dollop of sour cream or yogurt and a sprinkle of finely minced green onion or chives.

Fill a napkin-lined basket with warm store-bought rolls, biscuits, or crusty bread. Or serve assorted crackers or bread sticks.

Salad is always a nice accompaniment. For something simple, try combining seasonal greens with sliced oranges and toasted walnuts. To enhance an orange-flavored dressing, add a little walnut oil. Garnish the salad with julienned or finely grated orange rind and serve it in a clear glass or wooden bowl.

For dessert, serve ice cream in goblets accompanied by a plate of brownies dusted with confectioners' sugar.

Roast chicken salad night.   Roast the chicken yourself or buy it from your local delicatessen and cut it into serving pieces. You can make the food festive by arranging the chicken pieces on a platter lined with lettuce—green leaf, red leaf, or a combination. Garnish the

Family Meal Time Savers

☐ There's nothing wrong with buying nourishing store-bought food. Take advantage of the many delicious convenience foods that are now available, such as deli meats and prepared salads (tuna, egg) from your supermarket. Salad bars offer an inspiring assortment of healthful main dish salads that make an appealing meal.

☐ Buy seasonal produce and let it inspire your menus. A simple meal of the season's first sweet corn and a ripe tomato salad, along with bakery bread and sliced cheese will satisfy and delight.

☐ Take advantage of the weekends or whenever you have free time and excess energy to prepare all or part of a dish and then freeze it for future use. This makes especially good sense when using seasonal produce. Imagine having tomato and basil soup on an early winter evening when the pungent perfume of fresh basil is just a fleeting summer memory. Freezing part or all of a meal is a tremendous boon to the working parent.

☐ Pretty ovenproof casseroles save time and cleanup. Simply add some minced parsley or a sprinkling of paprika to highlight the food itself.

☐ One-dish suppers cooked in a skillet cut down on preparation time and cleanup—and can be a great way to use up leftovers. Brown onions and rice in a skillet with a bit of oil or butter. Add broth and cook until the rice is tender. Stir in leftover bits of meat or chicken and leftover or frozen vegetables. Season with a handful of chopped fresh herbs.

chicken with decorative lemon slices and fresh thyme or rosemary sprigs. (If you're roasting the chicken yourself, add one or both of these herbs to the cavity of the chicken before cooking for a boost of flavor.)

Make a simple dressing of lemon juice, olive oil, and seasonings, and spoon it over the chicken.

As an accompaniment, serve potato, macaroni, or rice salad tossed with a yogurt, light mayonnaise, or sour cream sauce. Add finely chopped red or green sweet pepper and minced fresh parsley, dill, or tarragon to the salad for color. Before serving, sprinkle the top with paprika.

Still want dessert? How about a store-bought angel food cake with a berry sauce? To make the sauce, puree a package of frozen berries in the blender and season it with orange or lemon juice and sugar to taste. Slice the cake, arrange it on dessert plates, and surround each piece with some of the sauce. Garnish with whole berries and a few sprigs of mint.

Taco night.   You'll be surprised at how fast you can assemble the ingredients for make-your-own tacos. Have ready heated taco shells and serve with bowls of chopped tomato, shredded lettuce, grated cheese, and spicy ground-meat filling. Let everyone serve themselves and assemble their own tacos.

Southwestern pottery or dishes are terrific here, although any colorful dishes will do.

For dessert, sliced fresh mangoes served with a sprinkling of lime juice will cool everyone down—even the cook!

Pizza night.   Make your own pizza dough or pick up ready-to-use dough from the supermarket or a pizza parlor. Children love rolling the dough (and you never have to worry about them "overworking" it) and choosing their own toppings. Have ready assorted toppings, such as tomato sauce, mushrooms, sweet bell pepper rings, onion rings, olives, sun-dried tomatoes, and cheese.

Either precede the pizza with antipasto from your local deli or serve it right along with the pizza.

Italian ice cream and pine nut cookies make a wonderful dessert.

EASY PRESENTATION IDEAS

☐ Minced fresh parsley, dill, or chives sprinkled on the top of soups or salads add both color and freshness.

☐ Line dishes with soft-leaf lettuce when serving grain or pasta salads or roasted chicken.

☐ Line dessert plates with doilies.

☐ Dress up store-bought sponge cake or gingerbread by sifting confectioners' sugar over the top before serving. If you place a paper doily on the cake first, the confectioners' sugar will fall in a lovely pattern. Carefully lift off the doily to reveal the pattern.

☐ Serve ice cream, pudding, gelatin, or fruit salad in elegant stemmed glasses or goblets.

SETTING THE TABLE

Food always looks more appealing when it is placed on a table that has been set with care. Take a moment to put out placemats and gaily colored napkins—even for a quick meal eaten in the kitchen.

Who says china has to match? It isn't important if the dishes have different patterns or if the glasses don't match. In fact, it's more fun.

Scour flea markets, country auctions, and tag sales for interesting buys. Also, keep your eyes open for flatware and serving pieces. Sometimes quality pieces—even sterling—can be purchased for a song. All that is needed is a good cleaning and an appreciative home.

Take advantage of white sales to purchase colorful placemats and napkins—matched or unmatched. Don't limit yourself to traditional table linens—you can transform patterned sheets and fabric remnants into tablecloths, placemats, and napkins.

Use your children's ceramic artwork as centerpieces for your table. Not only will the table look more festive, the kids will take pride in knowing that you have chosen a place of honor for their work.

Don't reserve candlelight dinners for entertaining. Small votive candles, a large candle with a hurricane shade, or even tapered candles make family meals special. Children love eating by candlelight and often argue about who will blow the candles out!

arty Planning

Parties are for fun and even the busy host and hostess can be included in the good times. A little planning can make the party enjoyable and relaxing for you. Here are some points to keep in mind.

DECIDE AND PREPARE!

Number of guests. If you plan to entertain indoors, the number of people you invite should depend upon the space you have to accommodate them. In general, for a casual sit-down dinner party, eight is a comfortable figure. A buffet is a wonderful way to entertain up to twenty people. For more than twenty, a cocktail party or dessert party is ideal. If you plan to entertain during the warmer months, consider a barbecue or picnic.

Creating a Party Mood

☐ Play background music low. Plan your selections in advance. It's fun to match music with food—Dixieland jazz with southern fried chicken, or Italian opera with pasta.

☐ For a romantic atmosphere, use bone-handled flatware, colored glass goblets, and antique china and lace.

☐ For a casual feel, mix textures and patterns. For example, pair checked mats and napkins with floral plates, all in blue and white tones.

☐ For a country mood, use florals in cheerful colors. Needlepoint and embroidery add texture.

☐ For a contemporary ambience, use simple dishes and flatware. Choose solid and striped linens and china and sleek crystal and flatware.

The menu. The size of your space and number of guests can be your guide for planning your menu. Select dishes that can be prepared completely or at least partially ahead of time. Vary the recipes in taste, color, and texture, but keep the overall menu simple. Now is not the time to try out all those new dishes you've been curious about.

Theme. If you center the party around a theme—an anniversary, birthday, historical event, holiday, or even sports event—let your menu and decorations playfully reflect it.

Advance preparation. Lists! Lists! Lists! They can keep you organized and prepared. Start off with a list of the things you need to buy and make.

Five days before the party, buy nonperishable foods and check your pantry for staples. Order wine, liquor, and flowers as needed. Check to see that your table linens are crisp and clean and that your china, glasses, and flatware are all sparkling. Select serving dishes. If you don't have enough plates or flatware, mix pieces from different sets. If necessary, rent or borrow chairs, glasses, and serving trays.

Two days before the party, buy the perishable foods. Vegetables and salad greens can be trimmed and cleaned and will keep beautifully if wrapped in dampened paper towels and plastic and stored in the refrigerator.

One day before the party, prepare dishes that are to be served cold or that can be made in advance and reheated. Be sure you have enough ice, and, if you don't, make or buy more.

That morning set up the bar and dining room table or buffet. Place the flowers or other centerpiece on the table and arrange any room decorations. Be sure there is a clear route between the kitchen and buffet table.

SETTING THE TABLE

Traditional "tablecloths" aren't necessary to set a festive party table. Other attractive possibilities include country quilts, pieces of yard goods, samples of lace and embroidery, pretty sheets, painted fabrics, even brown craft paper for a kid's party.

Let the time of year influence your table as well as your menu. Earth tones add a seasonal accent to autumn meals, pastels to summer ones.

(continued on page 416)

Two Simple Napkin Folds

The centuries-old art of napkin folding is easier than it looks and adds beauty to any table.

Bishop's Hat.

1. Fold the napkin diagonally in half to form a triangle and pull each corner up to the apex to form a square.

2. Turn over the napkin so that the open edges lie toward you.

3. Pull the two top flaps up and away from you, and fold the remaining two flaps back in the same way to form a triangle.

4. Turn the napkin over again and pull the two outer corners together so that they overlap. Then tuck one flap into the folds of the other to hold them in place. Turn the front of the hat to face you, position the napkin upright and pull the loose flaps down.

Bishop's hat.

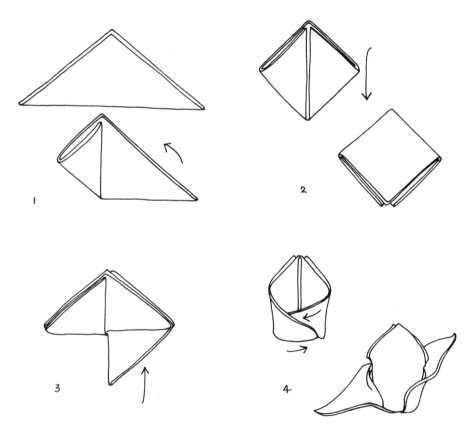

Four Feathers.

1. Fold the napkin in half diagonally to form a triangle. Place the folded edge toward you. Place your index finger on the center of this edge and, using the top layer of fabric only, bring the apex down to meet the left-hand corner.

2. Form a triangle by bringing the remaining top corner down and across to the lower left corner as before.

3. Bring the top corner down once more to meet the lower left corner, folding the triangle in half.

4. Fan out the folds slightly, then turn the napkin over so that the folds are underneath.

5. Lift the edge and roll the napkin into a loose cone shape as shown, stopping about halfway across. Fold up the bottom point and insert the napkin into a glass.

Four feathers.

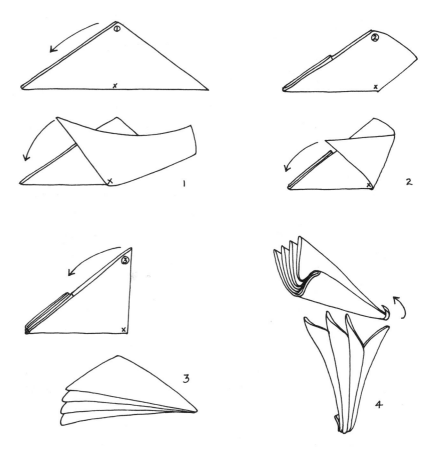

Caring for China, Silver, and Crystal

Antique china, delicate bone china, or fine porcelain decorated with platinum or gold, silver or silver-plate flatware, and crystal are all best washed by hand. Follow these tips:

☐ Use a rubber or plastic scraper to remove food on dishes.

☐ Line the sink with several layers of paper towels or a dish towel, or use a plastic dishpan. Do not overcrowd the dishpan or sink.

☐ Use moderately hot water and a mild detergent. Very hot water can crack china and glassware.

☐ Avoid using abrasive cleaners, scouring powders, or steel-wool pads.

☐ Wash glassware first, then silver, and then china in this order to keep your dishwater clean longer. Rinse in clean, moderately hot water.

☐ Air-dry glassware and china on a dish rack and polish with a soft lint-free towel. Buff silverware dry with a soft towel to prevent water spots. Be sure all silver is completely dry before storing.

☐ If you can't wash silver soon after use, rinse and dry it. Prolonged contact with acid or highly salted foods can discolor it.

Several patterns or shades in the same color scheme can be more effective than a straight one-color, one pattern look.

Sometimes the best ornaments on a festive table are decoratively folded napkins in varying materials and colors. For sit-down dinners, the traditional place for napkins is to the left of flatware. But you don't have to follow the rules. Tuck napkins in glasses or place them on top of the plate. For buffets, roll up the flatware in napkins and set in baskets on each table.

Napkin rings are always appropriate and attractive. For an especially lovely effect, tie the napkins with satin ribbons and tuck in a fresh flower. For Thanksgiving, you might fold the napkin in half twice to form a long rectangle and roll it up to form a bundle resembling a diploma. Wrap a beige or wheat-colored ribbon around the napkin twice and tie the ends under the napkin. Arrange a small bunch of dried flowers, secured with thread, under the ribbon in the center of the napkin.

If you keep centerpieces and candles low, they won't interfere with dinner conversation. Tapered candles or a grouping of votive candles make for intimate lighting, but you may have to supply some discreet electric lighting so everyone can see what they are eating!

Although flowers are the most common centerpiece, a collection of figurines, a basket of shells, or a bowl of mirrored holiday ornaments is a wonderful substitute.

For a natural centerpiece, arrange pots of fresh herbs on the table and decorate each pot with a ribbon. Or present the pots in pretty baskets or decorative pottery. If you are fortunate enough to have plenty of herbs on hand, cut them into bunches and arrange them in a glass vase or small pitcher in lieu of flowers. Food ingredients themselves can be used to create imaginative centerpieces. Just keep it simple and avoid clutter.

For formal parties, polish your china, silver, and crystal until it gleams.

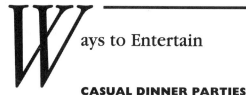

Ways to Entertain

CASUAL DINNER PARTIES

Sitting down with friends to enjoy fine food and wine can be done inside or out, elegantly or casually. Whatever the theme—a pizza party, barbecue, gumbo party—a dinner party offers the opportunity to entertain in a personal style. Once the decision has been made to give a dinner party, extend invitations and begin planning your menu. If possible, choose seasonally available items, taking into account foods that contrast in color, texture, and shape, and that will come together in a balanced, well-defined whole.

Select wines and nonalcoholic drinks to complement the menu. For eight dinner guests, buy four bottles of wine—less if you are offering other beverages.

The cocktail hour is a time for guests to gather together in anticipation of a very special evening. The time period should not exceed an hour—thirty minutes is preferable. Serve light appetizers. Don't overwhelm your guests with food that kills their appetites. Nothing should detract from the meal you have carefully planned and prepared.

The cocktail drinks can include liquor, wine, champagne, beer, and nonalcoholic beverages. For added appeal, decorate the drinks with unusual garnishes where appropriate. Strawberries and raspberries in champagne, for instance, or a slice of orange or lime where normally lemon would be used. Offering your guests special drinks adds to the excitement of the evening. Kir Royales, margaritas, iced Russian vodka, a particularly good sherry or vermouth, and a vintage wine are some examples. In any gathering there are sure to be some people who don't drink. Be sure to include an appealing nonalcoholic alternative— sparkling fruit juice sodas, homemade fruit punch, flavored seltzers.

There are no rules when it comes to serving the meal. You might choose to serve one course at a time, or bring out everything and let your guests help themselves. You can serve up plates from the kitchen, pass serving bowls at the table, or serve from a sidebar.

A grand finale in the form of a dazzling dessert is the most glorious way to end a perfect meal. Such a dessert need not be elaborate. Fresh fruit sorbets and ices garnished with seasonal berries and unusual fruits and an assortment of beautiful cookies are delightful.

Menu ideas.

PAELLA PARTY Paella is a wonderful party dish whose contents can be varied not only to suit your tastes but also your budget. The dish itself goes a long way and two paellas can easily serve twelve people.

Traditionally, a paella contains saffron rice (eliminate the saffron if it is too expensive for your budget and add a pinch of turmeric to color the rice yellow), chicken, seafood, and a combination of vegetables, including sweet bell peppers, onions, and tomatoes. However, there are ample variations. Use all chicken, only seafood, or even only vegetables, depending on your tastes and that of your guests. The essential ingredients are the rice and broth.

The different elements can be prepared ahead of time—browning the chicken and sautéing the vegetables, measuring out the rice and broth, and cleaning the seafood. Assemble the paella just before you pop the dish in the oven. Cooking time is roughly 30 minutes.

Precede the paella with a simple make-ahead soup and accompany it with a large green salad containing mushrooms and sliced almonds. Edible flowers (see page 407) can be used for a decorative touch. Add crusty bread and a pitcher of white or red sangria garnished with fresh fruit. For dessert, serve a store-bought apple tart accompanied by caramel ice cream or pineapple sherbet and crisp spice cookies.

Keep the Spanish theme in mind when choosing linens and dishes. Brightly colored Mediterranean placemats and napkins work beautifully, as do simple tumblers and ceramic dishes.

SUNDAY AFTERNOON BRUNCH Brunch is one of the friendliest ways to entertain. Quiches and breakfast casseroles containing eggs, cheese and ham or sausage are always a hit. Or, if yours is the kind of kitchen that your guests gravitate toward and you are comfortable cooking with an audience, make omelets, letting your guests choose their own fillings.

Greet your guests with an eye-catching centerpiece—perhaps flowers arranged in an enameled coffeepot, ceramic pitcher, or glass canister. Decorate the table with plants or pots of herbs tied with ribbon.

Serve juice and milk in glass or ceramic pitchers.

Transfer jams, jellies, and butter to small crocks, cake tins, or antique muffin pans.

Tuck napkins into rings, wrap them with ribbon, or roll them up and let guests pull them from a basket.

ENTERTAINING LARGE GROUPS WITH BUFFETS

With their easy informality and lively mix of food and guests, buffets are the ideal way to entertain large groups of friends. Buffets encourage people to mix and mingle and provide them with a greater variety of foods to sample as well. Buffets lend themselves to many styles and themes and offer infinite possibilities to fit any budget. In fact, with careful thought and preparation, buffets offer the best opportunity to entertain on a grand scale inexpensively (see pages 425–426 for amounts needed for feeding a crowd).

The food is displayed on one large "buffet" table or several small tables joined together in a U-shape. A wide array of food can be offered or the menu can be kept simple.

Although buffets do not have to be elaborate, the food should be arranged to appear abundant. If there are empty spaces, fill them in with ferns, ivy, gourds, or other items reflecting the theme of the party. For example, if you're having a Mexican buffet, decorate the table with dried and fresh chilies, sombreros, and colorful Mexican ceramics. A fanciful piñata in the center of the table creates an imaginative focal point.

Setting up and maintaining buffet tables.   If you are presenting a large assortment of dishes, use a centerpiece as the focal point from which all other dishes radiate. Elevating some dishes on napkin- or cloth-wrapped boxes or serving them from stands makes the presentation more dramatic and exciting.

The location of the buffet table should let guests move freely around it. Set the table for easy traffic flow—plates first, entrées and accompaniments next, flatware and napkins last. For easy carrying, wrap each set of flatware in a napkin.

Negotiating a buffet table is tricky, so try to make things as easy as possible for your guests. For example, place the bread selection and butter plate beside one another and have the butter at room temperature for easy spreading. Be sure there are serving pieces placed next to each dish.

Serve food in neat portions that can be simply scooped up and put on a plate—presliced meats, fried chicken, tacos, vegetable salads in vegetable cases—or in help-yourself casseroles or chafing dishes. If you are serving soup, offer it in easy-to-handle mugs, rather than soup bowls.

Do not crowd the table—allow plenty of room for guests to serve themselves neatly. Place serving dishes about 6 inches from the edge of the table to prevent guests from brushing against the food and getting it on their clothing. This also keeps spills to a minimum.

It is important that there be comfortable places for everyone to eat. Provide card tables, folding or lap trays, stools, etc.

Paper Goods

A large selection of colorful and sturdy plates and cups are available in both paper and plastic. Consider using them alone, or as supplements, when you're entertaining a large crowd and don't have enough dishes, glasses, or flatware to go around. For instance, a buffet dinner can be served on stoneware, and dessert on festive paper or plasticware. (Paper plates are invaluable for children's parties, too!) An added advantage is the quick cleanup afterward.

If you are seating guests at the dining room table or several smaller tables, set the tables with flatware and glasses beforehand so that it isn't necessary for guests to pick them up at the buffet table.

Prepare large amounts of your recipes in advance but set out only smaller serving dishes. Reheat in the kitchen and replenish the table as necessary.

Leave an unobstructed route between the kitchen and the serving table so you can bring out food without detours.

Remember to choose foods that lend themselves to advance preparation and will not suffer from sitting out for more than an hour or so.

It is not necessary to set out the entire meal at once. The buffet table can be cleared, and fruit and dessert served later with coffee.

Allow a case of wine (twelve bottles) for every twenty guests. If you are serving other beverages, allow just eight bottles.

Theme party buffets.

HARVEST TABLE   Choose natural decorations emphasizing autumn. A beautiful bright pumpkin makes a logical focal point with nuts, dried corn-on-the-cob, variegated gourds, and vivid red apples around it completing the effect. Use colorful autumn leaves (artificial fall foliage can be purchased in parts of the country where the leaves don't change) to fill in spaces on your table, and complete the setting by providing napkins in warm fall colors.

GRADUATION BUFFET   To cut costs, consider co-hosting a party with other parents. Use decorations in the school's colors to pull together all the other elements of the party.

Tie rolled white napkins with ribbons in the school colors to resemble diplomas.

For a chuckle or two, make a photo collage of the graduate's life and times: the first day of kindergarten, a visit with Santa, school plays and activities, sporting events—even the prom. However, be sure there's nothing *too* embarrassing.

NEW YEAR'S EVE OR WINTER SOLSTICE   For a change of pace from all the Christmas decorations, let the starry winter sky be the backdrop for your party. Cover the table with dark blue, dark purple, or even black cloth and affix colorful foil star cutouts to the tables, and even to the walls. Dust the table with Christmas tree tinsel. Hang star cutouts from the ceiling. All-white floral arrangements will add drama. If you have the time, assemble a music tape for the dinner hour of moonlight and starlight songs, such as "Moonlight in Vermont" and "Stardust."

Various ethnic groups have made a tradition of eating certain foods to bring luck and prosperity in the new year. The Italians eat lentils, which are said to resemble coins. Scandinavians eat herring, which swim together in great numbers, promising abundance and prosperity. A number of ethnic groups eat cabbage, which symbolizes paper money. Any and all of these foods can be served and are sure to be good conversation starters.

MIDWINTER GETAWAY PARTY   If you live where winter never seems to end, you can delight your friends with a taste of the tropics. Decorate the table with lush houseplants and ferns. A few orchids or large lilies, if your budget allows, will add to the effect. A basket of tropical fruits will make an equally splashy centerpiece. Choose a bright floral tablecloth.

Think tropical for the menu. Jamaican jerk chicken, seafood, and rice pilafs are very appealing. Garnish your platters with citrus and tropical fruits. Use hollowed-out coconut shells as serving dishes. Mix up a tropical fruit punch.

CHILDREN'S PARTIES   Have fun planning the party with your child! This is a wonderful way to spend time together and will help make the child feel more involved.

Sending out special invitations can heighten the sense of anticipation. Include a beginning time *and* an ending time for the party so parents will know when to retrieve their children.

When it comes to children's parties, more is not merrier. More can be disastrous! The rule of thumb for how many guests to invite is the age plus one for birthday parties. A four-year-old might invite five children; a five-year-old, six; and so on. Keep the number reasonable. A large group may be overwhelming not only for you but also for your child.

Keep the party short. Two hours is sufficient for everyone to have a good time.

Adult friends will be immeasurably helpful—wiping up spills, distributing ice cream, answering the phone, etc. Two adults for every six school-age children is a good ratio.

Balloons and streamers are colorful and fun. They also are relatively inexpensive and help put the children in a festive mood.

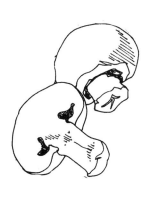

Don't make the mistake of planning too many activities for young children. Between the ages of three and eight, most children will enjoy only one or two games as an ice breaker. After that, its best to follow up with the cake, then present opening. From then on, the children are usually ready to play—with the birthday child's toys if he or she is good at sharing. If not, send the children out to the backyard or playground for some rough-and-tumble play.

Older children may enjoy planned activities, such as skating, bowling, miniature golf, or a trip to the beach.

Buy sturdy paper plates, cups, and napkins (have plenty) for easy cleanup. It is not uncommon for children to end up with more food on them than in them.

Serve finger foods to eliminate the need for knives and forks. Offer the children fun foods, such as hero sandwiches or pizza. If desired, the food can be cut into fanciful shapes with cookie cutters. Garnish platters with edible decorations. Avoid toothpicks; they can be swallowed accidentally.

Children live by their own set of social standards, just as adults do. If everyone gives out goody bags at the end of a party, you would be wise to plan to do likewise. If you don't like the idea of sending children home with a bag of candy, mix little toys in with the sweets. Or make a piñata and fill it with little toys and nuts in their shells. At the end of the party, the children will enjoy breaking the piñata and collecting the nuts and toys for their take-home bags.

COCKTAIL PARTIES

Unless you have invited just a few friends for cocktails before dinner, try to invite enough people to comfortably fill a room. When in doubt, invite more rather than fewer people. Unlike a dinner party and a buffet, it is not necessary to provide seating for everyone. In fact, inadequate seating works well here since it encourages people to mingle. Once people begin to sit down, the movement so important to a cocktail party is lost.

For a party of about twenty-four people, plan to serve six to eight different hors d'oeuvres and allow three of each kind per guest. If the hors d'oeuvres are hearty, two per person should suffice. If you like, you can add additional types of hors d'oeuvres for every ten to twelve more guests. Plan to pass trays for four or five of the different hot hors d'oeuvres. Then, on a buffet table, offer three or four dips and spreads accompanied by crackers and crudités. Balance your menu with both hot and cold as well as light and slightly more substantial selections.

The time of day influences how much food you should serve. For an early afternoon or late evening party, it's safe to assume that most guests will have eaten a meal, so they won't be too hungry. For a buffet centered around various sliced meats and cheese, ¼ pound of food per person should be ample. In the early evening (five or six o'clock), most guests will be hungry, so you should offer about ½ pound of food per person. If the food doesn't lend itself to figuring out per pound, figure as above, with two pieces of each type of hors d'oeuvre per person.

Presenting the hors d'oeuvres. The classic way to present hors d'oeuvres is to arrange them artistically on trays. For maximum dramatic effect, group only one type of hors d'oeuvre on each tray and allow the food to be displayed without crowding.

Decorate the trays imaginatively but simply. The decorations are meant to enhance the beauty of the food and not to overwhelm it. A single flower or fresh herb blossom highlighting the color or accenting the flavor is all that is needed.

Everything You Need to Know About Ice

There are approximately fifteen ice cubes to a pound. When planning amounts to buy or make for a party, use this table:

NUMBER OF GUESTS	AMOUNT OF ICE
For a 2-hour party:	
8	5 pounds
12	10 pounds
24	20 pounds
48	40 pounds
For a 4-hour party:	
8	10 pounds
12	20 pounds
24	40 pounds
48	75 pounds

The Perfect Drink

For uniform results, measure liquor with a jigger (1½ ounces). Put the ice in the glass first. If you are using sugar or fruit juice in a drink, put it in the glass before adding the liquor to allow it to dissolve better. For a clear cocktail, pour liquor over ice in glass.

If possible, chill glasses for beer and cold drinks.

Trays can be lined with doilies or decorative paper placemats if the food itself is not too moist. Or you can use a cloth napkin to line the tray or layer decorative leaves or ferns on the bottom to absorb any moisture. The trays can be passed either by the host, hostess, or a helpful friend.

The bar. The best place for the bar is in a foyer, hall, or any uncongested area where guests can circulate freely. You'll need a 6- to 8-foot table covered with a white or decorative cloth reaching to the floor to camouflage stored bottles, ice, and other setups. Use decorative pitchers and decanters for jugged wines, juices, and water.

If possible, have someone act as official bartender. Alternatively, set up the bar so that guests may help themselves. However, for more than thirty people it is advisable to have help.

Have an assortment of glasses and beer mugs in varying sizes and shapes. If you don't own enough glasses to accommodate your party, rent or borrow them. For outdoor parties, plastic is best. Small decorative bowls containing garnishes for the drinks should also be set out on the bar—sliced lemons, limes, oranges, cherries, olives, cocktail onions, lemon, lime, and orange twists, etc. Be imaginative and offer unusual choices for traditional drinks.

How much liquor to buy. The number of drinks (1½ ounces of liquor each) per bottle is twenty-two drinks per liter bottle; thirty-nine drinks per 1.75 liter bottle. A 750 ml bottle of wine provides six 4-ounce glasses.

Only you can be the judge of the drinking preferences of your guests. Today, more people than ever before are likely to drink beer, wine, or soft drinks, instead of hard-liquor cocktails.

□ For a cocktail-drinking crowd, plan on an average of three drinks per person for a cocktail party.

□ For wine, assume each guest will want two to four glasses.

□ Take into account the time of year and time of day the party is taking place. People tend to drink less during an afternoon event.

□ In very hot weather, drinks have a more potent effect, so encourage your guests to drink soda, juice, and nonalcoholic punch.

□ If the party is going to run 3 hours or longer, have coffee on hand.

Standard Bar Equipment

Cocktail shaker

Corkscrews

Can and bottle openers

Drink stirrers and swizzle sticks

Ice tongs and scoop

Ice tub

Ice chest

Ice bucket

Lemon zester

Jigger measures

Paring knives

Mixing glass and spoon

Citrus juicer

Blender for frothy drinks

Fine strainer

Wooden chopping board

Paper cocktail napkins

Decorative party picks

Short and long plastic straws

□ Be sure there is plenty of ice—enough for at least four cubes per drink.

The well-stocked bar should include

LIQUOR:

1 liter vodka (2 liters if you're having 20 or more guests)
1 liter gin
1 liter bourbon
1 liter Scotch (2 liters if you're having 20 or more guests)
1 liter dry vermouth
1 liter sweet vermouth
1 750 ml brandy
2 750 ml liqueurs (Grand Marnier, Bailey's Irish Cream, etc.)

MIXERS:

2 to 4 liters seltzer
1 quart each cola, diet soda, ginger ale, tonic water, orange juice, tomato juice
1 bottle Bloody Mary mix
3 limes, 1 lemon
Green olives, pearl onions

BEER:

2 six-packs lager beer
2 six-packs light beer
2 six-packs imported beer

The above quantities will vary depending on the tastes of your guests. It is always better to err on the side of excess. Most unopened liquor usually can be returned to the liquor store or saved for almost an indefinite period of time and used at a later date.

Nonalcoholic drinks should also be offered—always keep fruit juices, sparkling mineral water, and assorted sodas on hand.

Making Ice Cubes

□ **For crystal-clear cubes, boil water and let it cool before freezing in ice trays.**

□ **Prepare ice in advance, unmold from trays directly into plastic bags; tie shut and return to freezer.**

□ **To make decorative ice cubes: Fill an ice-cube tray with water and to each compartment add a mint leaf, strawberry or raspberry, green or red grape, a piece of lemon or lime, an olive, or a cocktail onion. Once the cubes are frozen, unmold and store in a plastic bag in the freezer. Select a cube to suit the drink.**

Cocktail Party Wine Guide

NO. OF GUESTS	BOTTLES WHITE 750 ML	BOTTLES RED 750 ML
4	2	1
6	2	2
10	4	2
12	6	2
30	9	4
40	13	6

Feeding a Crowd

Amounts for 50 Servings

The amounts below are based on serving sizes. When planning a party, remember that some people will eat 2 to 3 servings of a dish. Each of the entries is based on a meal with one entrée served with one side dish and one dessert. If you are serving more than one entrée or more than one side dish or dessert, adjust amounts accordingly.

	SERVING SIZE	AMOUNT TO BUY
Meats		
Bacon, sliced	2 slices	5 pounds
Chicken, roast	¼ small chicken	Thirteen 2-pound chickens
Frankfurters	2 frankfurters	10 to 12 pounds
Ground meat for meatloaf, meatballs	4½ ounces	15 pounds
Ham, roast	4½ ounces	15 pounds
Turkey, roast	4½ ounces	18 pounds boneless 40 pounds whole
Fish		
Fish fillets	4 ounces, cooked	16 pounds
Fish, whole, dressed	3 ounces, cooked	40 pounds
Scallops	4½ ounces	15 pounds
Shrimp, raw, in shell	4 ounces	25 pounds
Vegetables		
Beans	½ cup	10 pounds
Broccoli	½ cup	16 to 20 pounds
Cabbage	½ cup	12 pounds
Carrots	½ cup	10 pounds
Lettuce for salad	⅛ large head	7 large heads
Potatoes, baked	1 medium-size	25 pounds
Potatoes, mashed	½ cup	15 pounds
Tomatoes	3 whole slices	10 pounds
Fruits		
Bananas, sliced	3 ounces	10 pounds
Melon	8- to 12-ounce slice	30 to 40 pounds
Pineapple, diced	½ cup	5 pineapples
Strawberries, for sundaes	½ to ⅔ cup	6 to 7 quarts
for shortcake	¾ cup	8 quarts

(table continues)

Feeding a Crowd (*continued*)

Pasta and Rice

Macaroni	I cup cooked	3 pounds
Noodles, spaghetti	I cup cooked	6 pounds
Rice, long-grain	⅔ cup cooked	3 pounds

Bread and Crackers

Bread, sliced	2 slices	Four 2-pound loaves
Crackers	4 crackers	Four 8-ounce packages
Rolls	2 rolls	8½ dozen

Desserts

Cake, 9-inch, frosted, two-layer	¹⁄₁₀ of a cake	5 cakes
Cookies	2 to 3	10 to 12 dozen
Fruit cup, fresh	½ cup	6½ quarts
Ice cream	½ cup	2 gallons
Pie, 9-inch	⅙ of a pie	9 pies

Beverages

Coffee, ground	I½ cups	2 pounds
Coffee, instant	I½ cups	One 10-ounce jar
Juice, canned	½ cup	Five 46-ounce cans
Juice, fresh	½ cup	6¼ quarts
Lemons for lemonade	I cup prepared	3 dozen lemons
Milk	I glass	4 gallons
Tea, bags	I½ cups brewed	8 dozen tea bags
Tea, loose	I½ cups brewed	4 ounces loose tea
Tea, iced	12-ounce glass	3 gallons*

Miscellaneous Items

Butter	2 pats	2½ pounds
Cream, for coffee	2 tablespoons	4 pints (2 quarts)
Lemons, for tea	I slice	6 whole lemons
Salad dressing	2 tablespoons	Three 16-ounce bottles or 1½ quarts dressing

*6 ounces tea makes 3 gallons tea with ice

INDEX